The German
Secret Field Police
in Greece, 1941–1944

The German Secret Field Police in Greece, 1941–1944

ANTONIO J. MUÑOZ

McFarland & Company, Inc., Publishers
Jefferson, North Carolina

Frontispiece: German sign post in Paris. Notice the Secret Field Police sign (GFP). Ca. 1940–1941 (Bundesarchiv–Koblenz).

Library of Congress Cataloguing-in-Publication Data

Names: Muñoz, Antonio J., author.
Title: The German secret field police in Greece, 1941–1944 / Antonio J. Muñoz.
Description: Jefferson, North Carolina : McFarland & Company, Inc., Publishers, 2018 | Includes bibliographical references and index.
Identifiers: LCCN 2018002146 | ISBN 9781476667843 (softcover : acid free paper) ∞
Subjects: LCSH: Greece—History—Occupation, 1941–1944. | Germany. Heer. Geheime Feldpolizei—History. | World War, 1939–1945—Greece. | World War, 1939–1945—Regimental histories—Germany.
Classification: LCC D802.G8 M78 2018 | DDC 940.54/134309495—dc23
LC record available at https://lccn.loc.gov/2018002146

British Library cataloguing data are available

ISBN (print) 978-1-4766-6784-3
ISBN (ebook) 978-1-4766-3104-2

© 2018 Antonio J. Muñoz. All rights reserved

No part of this book may be reproduced or transmitted in any form or by any means, electronic or mechanical, including photocopying or recording, or by any information storage and retrieval system, without permission in writing from the publisher.

On the cover: officers in the Wehrmacht Geheime Feldpolizei (Army Secret Field Police) *left to right* Büttner, Wiese, Pätzke, Fenske, Gernert, Baucke, Göde, Klatt, Sowa, Grieger, Albrecht, Rüskriem, Gawehns, and Luecke (United States Holocaust Memorial Museum, courtesy of Instytut Pamieci Narodowej); *background* map of Greece © 2018 iStock

Printed in the United States of America

McFarland & Company, Inc., Publishers
Box 611, Jefferson, North Carolina 28640
www.mcfarlandpub.com

For all those who perished
as a result of the Nazi invasion of Greece

Acknowledgments

I would like to express my gratitude to various people who in one way or another assisted me in the creation of this study. First, I would like to thank my family. The writing of this work took a lot of time and effort, which was robbed from quality time with my loved ones. Because this research was privately funded, it proved financially costly. Yet my wife never complained whenever I would tell her that I needed to fly to Europe. I owe her a great deal that I shall never be able to repay for her moral support and assistance in facilitating this project. I owe special thanks to Dr. Victoria Muñoz-Terry for having helped me to digitize Wilhelm Krichbaum's 1947 study on the Secret Field Police. The prospectus would never have been as good if my daughters, Martha and Victoria would not have given me input and advice.

I am also grateful and appreciative of my mentor, Dr. Dolores Augustine, professor of German studies whose patience and friendship guided me through the process of preparing this study. Dr. Augustine is truly the ideal of what a professor should be: patient, critical and objective, slow to anger, and always supportive! This work is all the better because of Dr. Augustine's great insight, analysis and critique. Like Dr. Augustine, Dr. Mauricio Borrero, professor of Russian studies was helpful and discerning. I'd also like to thank Dr. Alejandro Quintana, whose input was also important. Special thanks go to Dr. Julia Sneeringer, who suggested a doctoral program specifically suited to my needs. Finally, I would like to acknowledge my beloved sister-in-law: professor of Spanish literature Dr. Maria del Carmen Caballero-Alonso. Before she passed away, Mari-Carmen helped me on the academic path. Her kindness, love and patience will always shine as a perfect example of the best in human nature. Mari-Carmen, child of light, we miss you terribly!

Table of Contents

Acknowledgments	vi
Preface	1
Introduction: The GFP and the German Army's Institutional Extremism	8
1. Greece: 1832–1940	21
2. Hitler's War Aims and the Balkans	33
3. Nazism, the GFP and Greece	42
4. Organization of the Secret Field Police in Greece	49
5. The Secret Field Police and the Subjugation of the People of Greece	74
6. The Participation of the Secret Field Police in the Holocaust in Greece	94
7. The Secret Field Police in Yugoslavia, Romania and Bulgaria	114
8. The GFP in the West and Scandinavia	125
9. The Secret Field Police in the Soviet Union	154
10. Towards a Reckoning	188
Conclusions	200
Appendix I: The Structure of the SS Command in Serbia, 1941–1942	205
Appendix II: Structure of the SD in the Occupied Regions of Western Europe	206
Appendix III: Commander of the Order Police "Serbia"	208
Appendix IV: Uniform and Rank Insignia of the Geheime Feldpolizei	210
Appendix V: Organization of the Secret Field Police	212
Appendix VI: Order of Battle—Secret Field Police Forces in France, Spring 1941	214
Chapter Notes	216
Bibliography	233
Index	243

Preface

In 2005, while doing research on the history of the German Police, I came across mention of what turned out to be an obscure, and little known German Army organization known as the *Geheime Feldpolizei* or Secret Field Police.[1] Little is known on the activities of the GFP during World War II. In academic as well as in amateur circles, the GFP is almost a complete mystery. A few authors have attempted to write about the GFP, but so far, their efforts have proved fragmentary and rudimentary. One of the issues that historians have had to face when attempting to document the history of the GFP is that this very secretive organization left few records behind that could actually be used to document its story. Shortly before the end of the war, most GFP documents and files were destroyed in order to try and conceal the activities of this secret police force. In addition, members of the GFP, starting with its wartime chief, Wilhelm Krichbaum, made a concerted effort to portray their organization as just another German Army intelligence unit. In 1947 Krichbaum authored a monograph for the U.S. Army Historical Division wherein he detailed all of the supposed duties of the GFP. Unfortunately for the researcher, Krichbaum failed to document the activities of the GFP in the Holocaust. At the end of the war, officials of the GFP were tight-lipped and evasive regarding their duties and their links to the SS. All of this has made researching the GFP extremely difficult.

Perhaps because of this difficulty, to date no one has written in any detail about the activities of the GFP. This is especially so regarding the activities of the GFP in Greece. Using primary source material, I have been able to produce a fairly detailed history of this elusive German Army organization. I have accomplished this by employing testimonials, prisoner of war reports, as well as primary and secondary sources, much of which has never been published before. In particular, I have been able to focus on the available archival data regarding the GFP's actions in the Holocaust. In addition, I was also able to spotlight their comportment in the occupation, repression, and atrocities committed against the general population in Greece. This work therefore, looks at which particular units and which specific members of the GFP in Greece were responsible for these actions. The list of GFP formations which served consistently throughout most of the occupation of Greece was relatively small, and their designations are known. A few operated in Greece only temporarily and were later reassigned to other areas of the Balkans. These units therefore altered their location, and even their commanders and personnel from time to time. By following the movements and actions of these GFP personnel as well as their units, I was able to obtain a more precise accountability of their criminal behavior.

In order to achieve a better understanding of the activities of the GFP in Greece, I needed to learn how this group was organized. Secret Field Police units operating in Greece like elsewhere, were subdivided into smaller commands that were dispersed to various regions, islands, and towns. By locating and identifying these units and their members, and tracking their movement, I hoped to attain a clearer picture of which GFP units and which personnel took part in the Holocaust and in which particular atrocity. It was thus very important to study the movements of these formations and also track their personnel to the various station posts. By cross-referencing this information with the massacre sites attributed to German forces, I was able to discover just exactly who did what.

Which units were dispatched to areas of Greece and what were their direct orders? Which men were temporarily assigned to GFP units at specific times, in order to help augment the formations that served with military units that committed atrocities? What GFP formation and which GFP personnel were dispatched to help expel Jews from certain parts of Greece? From what German army formation(s) did these men who were temporarily assigned to GFP units come from? What were their names and ranks? When were they placed on temporary assignment to the GFP for the purpose of these operations? When did they return to their former commands? What was the nature and character of some of the leading figures of the GFP stationed in Greece? I also tried to place GFP leaders who served in Greece in a social/biographical context. By doing this I was seeking to understand the roots of their participation in the Holocaust. For example, were the goals of the GFP officers in Greece aligned with the aims of the Nazis? These are some of the questions that existing scholarship has only minimally addressed, and which my study will consider in profundity.

As previously stated, GFP units were divided into numerous sub-commands, each of which were called a *Sekretariat*. These *Sekretariat* were then posted to various locations throughout the country. While this may seem inconsequential, it is extremely important in cases where we only have rudimentary knowledge of who committed a particular war crime. Quite often, witnesses to war crimes can only state that "the men"; or "some of the men" who committed the atrocity in "such and such a town" were from a specific unit. Worse still, are the instances when a survivor or witness can only remember that the perpetrators were *"Wehrmacht"* soldiers and nothing else. However, if we can identify which GFP units were operating at particular points in Greece at specific times of the war, then we can come closer to detecting which likely GFP formation (and their personnel) was or might have been implicated in a specific war crime.

Although this study focuses on the GFP's operations as well as their offenses in Greece, the most comprehensive and most violent war crimes of the Nazi Holocaust occurred in the USSR. Therefore, any study detailing the comportment of the GFP in Greece also requires that comparisons be made with their behavior in the Soviet Union and elsewhere in Europe. This is why I provide several chapters on the actions of the GFP in the East as well as in the West: to provide a comparison to their conduct inside and outside of Greece. One of the major stakes of this project therefore, is to consider how and why the GFP's actions in Greece contributed to the large-scale extermination efforts of the Nazi Holocaust. How does Greece fit into this effort? The simple fact is that by occupying Greece the Germans acquired Greece's Jewish population, directly threatening its extermination. The Nazis mostly succeeded in destroying Greece's Jewish population. In addition to this tragic event, the Axis occupation also had detrimental effects on this already economically poor and distressed country. Adolf Hitler and to a lesser degree his Italian ally, Benito Mussolini, were ultimately culpable in the deaths of about 530–560,000 Greeks during World War II, including 80 percent of Greece's pre-war Jewish population.[2]

Historians Klaus Geßner,[3] Robert Winter,[4] and Paul B. Brown[5] have established that the GFP (along with the Army, Order Police, SS and SD) was responsible for sending millions of Europe's Jews to their deaths—either by assisting the SS *Einsatzgruppen* in the killing fields, on the pretext of fighting the partisan war, or by assisting in the deportation of Jews and other persons to the Nazi killing machinery established in the death camps.[6] Paul Brown's research concentrated on dispelling the myths and misinformation which were weaved by Wilhelm Krichbaum in his 1947 monograph on the GFP, which he wrote for the U.S. Army. For example, Brown has dismissed the suggestion that the majority of the senior leadership cadre of the GFP were not Nazis, but merely "army intelligence officers." We now know that most of the top GFP officers were Nazi Party members, but what about the GFP officers in the field?

Paul Brown (like Winter), has also established that post-war exigencies, like the start of the Cold War, accelerated the release and "rehabilitation" of many former GFP men. Some of these men ended working in either the American or West German intelligence, or even the West German government. In 2010 Winter wrote an entire biography on the former head of the GFP, Wilhelm Krichbaum. In it he detailed his life before, during, and after the Nazi period. The wartime and post-war period were particularly interesting. During the early phase of the Cold War Krichbaum was recruited by Reinhard Gehlen,[7] the head of West German intelligence.[8] Three years after the Krichbaum biography, Winter published a book on the GFP during World War II. While it is a vital reference source on the topic, my only complaint is that it is too concise. Having a large interest on the history of the Secret Field Police, the length of the book (160 pages) left me wanting to read more. Nevertheless, both of Winter's books are required reading. While Geßner, Winter, and Brown have written general studies of the GFP, some scholars like Jean-Leon Charles and Philippe Dasnoy chose to concentrate on the history of the GFP in a particular region—in their case, northern France and Belgium.[9]

Experts on the field of the Holocaust such as the renowned scholar Raul Hilberg (1926–2007), referred to the GFP and its connection to the extermination of the Jewish population of Europe but only in passing.[10] Mark Mazower's 1993 book on the German occupation of Greece is a classic study, and required reading on the topic, including the Holocaust. Both of these works mention that GFP units were involved in the forced collection and deportation of the Jews of Greece, but do not go into great detail given that the topic of these studies concentrated on larger issues (the entire Holocaust, and the German occupation of Greece). Here again we see that there is room for further study on the activities of the GFP in Greece.

By now academics have established that the conduct of the German Army in the Soviet Union was very "hands-on" when it came to assisting the SS in committing atrocities. Consequently, in academic circles the German campaign in the East is now perceived more as a *Vernichtungskrieg* than as a normal military campaign.[11] The use of this particular term has by now become quite ubiquitous. This is thanks mostly to the hard work of researchers such as Hannes Heer and Klaus Naumann, who described the process fully in a massive study on the topic of German Army war crimes.[12] Many other historians have contributed to this theme, such as Christian Hartmann, Johannes Hürter, Ulrike Jureit,[13] Klaus-Michael Mallmann, Volker Rieß, Wolfram Pyta,[14] Götz Aly, Dieter Pohl, Thomas Sandkühler, Walter Manoschek, Michael Zimmermann, Christian Gerlach, Christoph Dieckmann, Sybille Steinbacher, Karin Orth, and Ulrich Herbert.[15] However this effort at dispelling the notion of the German Army's "clean hands" during World War II could not have been accomplished without the aid of earlier, ground breaking scholars like Raul Hilberg, Omer Bartov,[16] and Jürgen Förster to name a few.[17] The GFP's role as liaison between the German Army and SS, as well as intelligence gatherer, placed it in the forefront of this *Vernichtungskrieg*.

Present scholarship on the actions of the GFP has affirmed that the bulk of their mission in the West was counterintelligence. We know that the GFP behaved mostly as a regular intelligence arm of the Army and later of the SS Security Service in the West. In 1942, several GFP formations stationed in France and Belgium were disbanded, with their personnel being absorbed into the SD, or transferred into GFP units elsewhere in Europe. The selection process depended on the age and health of the GFP member. Younger and healthier members were transferred to GFP units earmarked for the Russian campaign, while older and less physically fit members remained in France and were absorbed into the SD. The GFP components which remained intact were employed in such relatively mundane tasks such as investigating sabotage, enemy intelligence efforts, desertions, and black marketeering. Former GFP personnel who had been transferred into the SD in France took part in the roundup of Jews, as well the requisition of their property.[18] In this they were assisted by several GFP units. The principle difference between GFP deportment in the West versus their behavior in the East has also been confirmed by scholars. While the GFP behaved ruthless in the East, its comportment in the West was measured. No study however, has been conducted on the behavior of the GFP in the Balkans. To what extent did they participate in the Holocaust and the wars of annihilation?

In the case of the Soviet Union, from the very start of the campaign, we know that the German Army played a central role in racial warfare. Various orders originating before and shortly after the invasion of the Soviet Union; such as the Barbarossa Jurisdiction Order and Commissar Order all worked to create the conditions where war crimes would occur on a regular basis.[19] The virtual *Vernichtungskrieg* that was waged in the East guaranteed that the German Army's comportment would be immoral. Given that the GFP quite often acted as liaison between the army and the SS, it had a greater and more active role in the physical annihilation of the Jews of the Soviet Union.

In writing the chapter on the activities of the GFP in the USSR (as a comparison to its actions in Greece) I have uncovered that GFP behavior towards the general Russian population was just as criminal as their complicity in the murder of Russia's Jews. Instances where GFP officials ordered the execution of non–Jewish Russian citizens proved to be just as common as their enthusiasm in the Holocaust. It would appear that the entire Russian population (not just the Jews) was targeted for destruction. This affirms the "war of annihilation" premise that many scholars claim occurred during the Russian campaign. It also appears that the GFP operated with stricter rules of conduct in the Nordic nations (The Netherlands, Denmark, and Norway). In these countries GFP forces were forbidden from committing crimes against the local population. Their mission was strictly military intelligence in nature. In fact, while GFP units were used to roundup Jews in France and Belgium from 1942–1944, they did not take part in the Holocaust in the Nordic countries.

The unique nature of this project is that it uses archival evidence collected from major repositories including rolls upon rolls of microfilm housed at the United States National Archives, College Park Maryland; copies of documents from The National Archives, Kew Gardens, Surrey, in the United Kingdom; wartime and post-war POW interrogation reports, as well as files held at the *Bundesarchiv* in (1) Freiberg, (2) Koblenz, and (3) Berlin regarding the GFP.[20] In addition to the U.S. National Archives and the Federal German archives located in Freiberg, Koblenz, and Berlin,[21] the United States Holocaust Memorial Museum holds a vast amount of primary source material that was made use of in this thesis. Not only does the USHMM offer documents, but a huge collection of maps—many of them dealing with German rear area security behind the lines in the USSR. The "Consolidated Wanted Lists" which was published after the war by the Central Registry of War Criminals and

Security Suspects,[22] was also of assistance in locating GFP personnel, what units they belonged to, and what crimes they were accused of committing.[23]

Under the Freedom of Information Act, I was able to obtain the files of two principal Secret Field Police members: Wilhelm Krichbaum and Philip Greiner. However, as is typical of many intelligence agencies that must provide information which they may still deem sensitive, those files were redacted. The transcripts from *The Trial of German Major War Criminals: Proceedings of the International Military Tribunal at Nuremberg* were also useful. The *Records of the Army Staff* (Record Group 319)—*CIC Collection–Declassified Files;* also, contain intelligence reports on the GFP and on the German police as a whole. Finally, GFP documents and identity cards, photographs, letters, and postcards on sale by private collectors were also studied. All of these sources have been referenced in order to create a history of the GFP's movements, operations, and conduct. My research also provides for a greater understanding of how these individuals came together as collective operating bodies of the German Army Secret Field Police. It also contains biographical coverage of GFP officials, including Wilhelm Krichbaum, the head of the GFP from 1939 to 1945. His biography also covers the period after the war, when he and other former GFP members were recruited into the OSS (Office of Strategic Services) and later, the *Bundesnachrichtendienst* (West German Intelligence).

The Introduction to this study attempts to formulate a link between the early history of the GFP in the nineteenth century, and their comportment up to and including World War II. I posit that since the second half of the nineteenth century, the German Armed Forces had a problem with institutionalized extremism that gave it a propensity for excesses that went beyond the norms of proper military behavior. This *mentalité* allowed for German army units (the GFP included) to become susceptible to committing war crimes. This theory has been proposed by Dr. Isabel Hull in her study on the German Army of Imperial Germany.[24] According to Hull, with the start of the Franco-Prussian War, the German General Staff operated under the premise of "military necessity" which created a "genocidal" military culture. This culture did not arise because of desperation, as many historians have argued. Instead, according to Hull, the culture's foundation lay in the German constitutional system of 1871 that ensured the supremacy of the military over the civilian branch of government; while also elevating Kaiser Wilhelm II (who some say was mentally unhinged) to the role of supreme decision-maker. This effectively denied non-military checks and balances on military leadership. Hull states that this system of no real checks and balances contributed to the institutionalized brutality of the German Imperial Army—a practice that simmered through the "shame" of defeat in 1918, and surfaced with greater vigor during the Second World War. The Nazi regime, instead of mitigating the existing brutality of the German Armed Forces, acted to amplify its violence. The GFP was a part of this military tendency in the German Army and was also affected by its psychology.

Chapter one covers the history of Greece from the establishment of the First Hellenic Republic until the Axis invasion in 1940/41. It also describes the social, political and economic troubles experienced during this initial one hundred ten-year history of modern Greece. The decision by Benito Mussolini to declare war on the Greek government of Ioannis Metaxas is also discussed. Why exactly did Italy invade Greece on October 28, 1940? Mussolini believed that the Greeks were ripe for conquest. Even though the brave and steadfast actions of Greece's army temporarily thwarted his plans, the Italian dictator's estimation of Greece's economic weakness and political division was not incorrect. To understand why Greece was so destabilized by 1940, one must know how it was that it found itself in that situation. Most works on the Axis occupation of Greece have not really explained in any great detail all of the social, economic, political and military events—some which were very nuanced, that left the Greek nation seemingly susceptible to foreign invasion.[25] The various key social, economic, military, and political issues which set the stage for the tragedy that occurred in Greece from 1941–1944 are covered in this chapter.

Chapter two is concerned with detailing Adolf Hitler's war aims from 1940–41. His military decisions are explained so that one can ascertain how it was that the German dictator eventually involved himself in the conquest of Greece and Yugoslavia. Greece constituted a significant amount of territory in the Balkans. It possessed strategically situated islands in the Eastern Mediterranean that would prove vital to both the Allied and Axis war effort. It appears that initially at least, Hitler desired a quiet Balkans to safeguard his oil supplies from Romania and Hungary. When Mussolini destabilized the military situation in the Balkans by invading Greece, Hitler was forced to take a more active role in that region of Europe. The pro-Allied coup that occurred in Yugoslavia in March 1941 was the deciding factor in the *Führer's* decision to invade Yugoslavia. The relationship between the German and Italian dictators is also discussed, as well as Hitler's plans for an invasion of the USSR and Mussolini's inept attempts to mimic the *Führer's* military successes.

Chapter two also describes how Nazi Germany's existing war aims were adjusted to fit the exigencies of occupying Greece and Yugoslavia. The German wartime economy regarding occupied nations worked very much as a parasitic system. The Germans would extract the resources and bring them to the Reich. Once they were occupied, Greece and Yugoslavia were immediately exploited for their resources. In particular, the Nazi exploitation of Greece's resources was so thorough that it created a famine during the winter of 1941–1942. This famine killed tens of thousands of Greek citizens and persisted in certain regions of the country as late as 1944. This extensive targeting of Greece for economic exploitation compounded an already shaky economy. Aside from robbing her resources, German interests now centered on defending their Balkan possessions from Allied capture. With Greece and Yugoslavia occupied, Hitler's oil supplies and the right flank of the projected invasion of the USSR were now safe. Other Nazi goals were now implemented, such as the destruction of the Jewish population. In Yugoslavia, the Holocaust was immediately put into effect. In the case of Greece, full implementation of *ha Shoah* had to wait until 1943 when the Germans became the sole warden of Greece and Yugoslavia. The GFP's role in all of these war aims is also discussed.

Chapter three covers the function of the GFP in the occupation of Greece. It includes a discussion of its role in the suppression of the Greek people, as well as its participation in numerous atrocities. Brief biographies of GFP officials are discussed. These biographies also include known individual traits and tendencies. The structure of the GFP command in Greece is also described in great detail. Chapter 4 is the meat and potatoes of the study, covering the participation of the GFP in the Holocaust. We know that the GFP took part in the Holocaust in Greece, but what we do not know in any great detail is which units and which personnel were involved in which of these Jewish deportations and murders on Greek soil. This chapter more clearly ties the GFP with the Holocaust in Greece. It does this by tracing unit movements and personnel transfers in order to ascertain which formation and which individuals were involved. Chapter four is filled with translated documents confirming unit and individual personnel transfers, including their sub-commands. Member lists for various GFP formations are also included. This extensive documentation of the GFP in Greece will better highlight its role in the Holocaust.

Chapter five covers the employment of the GFP in Yugoslavia, Romania, and Bulgaria.

A total of only one GFP unit served in each of these Balkan nations. In the case of Romania and Bulgaria—nations that were considered Axis allies, the behavior of these GFP units was limited. Although limited in their ability to serve, these GFP units made every effort to fulfill the goals of the Nazi regime and examples are given. Chapter six and seven are comparative chapters. Chapter six covers the employment of the Secret Field Police in France, Belgium, the Netherlands, Norway, and Denmark. It includes the dissolution of several GFP units stationed in the West in 1942, and the absorption of their personnel into the SD. The chapter also covers the operations, dispositions, and employment of GFP units in the West. It also lists the officers involved in key posts, as well as the GFP military chain of command. In addition, a substantive cross section of GFP formations employed in the West and their operations are also presented. Their unit histories are documented describing their comportment—all in order to establish whether there was a common behavioral pattern. Chapter seven is similar in presentation and length to Chapter six, only it concentrates on the operations of the GFP in the USSR. These two chapters are presented as a comparison of the deportment of the GFP in Greece. Comparing the behavior of the GFP in the Balkans with their comportment in the USSR and in the West, can help us to understand what level of violence they employed in Greece and what their goals were. Only through a comparison study can one arrive at a just and fair conclusion regarding the activities of the Secret Field Police in Greece.

This study's greatest contribution is in providing extensive documentation of the participation of GFP forces in actions that were criminal in nature. The study therefore adds further brick and mortar, solidifying established precepts with greater certainty and detail than has been documented before. By better detailing the history of the GFP in Greece, we can assess and properly understand the larger role which it played in Hitler's murderous plans. Finally, I should like to stress that this study will move forward our understanding of the role of the *Wehrmacht* in World War II. What were the Nazi priorities in Greece? Professor Mark Mazower states that the German occupation of Greece was part of the German military campaign that sought the subjugation of Europe. Further, that the economic effects of the German occupation did not cease with the German withdrawal in September/October 1944.[26] In fact, many believe that the German occupation had detrimental and long-lasting effects which still plague Greece today. Mazower's masterpiece on the German occupation of Greece describes fully the horror and agony that Greeks went through during the occupation.

While Mazower's work covered the general history of the German occupation of Greece, this study only concentrates on the actions of the GFP. I am seeking to find the answer to many questions dealing with the GFP that will hopefully allow for a better understanding of this organization. Did the GFP in Greece operate with the intent of supporting all Nazi goals? How was their comportment like in Greece? Was it like their behavior in the West? Was it like their comportment in the East? Did they attempt to preserve the basis of wealth and prestige of the Greek people as was the case in France and other Western countries? Finally, was the GFP a vital instrument between the German Armed Forces and Hitler's SS? These are but just a few of the many questions I shall attempt to answer.

Introduction
The GFP and the German Army's Institutional Extremism

The GFP as a Tool of Repression

It appears from all available evidence that the original mission of the GFP—protecting high ranking officers and army intelligence—was expanded during the Third Reich period to include more nefarious tasks. During the Second World War the GFP was utilized by Hitler and his henchmen as a tool of repression, and as part of the apparatus of extermination. Like the rest of the German Army, the GFP bended willingly to Hitler's will, and obeyed orders that were criminal in nature. Following Hitler's numerous decrees, the GFP acted on orders that contravened the rules of war as established by the Geneva Conventions of 1864, 1906, and 1929.[1] How was this possible? The answer lies in the history of the GFP and its parent organization, the German Army. The very manner in which the German military fought their wars prior to the Nazi period made it that much easier for the Nazis to easily re-task the German Armed Forces (the GFP included) for murder. The GFP's original mission—that of army intelligence and security was easily co-opted.

All of the original members of the GFP were Prussian police officers. Like the army, the Prussian police was not known for its liberal views. On the contrary, it reflected the monarchist and conservative tendencies of the Prussian State which had begun to develop as early as the reign of Frederick II. Frederick the Great believed that internal stability depended on *Ruhe und Ordnung* ("calm and order").[2] He also held that any means were justified in order for *Ruhe und Ordnung* to be applied. This conservatism and militarism was continually reinforced throughout the 17th, 18th, and 19th Century. The manner in which it was achieved was initially through (1) an alliance of the Prussian king and the nobility (the *Junker* class), who served in either the Prussian military or the government, and (2) through an efficient tax system that generated sufficient funds to finance the government and a large military.

Since the 19th Century the German military developed in a vacuum that prevented any checks and balances on its comportment. There were several reasons for this. First, the German constitution shielded the military from any civilian oversight or censure. Second, the German political structure and its base institutions provided no coordination that enforced the military's sense of self existence for the sake of the nation. Finally, once Otto von Bismarck left office in 1890, Germany had no cohesive foreign policy that might have guided or restrained the military's slide to activism.[3] In essence, Bismarck's principle that

"Germany is a satisfied nation" came to be questioned. This *mentalité* saw expression from 1904–1907 with the Herero and Namaqua massacres in German controlled Southwest Africa. On January 12, 1904, the Herero people rebelled against German colonial rule. General Lothar von Trotha crushed the Herero uprising using horrendous tactics. When the Nama tribe also rose up in rebellion in October, the Germans employed equally harsh methods. The German Imperial Army employed mass shootings in Southwest Africa. In total, some 100,000 Herero and Nama were killed.

It is obvious that in Southwest Africa the Germans pursued a policy of total annihilation. Today the German massacres of the Namibian Herero and Nama people are seen as the first Genocide to occur in the 20th Century. Unfortunately, this radicalism within the German military only increased in tempo when World War I broke out. The brutalization of the Belgian people during the German occupation is well documented. The employment of unrestricted submarine warfare, the bombing of enemy population centers, and the vast use of chemical weapons, all indicated the rising levels of violence which the German military was willing to undertake in order to succeed. Even the manner in which the German military conducted the war—to the point of self-destruction, indicated that it operated with little or no control. At the end of World War I German military culture did not learn the lessons of military excess. On the contrary, embittered officers walked away from the First World War believing they had acted with too much restraint. Many swore that they would act with more severity and harshness "in the next war."

The Creation of the GFP

The history of the GFP can be traced back to the Prussian Army of the 19th Century. This special army police force was created shortly before the start of the Danish-Prussian War of 1864. The original GFP force was built around fifty police officers who had been conscripted into the Prussian Army. Given that the GFP was organized shortly before the war, it arrived in the field too late to take part in the conflict. The Second Schleswig War (as it was also called) was fought for control of the duchies of Holstein and Lauenburg, and began over succession disputes when the Danish king died without an heir acceptable to members of the German Confederation. From February to May 1864 Prussia and Austria easily defeated Denmark. In October 1864, the Treaty of Vienna forced Denmark to concede the Duchies of Schleswig, Holstein, and Saxe-Lauenburg to Prussia and Austria. After the war, the Prussian army occupied the German provinces of Schleswig and Holstein. Schleswig contained a sizable Danish population which was opposed to the Prussians and Austrians. The GFP proved useful in seeking out pro–Danish elements in these provinces:

> During the wars of 1864 and 1866, the Secret Field Police appears for the first time in the Prussian army. It consisted of drafted police officers who were assigned to the protection of leading personalities and staff headquarters. The number of such officers at that time was very small, approximately 30-40 men. The GFP remained inconspicuous and the public was hardly aware of its existence. At the time of the war of 1870/71, the organization, which had now been activated in the German Army, had already expanded considerably. It consisted of police officers and police officials, mostly recruited from the civilian police force, and included also men form the criminal police. In charge was the Berlin Police President, Baron von Stiebitz, a friend of Bismarck's.[4]

The actual military campaign to defeat Denmark took only five months. However, neutralizing pro–Danish loyalists in the region took another seven months to achieve.[5] From the very beginning, officials of the GFP wore both civilian and military attire. Civilian attire was used when members were operating incognito in the general population. The conservative nature of its officers most likely allowed it to operate with great zeal against pro–Danish supporters. The fact that the GFPs mission was quickly expanded to include the search for opponents within the civilian population seems to affirm that from its inception, the GFP was used as a tool of repression. By 1865 the GFP included thirty-one police officials and one-hundred-fifty-seven field officers—all attached to the Prussian General Staff.[6] Although it was employed in hunting pro–Danish supporters, the GFP kept its original mission of protecting high ranking officers and army intelligence. It also served as the immediate bodyguard of the Kaiser and other important members of the royal family. This included guarding the Royal Palace, as well as apartments owned by the emperor all over Germany and outside the country.

During the Austro-Prussian War of 1866 the GFP was once again relegated to protection of the Kaiser and high ranking officers of the Prussian General Staff. The war came to an end so quickly that the GFP had no time to involve itself in anything more than protecting senior officers. The Franco-Prussian War of 1870–1871 was the next major conflict in which the GFP would be employed. This time however, the very nature of the war would once again expand the duties of the GFP. After the six-month-long Franco-Prussian War, Germany was united under the Prussians. The GFP was not disbanded but was instrumental in keeping an eye out for pro–French activities in the border provinces of Alsace and Lorraine. These two provinces had been part of the German states until 1648. In that year, they were given to France in gratitude for French support of German Protestants during the Thirty Years' War.

As for the Kaiser's personal security, from the very beginning it had been the duty of the GFP to protect Wilhelm I, and later his brother, Frederick III. Kaiser Frederick III had briefly ruled Germany from March to June 1888 before he succumbed to throat cancer. The GFP also protected Wilhelm II from the very moment he became head of Imperial Germany on June 15, 1888. In 1901, the officer charged with protecting the Kaiser was *Kriminalkommissar* (Criminal Commissioner) Gustav Steinhauer. Steinhauer had previously served as police commissioner for the Berlin police. In 1901, he accompanied the Kaiser to England.[7] He and several other GFP members never left the emperor's side; living in the palace and escorting Kaiser Wilhelm II wherever he went. When World War I broke out, the GFP escort was augmented and was never far away from the Kaiser. When war finally broke out in 1914 *Polizeikommissar* Kuntze took charge of Kaiser Wilhelm II's immediate security. By the beginning of the twentieth century, the principal peacetime mission of the GFP was guarding the German emperor. The secondary assignment remained protecting high ranking officers of the General Staff, while the third mission was to guard the headquarters of the army high command.

The Occupation and Suppression of Alsace-Lorraine

Border provinces in Europe have always been a source of contention and conflict. In the early 17th Century the provinces of Alsace and Lorraine were German regions that bordered the frontier of France. In 1648, at the end of the Thirty Years' War, France was given these two provinces by German Protestants as reward for France's assistance against the Holy Roman Empire. When the German Empire was declared in 1871 France was forced to return these two provinces to a now united Germany. Although these two regions contained a sizable ethnic German population, and the Alsatian dialect is German in origin, by 1871 these people felt themselves to be French. Most Alsatians had no desire to join the German Empire and were totally imbued in French ways. The very idea of being forced to become part of this new Germany was difficult for most of these people to accept. Worse still was the indignation of seeing German forces deployed and quartered in their towns and cities. For the French, the defeat suffered at the hands of the Prussians and their German allies in the Franco-Prussian War was never forgotten. Nor did the French government forgive the Germans for the shame of having to give up Alsace and Lorraine. From the very beginning therefore, French propaganda played a role in agitating the local populace against the German "occupation."

This French-sponsored resistance to the annexation of Alsace and Lorraine caused the Germans to react harshly against any local opposition. From the very beginning, it was felt that the Secret Field Police needed to be deployed in these two regions to help mitigate this resistance. Another factor which played a role in the manner in which the Secret Field Police would operate in Alsace-Lorraine was the way that the French had conducted themselves during the six-month long Franco-Prussian War. The Prussians had been shocked by the introduction of French guerrillas behind their lines.[8] French military reversals and desperation on the part of the French command is what prompted the creation of these "*francs-tireurs.*" The Prussians were not the only ones to encounter French civilians shooting at them from behind the lines. Units from other German states experienced similar events that moved them to act more harshly towards the civilian population.[9] During the war, GFP officials were responsible for investigating civilian attacks against the German military. They were also to determine if a civilian accused of sabotage was guilty or not.

The Secret Field Police entered these provinces shortly after the Prussian Army occupied these border regions. The GFP immediately assumed the role of suppressing pro-French activities. After the war ended, sporadic attacks against the German military continued in Alsace and Lorraine. The GFP investigated these acts of sabotage, while they also kept an eye on known pro-French leaders. In early 1880, explicit policies dealing with passports and their use were instituted. Initially, this only applied to the *Reichsland* regions of Alsace-Lorraine, where many serious cases of espionage had been reported.[10] This led to the activation of the border police in those areas, specifically directed against espionage efforts by France. Measures were also directed against recruiting agents for the *Légion Etranger* ("Foreign Legion") and former members of that organization in those provinces. At the time the Germans were concerned that the French were recruiting German nationals to serve in this military organization. Because of these tensions, the border police in Alsace-Lorraine worked closely with the GFP. While the German police kept a list of all military age men in these provinces, the GFP kept an eye on former members of the French Foreign Legion. It was the responsibility of the GFP to track down recruiters for the *Légion Etranger*. Touring bars and restaurants in civilian attire was another way of keeping an eye on local public opinion, and on individuals suspected of pro-French sympathies.

From 1871 to 1913 the GFP operated in this fashion. In 1914 Police Director Bauer was placed as head of all GFP forces in Alsace and Lorraine. The headquarters of the GFP was located in the city of Strasbourg (Alsace). Bauer had been a major in the Bavarian army reserve. In 1887, he had entered the German police and served as the police commissioner of Metz. He had also spent some time as police commissioner of the frontier town of Novéant. Bauer was fluent in the French language, and this most likely helped him to qualify for these police positions. Before being appointed as police commissioner for Strasbourg, he had served as police advisor to the Alsace-Lorraine Ministry. This ministry was a point of controversy and contention during German rule of these two contested provinces. The

GFP was tasked with investigating the activities and relations of the members of that ministry (and the population in general). Principally, the Prussians were concerned that some of the members of the ministry were pro–French. From the very beginning nationalist feelings on both sides were strained in Alsace-Lorraine:

> The widespread German feeling that Alsace is German land is by no means devoid of historic foundation; the common Alsatian speech is to this day Germanic and the French possession of Alsace is not very old. It is, however, one of those accidents resulting from the late crystallization of German national feeling that the people of Alsace were, by 1871, essentially opposed to annexation to Germany.[11]

Tensions and controversies continued for most of the history of the German occupation of Alsace-Lorraine. In January 1914, after years of political squabbles Governor-General Count Charles von Wedel (head of the Alsace-Lorraine Ministry), including his entire cabinet, resigned. Wedel had been leading a policy of conciliation with pro–French groups in the region, but this strategy had been strongly opposed by Prussian conservatives.[12] Governor-General Wedel had resigned in frustration over the impasse about what strategy the Germans should employ in Alsace-Lorraine. In order to smooth things over, Kaiser Wilhelm II decided to make Wedel a prince. He was to be succeeded as Governor of Alsace-Lorraine by Johann von Dallwitz, whom the Kaiser had tasked with trying to unite the *Reichsland* to Germany. The problem which prefaced Wedel's resignation had begun as a result of a clash that occurred in the town of Saverne a year earlier.[13] The squabble had been sparked by the actions of Second Lieutenant Günter von Forstner of the Prussian 99th Infantry Regiment.

In late 1913, Lieutenant Günter von Forstner was a member of the two-battalion strong Prussian 99th Infantry Regiment which was garrisoning the town of Saverne. Lieutenant von Forstner's insults towards Alsatians, spoken out of arrogance and rancor, began the incident known as the "Saverne Affair." A good number of the town's Alsatian population including local politicians, demonstrated their anger by picketing in front of the regimental barracks. The Prussian military overreacted and men were hurt. French newspapers used this incident to France's own benefit—highlighting how Prussian arrogance was once again slighting the "honor" of Alsatians. The Prussian military's high handed tactics with the local population of Alsace-Lorraine was a sore point throughout the German control of these two border provinces. The GFP was also involved in harassing the local population. Police Director Bauer was accused of personally interrogating many men and even women employing harsh methods:

> He took a cruel pleasure in torturing particularly the women whom he cross-examined, and liked to drive them to despair by his persiflage [teasing] and insulting raillery [playful insults]. Speaking French as he did quite correctly, he thought he was being witty in the French way. To assist him in his sinister task, he was surrounded by a gang of ruffians animated by the same passion for torture and all worthy supporters of such a chief.[14]

Police Director Bauer also played an important role in the "Hansi Case." Jean-Jacques Waltz was an Alsatian artist whose nickname was *"Hansi."* He was a staunch pro–French supporter who produced numerous anti–German postcards and paintings. He worked as an artist for the textile business, and drew postcards for local events. He began publishing satirical postcards and other works beginning in 1908 using the pseudonym "Hansi." He particularly liked poking fun at German tourists, depicting them as vulgar, obese and obnoxious people, whose ignorance was only matched by their arrogance. This negative portrayal eventually got the attention of German authorities. Hansi was ultimately jailed numerous times by the Germans for his pro–French activities. The last time he was tried was in July 1914 when a German tribunal in Leipzig gave him a one year sentence for making fun of the German Army.

The trial of Jean-Jacques Waltz caused national outrage in France and his case made newspaper headlines. During Hansi's hearing, Police Director Bauer warned the Imperial Council against freeing Hansi or allowing him to go free on bail. In spite of this Hansi was released by the military tribunal, pending the trial. The trial was a half-hearted attempt to appease the local population. Hansi received a one year sentence but he managed to escape to France. There he immediately joined the French Army as an officer and interpreter. He served in both world wars with distinction. When war broke out in August 1914, the German authorities listed him as a deserter. This was technically true since he had been born in Alsace in 1873–two years after the German annexation, so he was considered a German citizen. The GFP was assigned his case but Hansi was never caught, given that he was now living on French soil and beyond the reach of Germans authorities.[15] Police Director Bauer's warning that releasing Hansi on bail was a bad idea proved prophetic. Bauer's last position before the war broke out in August 1914 was as police commissioner of Strasbourg. When war broke out Bauer's position was elevated, becoming head of all GFP units on the entire Western Front.

The GFP During World War I

World War I would once again expand the ranks of the GFP, as well as the missions that it would perform. A month after the start of the Great War, the German Army GHQ for the Western Front was established in Charleville (Charleville-Mezieres, west of Sedan), which lies on the French side of the Franco-Belgian border. It was then that the Secret Field Police arrived to take over security duties for the German GHQ. The organization of the GFP during World War I was simple: each German army had one GFP unit attached—principally to protect the senior officers. Counterintelligence was also a role that was part of the GFP. The size of the GFP units at this time was around 30–40 men. Later in the war, the GFP would eventually employ dogs as part of their security apparatus. One study, written and published in 1931 described the observations of a member of the GFP during World War I. The officer interviewed was *Oberleutnant* (1st Lieutenant) Hans Witte, of the GFP. Witte wrote:

> Before the war, there were relatively few men involved in counter-intelligence operations. They were initially posted to central offices and assigned to frontier posts. When the war broke out [First World War] these men served as the core of the GFP for every army. Each army had a Field Police Commissioner and 8-10 field officers. As the war progressed, the necessity of the war dictated the employment of the GFP. For example, the region of Flanders eventually required three military field police commissioners and eighty field police officers.[16]

Witte explained that because of the stationary front lines in the West, as well as the neutral border of The Netherlands, and what he referred to as the "fanatical French and Belgian population" there was a need for a larger force of GFP men in the West.[17] Their job included intercepting (and reading) civilian as well as military mail, the discovery of hidden phone lines across the front lines, intercepting spies along the Dutch and Belgian border, and investigating cases of espionage and sabotage. By 1917 there were a total of three field police directors and eighty men assigned to the GHQ of the German Army in the West, while every army headquarters began the war with one police commissioner and about eight to ten men. This deployment increased or decreased, depending on the particular need of the army unit. Beginning in 1917, the men of the GFP were also tasked with tracking down deserters. The continuing stalemate and the dreadful losses of trench warfare had begun to demoralize men on both sides of the front lines. The morale of the fighting men was so low that in that year several French regiments refused to return to the front lines. The French high command resorted to executing the ringleaders in order to restore discipline. On the German side, the GFP sought deserters hiding immediately behind the front lines, but in some rare instances, a few German soldiers managed to reach their home towns but were pursued there by the GFP.[18]

In February 1917, the German GHQ stationed in Charleville was transferred to Bad Kreuznach. However, the GFP unit under Bauer remained at Charleville. Bad Kreuznach was the regional capital of the district in the Rhineland-Palatinate region of Germany. In June 1917, the operational area for the German First Army was moved to the region of Sedan, and its headquarters was placed in Charleville. This allowed for two GFP units to be posted in the town. The GFP unit for First Army was located in a building on Boulevard Gambetta. According to one French source, Major Bauer's official position was as representative of the GFP in the GHQ Great General Staff Headquarters. In March 1918, the principal German Army GHQ was moved to Spa, in Belgium. It was at this time that Major Bauer and his secret field police unit moved there from Charleville. Bauer's immediate superior in the GFP was Lieutenant-Colonel von Hahnke, however his immediate superior in the Great General Staff Headquarters was the "IIb" (communications) officer of that staff, *Oberst* (Colonel) Nikolai.[19]

What is interesting about this chain of command for the GFP is that during both world wars the communications officer and the intelligence officer for German units were always labeled as the "IIb" and "Ic" respectively.[20] One would think that the Secret Field Police, being principally an intelligence organ, would be answerable only to the "Ic" (intelligence) officer, but apparently, this was not always the case. The key is that both the "IIb" and "Ic" positions were staffed by officers who were always informed about everything that was going on in the front lines but also behind the lines. For example, the Holocaust in Europe was something that any German officer in an army staff charged with the position of "IIb" or "Ic" would have known about. Kurt Waldheim, who served as Secretary General of the United Nations and then became President of Austria, had actually served as both "IIb" and "Ic" during the Second World War while serving in the German Army in the Balkans. He never served in the GFP, but certainly had dealings with GFP officials during the course of his career. The issue of his controversy was that as "IIb" or "Ic" he would have surely known about the Holocaust.[21]

During the First World War, the entire counterespionage service, inclusive of the executive branch, was directly subordinated to the Army's Supreme Command. In addition to its intelligence duties, the GFP was still in charge of protecting high ranking officers, important personalities (like the Kaiser and his family), and certain high value buildings. The Secret Field Police Commissioners wore Army uniforms with light blue piping on their shoulder straps with light blue striping around the peaked caps. Their epaulettes only consisted of the Imperial eagle. Although the size of each GFP unit during World War I was equivalent to a platoon, an officer with the rank of major led each of these units. In general members of the GFP worked in civilian clothes, especially when engaged behind the lines. Uniforms were worn on the front lines or immediately behind the front lines. This was confirmed by a description of GFP personnel accompanying the Kaiser, on a tour of the Western Front. The Kaiser's visit to the Great General Staff in Charleville on July 24, 1915 was described thusly:

The moment the Kaiser arrived in Charleville, elegant gentlemen clothed in the latest Berlin fashion made their appearance in the streets, walking gravely up and down and scrutinizing the passers-by with a profound and piercing eye. This band of ruffians belonged to the German Secret Police, which sowed terror throughout the occupied territories during the occupation. Nobody was at all deceived as to the abominable task they were to begin. The Geheime Feldpolizei, as it was called, was a mighty force in the hands of the General Staff.[22]

There is a photograph in the private album of a British collector dated "1917," which shows GFP personnel with dogs at a camp, somewhere on the eastern front. In the photograph, you see several German shepherds and their GFP handlers. The sole surviving photograph is of a graduating class of trained German shepherds and their GFP handlers. The location where the picture was taken was at Uzjany, in Lithuania—one of the Baltic States that temporarily freed themselves of Russian rule thanks to the German successes against the Imperial Russian Army during World War I. It appears then, that dogs were used by GFP units in the Baltic States. It is unclear however, whether the GFP employed dogs in other battlefronts. The photograph was taken towards the end of the war, in 1917. Behind the dogs and their GFP handlers is a sign describing the training center, which included several wooden barracks and a large kennel. At the time, the dogs employed by the GFP were a relatively new breed that had been established in 1899. This new breed of dog was the "Alsatian." The "Alsatian" was later renamed the "Shepherd."

The wooden sign in the photograph has four rows of block lettering in various sizes and hung on the porch of "Building 17." The sign read as follows: *Dressur Anstalt Für Polizei-Hunde Oberkommando-Ost Geheime Feldpolizei A.A.D.* ("Dressur-Institute for Police Dogs, High Command East–Secret Field Police A.A.D."). The implication of employing dogs in the service of the GFP meant that not only could the animals be used as guard dogs for defensive purposes, but they could also be employed to take down a person in offensive operations, such as hunting down deserters or even guerrillas. While many military forces have employed the use of dogs, it is another indicator that the GFP had moved from being merely an intelligence gathering organization. The employment of dogs by the GFP indicated a more aggressive military mission.

Primary sources concerning the operations of the GFP during the First World War are scarce given that most of the documents were destroyed at the end of the conflict.[23] Fragmentary records do exist. One such example, dealing with Romania, gives us an eye into GFP operations in the Balkans. In 1916 Romania entered the war on the side of the Entente Powers. Three Romanian armies attacked the Austro-Hungarians on August 27, 1916. After almost two years of fighting the Romanian Army was crushed by the combined armies of the Germans, Austro-Hungarians, and Bulgarians. An initial peace treaty was signed by the defeated Romanians on March 5, 1918. This was to coincide with the demobilization of the Romanian Army. A more formal peace treaty was signed on May 7, 1918, in Bucharest, but the treaty was never ratified. Nevertheless, the Germans felt sufficiently confident that they began to transfer forces to the western front to support the St. Michael offensive that had begun in March 1918.

Although the Germans withdrew a large part of their forces to the West, a sizable part of Army Group "Mackensen" was kept on Romanian territory in order to assure that the Romanians would not renew offensive operations. There was also an economic reason for the Germans to keep forces in Romania. By 1918 Germany was starving and running short of resources. Food products as well as the oil fields at Ploesti were now vital to keeping the German war effort going. The Secret Field Police was tasked with keeping an eye on the movements and actions of senior Romanian officers and observe any suspicious troop movements. GFP forces were employed in small groups in the following towns: Buzau, Braila, Campina, Focsani, Ploesti, Predeal, and Rimnical-Sarat.[24] The GFP in Romania was led by *Feldpolizeidirektor Hauptmann* Hartenstein. Hartenstein's GFP-HQ was located in Bucharest. Secret Field Police units were attached to the headquarters of the German divisions in Romania. They were referred to as "political police" by the German command, and had far reaching powers of arrest. An attempt was made to bribe and recruit spies within the Romanian military and security apparatus but it appears that the end of the war and Germany's withdrawal in November 1918 ended whatever minor success the GFP may have made in this area. So critical was Germany's need for the resources available to Romania that German troops only withdrew at the very last minute. When they did retreat, they scoured the countryside for resources, thus slowing their withdrawal. Because of this, some units were caught and destroyed during their departure from Romania. In total, we know that about 90 percent of all GFP units stationed in Romania managed to return to Germany at the end of the war.

The GFP During the Inter-War Era

The time period between the end of World War I and the start of the Nazi period was a low point for the history of the GFP. At the end of World War I, the Secret Field Police had been disbanded. The Versailles Treaty had dissolved the General Staff, and with it all of its ancillary branches, including the GFP. The Treaty of Versailles had limited the German Army to 100,000 men and the duties of the GFP were deemed no longer necessary. In November 1918 chaos reigned in Germany following the surrender and the abdication of the *Kaiser*. In January 1919, the communists attempted a take-over of the Berlin government in what became known as the *Spartacist* revolt. Similar unrest occurred throughout Germany. In Bavaria, a "Bavarian Soviet Republic" was even briefly established in the spring of 1919. The Communist uprising eventually failed but disorder remained in many parts of the country. In Upper Silesia, the Polish population attempted a series of three risings against German rule from 1919–1921. The Treaty of Versailles had called for a plebiscite to be held in Upper Silesia two years after the Treaty was signed in 1919. The Plebiscite was carried out in March 1921. This vote would determine if the population was to live under German or Polish rule. Both sides feared cheating, so from the very beginning Poles and Germans employed propaganda and paramilitary units to threaten and cajole the local population.

A plebiscite police force was created in Upper Silesia in order to assure that no irregularities would occur during the voting. However, a great number of former GFP members managed to join this "plebiscite police force." These men had initially been selected as GFP officials not merely for their knowledge of police duties, but also for their loyalty to the Prussian King, and later the German Kaiser. Given their allegiance, most likely their devotion was to a unified Germany. No proof of documented irregularities on the part of these former GFP members exist. However, during the voting period the local Polish language newspapers complained about police intimidation. Various newspapers argued that the Plebiscite Police was harassing Polish voters. They also complained about police officers tampering with the election ballots.[25] These accusations were never followed up with an investigation, but it left lingering suspicions about the neutrality of the Plebiscite Police.

At the time, the region of Upper Silesia was composed of 60 percent Poles and 40 percent Germans.[26] The plebiscite results proved so confusing and divisive that both Poles and

Germans created small militia forces to assert their "results." Both sides accused each other of voter fraud, and constituent intimidation was rampant. Given all this, the Entente powers brought in French and British troops to keep the peace. In the end, the Allies asked the Council of the League of Nations to step in and decide the matter. It eventually decided in favor of Poland.[27] In light of this incident, it is perfectly reasonable to question whether the "plebiscite police force" should have been allowed to include former GFP officials. Although we have no proof that these officials were involved in any voting irregularities in Upper Silesia, their selection should have been questioned. Once the war had ended and the Kaiser had abdicated, the German Army was forbidden from reactivating the GFP. However, the Weimar Republic needed an intelligence arm to help protect the new democratic government from threats which it perceived as coming both from the Left and Right:

> Since the Republic too was obliged to adopt protective measures against espionage and also against economic espionage, the police were entrusted with the mission. The "Central Police Agencies to Combat Foreign Espionage" were created; one at Berlin, one at Munich and one at Dresden. The Central Police Agency at Munich was for many years commanded by Bauer, frequently mentioned as Chief of the GFP during the World War. Many former Field Police officers served as criminal investigators in the Central Police Agencies even after 1933.[28]

In 1920, the *Reichswehr* established the *Abwehr*.[29] The *Abwehr* was a German military intelligence organization which existed until the end of World War II.[30] The *Abwehr* was large and contained many departments. The GFP was but one force that was nominally under the command of this army intelligence force. The *Abwehr* was led by Admiral Wilhelm Canaris from 1935 until 1944.[31]

The GFP and the Early Nazi Period

When the Nazi Party came to power in 1933 the initial GFP unit created was *Gruppe Geheimefeldpolizei z.b.V.*[32] The new GFP was formed under SD auspices and was created in September 1933. The Secret Field Police quickly became a trusted institution, given that the men assigned to the GFP were either Nazis or conservatives, totally opposed to democratic principles. The first GFP unit was composed of one field police director, and thirty-two field police officials. In addition, the unit contained seventeen men drawn from the Army. During the Third Reich period, the GFP was expanded greatly. The initial stages of the reorganization and expansion of the GFP was the establishment of the *Geheimes Staatspolizeiamt* (Office of the State Secret Police) in mid–October 1936. This was done under the auspices of *Kriminalrat* (Criminal Police Superintendent) Dr. Herbert Fischer and *SS-Sturmbannführer und Leutnant der Reserve* (SS Major and Lieutenant of the [Army] Reserve) Walter Mosig (born May 24, 1907).[33] Dr. Herbert Fischer was Field Police Director from 1937–1938. He was also the leader of the secret field police unit that took part in the Spanish Civil War under the tutelage of the "Condor Legion."

Wilhelm Krichbaum's post-war report on his organization claimed that *Gruppe Geheime Feldpolizei Legion Condor*, which operated in Spain from June 1938–March 1939, was not part of the GFP. In spite of this claim, we now know that this unit was definitely a part of the GFP, and that it was the forerunner of one of the most active and brutal GFP units of the Second World War. Created on June 1, 1938, the principal task of this GFP unit in Spain was to work in unison with the *Servicio Informacion Policia Militar* (Spanish Nationalist Intelligence Service) that was to turn over to the GFP all German members of the International Brigades which became prisoners of the Nationalists. Those Germans serving in the International Brigades (principally in the *Thaelmann Bataillon*) which were turned over to the GFP were eventually sent to concentration camps in Germany. A total of seventy-five German communists and about seven hundred other International Brigade members were interrogated by the *Gruppe Geheime Feldpolizei Legion Condor*. Most of those men captured, especially the German nationals ended up in Nazi concentration camps. Their end in these camps was most likely an unhappy one. Members of the GFP who served in Spain from 1936–1939 were eventually used to help form *Gruppe Geheime Feldpolizei 570* (GFP-570). This unit would eventually serve in Russia and would establish itself as a particularly brutal formation.[34]

Another GFP unit also saw service during the early Nazi period. This turned out to be *Gruppe Geheime Feldpolizei 540*, which was composed of thirty men under the command of *Oberregierungsrat* (Senior Government Official) Dr. Hultsch.[35] It took part in the *Anschluss*—the German absorption of Austria into the Reich in early 1938. Members of the GFP in Austria were employed in arresting known Nazi opponents, as well as helping to protect Hitler's life when he entered Vienna on March 15, 1938. The GFP also took part in the occupation of Czechoslovakia in March 1939. The incorporation of the Sudetenland into Germany in October 1938 left the rest of Czechoslovakia weak because the principal Czech defenses were located along the Sudetenland. Once the Germans occupied this region, the rest of Czechoslovakia was basically defenseless.

Hitler threatened Czechoslovakia's president, Emil Hacha, with the destruction of Prague and the rest of his country if he did not accede to the German occupation. On March 15, 1939, under a light snowstorm, German forces crossed into the Czech territories of Bohemia and Moravia. As they had done in Austria, the GFP was assigned the task of arresting important civilians, as well as high ranking military personnel who might oppose the Nazis. The eastern part of the country (Slovakia) was not occupied by the Germans, but was made a puppet satellite state under the rule of a defrocked Catholic priest named Jozef Gašpar Tiso. Father Tiso quickly expanded the *Hlinka Garda* (Hlinka Guard)–the Slovak version of the Fascist storm troopers, which had been created by Karol Sidor in October 1938. Under Father Tiso and the Hlinka Guard, the Jews of Slovakia began to be persecuted.

Even though the GFP had already been in existence since 1933, the official date of activation was July 21, 1939. Less than a month later on August 1, the OKW established "Regulation No. 150." It began by stating "The Secret Field Police is the executive organ of the intelligence service of the field army." This initial sentence concisely explains the principal rationale behind the restoration of the GFP during the Nazi period. However, this mission would soon be expanded to other, more nefarious assignments. During World War II the GFP was made subordinate to the *Ausland/Abwehr Amt* (foreign intelligence department) of the OKW:

> Due to the close relationship between the GFP of earlier wars and the intelligence service as mentioned in the introduction, the mobilization preparations for the GFP were turned over to the *Amt Ausl/Abw* (*Amt Ausland Abwehr*) in the OKW, located at Berlin, Tirpitzufer 72–84 and headed by Admiral Canaris. Of the three branches of this department, only Intelligence Branch III (German Abbreviation *Abw 3*) handled pure intelligence work, so that matters pertaining to the GFP were also handled by this office and the creation of a service annual, preparatory induction measures for military areas as well as the procurement of equipment for the GFP was turned over to a specific section of *Abw 3*.[36]

Although the GFP was to be an army organization, its association with the Third Reich was deeper than this affiliation. Although recruits for the GFP came from the *Landespolizei*, including the *Grenzpolizei* (Border Police), as well as the *Gemeindepolizei* (Municipal Police), many came from SS organizations. For example, a good number of its members were drafted from the *Geheime Staatspolizei* (State Secret Police), as well as the *Kriminalpolizei* (Criminal Police). These two police organs were a part of the *Sicherheitsdienst* (the SS Security Service).

In fact, the entire German police apparatus was soon placed under the control of the SS. This close affiliation with the Nazis made the GFP a lynchpin of cooperation between the army and SS. Their very title and position gave GFP officials far reaching powers of arrest. they could also pass check points without being investigated, commandeer men and equipment, as well as demand services from any military and civilian office. The fact that many of its members were former *Gestapo* or *Kripo* officials, also gave the GFP added weight and influence. This close association with the SS became very clear when in 1942, when numerous GFP units operating in France were disbanded and their personnel were transferred over to the Security Police and SD. This was done in order for the SD to create station posts and units that would be located throughout occupied France.

Expansion of the GFP During the Second World War

When World War II began, the GFP was still relatively small. However, the expanding conflict and the increasing demands of the war would continue to require the GFP to enlarge its numbers. By July 1941 the GFP had eighty-three units operating in the field. Each of these formations were the size of a small company. The *Luftwaffe* (Air Force) was even tapped as a source for GFP recruits. In 1940 one GFP unit was created from personnel drawn from the *Luftwaffe*.[37] This GFP formation was numbered "GFP-637(L)," where "L" stood for *Luftwaffe* (Air Force). It was created on February 15, 1940, in Dresden (Military District IV). In 1941, it was operating under *Luftflotten Kommando 2* and was stationed in Brussels. In July 1943, it was moved to Italy and initially stationed in Frascati, near Rome. It was later transferred to Padua in northeastern Italy. The pressure for additional GFP units would force the recruitment of further Army and Air Force personnel. Nineteen-forty-one was a year of great expansion and reorganization for the Secret Field Police. Preparations for *Unternehmen Barbarossa* ("Operation Barbarossa"–the planned German invasion of the USSR) also required a reorganization of the GFP field units. Field units of the GFP that were assigned to the Russian campaign were to be larger in size. Most of these formations would contain about ninety-five men each, instead of the standard 50–60 man groups which had operated in the West.

On October 15, 1941, an 84th GFP unit was created (GFP-741). This formation was an upgrading of *Kommissariat der GFP für Deutsche Afrika-Korps* which had been established May 19, 1941.[38] During the winter of 1941/42 an 85th GFP unit (GFP-742) was created from *Luftwaffe* personnel. GFP-743 (the 86th unit) was created in 1943 and sent to France under Army Group "B." The 87th GFP unit (GFP-751) was established on August 2, 1943, and was sent to Italy in September to serve under 14th German Army (*Armee Ligurien*). In the winter of 1943/44 the 88th and 89th GFP units were created: GFP-744 (using *Luftwaffe* personnel) and GFP-745. GFP-744 remained in Germany and was sent to the region of Schleswig-Holstein, by the Neufahrwasser Channel. GFP-745 was sent to operate under Army Group South on the Eastern Front.[39] There was also "GFP z.b.V."—charged with protecting important Nazi officials during the war.[40] The individuals which "GFP z.b.V." protected included: Hitler (at Obersalzberg), Hermann Göring, Joachim von Ribbentrop,

Heinrich Himmler, Joseph Goebbels, Wilhelm Frick, Hans Frank (in Prague), Arthur Seyss-Inquart (in Den Haag), Joseph Antonius Heinrich Terboven (in Oslo), Karl Dönitz, Werner Best (in Copenhagen), and Ernst Kaltenbrunner.[41]

Thus, the total number of Secret Field Police units created during the Second World War turned out to be around ninety company-sized formations. The Nazi dictatorship only lasted about twelve years, yet it saw the expansion of the Secret Field Police to levels that it had never experienced before. Surprisingly, this rapid growth happened very smoothly and without incident. The GFP was absorbed into the German dictatorship during the period of the Nazi *Gleichschaltung*—the process through which the Nazis established a system of dictatorial control over all aspects of German society.[42] This rapid and smooth transition, coupled with the acceptable manner in which the GFP followed the criminality of the Nazi regime, could only have occurred if the Secret Field Police had already been predisposed to totalitarianism and extremism (which its history affirms). In this the GFP was likely a perfect model of German society in the early twentieth century: extremely conservative at heart. This right-wing propensity on the part of most Germans was fittingly illustrated during the relatively democratic period of the Weimar Republic, when it was depicted as "a republic without republicans."[43]

The GFP, the Nazis, and the Institutional Extremism of the Wehrmacht

The institutional extremism of the German Armed Forces throughout the nineteenth and twentieth century led it to its collusion with the Nazi regime and its exterminationist ideology. The *Gleichschaltung* brought German society closer to the Nazi fold. It allowed for the Nazis to co-opt most of German society and her most important institutions. The German *Wehrmacht* was the most important of those German establishments. The propensity for extremism and radicalism within the German military made this co-opting by the Nazis that much easier. The Secret Field Police was a recognized intelligence instrument of the *Wehrmacht*. Its military duties made it a center for the very kind of conservative and reactionary individual that made institutionalized brutality and extremism possible. It is no surprise therefore, that men in the GFP easily followed the SS into murderous behavior during World War II. In fact, the Nazis chose to give the GFP many crucial roles during the war. They did this because they trusted the GFP on account of its long-established antidemocratic tradition.

1

Greece: 1832–1940

The Changing Face of Europe

In many ways, the problems that plagued Greece during the early half of the twentieth century were issues that most of Europe was facing during the same time. The early half of the twentieth century was a very precarious period in which democracy did not establish itself very well in many of the European countries (with, perhaps, a couple of exceptions). Woodrow Wilson had wanted to support these newly created fledgling democracies but domestic American politics prevented the American president from obtaining the required funding to prop up the new European democracies. Many now believe that not fully supporting the new democracies of Europe after the end of World War I was a mistake. In fact, many now realize that the rise in Fascism was due in part to the failure of democracy in Europe.[1]

The issue of sustaining these democracies meant embracing a changing political landscape, where the old centers of power (the monarchies and nobility) were at odds with the rising political awareness of their people and their demands for an increasing voice in government. Industrialization exacerbated the changing communal and economic structure of old Europe with its old social contracts of the mass poor and the minute but privileged elite, into a system of commoditization that affected all aspects of human life. This ultimately exacerbated the breakdown of various forms of social order, human relations, and class divisions.[2] Continued imperialist expansion in the nineteenth century by European powers only served to increase tensions in a society that was already undergoing social, economic, and political stress and (most importantly) rapid change.[3]

The rise of nationalism was another major factor that led to dramatic alterations of the socio-political face of Europe.[4] The nationalist wave that spread throughout Europe in the nineteenth century eventually helped to bring down some of the old European empires. The idea of one nation with a common land, common ethnic origin, language, customs, and even a common religion was gaining momentum and spreading in popularity. Two supra-nationalist states which were greatly threatened and eventually destroyed by this political idea called "nationalism" were the Austro-Hungarian and the Ottoman Empire. One of the numerous peoples in Europe who sought their own nation was the Greeks. In the case of Greece, its rise as an independent nation carried with it special problems that were particular to Greece alone.

For one thing, Greece was a relatively poor country with no industrialization and completely dependent on an economy based on fishing, herding, and farming. Because of Greece's particular geography farming land was limited. There were other factors that contributed to Greece's instability in the early half of the twentieth century. Many of these problems that were specific to the Greek nation had begun in the eighteenth and nineteenth centuries. From 1832 until the end of World War I Greece grew at the expense of the Ottoman Empire. This constant expansion through numerous wars left Greece politically divided and economically weakened. This while also dealing with the European issues already described.

From the Byzantine Empire to the Creation of the Greek Nation in 1832

Greece's relationship with the Ottoman Empire can be traced back hundreds of years to the Byzantine Empire,[5] the rise of Islam in the seventh century, the arrival of the Seljuk

Territorial expansion of the Greek State, 1823–1947 (map by author).

Turks to the Middle East in the ninth century, and their eventual adoption of Sunni Islam. The Seljuk Turkish victory against the Byzantine forces of Emperor Romanos IV Diogenes at the Battle of Manzikert in 1071 spelled the beginning of the end for the Byzantine Empire since most of Anatolia (the heartland and economic base of the Byzantine Empire in the eleventh century) was captured by the Seljuk's after that battle. However, the Byzantine Empire would linger and decline slowly until the year 1453 when the nineteen-year-old Ottoman Sultan, Mehmet II finally conquered its capital, Constantinople, renaming the city "Istanbul" and ending Byzantine rule forever. From this point on, the Ottoman Empire began to expand into the Balkan Peninsula and soon conquered the many people's living there (including the Greeks).

It was not until the Greek War of Independence which lasted from 1821 to 1832 that Greece gained its freedom from the Ottomans. This war was not one war, but a series of conflicts between six nations. The bulk of the fighting (and dying) happened between the Greek revolutionaries and the Ottomans who wished to retain control. The Egyptians, nominally under the control of the Ottomans, also joined in the war against the Greeks. There was even a period of time when two separate Greek factions within the nationalist movement to establish a state, fought one another. Eventually the chaos and killings became so great three European powers: Russia, France, and the United Kingdom felt they had to get involved (on the side of the Greeks) in order to end the violence.[6] Territorially speaking, the unification of most of what would become modern-day Greece began with the founding of the Greek nation in 1832. Britain and France imposed a monarchy on the Greeks but a fierce desire to decide their own fate caused an uprising in 1843 that eventually forced the king to acknowledge a constitution and a parliament as the representative assembly of the people.[7] This was firmly established by Charilaos Trikoupis, the Greek politician who curbed the power of the monarchy to interfere in the assembly by issuing the rule of vote of confidence to any potential prime minister.

A New Nation and Continuous Wars

Throughout the various military and economic crises which Greece experienced, well meaning politicians were always willing to step forward and try to lead the nation through the teething problems which always occur with a young nation. One such politician who became the symbol of this goal of Greek unity and economic prosperity was Eleftherios Venizelos. Venizelos also represented liberalism in modern Greece. One of the ways he did this was by having Greece join the Balkan League.[8] Not everyone in Greece believed in Venizelos and of the ideas for which he stood for. Some saw him as overreaching and of undermining the monarchy during the First World War.[9] He had also been blamed for the disastrous campaign in Anatolia against the Turks in the early 1920's. He hailed from the island of Crete and had been responsible for helping to eventually unite his island home to the Greek nation. He later became Prime Minister of Greece and saw the nation through many turbulent decades of economic upheavals and military campaigns. Many saw him as the father of his country.[10] Another accomplishment of Eleftherios Venizelos was his ability to have Greece ally itself with other countries in the Balkans against the Ottomans.

The remainder of the nineteenth century and shortly up until the beginning of the First World War, many of Greece's politicians and military leaders continued their attempt to unite all Greeks into one nation, while others felt they should concentrate on strengthening the economy. Some felt that both could be accomplished. The quest for Ottoman lands which held a sizable if not overwhelming Greek population seemed to be a perpetual goal, especially for politicians like Venizelos. For example, after war broke out between the Ottomans and Russia, Greece joined on the side of the Czar and the Russian Empire. After Russia won, Greece gained parts of Epirus and Thessaly from the Turks and these regions were added to the Greek nation. Later on, during the Balkan Wars of 1912–1913 when Bulgaria, Serbia, Montenegro and Greece were all trying to gain additional territories—at the expense of the Ottomans—squabbling and factional fighting broke out amongst these "allies,"[11] whose only evident uniting bond was the expansion of their own kingdoms at the expense of the Ottoman Empire. In spite of this infighting, everyone walked away with something, with the Ottoman Empire coming out the losers once again.

The Continued Weak Economy

The establishment of the nation of Greece so relatively late in the history of Europe meant that for all intents and purposes, this newly created nation state was far behind most of the European countries in economic, scientific, and technological development. Even farming equipment was non-existent and rudimentary—still dependent on techniques that had been used as far back as the latter middle ages. As a result, Greece was financially poor and underdeveloped. Infrastructure projects only served to drain the already small coffers of the government and added to the worsening economic condition of the country. The Greek nation was too weak economically speaking to manage the large infrastructure projects that were needed in order to modernize the nation. All the while, as Greece's king and politicians attempted to bring Greece into the twentieth century, the little nation of Greece continued its attempts to unite all Greeks under one nation. Although Greece had many talented and good willed individuals in the government, many differed as to how to help the nation grow.

In 1893, the weak Greek economy was forced to declare public insolvency and to accept the imposition of an International Financial Control authority to pay off the country's debtors. Many Greek politicians from the left, the right, and even the pro-monarchist supporters had their own ideas about what should be done to get Greece through the economic crisis. The royalist supporters of the Greek King, George I believed that too much power had been ceded to the Greek parliament and squabbling amongst the politicians was impeding action that needed to be taken.[12] Others thought a military dictatorship might solve the nation's woes, while still others believed that improving the economic lives of the poor would ultimately lead Greece to prosperity. There were also those who believed that the few rich oligarchs in the nation needed to lead the way by having a freer hand in the economy and in labor relations with company owners.

For years, the Greek government had been trying to strengthen its economy. For example Greece eventually joined the Latin Monetary Union in 1867. Spain and Romania considered joining for a while, but decided against it. The LMU had been established in 1865 by France, Belgium, Switzerland, and Italy. Its goal was to attempt to base their paper currency on the value of a specific amount of silver and gold in their coins. The LMU failed for three basic reasons: (1) the value of silver was declining as the nineteenth century was coming to an end, (2) some states that later joined the LMU (Rome—i.e., the Papacy) were minting silver coins that were slightly less in silver content than the coins of other LMU members and exchanging them for silver coins with the higher actual weight, (3) German traders, in particular, were known to bring silver to LMU countries, have it minted into coinage then exchanged those for gold coins at the discounted exchange rate.[13]

According to the National Bureau of Economic Research, there were twelve countries which had been placed on "super-sanctions" between 1870 and 1913 during the classical Gold Standard Period. Of the twelve countries listed, Greece was placed (from 1898–1913) under "the International financial body that administers the finances of the defaulting republic."[14] In fact, according to the same source, Greece had defaulted earlier—in 1826 and had resumed the Gold Standard in 1880, but had defaulted again in 1894 again in 1898. Part of the reason for the default in 1898 had been the disastrous loss of the Greco-Turkish War and the huge war reparations which Greece had to pay the Ottoman Empire. Ostensibly therefore, the incessantly weak economic condition of the Greek nation was not simply because it employed the Silver and Gold standard for its currency, but was more closely tied with the lack of foreign capital investments, the relative backwardness of its agricultural output, the lack of a substantial industrial base, and the continuous wars that fledgling Greece waged from its inception in 1832 to 1922—a period spanning ninety years, or almost a century.[15]

The Rise of Ioannis Metaxas

Metaxas was born to a family that had received noble title in the 17th Century while the Venetians controlled the island of Kefallonia (Cephalonia). Born in 1871, he attended the Evelpidon Military College, graduating a 2nd Lieutenant in 1890. The relationship between Metaxas and the Greek royal family had begun while he was a junior officer serving on the staff of the Crown Prince Constantine in 1897. In 1889 Princess Sophia, the sister of Kaiser Wilhelm II, married her third cousin Constantine I, Duke of Sparta and heir of the Greek throne. Thus, began a close and friendly relationship between the German and Greek monarchies. Metaxas and a few other pro-monarchist officers were soon selected for further training at Berlin's *Kriegsakademie* (War Academy). According to one contemporary source, Metaxas performed so well that he was referred to as "the little Moltke"—a reference to Field Marshall Helmuth von Moltke, the creator of a new, more modern method of directing armies in the field. His rise in the Greek Army continued, becoming a captain in 1907.

Although a section of the army supported the monarchy, a good number of officers wanted change from the continued economic and political chaos that seemed to be unsolvable by the current regime. Forming the secret "Military League," these officers engineered a *coup d'état* in August 1909 that allowed for Eleftherios Venizelos and his Liberal Party to assume a majority in the Greek Parliament in 1910.[16] Venizelos understood the resentment and division in the military. He therefore attempted to placate the pro-monarchist elements in the army by subverting some key officers. Metaxas was actually asked to become an assistant to Venizelos, and he accepted the job. This conciliatory act on the part of Venizelos was followed by a reinstatement of Crown Prince Constantine as Inspector-General of the Greek Army. Most Greek historians believe that Metaxas took the post in order to act as informer and spy for the Greek royal family. The reinstatement of the Crown Prince Constantine into Greek Army affairs coincided with Venizelos' invitation of a French Army military mission to Greece. The officers in this mission were tasked with reorganizing the Greek Army.

The Balkan Wars of 1912–1913 gave Metaxas the opportunity to employ the knowledge he had gained in his 20+ years in the Greek Army. The "little Moltke" proved an able and effective staff officer. During the war, he was promoted to the rank of major. His performance was so prodigious that he was selected after the war to serve in the diplomatic negotiations that took place after the war. By then he had been promoted to lieutenant-colonel. Upon the death of his father in 1913, Crown Prince Constantine became Constantine I, king of Greece. If there was a year where both the monarchists and republican liberals worked in relative cooperation, it would be 1913. Fresh from their victory over the Turks and having gained additional territory, the goals of the opposing political forces in Greece briefly seemed to coincide.

World War I

The Greek king, Constantine I assumed the Greek throne on March 18, 1913, after his father George I had been assassinated by a Greek Anarchist. George I had been visiting the newly acquired city of Thessaloniki (Salonika) when Greece acquired the region after the successful Balkan Wars of 1912–1913.[17] The start of the Great War in 1914 soon broke the brief peace between Greeks backing Venizelos and the Liberal Party and pro-monarchist supporters. The disagreement between the Greek King Constantine I and Eleftherios Venizelos over whether Greece should enter World War I divided Greece along two principal factions: those who supported the monarchy and its policy of neutrality, and those who were allied with Venizelos and his desire to support the Allies against the Central Powers (which of course included the hated Turks).[18] The Balkan Wars of 1912–1913 provided a vital boost for a man who would loom large in Greek politics in the 1930s. This turned out to be Ioannis Metaxas. Metaxas early military career made him a devout monarchist. During the Balkan Wars, he not only served as a general staff officer in the Greek Army but also participated in diplomatic negotiations that led to solid alliances with other Balkan nations.[19]

World War I was the one single event which showed that the nation of Greece was divided as to what political goals and aims it should pursue. Between 1914 and 1917 the nation of Greece remained ideologically as well as physically divided, with Venizelos ruling from Salonika and Constantine I ruling in Athens. The Allies wanted to oust Constantine I from the Greek throne since he was related by blood and marriage to Kaiser Wilhelm II, but could not do so because he was being protected by Czar Nicholas II. When the Czar was overthrown in 1917, Constantine I did not formally abdicate the throne but was forced to leave Greece, assigning his second son Alexander to succeed him. Venizelos now had a free hand and Greece joined the Entente against the Central powers on June 29, 1917. Ioannis Metaxas and other pro-monarchist officers were arrested and forced to leave Athens by the French, who now installed Venizelos as Prime Minister. Venizelos and his supporters felt triumphant after having finally won the struggle with the king. However, in areas where the king had strong support by officials of the Greek government—both minor and important were purged of pro–Venizelos supporters. In retaliation, Venizelos did the same thing when he assumed office in Athens.[20] Around 1,500 pro-monarchist Greek officers were cashiered and Venizelos ruled under martial law from 1917–1920. Metaxas and his immediate family were brought by the French to the island of Corsica, where they were forced to remain there for the duration of the First World War. This policy of punishing political opponents through exile or loss of either a civil or military position became commonplace in Greek politics.[21]

The height of popularity for Venizelos was during the period 1917–1920. This was due mainly to the fact that Greece had joined the winning side of the Great War, and Venizelos had been instrumental in this. This gave Venizelos tremendous popularity in Greece, since the Treaty of Sevres had apparently won Greece additional territories from the Ottoman Empire and integrated more Greeks into the nation. In July 1918 Sultan Mehmet V had died. In his place, Mehmet Vahdettin VI assumed the Ottoman family dynasty and rule over the Caliphate, which was based in Istanbul (formally known as Constantinople). Concerned with preserving the family position Vahdetin VI signed the Treaty of Sevres:

> Vahdettin signed the Treaty of Sevres in August 1920. The document left only the smallest of a state in Asia Minor for the Turks, recognized an independent Armenia, gave Izmir and Eastern Thrace to the Greeks, and internationalized the straits. The Entente powers did not have the will to enforce these terms, and accepted a Greek offer to do so. The Greek-Turkish war which ensued until 1922 ended with a Turkish victory, in which Kemal and Ismet Pasha played a key role.[22]

The Greco-Turkish War, 1919–1922

The Greek Army landing on Asia Minor and the Turkish military's eventual rebuke of the Treaty of Sevres sparked the Greco-Turkish War (1919–1922) which ended disastrously for Greece. The war began well enough for Greece, but political events at home and abroad soon caused the Greek military effort in western Anatolia to flounder and then collapse. British Prime Minister David Lloyd George had initially encouraged Venizelos to expand the Greek Army's hold in Anatolia. This was aided by the Allied occupation zones which protected the flanks of the advancing Greek Army and by the fact that the Turks had to maintain military units to cover these Allied zones—thus denying the Turkish Army the ability to concentrate its entire might against the Greek advance. Landing first at Smyrna, the Greek Army quickly expanded its control of western Anatolia in a series of offensives.

In October 1920 King Alexander was bitten by his pet monkey. The wound was not properly treated and within a matter of days he died of bacterial infection of the blood—more commonly known as "sepsis." Because of his sudden death, the elections that Venizelos had called for the beginning of November took on a more divisive character, with Monarchists and Liberal Venizelos supporters leveling accusations and counter-accusations at one another. Even though the monarchists had no actual plan for achieving a fair and just peace with the Turks, they undermined the war effort by campaigning on a platform of a peace treaty with Turkey. The Venizelos administration had placed Greece on a war footing since 1917. Weary of conflict and tired of martial law, the majority of the Greek people opted for a treaty with Turkey and an end of the war.

The unexpected political defeat forced Venizelos and many of his important supporters to leave the country. To this day no one really knows why Venizelos decided on early elections. Perhaps he was hoping that the war would solidify his party's position in parliament, perhaps he wanted to forestall a possible return of the king. In any event, it is one of the biggest mysteries of the period. A pro-monarchist government was now installed. Prime Minister Dimitrios Gounaris now did what was common in Greek politics; his administration purged officials within the government and the military of pro–Venizelos supporters. Hundreds of pro–Venizelos bureaucrats as well as military officers were cashiered. At the same time Gounaris called for a plebiscite to have the Greek people vote on whether they wanted the Greek king to return. This angered the Allies, who still remembered the pro–German stance of the king. They threatened to withdraw military support for Greece if the king returned. In spite of this, a majority of the Greek people voted for the king's return.

The reinstatement of Constantine I allowed for Ioannis Metaxas to return home to Greece and (more importantly) avoid the death sentence that had been place on him in absentia by Venizelos. Metaxas had been found guilty in January 1920 for his role in an anti–Entente uprising in Athens in December 1916. Other pro-monarchist officers were now reinstated during the period following the return of the king. Metaxas however retired from the Greek Army even though he had been offered the post of Chief of Staff of the Greek Army in Anatolia. Metaxas refused to support the campaign in Asia Minor, claiming that Allied support for the Greek campaign was floundering and the dismissal of competent army officers because of pro–Venizelos sentiment would prove disastrous. His grim predictions about this campaign would ultimately turn out to be proven true.[23] Leadership of the war effort was now given to General Anastasios Papoulas, a monarchist supporter. Similarly, the ranks of the Greek Army were staffed with pro-monarchist officers, many who lacked practical combat experience.

Meanwhile, events outside the country were working against the Greeks. The French and Italians finally withdrew their forces from Anatolia, opening a flank that the Turks quickly exploited. Worse still, Italy and France began to sell arms to the Turks. Russia, now controlled by Vladimir Lenin and the Bolsheviks, decided to militarily support the Turkish revolutionary government. The withdrawal of Allied forces also allowed for the majority of the Turkish Army to concentrate on the Greek advance. A Greek Army was finally stopped along the Sakarya River in September 1921. Its forces spent and exhausted, the Greeks pleaded for Allied help. Still angry that Constantine I had returned to Greece, the British and French ignored the Greek plea for military assistance. In March 1922, they offered to mediate an armistice. Sensing they had the military advantage, the Turks refused. The final campaign of the war lasted from August to September 1922 and witnessed the complete defeat of the Greek Army and the expulsion of Greek forces from Asia Minor.

The massacres that both sides perpetrated throughout the war also left a lasting legacy of hatred between the Greeks and Turks that has lasted to the present. The expulsion of the Greek populace from western Anatolia now began. The Greco-Turkish War uprooted around two million people. During and shortly after the war, approximately 1,500,000 Christians (mostly Greeks) and 500,000 Muslims (mostly Turks) were forced to leave their homes during a population swap between Greece and Turkey. This massive refugee problem now worsened the already fragile Greek economy. The economic and social pressures involved in absorbing 1½ million refugees soon sparked anger from the general population, who now began to resent and disparage these unfortunate people. Many Greeks referred to these refugees a "Turks," refusing to see them as fellow Greeks. While the Balkan Greeks had suffered greatly on account of the war, the Anatolian Greeks had lost far more. They had lost their homes, their personal property, their shops, their farms, their animals, and countless family members killed in the war. Needing to find work, these unfortunate people now inadvertently helped to further depress the already low wages that existed in the country. Suicide rates increased in Greece as desperate people found no way out of their economic predicament. This event was not unlike the current suicide spikes in modern Greece on account of the severe economic crisis that began in 2008.[24]

With the failure of the Greek Army in western Anatolia, the government of Petros Protopapadakis had collapsed. In the face of this catastrophic military and civilian disaster, the monarchy was blamed. Greece was now plunged into further political and economic chaos. From August to September 1922 Nikolaos Triantafyllakos became temporary Prime Minister. Leading officers in the Greek Army now rebelled and forced the abdication of Constantine I as well as Prime Minister Triantafyllakos. As a result, George II came to the throne on September 27, 1922. In October 1923, the Republican "Revolutionary Committee" headed by Colonel Stylianos Gonatas, Admiral Phocas and Colonel Nikolaos Plastiras, asked George II to leave Greece while the National Assembly debated the topic of what future form of government Greece should have. The king complied but he refused to abdicate. Perhaps as a counter to the activities of the "Revolutionary Committee," Ioannis Metaxas had established the "Freethinker's Party" in November 1922.[25] The party was pro-monarchist and its manifesto had actually been declared a month earlier when its goals were published in the daily paper, *Nea Imera*. He left Greece on December 19, 1923, and headed into exile in Romania, where his wife was from. In the wake of the king's departure, and the ouster of Triantafyllakos, Dr. Sotirios Krokidas was appointed interim Prime Minister.

The Second Hellenic Republic

When the Second Hellenic Republic was proclaimed on March 25, 1924, the king was officially deposed, stripped of his Greek nationality and his possessions and properties in Greece were seized by the New Greek government.[26] Ioannis Metaxas soon returned after the establishment of the Second Hellenic Republic, claiming to support it. However, from the very beginning the New Greek republic had to deal with numerous issues that were virtually insurmountable. These included the fact that Greece was still dependent on agricultural exports for its economy, the problem of settling huge numbers of refugees from the Greco-Turkish War, as well as other foreign and domestic issues such as income inequality between the minority wealthy and overwhelming poor. Immigration (principally to the United States) which had always acted as an "exhaust valve" for many nations (Greece among them), especially during economically depressed periods actually decreased dramatically during the inter-war years because of restrictive U.S. legislation during that time period.[27] Before the First World War, about 300,000 Greeks had immigrated to the United States. The new inter-war quota however only allowed 100 Greeks to immigrate to the United States per year.[28]

Between 1928 and 1930 Greece's Prime Minister, Eleftherios Venizelos had managed to sign several foreign peace treaties: with Italy's Benito Mussolini (in 1928), and even one with Mustafa Kemal of Turkey in 1930. The internal situation of Greece throughout the twenties and thirties was politically and economically chaotic. The problem of absorbing 1½ million refugees (from lands that now belonged to Turkey) further burdened Greece, bringing it additional social, economic, and political disorder. Land was not available for these refugees who were mostly farmers. Foreign investment for agrarian Greece was also difficult to acquire. Communism and Anarchism was becoming popular among the poor and destitute.[29] As a result, in 1929 Venizelos passed legislation that severely restricted the civil liberties of Greeks. These laws were specifically established in opposition to inroads that were being made by the communists, their left-wing supporters, and trade unions among the Greek lower classes. These new laws were not popular with the very people who were the core of Venizelos's supporters. Nevertheless, the final nail on the coffin of the political career of Eleftherios Venizelos was the Great Depression.[30]

The liberal government of Venizelos had done its best to balance the economy in a manner that would both benefit the poor and the business class. Unfortunately, events outside as well as inside Greece always seemed to work against the stabilization of the Greek economy. The stock market crash in America in 1929 initially did not affect Greece's already weakened economy but by the beginning of 1932 the situation was already being felt and was quite a surprise to many in the Greek government:

> ...the Greek economy was caught unprepared for the Great Depression, as the conviction of a continuation of the years of growth had led to an expansion of commercial activity and the excessive increase in bank loans. Hence, when the crisis broke out, enterprises naturally found themselves confronted by a plethora of obligations, while banks saw their assets immobilized.... Consequently, the initial effect of the crisis was an immediate restriction on bank loans and a general shrinking of economic activity.[31]

That same year Venizelos was forced to resign. Part of the reason was external (the Great Depression), but another was one of Venizelos own making. He insisted on keeping the Greek currency under the Gold standard—which pushed the Greek economy into a deep recession and forced him to devalue the *Drachma*. He thus alienated many supporters who came from the lower working classes because they were the ones who felt the brunt of the depression the most.[32] There was still strong support for Venizelos within the Greek Army. These pro–Venizelos Greek Army officers staged two abortive *coups d'état* attempts in order to try and restore him to power. These occurred in March 1933, and March 1935. In the latter, Venizelos himself was implicated and he was forced into exile in France.[33]

The Dictatorship of Ioannis Metaxas

After a hasty and rigged election, King George II now returned to Greece in 1935. Elections were held again in 1936 with the balance of power depending greatly on the Communist Party, which held just 5 percent of the seats in Parliament. The Republicans and Monarchists both courted the Communist Party members of Parliament. Loathing the Communists, fearing another coup, and acting on fears of further national economic instability on account of increasing labor strikes, on April 13, 1936, King George II appointed Ioannis Metaxas, as interim Prime Minister of Greece.[34] The continued labor strikes and unrest throughout the country was sufficient cause for Metaxas to declare that a state of emergency existed in Greece, beginning on August 4, 1936. With the full support of the king, Metaxas instituted a military dictatorship that would rule Greece until the Axis invasion of 1941.[35] His dictatorship came to be know as the "4th of August" dictatorship, after the date it began.

Metaxas abolished all political parties, including his own—the "Freethinker's Party." His party had never garnered many votes. The height of popularity for the Freethinker's Party was in 1926 when it gained 151,660 votes in the General election. In order to control the situation, Metaxas also introduced censorship, severely curtailing what information newspapers and radio stations could report. Any articles that were negative of the dictatorship were prohibited. Newspaper reporters were jailed for breaking the censorship laws and political leaders were imprisoned for anti-government activities.[36] Although internally Metaxas crushed all dissent and opposition, employing Fascist-style policies to achieve this goal, he was surprising neutral in his foreign policy. He did openly praise the existing right-wing regimes of Europe, but he followed a neutral course, making sure to have friendly relations with democratic states like France and the United Kingdom. In spite of this, relations with Germany relatively friendly and cordial. In fact, by the 1930s Nazi Germany was Greece's largest trading partner.

Mussolini Sees Greece as an Easy Target

In the early twentieth century, the nation of Greece was experiencing economic woes that were reflected in its ever-growing political instability. Although industrialization was in its infancy in Greece, the changing economic and communal patterns that came with it altered the social structure of this relatively young European state. Another problem which plagued Greece was the issue of having to absorb a huge refugee population after the catastrophe of the Greco-Turkish War (1919–1921). The majority of the Greek population was poor and prosperity seemed impossible to achieve. This also exacerbated social tensions, which led to the rise of radical political groups from both the left and right. The continuing conflict between republicans and monarchists in the country only led to greater political discord. The Great Depression eventually reached Greece, slowing or completely halting whatever economic growth and modernization efforts the country had managed to achieve. When Metaxas established his dictatorship, he seemed to want to unite the Greek nation and forge it into a power for change in the way that one brings the fingers of a hand together into a fist—thus making that hand strong and robust.[37]

However, the attempts by Metaxas to mimic Fascism and Nazism mainly failed because the Greek populace, since the rise of their civilization in classical times, had been bred to live as freethinking and independent minded people. Nevertheless, these apparent internal political, economic, and social weaknesses were not missed by Benito Mussolini, Italy's dictator. Mussolini believed that Greece was ripe for conquest. He also believed that the internal problems of Greece would make the subjugation of the Greek nation an easy affair. However, he failed to understand that the greatest loathing for a Greek was that the will of others be imposed on them by force. This inclination towards freedom of thought and independence had been seared into the Greek psyche since time immemorial.[38] To be forcibly ruled was a detestable thing for a Greek. To be ruled by a foreign power was an even greater calamity. On October 28, 1940, the Italian envoy to Greece presented Metaxas with demands by Mussolini to have occupation rights to strategic Greek positions. The demand was in essence a surrender of Greek sovereignty. Most historians will relate that the reply Metaxas gave was brief and in the French language: "So it's war." However, a popular myth has grown from this event: that his reply was simply "Ochi!" ("No!").

Whichever is the case, Metaxas refused to yield to the Italian demands and prepared to defend Greek independence. A few hours after this meeting between the Italian envoy and Ioannis Metaxas, the Italian Army invaded Greece from their bases in Albania. Although the Greek nation was saddled by domestic woes when Italy invaded, the Greek people did what they had done so many times before: they stood up to the foreign despot and fought bravely. The smaller Greek Army not only held off the larger Italian force, but even managed to counterattack, pushing deep into Italian held Albanian territory. It was at this point in time that Adolf Hitler sealed Greece's fate by deciding to assist the Italian dictator's floundering campaign. Luckily for Metaxas, he did not live long enough to see the Greece that he loved defeated and prostrate. On January 29, 1941, after a short but severe illness, Metaxas died of a bacterial infection of the pharynx. His health had deteriorated after several months of tirelessly working to defend his nation from Italian aggression. Upon his death, George II appointed Alexandros Koryzis as the new Prime Minister, but he continued the "4th of August" dictatorship until the Greek capitulation.

The Prewar Jewish Community in Greece

The prewar Jewish community in Greece was principally divided into two groups. The first was the Romaniot Jews (sometimes spelled "Romaniote"), who had existed in Greece and the surrounding regions for about 2,000 years.[39] The Romaniotes were located on some Ionian islands like Corfu, Rhodes, Lesbos, Chios, and Samos. On the mainland, a fairly sizable number of Romaniot Jews lived in Athens, Thebes, Ioannina, Chalcis, Arta, and Corinth. Romaniote oral tradition tells of Jews arriving in Ioannina, Greece shortly after the failed rebellion in Jerusalem in 70 A.D. against the Romans. The Romaniote Jews were completely assimilated into Greek life. The only thing that set them apart from their neighbors was their practice of Judaism.

The second group of Jews living in Greece was the Sephardic Jewish community, which had arrived beginning in 1492 when Queen Isabella I (of Castile & Leon) and King Ferdinand II (of Aragon) had expelled the Jews of Spain following the Alhambra Decree of March 31, 1492.[40] Most of those Sephardic Jews who reached Greece managed to settle in northern Greece. Under the Ottoman Empire, the city of Salonika (Thessaloniki) became the center of that Sephardic Jewish life for hundreds of years. In fact, it remained predominantly a city with a Jewish majority.[41] Like the Romaniote Jews, the Sephardim were totally integrated into Greek society. Of the approximately 70–80,000 Jews living in Greece during World War II, around 80 percent perished. From 1941–1943, some 14,605 Greek Jews were living in the Italian zone of occupation and were temporarily protected from the clutches of the Nazis. After the Italian surrender these Greek Jews were once again threatened. The lucky ones managed to make it to Allied controlled Italy. Most however, only had two choices: hide and hope not to be caught, or join the partisans and hope not to be caught. Eventually some 6,320 of them were captured and murdered by the Nazis.[42]

Conclusions

Greece was a relatively young nation that had been born out of a struggle for independence. Yet its roots lay deep in the past; in the history of the Byzantine Empire. Its people had a rich culture with unique customs. Their major religion (Eastern Orthodox Christianity) had deep roots in Greek society, and the population was industrious. Antisemitism was almost non-existent, and the nature of most Greeks was friendly and peaceful. Yet, in spite of all these positive aspects, history had not been kind to Greece. The region of the Balkan peninsula where Greece was established was principally mountainous, with a lot of coastline. The land was therefore not conducive to industrialization. During its first one-hundred-year history, Greece continued to suffer from conflict and growing pains. Economic, political, and social upheavals, both internal and external, caused the little nation of Greece to flounder in what seemed like a continuous sea of troubles. It was within this historical construct that Greece found itself engulfed in the greatest conflict in the history of mankind. The Greek people had not wished it, but nevertheless it was thrust upon them by evil men. Greece, like other nations of the world, suffered terribly as a result of this aggression. In the case of Greece, the occupation was particularly devastating, given its already weakened state just prior to the war.

2

Hitler's War Aims and the Balkans

Fall of 1940

In the fall of 1940 Adolf Hitler was disinclined to absorb Greece and Yugoslavia as part of his conquests. He had been devoting most of his attention and energies to planning the upcoming invasion of the Soviet Union. In fact, the German dictator considered the Balkans a mere "sideshow."[1] That is to say his concerns were directed towards planning the destruction of the USSR. Hitler hoped that the defeat of Russia would force England to sue for peace. Compared to this planned undertaking, the Balkans was indeed a "sideshow." In any event, Hitler's initial reluctance in occupying Greece and Yugoslavia had practical foundations. The German dictator wanted to assure that the vital oil fields at Ploesti in Romania, and near Lake Balaton in Hungary were safe from Allied attack. As the war dragged on these oil fields became even more vital to the German war machine. Hitler also wanted to assure that the right flank of the upcoming Russian campaign would be secure. Therefore, having the Balkan nations either on his side or neutral allowed for these goals to be achieved.

Where to Attack After the Fall of France?

When the Germans defeated the French Third Republic in the summer of 1940 Hitler and the Nazis were exuberant, believing that they were on the brink of winning the war. In spite of France's surrender the German dictator still faced a very defiant United Kingdom. Hitler had a grudging admiration for the English people, perhaps because of his belief that the English people were Aryan. In fact since the mid–1920s the Nazi dictator apparently desired friendship, and even considered a possible alliance with the English.[2] For whatever reason, the Führer offered peace terms in July 1940 to the English people and their new Prime Minister, Winston Churchill.[3] However with Hitler's false promises of peace still fresh on their minds, Churchill and most of his cabinet ministers absolutely refused to consider Hitler's peace offer, believing it to be just another stratagem on the part of the Nazi leader.

Churchill was also determined to avoid the political errors of his predecessor, Neville Chamberlain who had trusted Hitler's promises too readily. When addressing Parliament regarding the Czechoslovakian crisis he had stated that at Munich "Herr Hitler was speaking the truth."[4] In all fairness to Chamberlain, the English people (as well as many others in Europe) were hoping that the Munich agreement would bring real peace. When Chamberlain returned to London, he was hailed as a hero.[5] The American President, Franklin Delano Roosevelt even chimed in on the topic of peace with the Nazi dictator as late as September

1941, when he listed eight reasons why an accommodation with Hitler and the Nazi regime was impossible.[6] Winston Churchill needed no urging from his good friend, the American president. He was dead set on defeating Nazi Germany at whatever cost. This was proved by his famous speech to the House of Commons on June 4, 1940, when he said:

> We shall go on to the end. We shall fight in France, we shall fight on the seas and oceans, we shall fight with growing confidence and growing strength in the air, we shall defend our island, whatever the cost may be. We shall fight on the beaches, we shall fight on the landing grounds, we shall fight in the fields and in the streets, we shall fight in the hills; we shall never surrender....[7]

Another possible cause for Churchill's intransigence might have been the realization that making peace with Hitler would have emboldened the far right in England. These were Englishmen who had joined the British Union of Fascists. This political party had been created in 1932 by Sir Oswald Mosley and had reached some 20,000 members by 1939. In 1940 it had been proscribed by the British government. Sir Oswald Mosley and 740 other British Fascists were then imprisoned for the duration of the war. If peace was made between the United Kingdom and Nazi Germany, Mosley and his men would be free to continue their Fascist activities. Peace with Germany therefore, would have set England on the road to Fascism. Consequently, Churchill would have never sought peace terms with Hitler or any other Nazi that might replace him, believing correctly that Nazism was a plague that needed to be expunged from the world.

Reluctantly, the German dictator issued Führer Directive No. 16 on July 16, 1940, ordering that preparations be made for an invasion of England. This was codenamed operation *Seelöwe* ("Sea Lion"). Army forces were assigned to planned beachheads, landing barges were collected by the German navy, and other specialized equipment was gathered. These preparations did not go unnoticed by the British. The landing barges were quickly discovered along French and Dutch canals and rivers and were systematically destroyed by the Royal Air Force. Given that Hitler's heart was not in this invasion, the plan was allowed to die. On October 12, 1940, Hitler issued an order, releasing army troops assigned for operation *Seelöwe* to be sent to other fronts. The planned invasion of England never materialized. In any event, while the British navy controlled the seas, an invasion of England would have proved catastrophic for the Germans. When Mussolini declared war on Greece at the end of October, Hitler was furious. Reluctantly he ordered that preparations be made to come to the assistance of the Italian dictator.

The Führer no doubt continued to entertain hopes that perhaps the United Kingdom would come to some sort of accommodation with the Third Reich. Hitler rightly believed that Winston Churchill and the British were hoping the USSR would join the war on their side. He reasoned that if the Soviet Union was conquered, then the last hope for the United Kingdom to defeat Nazi Germany would be removed.[8] With this hope gone, the German dictator believed England would sue for peace.[9] Hitler appears not to have entertained the likelihood that America might enter the war on the side of the British. If he did, he merely brushed this possibility aside, given that the United States was not presently on the dictator's crosshairs. Churchill was indeed banking that Joseph Stalin and the Red Army would join the war to help defeat Hitler. If the Soviet Union declared war against Germany, the Nazis would have to fight on two fronts. Having to fight on two fronts is part of the reason why Imperial Germany lost World War I. The entry of the USSR in the war on the side of the Allies would have obviously been a strategic advantage for the British and a nightmare for the Germans.

In the end the German dictator would provide the British prime minister with the two-front war that he wanted. Planning for the invasion of the Soviet Union, which Hitler codenamed "Barbarossa" had begun as early as the fall of 1940. The Führer appears to have made the decision to invade the USSR for several reasons. It was not merely to crush England's hope that Russia would become an ally against Germany, but was also made on political grounds. In his rambling manifesto, *Mein Kampf* ("My Struggle"), he declared his intention to destroy the Soviet Union in order to create additional "living space" for the German people. He wrote that Germany's future lay in conquering the East, of which the USSR comprised a great portion of those lands. We may also speculate that in the fall of 1940 with the English defiant and undefeated, Hitler was struggling to find a strategy that would gain him ultimate victory in Europe. Unable to invade England and complete his conquest, the Führer now turned his gaze eastward.

The Italians Destabilize the "Soft Underbelly"

As 1940 ended, there were many concerns that worried the German dictator. By the autumn, the Balkans seemed to be taking up more and more of Hitler's attention. In November, British forces had landed on the Greek islands of Crete and Lemnos. British encroachment in the Balkans would threaten not only the ultimate success of Mussolini's ill-conceived invasion of Greece, but it also endangered part of the rear area for the planned German invasion of the USSR. In addition, Hitler's oil supply was in jeopardy, as well as Europe's "soft underbelly." If the Allies were able to establish a foothold in the Balkans, then the strategic oil fields in Romania and Hungary would be threatened and the Mediterranean basin region would be open to Allied air and land attack. This would have severely limited Hitler's ability to wage war and would force the German dictator to divert substantial military resources to protect this region of Europe. The right wing of Hitler's Russian adventure would also be put at risk from Allied attacks emanating from the Balkans.

Events in Libya and Egypt in the winter of 1940–41 would underline that Axis vulnerability in the Mediterranean area of operations. Mussolini had declared war on the Allies on June 10, 1940—when it had become quite apparent that the Germans would defeat France. Clearly the Italian dictator was hoping to get in on the spoils of war. Italy's entry into the conflict however, opened several battle fronts throughout most of the Mediterranean basin, and in East Africa. In August 1940, the 10th Army under General Rodolfo Graziani, comprising some 150,000 troops was ordered to invade British held Egypt from Italian-controlled Libya. The British in Egypt were outnumbered, having perhaps 63,000 British and Commonwealth forces. From December 1940 to February 1941 36,000 troops under Lieutenant-General Sir Richard O'Connor counter-attacked.[10] The small Allied force almost destroyed the entire Italian 10th Army, capturing some 100–115,000 prisoners and conquering most of Cyrenaica (eastern Libya).[11]

Several months before the Italian military reversals in North Africa, Mussolini decided to up the ante by invading Greece. By doing so he destabilized the Axis military situation in the Balkans and the Mediterranean even further. These unexpected military reversals required not only Hitler's attention, but a diversion of sizeable German military forces. It also ended up delaying Hitler's invasion of the USSR by about six weeks. Six weeks of critical summer weather that could have proved decisive for Germany's Russian gamble. So important were these six weeks of delay that after the Nazi invasion began, the USSR thanked Greece and Yugoslavia for having been the cause of this German delay. Anthony Eden also praised the brave Greek defense and defended the employment of British troops in the Balkans, citing the same reason. Even Adolf Hitler agreed when he reportedly said:

> If the Italians hadn't attacked Greece and needed our help, the war would have taken a different course. We could have anticipated the Russian cold by weeks and conquered Leningrad and Moscow. There would have been no Stalingrad.[12]

Therefore, Germany's diversion into the Balkans ultimately proved detrimental to the Axis war effort. It also partly explains Hitler's growing frustration with the Italian dictator.

When Mussolini finally launched his invasion of Greece it was from his recent Balkan acquisition: Albania. Although the Italian dictator had physically invaded and acquired Albania in 1939, he had begun the conquest of this small Balkan nation as early as 1931. This had occurred through Italian investments, which eventually increased and augmented its control of the Albanian economy.[13] The Italian military occupation in April 1939 was virtually a bloodless one which lasted about a week, expelling King Zog's government and establishing direct Italian rule.[14] Mussolini was exuberant and boasted that Albania would be Italy's bridgehead in the Balkans.[15] This small nation was to become another Italian colony. Greece would be next on the Fascist dictator's Balkan "hit list." The Italian invasion of Greece in the early morning hours of October 28, 1940, quickly turned into a military disaster that progressively worsened by the spring of 1941.[16] This Italian aggression against a neutral nation was set in motion by the Italian dictator without consultation or agreement with Adolf Hitler. By all accounts, Hitler was furious with the Italian dictator.[17] Not only because of his inept military blundering, but because Hitler had been slowly courting the government of Ioannis Metaxas.

Surprisingly one of the principal reasons for Mussolini's decision to invade Greece while simultaneously trying to capture Egypt was to try and "one-up" the German dictator. According to Count Galeazzo Ciano, Mussolini complained: "Hitler always faces me with a *fait accompli*. This time I am going to pay him back in his own coin. He will find out from the papers that I have occupied Greece."[18] The Italian mess in Greece would require detailed planning, but the German dictator needed to address the calamitous state of affairs in North Africa immediately. To stabilize the situation Hitler sent General Erwin Rommel and three elite German divisions to Libya. These units would eventually come to be known as the *Afrika Korps* and its commander as the famed "Desert Fox." With this small force, Rommel was able to counterattack and retake eastern Libya from the British. Rommel even exceeded Hitler's expectations when in the spring of 1941 he launched an invasion of Egypt that quickly reached the town of Tobruk. This small German force had stopped the Allied advance into Libya and had actually pushed them back into Egypt. It was inconceivable to Mussolini that three German divisions were accomplishing what an entire Italian army could not achieve. Instead of being grateful to Germany for helping to prevent an Italian collapse in North Africa, he gritted his teeth in frustration and envy.

The Balkan campaign which Hitler was now forced to take part in would involve the deployment of dozens of German divisions and an equal number of air force squadrons. When Yugoslavia's regent was overthrown and a pro–British government was installed, the plan to defeat Greece was expanded to also include Yugoslavia. These invasions would be followed up by an occupation army that by mid–1943 would number in the hundreds of thousands. Thus, the conquest of Yugoslavia and Greece—something which the Führer wished to avoid in 1940/41, would become a drain on German military resources. The Third Reich found itself part-owners of two additional countries which they were not yet planning to plunder or invade. As previously stated, at the end of 1940 Hitler's gaze had begun to turn East, to the USSR where he hoped its conquest would win Germany *lebensraum* (living space) while also forcing the United Kingdom to sue for peace.[19]

Hitler, Mussolini and the Balkans

The decision by Adolf Hitler to invade Greece and Yugoslavia was made on military and political grounds. The immediate reason for the German invasion was to save the floundering campaign of the Italian army, which had launched an attack against Greece in October 1940. The relationship between Hitler and Italy's Fascist leader Benito Mussolini proved to be stormy and mercurial. This strained alliance set the tone for future dealings between both totalitarian regimes. The tensions which existed between these cobelligerents was confirmed by the difficulty which both dictators found in trying to cooperate. An example of this complicated union were the numerous occupation troubles which the Germans and Italians experienced after they conquered Greece and Yugoslavia. Both Hitler and Mussolini were often at odds as to how to rule these conquered nations. Artificial occupation zones created to delineate Italian and German spheres of control produced a bureaucratic nightmare that only benefited the enemy. These problems gave rise to tensions between the Axis powers. Mistrust grew to dislike between the Germans and Italians, which eventually turned into contempt. This is a perfect paradigm for the relationship that developed between Hitler and Mussolini during the war. Their military union was therefore more a form of expediency than an actual coalition.

Stabilizing the "Soft Underbelly"

The Mediterranean basin was viewed by Hitler and his opponents as the "soft underbelly" of Nazi controlled Europe. Before Mussolini involved himself in the war, there was very little that the Allies could do to diminish Hitler's hegemony in Europe through the Mediterranean region. Therefore, a stable Balkans and a neutral Italy was ideal for Hitler's strategic plans in 1940–41. By the spring of 1941 Adolf Hitler had bullied and/or cajoled many states in central and southeastern Europe into either joining in his planned invasion of the USSR or remaining neutral in the war. In November 1940, the Führer had compelled the leaders of Hungary, Romania, and Slovakia into joining the Tripartite Pact. The Hungarians and Romanians would eventually provide entire armies for Hitler's Russian adventure. Even the puppet state of Slovakia, which had been created when the Czech regions became just two more German provinces (Bohemia and Moravia),[20] provided a few divisions for the Russian campaign. On March 1, 1941, Bulgaria signed the Tripartite Treaty. In the case of Yugoslavia, the Nazi leader saw its regent Prince Paul, as the key to limiting British influence in the Balkans. Prince Paul had assumed control of the Yugoslav government after his cousin King Alexander I had been assassinated in Marseilles in 1934. He was to rule in this capacity until Prince Peter II could reach adulthood and assume the throne. Yugoslavia was therefore the "missing key" in Hitler's Balkan plans. However, that "key" seemed to have been found by the Nazis when the Yugoslav regent signed the Tripartite Treaty in the same month as the Bulgarians.

Once Mussolini blundered in Greece and Hitler realized that he had to save his Fascist ally, the Nazi leader even tempted Prince Paul with territorial gain, offering the region of

Salonika if Yugoslavia joined Germany in invading the Hellenic kingdom. The Serbian leader politely declined the offer and once again warned the German dictator of pro–Allied sentiment in Yugoslavia. In the face of this reluctance, Hitler pressed Prince Paul with a combination of threats and ultimatums. The Yugoslav leader however was wary of allying himself with Nazi Germany. He was concerned because his nation and in particular his armed forces, were overwhelmingly pro–Allied. The Serbian regent even prophesied that if he were to sign a treaty with the Germans, he would be overthrown by his own military within six months. Based on his dire warnings, the Führer relented somewhat and agreed to guarantee Yugoslavia's territorial integrity, publicizing openly in the newspapers of Europe that Germany would not use Yugoslavia's railroad system or violate her borders. After the false promises, which Hitler made at Munich, few people believed in the Führer's assurances or German declarations of peaceful coexistence. Reluctantly, Prince Paul signed the treaty on March 25, 1941.

Hitler's Decision to Invade Greece and Yugoslavia

Two days after Prince Paul signed the treaty with Germany, Yugoslav Air Force officers overthrew the prince-regent and installed the seventeen-year-old Peter II as the king of Yugoslavia. The second thing which the military junta in Belgrade did after ousting Prince Paul was to annul the Nazi-Yugoslav treaty. Hitler was seething with anger that his plans for Yugoslavia had been thwarted. Grudgingly, the Führer directed that the planned invasion of Greece should now also include the invasion of Yugoslavia. The start date for the attack now had to be pushed back to April 6, 1941, in order to accommodate the conquest of that country. The German plan for the invasion of Greece was codenamed *Marita*. It had been ordered by Adolf Hitler in November 1940—a month after Benito Mussolini's ill-fated invasion. Once the *coup d'état* in Belgrade occurred, the plan was expanded to include Yugoslavia. Hitler's decision was not made simply because the Italian Army was losing and Mussolini needed to save face. Once the Italian dictator involved himself in the war, the "soft underbelly" of Europe (the Mediterranean region) became an active war zone. The Italian war effort in North Africa was also being waged ineptly. In a meeting held on November 18, 1940, between Count Galeazo Ciano and Adolf Hitler, the Führer expressed how unhappy he was at the way Mussolini was waging war.[21] The Italian invasion of Greece in October 1940 further destabilized the Axis military situation. British and Commonwealth forces soon entered Greek territory. This move completely undermined Hitler's plans to safeguard his oil supply and the right flank of the planned invasion of the USSR. The Führer therefore, felt he had no other choice than to invade both of these Balkan nations in order to stabilize the Axis military situation.

British Military Aid to Greece

On February 22, 1941, British Foreign Secretary Anthony Eden met with King George II and Prime Minister Alexandros Koryzis on behalf of Prime Minister Winston Churchill. Based on the conversation between the British and Greek leaders, the decision was made to send further military help to Greece. Approximately 58,000 British and Commonwealth forces arrived on April 2, 1941. The British sent the following units to Greece: British First Armored Division, Sixth and Seventh Australian Infantry Division, Second New Zealand

Infantry Division, and the Polish Independent (Carpathian) Infantry Brigade. These 4½ divisions were organized into a corps-sized organization called "W-Force." Two days later the Germans launched their offensive against Greece and Yugoslavia. By April 9, 1941, the Germans had captured Salonika. On that date, "W-Force" was covering the Greek withdrawal from southern Albania and was located along a defensive line stretching from Florina-Edessa-Veria-Katerini. Unfortunately, the Germans had broken through behind that defense line by Florina and had taken Kozani by April 17. Ten days later German troops reached Athens. Once mainland Greece was occupied, Crete became the center of Allied resistance.

The British managed to evacuate around 50,000 troops from the Greek mainland, of which 31,246 ended up defending the island of Crete by mid–May.[22] In late April Greek forces on Crete included 9,000–10,000 men of the Greek Fifth Infantry Division. In the midst of this Balkan debacle, Churchill sent a detailed message to the Soviet dictator on April 19, 1941, warning him of Germany's impending attack on the USSR.[23] This was based on deciphered German military messages alluding to the upcoming invasion. One of the most closely guarded secrets of the war is that British intelligence had broken the German code for their military ciphering machine. Throughout the war the British were apprised of German intentions and this proved to be an important factor in defeating Nazi Germany. Stalin mistrusted the West as much as he doubted Hitler's intentions. He even had misgivings about people within his own government. Although his intelligence service was cautioning him that Germany was about to attack, the Communist dictator chose to ignore their advice. This was likely caused by Stalin's own suspicions brought on by his inherent paranoia.[24]

The end of the Italian/German campaign against Greece came shortly after the defeat of Greek, British and Commonwealth forces fighting on Crete. Lasting from May 20 to June 1, 1941, the battle ended in an Axis victory, but the allied defenders had inflicted a heavy blow on the enemy. Although the British and Commonwealth forces fought hard, and the Greeks (who were defending their country) fought even harder, the Germans eventually overwhelmed the allied defense. German losses were high, including 3,674 killed or missing in action, with an additional 2,000 wounded. Material losses were huge, with over 284 planes lost and hundreds damaged. The German parachute corps was so wrecked by this battle that Hitler never again committed the unit to a similar engagement. A year later, when the Italians suggested a combined Italian and German parachute assault against the strategically important island of Malta, the Germans completely refused to consider the plan.

Hitler's Initial Attitude Towards Greece

Although he never attained a college degree, Hitler was well read and well informed about European affairs. He knew that earlier in his military career Greece's leader, Ioannis Metaxas had been trained by Imperial Germany.[25] During his career as a politician, the Greek leader would also be accused of having been a Teutophile at heart. Metaxas refuted this accusation, claiming it was not true. His supporters were particularly vocal about rejecting the idea that Metaxas favored Germany, especially after the Nazi invasion of Greece. Adolf Hitler likely wished to attract Greece into the Nazi fold, seeing the dictatorship of Ioannis Metaxas as an attempt to create a Fascist state similar to the one established in Italy and other European nations.[26] Most likely Metaxas believed that using centralization along Fascist/Nazi lines would homogenize what seemed to be a diverse and disparate

Greek society. He also probably thought that an authoritarian regime would produce a rapid and more efficient modernization of the Greek nation.[27] Metaxas shared Hitler's hatred of Communism, as well as of liberalism and parliamentary democracies. However, he was not a racist and his attempts to mimic Fascism did not include the persecution of any minorities in Greece.[28]

Perhaps because of this authoritarian tinge, or maybe even because Greece had been the cradle of Western Civilization, Hitler seems to have had at least a grudging respect for the Hellenic kingdom. An instance of this is the episode described by Wilhelm Keitel after the Germans defeated the Greek Army. Keitel related how Hitler wanted his military to enter Athens without any pomp and circumstance in order to avoid injuring Greek national pride.[29] In addition, during a speech to the *Reichstag* on May 4, 1941, Hitler said the following about the valor of the Greek nation and its soldiers: "Historical justice obliges me to state that of the enemies who took up positions against us, the Greek soldier particularly fought with the highest courage. He capitulated only when further resistance had become impossible and useless."[30]

Of course, whatever "admiration" Hitler may have had for Greece and its authoritarian leader would not prevent the Führer, and Benito Mussolini from being ultimately culpable in the deaths of approximately 563,500 Greeks during World War II, including 80 percent of Greece's pre-war Jewish population. The waning Italian military campaign against Greece, as well as the appearance of British Commonwealth forces on Greek soil, is what finally forced the Führer to act. Although the campaign to occupy Greece and Yugoslavia was successful and Germany gained some immediate economic benefits, opening the Mediterranean region to the war eventually forced Germany to divert vast military resources for its safeguard. Initially at least, the invasions of Greece and Yugoslavia allowed the Germans to exploit both nations for their resources. They proceeded to do this with great energy.

The Immediate Economic Effects of the German Occupation of Greece and Yugoslavia

Before Mussolini's ill-fated attack on Greece, the German dictator had no immediate political or economic interest in the Balkans other than to secure treaties or alliances with various nations. He did this in order to safeguard the Balkans for the Axis. Hitler's initial lack of interest in physically occupying this region was therefore not driven by a desire for peace as much as a wish to secure his strategic plans with the least amount of effort. Once Italy undermined the Axis military situation, the German dictator had to take a more "hands on" approach in the Balkans and in the Mediterranean region as a whole. Nazi Germany reaped some immediate benefits from the occupation of Greece and Yugoslavia. The Germans economically plundered both countries. All sorts of minerals, foodstuffs, and luxury items were removed and brought back to the Reich. For example, Chromite ore which was a substitute for producing aluminum was in great demand by the German aircraft industry. At the beginning of the war, Germany only had a stockpile of 250,000 tons of this strategic material. Greece produced about 42,000 tons per year. These and other resources were systematically stolen. Plundering Greece therefore, proved economically beneficial for Nazi Germany.[31]

Greece was also hard hit by this exploitation with regard to foodstuffs. The plunder was so immense that it caused a great famine. The food shortage lasted the entire Axis occupation but reached its peak early on, during the winter of 1941–1942.[32] Although the

Catholic Church as well as many nations sought to send food aid for the Greek people, the war delayed and/or prevented delivery of food shipments. As a result, hundreds of thousands of Greeks eventually died of starvation and malnutrition. It appears that the poorer sections of the urban working class and the elderly were almost wiped out by the famine.[33] Although Germany benefited from vast amounts of seized foodstuffs, the German occupation of Greece and Yugoslavia proved detrimental. Partisan groups appeared immediately in Yugoslavia, where German treatment of the population was harsh from the very beginning. As the Germans pressed their advantage in Greece, a resistance movement eventually coalesced. Greeks now organized against the German and Italian occupation, striking at their oppressors whenever and wherever they could. In turn, the growing partisan movement required more Axis forces. It also resulted in increasingly harsher reprisals towards the Greek population.

Officers of the Wehrmacht's GFP, Gniezno, Poland. Left to right: Wiese, Luecke, Baucke, and Grieger (U.S. Holocaust Memorial Museum, courtesy Instytut Pamięci Narodowej).

3

Nazism, the GFP and Greece

The GFP Within the Context of the Nazi Occupation

To realize his objectives Hitler and his henchmen created and maintained a dictatorship which was ruthlessly effective. This regime was created in a manner that would ultimately achieve a Nazi utopia, but one that became a nightmare for millions. Luckily for the world that Hitlerian vision only lasted about twelve years. Before it was all over, about fifty to seventy million people would be killed around the world on account of the Second World War. The Nazis were never specific about what they planned to do but their actions pretty much gave the world an idea of what they were attempting to achieve:

> No comprehensive Blueprint for the New Order was ever drawn up, but it is clear from the captured documents and from what took place that Hitler knew very well what he wanted it to be: a Nazi-ruled Europe whose resources would be exploited for the profit of Germany, whose people would be made the slaves of the German master race and whose "undesirable elements"—above all, the Jews, but also many Slavs in the East, especially the intelligentsia among them—would be exterminated.[1]

The Nazis went about accomplishing their goals by first entrenching themselves in the German nation. They did this by creating institutions that (1) assured their continued position within the country and (2) would ultimately have the capability to assert Nazi control abroad.

The Nazis usurped existing organizations within Germany, and employed them to keep control. Some of the existing sections of power included the *Ordnungspolizei* (Order Police), *Gemeindepolizei* (Municipal Police), *Gendarmerie* (Rural Police), and *Kriminalpolizei* (Criminal Police). They even created new instruments of repression. These included the *Schutzstaffel* (SS), *Sicherheitspolizei* (SS Security Police), *Sicherheitsdienst* (SS Security Service), and *Geheimstaatspolizei* (State Secret Police). These became the principal security organs of Nazi control. These organizations were employed as tools of repression and terror. They would also be used to maintain control in conquered territories and subject nations. Like the rest of Germany, Hitler needed to Nazify the German Army so as to make it more pliable to his will. In order to assure that all aspects of German life became indoctrinated in National Socialist ideology, beginning in 1933 they initiated the period of the *Gleichschaltung*—the process by which the Nazis set up a totalitarian system of control over all aspects of German society.

All features of private and public life, including civilian and military institutions, were penetrated by the Nazis and made to march in lock step with their ideology. The army was one part of German society that was particularly targeted by Hitler. Surprisingly, usurping most of German society proved relatively easy. A good number of government employees working for the Weimar Republic were men who had served Imperial Germany. As a result, they tended to have conservative or right-wing views. German society at this time was principally conservative, given that its democratic institutions were relatively new. In fact, it's fair to say that the Weimar Republic was a republic without republicans.[2] The police in particular, contained a large percentage of men with extremely conservative views. The German Army was similarly inclined towards right-wing ideologies. Although its behavior was initially honorable, the war had a negative effect on its comportment. As the conflict progressed and intensified more episodes of un-soldierly conduct occurred. This immoral conduct was encouraged and made general policy by official German orders and decrees. In essence, the army was made an instrument of repression. This proved particularly true in the East, where many of the so-called *Untermenschen* lived. Criminal behavior was especially common along the Russian front.

Like the army, the *Geheime Feldpolizei* was co-opted by the Nazis. In many ways it proved easier for the men of the GFP to accept National Socialist ideology. In fact, the overwhelming majority of the senior leadership cadres of the GFP were avowed Nazi Party members.[3] The key to understanding how easily the GFP was absorbed into the Nazi structure lies in its history. Created by the Prussian Army in 1864, its initial mission was to protect the Prussian king as well as high ranking generals of the Prussian Army. By the time the Nazi Party assumed power in Germany, the GFP had seen service in the Danish-Prussian War, occupation of Alsace-Lorraine, and World War I. Its ranks were filled with die-hard conservative officials who at the very least supported an authoritarian government. The organization had been disbanded by the Treaty of Versailles but had been resurrected by the *Abwehr* (German Army Intelligence), as the initial intelligence arm of the *Wehrmacht* (German Armed Forces). Many of the officers who served in previous wars now returned to serve a new master.

From the very beginning of the war its membership was quickly expanded by filling its ranks with draftees from the *Gemeindepolizei*, *Kriminalpolizei*, *Gestapo*, *Gendarmerie*, as well as men from the *Grenzpolizei*. This meant that the GFP became even more saturated with Nazi Party members or at the very least, men who approved of the Nazi agenda. The GFP was therefore fully corrupted and imbued with Nazi ideology by the time war broke out. This is something that Wilhelm Krichbaum, the head of the GFP during the war, failed to mention during his postwar interrogation. According to Krichbaum, the role of the GFP only covered the following missions:

> ...to prevent sabotage and espionage, graft, damage to Army property and the undermining of morals. The GFP also acted as a fact-finding organ of the courts-martial, under the authority it came in such cases. In addition, the GFP had to carry out certain measures designed to maintain discipline, in the same manner as the military police services especially charged with this task. Tracing of deserters, tracing in general, and counterintelligence tracing in the theater of war was also part of their mission.[4]

His omission was done in order to shield himself and his organization from criminal prosecution. We know GFP officials committed war crimes and willingly cooperated with the Nazis. This proved especially true with regard to the campaign against the Soviet Union, where it was common for GFP units to directly assist in wholesale massacres and shootings of captured soldiers, partisans, and even civilians. Similarly, the GFP in the Balkans behaved in a criminal manner. However, it appears that their actions were selective depending on the country or area. This area of Europe was a nether region that contained a hodge-podge of ethnic groups. It was home to people of Latin, Aryan, Slavic, Turkic, or Gypsy origin.[5] The region also contained many religions: Catholicism, Eastern Christian Orthodoxy, Islam, and Judaism.

This hodge-podge of peoples and religions presented a particularly difficult "racial task" for the Nazi occupation forces. It was not a problem that could be resolved by employing a single brush stroke, as it appears happened in the case of the USSR, where brutality and genocide were bywords. Sorting out and deciding what to do with these various disparate peoples must have appeared a racial jumble for the German security and occupation forces. As part of the security apparatus in the region, the Secret Field Police would take on active role in this "task." Once these regions were occupied by the Germans, they began to segregate those considered racially inferior in preparation for their extermination. The GFP took part in that process. However, the level of cruelty and harshness with which the Germans proceeded in the Balkans depended on the country in which they operated. For example, their comportment in Yugoslavia was harsh from the start of the occupation. However, their brutality and severity in Greece only increased with time. Although the deployment of the GFP in the Balkans was small, it proved critical, especially with regard to the Jewish Holocaust. About five to six GFP units operated in the Balkans for most of the war. Of those, three were permanently stationed in Greece from 1941–1944.

In order to comprehend the actions of the GFP during the German occupation of Greece and its place in that history, one must first understand what were Adolf Hitler's war aims, how it was that the Nazi dictator decided to invade Greece and Yugoslavia, and how the GFP played a role in attempting to achieve those goals. As previously stated, Hitler's initial wave of conquests did not embrace the occupation of the Balkan Peninsula, of which Greece comprised a significant portion. Mainland Greece is composed of an area approximately 50,942 square miles and has a coastline of about 8,498 miles. With the exception of the central region of Thessaly, Greece is a land of long coastlines and narrow valleys covered by mountain peaks as high as 8,000–10,000 feet. The mainland is covered by three seas: the Adriatic, Mediterranean, and Aegean. The nation of Greece has more than two thousand islands, of which one hundred and seventy are populated. Greece therefore, presented an occupation nightmare for the Axis. Once Hitler had no choice but to invest himself in Greece, he committed his military to its safeguard and he plundered the nation as much as possible. Initially, the German occupation force in Greece was limited, with the bulk of the Axis forces composed of Italian troops. The fact that the nation of Greece was divided meant that the Germans could not get their hands on all of Greece's Jewish population. The Italian zone proved to be a temporary haven for Greek Jews fleeing the clutches of the Nazis.

The various conditions which made Greece a target for aggression during the Second World War have already been listed. What exactly however, were the long-term plans of Nazi Germany towards Greece? German goals in Europe were divided into three policies: (1) absorption, (2) forced cooperation, and (3) despoliation (exploitation).[6] The policy of absorption dealt with regions of Europe destined for "Germanization" and earmarked for absorption into the *Großdeutschen Reich* ("Greater German Empire"). With regard to the second policy (forced cooperation), the nations in question included Norway, France, Belgium, the Netherlands, Greece, Czechoslovakia, and to a certain extent, the Baltic States of Estonia, Latvia, and Lithuania. These comprised full economic cooperation and in part, as to certain groups in these nations—political cooperation as well.[7] The regions earmarked for the third policy (despoliation) were the "Government General" of Poland, the General Commissariat for White Russia as part of the General Commissariat *Ostland*, the administration of the Ukraine, as well as other Russian occupied territories. The main task of the Nazis was to draw raw materials, food, and labor. Greece was one of the nations designated for forced cooperation, but it appears that it also suffered exploitation. Throughout the war, the Nazi economy was dependent on a parasitic system of exploitation. Germany wasted no time in plundering Greece's natural resources:

> Greece was systematically robbed. Until the beginning of June in the port of Salonika large amounts of chromium ore, zinc, tin, copper, and lead concentrates were being shipped in the direction of Germany. German industrial managers increased the annual production of industrial metals and bauxite, manganese, nickel, molybdenum and pyrite under their control, so that the total value of annual commodity exports amounted to 45–50 million Reich marks. But even large petroleum and coal reserves (10,000 tons) and the most important agricultural export products were taken away, including 71,000 tons of raisins, 18,000 tons of oil, 7,000 tons of cotton, 3,500 tons of sugar, 3,000 tons of rice and 305 tons of silk cocoons.[8]

The Germans helped to create the conditions which exacerbated the desperate Greek economic situation. Nevertheless, the Nazis made sure to appropriate as much of the Greek economic surpluses as possible:

> In addition, the economic officers confiscated the machine tools of the Bodsakis Arms Factory and large parts of the rolling stock of the Greek national railroad. However, the most important booty was tobacco. Under the direction of Otto Loose the tobacco harvest for the years 1939 and 1940 were seized and taken away. It was 85,000 tons' Oriental tobacco with a value of 175 million Reich marks. This was sufficient for a full years' supply of cigarettes for the Reich Treasury and tobacco tax revenue of 1.4 billion Reich marks.[9]

In addition to stealing the resources of the land, the Nazi regime ended up bleeding the nation dry by forcing the Greek central bank to loan Germany 476 million *Reichsmarks* which was never reimbursed.[10] Finally, a special currency called the *Verrechnungsschein für die deutsche Wehrmacht* (Accounting Money for the German Armed Forces), or *Befehlsgeld* ("Command Money"), was created for disbursement of soldiers' pay in countries in which local purchases of the German military personnel were restricted for political reasons. There was also a problem in certain nations where the overall shortage of goods threatened uncontrolled inflation if the *Reichsmark* was widely used. This had initially happened in Greece where the plundering of the nation's resources had been large and thorough, causing a man-made famine.[11] An attempt was made by Pope Pius XII and the Catholic Church to help relieve the suffering as much as possible. The Pontifical Relief Commission provided food and medicine to many countries suffering from the depredations of the Nazi occupation, including Greece.[12] Nevertheless, the support which the Catholic Church could give was insufficient to stop the famine. Greeks continued to die, with the majority being the very young and the very old.

As stated, Greece's geography proved to be a challenge for the Axis occupation forces. With the exception of the central region of Thessaly, which has relatively flat terrain, most of Greece is composed of jagged, mountainous areas—all of which are ideally suited for guerrilla warfare. The long coastline of the country and the thousands of islands was also a garrison nightmare for Axis forces. It was virtually impossible for the Germans and Italians to watch every island and the entire coastline of Greece. As a result, it was fairly easy for the Allies to insert spies and commandos, and to supply the growing partisan bands. The Greek nation also included strategically important islands like Crete, Rhodes, Leros, Corfu, Lesbos and Cos. The initial military campaign on the mainland had not been very costly for the Germans. The capture of certain Greek islands however was another matter. As stated earlier, in capturing Crete, the German parachute force was so roughly handled that Hitler refused to employ it in any further large-scale parachute operations.[13]

Another problem for the Germans was that they had to share the occupation of Greece with Italy and Bulgaria. The various occupation zones that were created after the Axis conquest soon presented Germany with difficult logistical and bureaucratic problems. In the case of Jews fleeing the clutches of the Nazis, the Italian and Bulgarian zones became temporary havens. This turned out to be a partial blessing for the Jewish population since treatment of Jews was far better in the Italian zone and (to a lesser degree) in the Bulgarian occupation zone. However, it should be noted that simply being located in the Italian zone did not necessarily mean that as a Jew you were safe. The Italian zone was further delineated into sectors marked "A," "B," and "C." Although technically part of their conquest, sector "A" was wholly controlled by the Croatian Facist *Ustashe* government of Dr. Ante Pavelich. The *Ustashe* were fanatics that began to persecute the Serbian and Jewish population under their control. Sector "B" was an area where all civilian and military control was under the Italian Army. Sector "C" was an area where the Italian Army only controlled major strategic points.[14] This meant that to be fairly safe, a Jew needed to be in areas marked as part of Sector "B" of the Italian occupation zone. The Nazis initially welcomed the military forces of Italy and Bulgaria as a cheap way to occupy and control the Balkans. The Italians occupied parts of Yugoslavia and most of Greece, while Bulgaria occupied eastern Thrace.[15]

For the most part, the Italian occupation zone protected some of Greece's Jews until September 1943, when Italy surrendered and withdrew from the war. In the Bulgarian occupation zone Jews with Bulgarian passports were protected, but Greek Jews were handed over to the Nazis. Throughout September 1943, the Germans in the Balkans and Eastern Mediterranean were scrambling to detain, disarm, and intern as many Italian troops as possible. The Nazis feared that their former ally would turn over their weapons to the Greek or Yugoslav partisans or (worse still), that some Italian units would join the guerrillas and turn their guns against the Germans. Because of this the German Army rushed in as many units to Greece and Yugoslavia that they could afford to spare from other fronts. German fears regarding Italian forces were soon realized. As a result, some Greek islands that had been fairly peaceful throughout the occupation now became battle zones and killing grounds between German and Italian troops.

The British attempted to support those Italian units that wished to resist the Germans, by landing troops on the islands of Cos, Leros, Castellrosso, and Rhodes.[16] On September 18, 1943, English forces also landed on Symi, Stampalia, and Ikaria. The Germans spent the remainder of 1943 expelling the English from these islands. The wholesale murder of large numbers of captured Italian soldiers by the German Army—around 5,200 of them on the islands of Cephalonia and Corfu in September 1943–was now added to further tarnish the already muddied escutcheon of the *Wehrmacht*. Even as late as the summer of 1944 German forces were encountering wandering Italian soldiers—some in groups, some singly in the mountains and forests of Yugoslavia and Greece. The Secret Field Police was also involved in these illegal shootings, with members of GFP-510 and GFP-621 taking part in controlling the executions with the assistance of army units.[17]

A more mundane issue which the GFP had to deal with in Greece was the continued desertion of men from German units. The relative closeness of neutral Turkey was a temptation for many unhappy German soldiers. The particular geography of the country, with its hundreds of islands, made it very difficult to prevent these desertions. As the war progressed, the German military there began to experience more and more men leaving their post. It was up to the GFP to investigate these cases and to attempt to locate the runaway soldiers. A typical example of this issue can be seen by a text dated "11 August 1944" from the *Kommandant Ost-Aegaeis* to the commander of Army Group "E." The document was

3. Nazism, the GFP and Greece

Geographic Regions of Greece (map by author).

written based on reports from the 510th Secret Field Police Group which was stationed in the eastern Aegean islands during this time. Among other things, it said that the German Council General in Izmir, Turkey had been contacted by his Turkish counterpart. The Turks had relayed that they were holding in internment five German soldiers who had apparently managed to reach Turkish territory and had requested asylum. Those soldiers were:

Otto Meyer (born 26 November 1908) from Saarbrücken
Otto Alt (born 24 May 1910) from Meckenberg
Ernst Neumann (born 28 March 1920) from Kaminche
Werner Plevnia (born 4 May 1909) from Nauen
Friedrich Brink (born 26 January 1904) from Greifswald

The same document listed German soldiers who had either deserted or were AWOL from their posts:

6.6.44—Private Bruck, First Company, XII Battalion, 999 Penal Formation
6.6.44—Private Schmoll, First Company, XI Battalion, 999 Penal Formation
7–8.7.44—Private Pochoyka, Second Company, XII Battalion, 999 Penal Formation

14.7.44—Private Schmidt, Fourth Company, XII Battalion, 999 Penal Formation [turned himself in on 23.7.44]

23.7.44—Corporal Taflinsky, Third Company, Grenadier Regiment Rhodes[18]

By the beginning of 1944 investigating desertions became a larger mission for the Secret Field Police. But what about the actions of the GFP on the Greek population? As we shall see, the fate that befell these Italian soldiers on Cephalonia and Corfu was but a taste of the treatment handed out to Greeks at the hands of the Germans. In this the GFP proved to be fully complicit.

The Axis Occupation of Greece. Greece was occupied by three powers: Italy, Germany, and Bulgaria. When Italy surrendered in September 1943 Germany assumed occupation duty in former Italian controlled territories. The Bulgarian occupation force of three divisions withdrew from Greek Thrace in the late summer of 1944 (map by author).

4

Organization of the Secret Field Police in Greece

Locating GFP Units in Greece

The problem in writing the history of the GFP is that very little documentation survived the war. We know that GFP units took part in punitive measures against the population of Greece and Yugoslavia. What has been lacking are the particulars, such as which GFP official and what GFP unit took part in a particular reprisal. By being able to document which person or persons was involved with any specific crime, we can come closer to an understanding of the level of complicity in war crimes which the GFP was involved. What height of criminality can we ascribe to the Secret Field Police in this region of Europe? What were their crimes? Were the members all behaving in a similar manner? Where there so-called "dissenters" who opposed certain severe policies such as the physical torture of prisoners, mass arrests, executions, or organized deportations and massacres? What was the nature of the leadership cadre of the GFP in Greece and Yugoslavia? Did they all have a common background? Were they all cut from the same mold? Were they all avowed Nazis through and through? Knowing these questions will allow us to understand how the GFP operated in Greece.

In order to discover with greater certainty and accuracy which GFP personnel and GFP formation was involved in a particular crime, I have begun by tracing the location of these units during the period of the German occupation. Once unit locations had been established, primary sources and secondary documents and references were researched to see if a connection could be made between a particular act and a specific GFP unit. Knowing the unit posting of GFP officials, as well as their time and position in that formation was critical in my ability to be able to identify if that official may or may not have taken part in a war crime. I performed an overlay, employing a map of known German wartime crimes (*Kriegsverbrechen*) and overlaid those known sites with a map of German military and security unit locations on the date the crime was committed. Those units stationed on or near the region where a reprisal action took place were studied first. Lastly, I also depended on luck in combing through dozens upon dozens of microfilm rolls containing hundreds of thousands of wartime documents. Sometimes luck elicited a great find that cleared away the veil of doubt, bringing into the sunlight the truth about what happened in Greece so long ago.

Secret Field Police Units in Greece

The number of secret field police units that served in Greece were few in number. Although some Secret Field Police formations made brief appearances in the Balkans, the four principal units which spent most of the war operating on Hellenic soil were: GFP-510, GFP-611, GFP-621, and GFP-640. However, their actions had a definitive impact on the people of Greece. Although numerically small, the officials in these GFP formations held vast powers of arrest. Secret Field Police officials operated almost without limit. They could commandeer any vehicle, building, installation, or any men in order to obtain their goals. Within the German military, they were considered extremely influential and omnipotent. As we shall see, their participation in the suppression of the Greek population and in the Holocaust proved extremely critical. A clearer picture of which GFP officers led which unit can be obtained from the history of each formation and the following table[1]:

Table 1—GFP Unit Postings in Greece, 1941–1944

	Fall 1941	*1942*	*1943*	*1944*	*1945*
GFP-510	Salonika	Salonika and Rhodes	Salonika, Rhodes, then Athens	Rhodes, Leros, Samos, then Athens	Croatia
Commander	Karl Eschweiler	Karl Eschweiler, then Alois Uch	Alois Uch	Hans Behan then Manshausen	Manshausen
GFP-611	Athens, detachment on Crete	Athens, detachment on Crete	Mainly on Crete but also on Corfu	Mainly on Crete but also on Corfu	Croatia
Commander	Otto Begus then Ludwig Albert	Ludwig Albert	Ludwig Albert, then Bernhard Schulze	Bernhard Schulze, then HeinrichDeubel	Heinrich Deubel
GFP-621	Salonika	Salonika	Salonika	Salonika Ioannina, and Larissa	Croatia
Commander	Rhode	Rhode	Heinrich Deubel	Heinrich Deubel, then Alois Uch	Alois Uch
GFP-640		Athens	Athens & Piraeus then Bulgaria	Sofia, Bulgaria	Croatia
Commander		Gottfried Törkler	Gottfried Törkler, then Otto Begus	Dr. Otto Begus	Otto Begus

Leitender Feldpolizeidirektor beim Oberbefehlshaber Südost:
Principal Post: Athens (Spring & Summer 1941), then Salonika (Fall 1941–October 1944)
Commanding Officer: *Oberfeldpolizeidirektor* Roman Loos
Other Members: *Feldpolizeisekretär* Busse, *Feldpolizeisekretär* Leo Eder, *Dolmetscher* Reinhold Walther, *Wehrmachtsangehörige* Hermann Wilhelm, *Feldwebel* Ogrowsky, *Gefreiter* Malasch

Geheime Feldpolizei Gruppe 510
Principal Post: Salonika (Macedonia) [1941–1943], Rhodes & surrounding islands [1943–1944]
Group Leader: *Feldpolizeidirektor* Karl Eschweiler [1941–1942], *Feldpolizeidirektor* Alois Uch [1942—February 1944],[2] *Feldpolizeikommissar* Hans Behan [1944], *Feldpolizeiinspektor* Karl Manshausen [1944–1945]

4. Organization of the Secret Field Police in Greece

Geheime Feldpolizei Gruppe 611
Principal Post: Athens (Attica) [1942–1943], Crete & Corfu and surrounding islands [1941–1944]
Group Leader: *Feldpolizeikommissar* Dr. Otto Begus [1940–1941], *Feldpolizeikommissar* Albert [1941–1943], *Feldpolizeikommissar* Bernhard Schulze [1943—February 1944], *Feldpolizeikommissar* Heinrich Deubel [March 1944–1945]
Deputy Commander: *Feldpolizeikommissar* Bernhard Süsse [September 1940–June 1941].[3] Note: Süsse would eventually lead his own GFP unit on the Russian Front. In 1945 he was commander of GFP-744 under Army Group "Courland."[4]
Other members [under *Kommissariat 111*]: *Feldpolizeiinspektor* Ferdinand Friedensbacher [leader of *Sekretariat 1*], *Feldpolizeisekretär* Schenk [leader of *Sekretariat 2*], *Feldpolizeisekretär* Baar [leader of *Sekretariat 3*], *Feldpolizeisekretär* Murrer [leader of *Sekretariat 4*], *Feldpolizeikommissar* Hartmann [leader of *Kommissariat 110* until August 1943], *Feldpolizeibeamter* Friedrich Schubert

Geheime Feldpolizei Gruppe 621
Principal Post: Salonika (Macedonia) [1941–1944], Ioannina (Epirus) & Larissa (Thessaly) [1944]
Group Leader: *Feldpolizeikommissar* Rohde [1941—December 1942], *Feldpolizeikommissar* Heinrich Deubel [January 1943–February 1944], *Feldpolizeidirektor* Alois Uch [March 1944–1945]
Other known members: *Feldpolizeikommissar* Paul Härtel, *Feldpolizeisekretär* Wilhelm Pranz, *Feldpolizeisekretär* Georg Koch, *Gefreiter* Hermann Westhauser (1943–1944)[5]

Geheime Feldpolizei Gruppe 640
Principal Post: Athens (Attica) [1942–1943], Piraeus (1943–1944) Port town SW of Athens
Group Leader: *Feldpolizeikommissar* Gottfried Törkler[6] [1942–January 1943], *Feldpolizeikommissar* Dr. Otto Begus [February 1943–1944]

GFP-510

This secret field police formation was created on August 26, 1939, in *Wehrkreis XVII* (Austria).[7] *Feldpolizeikommissar* Karl Eschweiler led GFP-510 in 1941 and part of 1942 when he was transferred to the Russia Front. He was replaced by *Kriminal Kommissar* Alois Uch in 1942. Alois Uch was also a member of the SS, with the rank title of *SS-Obersturmführer*.[8] In 1944 Alois Uch was replaced by *Feldpolizeikommissar* Hans Behan. That same year GFP-510 was transferred to Athens where it remained until the general German withdrawal from Greece in October 1944. In 1944 Hans Behan was replaced by *Feldpolizeikommissar* Manshausen, who led the unit until the end of the war. GFP-510 took part in the Polish campaign under the 14th Army. In 1940, it was operating under the 12th Army. In 1941, it took part in the invasion of Yugoslavia under 12th Army. The unit remained in the Balkans and eventually became a part of the German occupation of Salonika April 1941. It established operations there and even ran a "detention center" (jail) for suspects. Since there was no *Gestapo* (State Secret Police) office in Salonika, the GFP jail served as the interrogation center and performed all of the functions which would normally be done by the *Gestapo*. Reports from prisoners who experienced this GFP jail first hand stated that Greeks and captured British soldiers were ill-treated.[9] GFP-510 was stationed in Salonika from 1941–1943, then moved to Kalamaki (Athens) from 1943–1944. In the Fall of 1944 the unit was withdrawn from Greece and withdrew through Macedonia and then Bosnia-Herzegovina. By 1945 it was operating in Croatia under *Heeresgruppe "F"* of *Oberbefehlshaber Südost*.

GFP-611

This GFP unit was raised on August 26, 1939 in *Wehrkreis XI* (11th Military District). During the campaign in the West, GFP-611 served in Rotterdam, Amsterdam, Dunkirk, and Paris. Later it was part of the security apparatus for the German XVIII Corps stationed in the Bordeaux area. GFP-611 was initially stationed in Lille, France in June 1940. It was later moved to Bordeaux, where it remained until January 1941. At the beginning of 1941 it was serving under the German First Army in France.[10] In the spring of 1941 it took part in the German invasion of Yugoslavia while operating under 12th Army. It briefly moved through Belgrade, Serbia in 1941, but settled in Athens, Greece that same year. It was stationed in Ampelokipoi, the central district of Athens. We know that GFP-611 was located in Athens in 1941 because letters using the unit's Field Post Number (10448) were posted by its members from the Hellenic capital.[11] According to one immediate postwar report, GFP-611 was sent to the Balkans in September 1941. On its way there, the train carrying the unit was involved in a serious crash and many of its members had to be hospitalized. This same source stated that because of this serious accident, GFP-611 was disbanded and its survivors returned to France.[12] The idea that GFP-611 was disbanded in the Fall of 1941 is incorrect. The following passage explains the correct chain of events:

> Head of 611 was an Austrian, Otto Begus from Salzburg, whose role in major Nazi war crimes in Greece would be investigated by Austrian prosecutors after the war. After the German conquest of the Balkans in April 1941, Begus' unit was deployed to Athens. Friedensbacher himself arrived in Athens some weeks later; he had been wounded in a railway accident in Transylvania during his transfer from France to Greece and had been sent to a military hospital in Vienna. Begus was soon replaced by another captain (*Feldpolizeikommissar*).[13]

GFP-611 remained stationed in Athens throughout 1942 as well as for part of 1943. In spring 1943, its headquarters was shifted from Athens to Crete. Its headquarters was now located in Heraklion, Crete. It operated there as well as on the island of Corfu from 1943 to 1944. GFP-611 investigated a raid on July 5, 1943, where apparently, a German airfield in Heraklion, Crete was attacked by British commandos. A total of sixteen Ju-88 bombers and a Klemm Kl.105 reconnaissance plane, all belonging to the *Luftwaffe's* I. Gruppe / L.G.1, were destroyed. GFP-611 was particularly active on the island of Crete between July and September 1944. this increase in activity was proportional to an equal increase in attacks by the Cretan underground, as well as by British commandos.[14] In April 1944 the roundup of the Greek Jews on the islands of Corfu and Crete began. GFP-611 was extremely involved in these roundups:

> Next higher in the reporting chain, Department Ic of the Corps Group Ioannina, agreed with the point of view of the Geheime Feldpolizei and the Ic branch office, and in a report about the island of Corfu informed Department Ic/AO at Army Group E headquarters that "2,000 Jews are still present, most of them inhabiting the city's outskirts." The deportation of these people, in the opinion of this officer, "would provide a not insignificant relief of the shortage of food supplies. At this time, the SD and the GFP are busy preparing the deportation of these Jews."[15]

During the spring and summer of 1944, GFP-611 took part in the capture of Greek Jews on these islands, as well as performing their "regular" army intelligence duties.[16] In September 1944 GFP-611 was transferred from Crete to Athens. From there it went on to Belgrade,

Serbia as part of the general withdrawal of German forces from Greece that began in October.[17] The unit was attached to *LXVIII Armeekorps* (68th Army Corps) and assigned to frontline reconnaissance units in order to better gather intelligence. From reports obtained after the war, it appears that close cooperation existed between the command staff of *Heeresgruppe "E"* (Army Group "E"), via the "Ic" (army intelligence officer) and the *SD, Sipo* and *Geheime Feldpolizei*.[18] Beginning in 1945 GFP-611 operated under Army Group "E" and in the region of Croatia.

GFP-621

This Secret Field Police unit was raised in *Wehrkreis I* (Military District I—Königsberg) on February 28, 1940.[19] It was established on August 28, 1940.[20] The Field Post number for GFP-621 between January 2 and April 27, 1940 was "36710." In 1940, it was assigned to the *Militär Befehlshaber Belgien/Nordfrankreich* (German Army Military Commander "Belgium and North France"). In the spring of 1941 GFP-621 was assigned to the German 12th Army and took part in the Balkans campaign that same year. In 1941, the unit was assigned garrison duty in Salonika, Greece. It remained there until the German withdrawal in October 1944. It was while operating in Salonika in 1942 that members of GFP-621 apprehended five Jews out of a group of 18, who were attempting to leave Greece to Italy by way of Salonika-Athens. GFP-621 discovered that several of these Jews had recently been issued with Italian passports—leaving the German command to speculate that the Italian consulate in Salonika was issuing Italian passports to Greek Jews who were trying to evade apprehension.[21] The deportation of Salonika's Jewish population began between mid–March and June 1943. According to historian, Mark Mazower, many Greek collaborators, including contacts aiding the secret field police, benefited from the abandonment of Salonika's Jewish businesses and homes.[22] Deportations of Greece's Jews continued into the spring of 1944. One source states that GFP-621 also operated a section of secret field police officials on the island of Chios in 1943.[23]

By the spring of 1944 GFP-621 had extended its area of operations to Ioannina and Larissa. Ioannina is the largest city in northwestern Greece. It lies at the heart of Epirus, the most mountainous region in the country. On March 27, 1944, the SS began the roundup of the 1,725 Jewish residents of Ioannina. During this operation, the Germans employed Waffen-SS drivers and eighty trucks from the Fourth SS Police Armored Infantry Division, local Greek gendarmes, German SD and SS personnel as well as one secret field police unit. According to one account German soldiers, watched on by GFP personnel began to comb the emptied Jewish homes for valuables. Some imprudent Greek civilian opportunists also tried to profit from their neighbor's misfortune, and paid with their lives.[24] In total 48,974 Greek Jews were deported to Nazi extermination camps. The GFP-621 was involved in these deportations and while they were not responsible for immediately gassing 37,386 of these northern Greek Jews upon arrival at Auschwitz-Birkenau,[25] they nevertheless were part of the machinery that helped to get them to these death camps for extermination. In the case of Ioannina, the GFP-621 was directly involved in the roundup of the Greek Jews.[26] The description of the roundup of the town's Jewish population clearly implicated the GFP:

> As if carrying out a military assault, Wehrmacht and police forces arrested almost the entire Jewish community of Ioannina. According to a Geheime Feldpolizei report, this raid took place "under the direction of Major Hafranek [or Havranek] of the Ordnungspolizei, including the Wehrmacht, the Feldgendarmerie, Ordnungspolizei, and Geheime Feldpolizei 621...."[27]

GFP-621 also took part in interrogations of captured Allied commandos. It was ordered to interrogate captured British, Greek and American commandos in the spring and summer of 1944. A Briton and three Greek nationals were captured by the Germans on April 7, 1944, operating on the island of Alimnia, just off the island of Rhodes. These four men were eventually interrogated by GFP-621. In addition, two Greek nationals and an American were captured while taking part in a raid on the island of Calino (Kalymnos) on the night of July 30–31, 1944.[28] The ultimate fate of these commandos is unknown but it was common German practice to hand over "saboteurs" (as all Allied commandos were referred to by the Germans) to the SD for elimination. In fact, a telegraph sent by Kurt Waldheim from Vienna (where he was studying to receive his PhD), and dated "14 April, 1944" to his intelligence headquarters in Army Group "E," requested the following information regarding the fate of these British, Greek and American commandos:

(1) Where are the men?
(2) Already interrogated?
(3) Interrogation completed?
(4) Special treatment when?

The reply came back as follows:

(1) The men with [Army Group] E
(2) Interrogation not yet complete (very obstinate)
(3) The men are to be handed over to the SD tomorrow, but will be further interrogated there. The date for the special treatment will be set by the SD.[29]

There is no doubt as to what "special treatment" meant: elimination. The Secret Field Police official in Rhodes was GFP Inspector Manshausen, while *SS Obersturmführer* and *Kriminal Kommissar* Alois Uch was in charge in Salonika. GFP-621 operated under the command of Army Group "E" beginning on December 1, 1943. During this time, Army Group "E" sent out a flyer, directing that all *Wehrmacht* personnel were to cooperate fully with the *SD*, *Sipo* (Security Police) and *Gendarmerie* (the military police). In addition, the memo listed disciplinary matters and deployment orders pertaining to NCOs and members of GFP-621.[30] A report dated "May 8, 1944" stated that on March 26, 1944 members of the coast watch from *Sturm Division Rhodes* had captured an "Allied sabotage troop of Englishmen, Americans, Russians, and Poles" aboard a Greek fishing vessel off the coastal island of Cephalonia.[31] On August 12, 1944, a *Sekretariat* from GFP-621 was attached to *Marine Einsatzkommando 20* (led by *Oberleutnant* M.A. Broekeron) in the coastal town of Kavalla.[32] This fishing town is located about 80 kilometers east of Salonika. When the Germans withdrew from Greece in the fall of 1944 GFP-621 was part of the rear-guard forces, making sure that vital port facilities and other important buildings would be dynamited in order to deny their use by the Allies. The unit ended the war in 1945 under Army Group "E" in Croatia.

GFP-640

This secret field police group was created on September 19, 1940 in Danzig (Gdansk) in *Wehrkreis XX* (Military District No.20).[33] The formation had not taken part in the campaign in the West but had remained in Poland. In 1942 GFP-640 was attached to the German 12th Army, which was serving in occupation duty in Serbia (Yugoslavia). It was then stationed in Athens sometime in the same year and remained there throughout 1943. Its headquarters' in Athens was located in a four-story stone building at the corner of Gladstonos and Patision Streets. The headquarters also contained a small prison and interrogation room. The GFP offices were located on the fourth floor. The building also housed the offices of the pro–Nazi Greek organization "National Socialist Patriotic Organization," whose acronym was ESPO. ESPO was created in the summer of 1941 by Dr. Spyros Sterodimas. Its members were ultra-nationalists and fascists who were rabidly anti-communist and anti–Semitic. Most Greeks were not anti–Semitic and were very patriotic. Because of this, ESPO was detested by almost everyone in Greece. This fact meant that from the very beginning of the creation of ESPO, its members became targets for Greek patriots. It was therefore deemed safer for its members to be housed in the same building as the GFP. Its Greek members also served as informers for the Germans and the GFP took full advantage of this.

The goal of ESPO was to recruit Greek volunteers to (1) fight on the German side or (2) work inside Germany. The building was therefore a high value target for the pro–Allied Greek resistance movement. On Sunday, September 20, 1942 a powerful explosion shook the center of Athens and totally destroyed the building housing the headquarters of GFP-640.[34] The unit took casualties and as a result of this attack, GFP-640 was shifted to the town and port of Piraeus in 1943.[35] Piraeus lies some twelve kilometers southwest of Athens. Some time in the second half of 1943 GFP-640 was transferred to Sofia, Bulgaria to serve under the German Military Commander "Bulgaria." The unit remained in Bulgaria until early September 1944 when Bulgaria declared war on Germany and German units were forced to withdraw from the country. In October 1944 GFP-640 was attached to Army Group "E." In 1945, it was operating in Croatia under Second Tank Army of Army Group "F." According to one report, the last posting for GFP-640 was operating under Second Army in East Prussia.[36]

The Officer Corps of the GFP in Greece

Some records regarding the officers who served in these Secret Field Police units survived the war. One such document dated "10 April 1944" details the Order of Battle for German formations stationed in and around Athens. The document listed *Feldpolizeikommissar* Hans Behan as the commander of GFP-510.[37] It placed the headquarters of this unit while in Athens as "No.32 Patissia Street."[38] It listed the strength of GFP-510 as having eleven civilian officials acting as officers (including Behan), 104 NCOs, and 81 enlisted men.[39] We know that in 1945 *Feldpolizeikommissar* Hans Behan was the *Kriminalbezirksinspektor* ("Criminal District Inspector") of Vienna.[40] It appears that after serving as head of GFP-510 in 1944, he was detached from the unit, promoted and transferred home to the Reich. Other officers who served as commanding officer of GFP-510 included *Feldpolizeidirektor* Karl Eschweiler and *Feldpolizeikommissar* Alois Uch. By 1945 Alois Uch was likewise detached from occupation duty in Greece and was posted to the Reich as a *Kriminalinspektor* in the city of Vienna.[41]

From 1940–1941 GFP-611 was led by *Feldpolizeikommissar* Dr. Otto Begus. In the Fall of 1941 *Feldpolizeikommissar* Albert assumed command of the unit. Albert was replaced by *Feldpolizeikommissar* Schulze in 1943. Schulze led GFP-611 until February 1944. In March 1944, the unit was handed over to *Feldpolizeikommissar* Deubel, who led it until the end of the war. GFP-621 was led by *Feldpolizeikommissar* Rohde until January 1943, when *Feldpolizeikommissar* Deubel assumed the post. Deubel led GFP-621 until February 1944 when he was reassigned as head of GFP-611. *Feldpolizeikommissar* Alois Uch led GFP-621 from March 1944 until the end of the war. Other members of GFP-621 included *Feldwebel* F. Ulbricht and *Feldwebel* Kerwell. Both of these sergeants were accused of ordering the machine gunning of Greek civilians while serving in Greece. From 1942 to 1943 GFP-640 was led by *Feldpolizeikommissar* Törkler. In February 1943 Törkler was replaced by *Feldpolizeikommissar* Dr. Otto Begus. The unit operated in the region of Athens from 1942–1943. It was transferred to Sofia, Bulgaria in 1943 as part of the German military mission to that satellite state. After Bulgaria switched sides and declared war on Germany on August 23, 1944, GFP-640 withdrew from Bulgaria, following the general German withdrawal. It ended the war in Croatia.

The Officer Cadre of the Secret Field Police in Greece

This section presents a concise history of the senior GFP officials that served in Greece. It would seem that the nature and character of the leadership cadre of the GFP would be important because it can give us an insight on how they may have operated and why. Were there common threads in each biography? For example, were they all conservative in nature? Was there an episode or incident in their career that can shed some light about their base instincts? For example, one such episode can be found in Heinrich Deubel's biography. Were the majority of GFP officials in Greece committed to a Nazi victory, or were they merely careerists only concerned with promotion? Was it perhaps a combination of both? Were there GFP members who attempted to ease the suffering of the Greek population? Finally, does the biographical data help us to understand their actions, good or bad? Unfortunately, some of these biographies are brief, depending on how much documentary material is available. Again, we see here how effective the GFP was at the end of the war, in destroying a large segment of their personnel and unit files. However, this section containing individual biographies is the most detailed biography yet collected on these officers. These biographies were gathered employing existing documents, interviews from captured POW reports, and post-war testimonials. This list is not presented by rank, but in alphabetical order.

Principal GFP Officials in Greece

1. Ludwig Albert

Albert began his career with the police and rose to the rank of superintendent, becoming one of the most capable police officials of the Nazi period.[42] In 1940 he was accepted as the *Feldpolizeikommissar* in the Secret Field Police and handled special cases that were assigned to him. Ludwig Albert led one of the most active GFP units in Greece from 1941–1943. Albert led GFP-611 during a period of time where his command was complicit in crimes committed in Athens as well as on the island of Crete. Responsibility for those crimes which occurred on his watch should fall on his shoulders. In 1943 he was transferred to the Eastern Front, where he led several GFP units until the end of the war. At the end of World War II Albert was apprehended by the U.S. Army which interrogated him. Based on his history and what was known of him at the time, he was classified by a court as a "follower." Beginning in 1949 he worked as a security officer in the Frankfurt region for the general intelligence agency in Karlsruhe. Ludwig Albert later went on to serve in the Gehlen intelligence organization for the West German government. He was arrested in 1955 on suspicion of working for the USSR. Before he could be brought to trial, he decided to commit suicide. His death was an indication of his guilt as a mole for Soviet intelligence. His brief biography could lead one to speculate that this man was perhaps an opportunist at heart.

2. Dr. Otto Begus

Begus was born in Bozen (Bolzano) in the South Tyrol area on September 25, 1889. He was the son of a local merchant. In 1916, he served as an officer candidate in the Fourth Tiroler Kaiserjäger Regiment. He served on the Italian front during World War I. Although he spoke fluent Italian, he grew to despise all things Italian on account of the fact that he was bayoneted by an Italian soldier during the war. Begus received several awards and decorations for his service in the Great War. He was the holder of the *Ehrenzeichen für Frontkämpfer* (Front Fighters award), which was issued to men who had served in World War I from 1914–1918. Begus also held the "Field Combat Medal" and the "Blood Order, 2nd Class." From April to July 1921 he briefly served in *Freikorps Oberland* in Upper Silesia in Silesia. He later studied law at Innsbruck University and eventually became an Austrian police official in 1928. More telling regarding the political conviction of Begus was the fact that he was one of only a select few recipients of the *Ehrenzeichen vom 9. November 1923*. This was one of the most prestigious decorations in the Nazi Party. Instituted in March 1934 it was awarded to men who in one way or another had taken part in the 1923 Putsch. Only true Nazis were awarded this honor. In addition to being a Nazi Party member, Begus also joined the SS. Begus had a relatively low SS membership number: "189,613."

In September 1933 Begus was the Police Chief for the Viennese district of Schmaltz. He was accused of pro–Nazi activities, arrested, and sentenced to six months in jail. He escaped to Germany to avoid imprisonment. In 1934, he served briefly as a detective in Munich. He returned to Austria and was involved in the murder of the Austrian Chancellor, Engelbert Dollfuss. He was arrested for complicity in the Austrian chancellor's murder, and served six months before escaping once again. Begus was given a temporary post in the Berlin Police, but in the beginning of 1936 he was sent to Ethiopia. There he became military instructor of the Negus Imperial Guard and fought against the Italians until Ethiopia surrendered in May 1936. He escaped to the Sudan and was eventually repatriated to Germany by the British.[43] In July 1936 he was appointed as Commissioner of the *Kriminalpolizei* (Criminal Police) in Frankfurt. In April 1937, he joined the Berlin Gestapo but was hospitalized briefly from March 23–31 in a Berlin hospital for an illness obtained while in Africa.[44] Two years later in 1938 he became commissioner of the *Kriminalpolizei* in Salzburg. In November 1939, he was made a *Feldpolizeikommissar* (equivalent to a captain's rank) and assigned as the commander of GFP-611, which was stationed in Rotterdam at the time. Begus continued to lead GFP-611 during 1940 (in the Low countries and Lille, France), and in 1941 (in Bordeaux, France). Otto Begus also held rank in the SS and was also a reserve army officer, holding the additional titles of *SS-Sturmbannführer und Hauptmann der Reserve* (SS Major and Captain of the Reserve).

Dr. Otto Begus continued to serve as commander of GFP-611 for the Balkan campaign. He traveled with the unit as it passed through Romania and Bulgaria before serving in Greece. In the fall of 1941 he was detached from GFP-611 and assigned as commander of *Kommissariat 110* in Athens. He served in that capacity until the beginning of 1943 when he was reassigned to the RSHA (*Reichssicherheitshauptamt*). In February 1943 Begus was posted to *Amt VI-F* (Department VI-F, Foreign Intelligence Service) of the Reich Main Security Office and stationed in Athens. On November 11, 1943, Begus was promoted within the SS as an *SS-Sturmbannführer* (SS Major).[45] This promotion is also indicative of the approval that the SS organization had in the "job" which Begus was performing. In June 1944, he was assigned as head of Amt VIS in Verona, Italy. He was apprehended there by Allied forces on May 29, 1945. After the war, Dr. Otto Begus was investigated by the Austrian government in complicity in numerous war crimes in Greece.[46] The biographical data points to the conclusion that Dr. Otto Begus was a die-hard Nazi, completely committed to Hitler's goals.

3. Heinrich Deubel

Heinrich Deubel was born in Ortemburg, Bavaria on February 19, 1890.[47] The son of a mail carrier, in 1908 Deubel joined the German Army and served in World War I. Because he joined in 1908 he received the *Prinzregent Luitpold* German Army Recruitment Medallion, which was awarded from 1886–1912. On October 11, 1914, he was promoted to *Vizefeldwebel*. He took part in the First World War but was captured early in the war and therefore spent most of the war in a British POW camp.[48] In 1920 he was promoted to the rank of *Leutnant*, but in that same year he was discharged from the army. He joined the Nazi Party and SS quite early, earning him the Nazi Party number of 14 178 and SS number of 186.[49] In the 1920s Deubel joined the *Freikorps* and was also involved in promoting the Nazi Party as well as in Anti-Semitic activity. He quickly rose through the ranks of the SS. In 1928, he was listed as part of *SS-Standarte 6*, but in 1931 he was reassigned to *SS Standarte 31*.[50] In 1934 he was eventually given command of an infamous post: concentration camp commander of Dachau. On December 12, 1934, Deubel assumed command of Dachau after its former commander, Theodor Eicke, was promoted to oversee all of the concentration camps. Deubel had been personally nominated by Eicke to be his successor. At the time, he held the rank of *SS-Oberführer*, which had been awarded to him on November 9, 1934.[51] He was camp commander until April 1936 when Hans Loritz replaced him. He was then posted to another, smaller camp named "Columbia-Haus" in the Templehof area of Berlin.[52] He ran that camp until he was finally removed from

Feldpolizeikommissar Heinrich Deubel, seen here wearing the uniform of an *SS-Oberführer* in 1934. Deubel ran afoul of the *Reichsfuhrer-SS*, Heinrich Himmler, who would sideline his career for an incident that occurred on Christmas Eve in 1934. Desperate to regain his standing within the Nazi Party, Deubel sought numerous positions within the Third Reich until 1942, when he would be appointed to the *Geheime Feldpolizei* and eventually posted to Greece (Bundesarchiv, Berlin-Lichterfelde).

office on September 22, 1936. In April 1937, he was listed as an officer in the staff of *SS Oberabschnitt Süd*. However, by June 1, 1937, he had been transferred to *SS Oberabschnitt Main*.

Deubel's downfall from what seemed like a bright career in the SS had begun almost as soon as he took office at Dachau. He had run afoul of the head of the SS, Heinrich Himmler for two reasons. First, in Himmler's eye he had embarrassed the SS over a violent incident which occurred on Christmas Eve 1934 at the Passau train station. The scuffle involved Deubel, an SS private, a policeman and numerous German citizens. Deubel came to the aid of the SS man, who had been removed from the line by a policeman for taking too long at the ticket window. Deubel then threatened to take the policeman to Dachau and flog him with a whip. This was at a time when the SS was becoming notorious for their brutality. The episode incensed Himmler because it even made the news in foreign newspapers. The incident earned Deubel a written rebuke from the *Reichsführer-SS*. Second, he gained a reputation with the guards at Dachau and with the detainees as a fairly lax camp commander. As a matter of fact, Deubel had apparently released several prisoners from Dachau who were accused of being communists. This was affirmed in a 1948 deposition given by a woman named Maria Mark Miller.[53] After Deubel's removal, he could no longer serve in the SS, so he went to work for the German customs office (*Zollamt*).

In 1939 Heinrich Deubel was promoted to Customs Inspector, and in 1941 was promoted once again to District Customs Commissioner (*Bezirkszollkommissar*). He also held the rank of a reserve lieutenant in an army convalescent company. In the spring of 1941 he was posted to France as a customs border patrol officer. He served in this capacity until 1942 when he managed to finagle his way into the Secret Field Police. On December 31, 1942, Heinrich Himmler sent an order to the SS Personnel Office, giving Deubel the initial rank of *polizeiverwalter* ("police administrator").[54] That year the GFP in France went through a large reorganization. Entire GFP units were disbanded and their men were sorted into two groups: those fit for frontline service and those who were not fit. The younger, more physically healthy men were posted to GFP units on the Eastern Front, while the others were kept to help staff the numerous SD station posts throughout the country.

Deubel saw an opportunity to "rehabilitate" himself in the eyes of the Nazi regime by volunteering for service in the GFP. The Customs Department was closely linked to the Frontier Guard. Given this connection as well as his rank as a *Bezirkszollkommissar*, Deubel was accepted and was assigned to the Secret Field Police in December 1942. The order, for this transfer, dated "31 December 1942," came from the headquarters of the *Reichsführer-SS* to the *SS-Personalhauptamt* (SS Personnel Main Office). A month later he was posted as the new commander of GFP-621. Having learned the pitfalls that come with notoriety, Deubel kept a low profile while serving as a *Feldpolizeikommissar* in the GFP. He was commander of GFP-621 until February 1944, when that position was given to another officer. A month later in March, he was assigned as the new commander of GFP-611. In late 1944, his unit withdrew from Greece and headed north. In 1945, he and GFP-611 were operating in Croatia, where they remained until the end of the war. In 1948, he was considered for prosecution but the German court could not find that he had committed any verifiable crimes while serving as camp commander at Dachau. It appears that his brief career in the Secret Field Police went unnoticed. He died inconspicuously in 1962.

4. Leo Eder

Leo Eder was born on September 25, 1881, in Adelereid, about ten kilometers NW of Augsburg in the Swabian region of Germany. He began his career as a police messenger and slowly worked his way to *Hauptwachtmeister* (Police Sergeant Major). He joined the Nazi Party in 1937. To dedicated Nazis, Germans who joined the Party so late after their takeover were not true believers. The implication was that Eder had joined the Nazi Party as a means to guarantee his career. However, a *Politische Beurteilung* (political assessment) by the office of the Nazi *Gauleiter* for Munich/upper Bavaria, dated April 16, 1938, painted a far different picture:

> Hauptwachtmeister of the Police Leo Eder has been a party member since January 5, 1937. Within the N.S.D.A.P. he holds the position of Block Warden at our local NSV group. Party member Eder belongs to the RDB, the NSV and the RLB. His wife belongs to the *N.S. Frauenwerk*. He also subscribes to the *Völkischer Beobachter* and the *Frauen Warte*. His attitude towards the movement is impeccable, and party member Eder also affirms his unswerving support to the Nazi state.[55]

It appears from this document that Eder was a faithful Nazi Party member. Not only was he a member of numerous Nazi Party organizations, but his wife was also a member of the National Socialist Association for Women.[56] Although he was advanced in age, Eder found himself as a member of the principal GFP staff for the Balkans, which was headed by Roman Loos. When assigned to this headquarters in 1941, Eder was sixty years old and had been promoted to the rank of *Feldpolizeisekretär*.

5. Karl Eschweiler

Karl Eschweiler was born on April 15, 1900. From all accounts Eschweiler was a career policeman. Since 1928 he was *Kriminalrat und Berufsbeamter* (police superintendent and civil servant).[57] Eschweiler became interested in the Hitler movement in the early 1930s, obtaining Nazi Party Number 2 026 982.[58] When the headquarters for the GFP was established in Berlin for the *Heer* (Army), Eschweiler was one of its staff members. Before being promoted and posted to GFP-510 in 1941 he had been in charge of GFP-501.[59] In 1941 he assumed command of GFP-510 and held this post until sometime in 1942. By May 1945 he was Deputy Field Police Director of an army group in the central sector of the Russian Front. After the war, he became a witness in the Denazification proceedings against Wilhelm Krichbaum.[60] Karl Eschweiler claimed that around 3,000 men served in the GFP. This was in contrast to his chief, Krichbaum who stated that only 2,000 men served in the GFP during the war. Eschweiler also alleged that of 3,000 men in the GFP, a mere 1 percent were members of the Nazi Party. This microscopic percentage of Nazi Party members in the GFP has since been disproven.[61] Like his boss, Eschweiler was a principal figure in the postwar attempt to hide the more criminal acts of the GFP and to paint the organization as simply an army intelligence unit.

6. Ferdinand Friedensbacher

Ferdinand Friedensbacher was in many ways a typical example of the type of Secret Field Police officer who served in Greece during the war. He was born in 1912 in the Tyrolean village of Kitzbühel. Friedensbacher was a single child of a landlady who farmed a chalet near the village. He won the first known downhill race at Kitzbühel on March 28, 1931— becoming very well known locally, and generally known regionally. He was therefore a relatively well known Tyrolean downhill skier. Friedensbacher had attempted to gain entry into the Austrian Army, with the ultimate goal of obtaining a civil service job after his term of service. In 1935 Friedensbacher was transferred over to the *Gendarmerie* (Rural Police)—

given that no full-time positions were open in the Austrian Army. The Rural Police force knew of his athletic skills and had accepted him, but his term of service was initially temporary. In fact, in January 1936 he was still listed as a "probationary *Gendarmerie*."[62]

During this time in the Austrian *Gendarmerie*, Friedensbacher met and fell in love with a local woman from Innsbruck whom he eventually married and who bore him several children. This link to Innsbruck—more than anything else—is what eventually persuaded Friedensbacher to accept a post with the *Kriminalpolizei* after the Nazi *Anschluss*. If he had not, he would have been posted elsewhere. In July 1939, he was transferred over to the *Gestapo* (*Geheime Staatspolizei*) under Section II C [Internal Security]. In November 1939 Friedensbacher was detached from the *Gestapo* and transferred over into the German Army. He was sent to Hannover and assigned to Secret Field Police Group 611 which was in the process of forming. In 1940 Friedensbacher served with GFP-611 in the Netherlands, Belgium and France. In 1941 Friedensbacher's unit was posted to Athens, Greece. Friedensbacher arrived a bit later, given that he had been wounded in a railroad accident in Transylvania. In the summer of 1941 GFP-611 was flown to the island of Crete. The Secret Field Police established their offices in Chania, Heraklion, and Rethymno. In the 1970s the Austrian government tried Friedensbacher for war crimes committed on the island of Crete while he was an official of the GFP, but he was exonerated of all charges. The amazing thing is that during the trial, he freely admitted shooting and killing a citizen who was suspected of being the local leader of the Greek underground.

7. Paul Härtel

Paul Härtel was born on February 23, 1905. In 1925 at age twenty, he joined the German Police. Three photographs exist of Paul Härtel in police uniform and are contained in his *SS Personalnachweis*, located in the *Bundesarchiv*, Lichterfelde in Berlin.[63] One of those photographs appears in this book. On August 18, 1939, Härtel was transferred over into the Secret Field Police. This was done as part of an expansion of the GFP in preparation for the start of the Polish campaign. Härtel received the rank of *Feldpolizeiobersekretär* in the GFP. According to the head of the GFP, Wilhelm Krichbaum, the rank of *Feldpolizeiobersekretär* was changed after a few weeks in 1939 to *Feldpolizeiinspektor* (Field Police Inspector) due to difficulties involving payroll regulations.[64] Härtel was assigned to GFP-621 and served in that unit the fall of 1943. Given that GFP-621 was stationed in Salonika, northern Greece was the unit's area of operations. In the summer of 1943 as the Italians were on the verge of leaving the war, guerrilla activity rose in the region of Ioannina. Based on

Feldpolizeiinspektor **Paul Härtel, member of *Geheime Feldpolizei Gruppe 621* (Bundesarchiv, Berlin-Lichterfelde).**

Härtel's intelligence, which he claimed he had acquired from prisoners during interrogation, the Second Battalion of *SS Polizei Gebirgsjäger Regiment 18* launched a punitive attack on the village of Mousiotitsa, killing about 153 civilians. Härtel was therefore partly responsible for the massacre given that he selected the village that was to be punished. In the Fall of 1943 Härtel left the GFP and was posted the *Feldpolizei Inspektion* (Inspectorate of the Field Police), in Germany. In 1945, he was attached to the police administration in Graudenz as a *Polizeiobermeister*. In 1965 when he turned sixty, he retired from work on a police pension.

8. Roman Loos

Roman Loos was born in Prussia on September 29, 1896.[65] Loos served in World War I when he joined the Kaiser's army on April 15, 1915. After training he was assigned to the 99th Infantry Regiment. Loos was discharged from service on December 1, 1918. After the war, Loos attended college. Sometime in the 1920s he moved to Vienna, Austria. Before working for the Gestapo and GFP, he had served as an Austrian police official in Vienna. This was prior to the *Anschluss* of 1938. He was not an early Nazi Party member, but his number was low compared to most: 1 527 590. In February 1935, he was given an SS rank and attached as an officer of *SS Standarte 89*, which had been created in June 1933 and stationed in Vienna. This SS regiment became infamous when ten of its members assassinated the Austrian Chancellor, Engelbert Dollfuss in July 1934. After the German annexation of Austria, Loos's career took off. By 1940 Loos was married, had two children, and was the *Polizeioberkommissar* ("Police Commissioner") of Vienna. He was described by a member of the GFP as being six feet tall with an oval face, dark hair and black eyes with clear cut features. In his service reviews, he was described by his superiors as a very experienced police officer. In fact, Wilhelm Krichbaum remarked that Loos was "the best horse in the GFP stall."[66] Like Dr. Otto Begus, Roman Loos was a supporter of the Nazi Party and of union between Austria and Hitler's Germany. In 1937 Loos was rewarded for his early support of the Nazis in Austria by being posted to the senior SD headquarters in Munich. Another example of how valued the Nazis considered Loos was the fact that he received the coveted German Cross in Silver.[67] This award was given to men who, according to the Nazis, performed their duties meritoriously but did not actually serve in combat.

Although Loos was reserved and quiet about his dealings, some of those around him were not. For example, *Feldpolizeisekretär* Busse, who was part of the headquarters staff led by Roman Loos in Salonika (LFPD Südost), admitted during a drinking party and under the influence of alcohol that everyone in the headquarters were all members of the Gestapo. A corporal named Malasch, who was also on the staff of LFPD Südost overheard Busse bragging about this.[68] In the early 1960s Roman Loos was investigated for war crimes committed in the Balkans by members of the Secret Field Police while he was in overall command. However, Austrian prosecutors could not gather enough evidence to proceed with a trial. This is not surprising given that during his tenure as head of the GFP in the Balkans, Roman Loos kept a low profile. In fact, Loos was described by one post-war account as "wily" and "skillful at avoiding the limelight."[69]

9. Bernhard Süsse

Bernhard Süsse (born 1894) was a former criminal police official before being assigned to the Secret Field Police. He rose through the ranks of the police, becoming a detective before being chosen for the GFP. He was deputy commander of GFP-611 from September 1940 until June 1941, when he was assigned as commander of a GFP unit on the Russian Front. In 1944, he was leading GFP-744(L) in and around the town of Ostrov (south of Pskov), in the region immediately behind the lines of Army Group North. At this time GFP-744(L) was under the command of Army Group "Courland." This GFP unit was primarily composed of air force personnel who had been trained in the role of GFP officials. In 1945, he was promoted to *Kriminalkommissar*.

10. Gottfried Törkler

Gottfried Torkler was originally from Berlin. He had several scars on his face from injuries acquired as a young man because of dueling, which had been popular in his youth. Before the war, he had served as criminal inspector in the State Police office in Karlsruhe. In 1941, he was transferred to Berlin. He was of slim build, was five feet six inches tall, and was fifty-six years old in 1942. That same year Törkler led GFP-640 while it was briefly stationed in Belgrade, Serbia. Later that year the unit was transferred to Athens. Torkler became renowned for many illicit financial transactions as well as for his sadism towards the Greek population.[70] He was also heavily involved in Black Market activities and had become rich as a result. Torkler led GFP-640 until the middle of 1943 when he was transferred, and sent to serve under the headquarters of the *Befehlshaber der Sicherheitspolizei und SD "Paris."* One document printed by the RSHA in 1944 listed Gottfried Törkler as receiving the *Kriegsverdienstkreuz, 1. Klasse mit Schwerten* (War Merit Cross, 1st Class with Swords).[71] This award was issued to soldiers for bravery not directly connected with front-line actions.

11. Alois Uch

Alois Uch was born on March 2, 1899. He was an active member of the *Sicherheitsdienst* when he was posted to the Secret Field Police. He was a long-time Nazi Party member who had served in the SD before the war. From 1942 to 1943 he served as the commander of GFP-510. In 1943, his official rank was an *SD-Obersturmführer und Feldpolizeikommissar*.[72] Alois Uch was heavily involved in the Jewish deportations that took place in Salonika in 1943. *Feldpolizeikommissar* Uch was appointed commander of GFP-621 in March 1944. He remained with GFP-621 as it withdrew from Greece in the fall of 1944. Sometime in 1945 he was detached from the GFP and sent to the Reich, where he became a *Kriminalinspektor* in Vienna.

The Central Command Structure of the GFP in the Balkans

Once the Germans occupied Greece and Yugoslavia, they had to establish permanent commands to control their military forces. It was in this way that in 1941 a senior leadership post for the Balkans was created for the GFP. Overall command of the GFP in the Balkans was given to *Oberfeldpolizeidirektor* Roman Loos, who held the title of *Leitender Feldpolizeidirektor beim Oberbefehlshaber Südost*, ("Senior Field Police Superintendent by the Supreme Commander South East").[73] Loos held this title and command position from 1941–1945. *GFP Südost* was originally located in Athens, but in the fall of 1941 was shifted to Salonika where it remained until the spring of 1943. It was then transferred to Belgrade (Yugoslavia) where it remained from 1943 until the autumn of 1944. It ended the war stationed in Zagreb, Croatia after German forces withdrew from Greece and Serbia in the fall of 1944. Luckily, a series of interrogation reports survived the war which brings light to the organization and activities of the GFP in the Balkans.

In July 1944, the British military in France captured a *Gefreiter* (Corporal) named Malasch who was very forthcoming when he was interrogated by British Army intelligence.[74] He willingly gave information about his service in the German military, and went on to describe how he had previously served as a communications expert with the GFP. He told his interrogator that he had served on the headquarters staff for the GFP in the Balkans. This was the principal HQ command for the GFP in the region which was led by *Oberfeldpolizeidirektor* Roman Loos. Malasch worked for the GFP headquarters from July to December 1942. This was confirmed by his *Soldbuch*. The *Soldbuch* was the ID booklet which all German military personnel had to carry on their person at all times. The importance of

The Various Regions of Greece (map by author).

4. Organization of the Secret Field Police in Greece

this former staff member under Loos's command is that he provided eyewitness testimony to events which took place regarding the Secret Field Police in this region of Europe.

Malasch surrendered to Allied forces in Normandy on July 17, 1944. His documents and the interrogation credibly established that in his last post he had served as a signals expert for the headquarters of Second Battalion / Grenadier Regiment 989 of the 277th Infantry Division. This German division had been brought up to the Normandy front in early July from southern France.[75] It appears from the testimony given by Malasch that his loyalty did not lie precisely with the Germans. The Prisoner of War statement which Malasch gave, claimed that he was half Austrian and half Czech. He also said that previous to being drafted into the German Army he had served eighteen months in the Czech Army. A thorough investigation by the Allied interrogator appeared to give credence to what Malasch testified during his debriefing:

> PW is half Austrian and half Czech, and served for eighteen months in the Czech Army. He was sentenced to eighteen months' imprisonment for expressing in the company of Croats, some of whom betrayed him, his intention of going over to Marshal Tito with his section. In prison, he was planning a mass escape to be followed by partisan warfare, when he was released before his time. He served in the GFP in Greece from July to December 1942 as a signals expert. His information is considered completely reliable, though dated, and it must be remembered that the period described is before the Abwehr was taken over by the RSHA.[76]

On the basis of this lengthy questioning, Allied interrogators were able to put together a schematic diagram of Roman Loos's staff as it existed in December 1942.[77] The deposition claimed that Loos' headquarters was composed of only nine men. Roman Loos was said to be originally from Prussia. He was six feet tall and had a strong build with dark hair, black eyes, and an oval shaped face. His features were said to be clear cut. In 1942, he was fifty years old. Roman Loos was assisted by eight officials. These included *Feldpolizeisekretär* Leo Eder, *Wehrmachtsangehörige* Hermann Wilhelm,[78] who served as the personal driver for Loos. The unit interpreter was Reinhold Walther. In addition, there was a communications NCO named Rudolf Harramach.[79] Other members of Loos' headquarters included *Feldwebel* Ogrowsky, as well as *Feldpolizeisekretär* Busse, Schenk, Baar, and Murrer. Malasch recalled that on one occasion he traveled with Loos on an inspection tour of the *Sekretariate*. He remembered that upon meeting the head of one *Sekretariat*, the first words which came out of Loos's mouth were "Where is your soundproof chamber?." It appears that Loos felt that every *Sekretariat* should have a soundproof room. Obviously, the need for a soundproof chamber meant that those interrogated were going to undergo excruciating pain during questioning and were likely to scream out. From this we can gather that torture was to be employed by the GFP in obtaining information and/or confessions.

Malasch stated that the GFP had tremendous powers of arrest and could even commandeer whatever men and vehicles were necessary in order to achieve a particular task. He says that they were feared and were avoided even by members of the German Army. The testimony by Malasch also described this GFP headquarters as owning several vehicles, some of which were civilian automobiles and others, which were military vehicles. The civilian cars were either English or French-built with Greek license plates. The private cars with Greek license plates were employed in undercover operations. Immediately below the *GFP Südost* headquarters were the two *Kommissariat* staffs established for Greece: *Kommissariat 110* and *Kommissariat 111*. Each *Kommissariat* command had around twenty-eight men. Of this number, fifteen were auxiliary personnel. *Kommissariat 110* was commanded by *Feldpolizeikommissar* Dr. Otto Begus, who had led GFP-611 in 1940 and in the first half of 1941. Later *Feldpolizeikommissar* Hartmann assumed command of *Kommissariat 110* until he was killed in the summer of 1943. *Kommissariat 111* was led by *Feldpolizeikommissar* Gottfried Törkler.⁸⁰ The structure of the *Kommissariat* commands in 1941 looked like this:

Each of the two *Kommissariat* possessed numerous weapons. These included pistols for every member of the unit, as well as a few machine pistols, some hand grenades, and even two light machine guns (MG34). Each *Kommissariat* had four sub-posts called *Sekretariat*. The *Sekretariat* were GFP station posts having a small group of GFP personnel (usually eight to sixteen men). The smallest GFP sub-group to the *Sekretariat* was the *Aussentelle*. The *Aussentelle*, or "Outer Station Post" usually contained anywhere from three to six GFP personnel. The manner in which the GFP was organized was based on the rank of the officers leading the unit. For example, the *Kommissariat* were usually led by a GFP member with the rank of *Feldpolizeikommissar or Feldpolizeiinspekteur*, while the sub-commands called the *Sekretariat* were led by a *Feldpolizeiobersekretär* or *Feldpolizeisekretär*. Finally, the lowest sub-group was referred to as the *Außenstelle*. The *Außenstelle* was usually led by a *Feldpolizeisekretär*. It is interesting to note that every GFP official was permitted to bear the rank of captain and allowed to wear any uniform that they deemed necessary.⁸¹

In December 1942, the headquarters for *Kommissariat 110* was in the town of Chania, on the island of Crete. This had been the base of operations for *Kommissariat 111* while it was operating on the island from 1941–1942. In 1941 *Kommissariat 111* created two station posts on the island. One *Sekretariat* was located in Rethymno, and another *Sekretariat* was

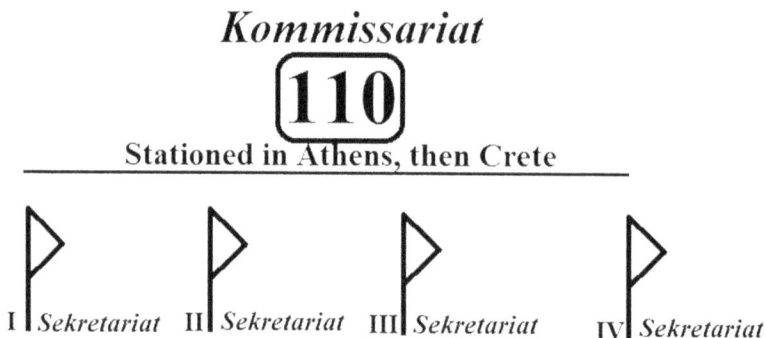

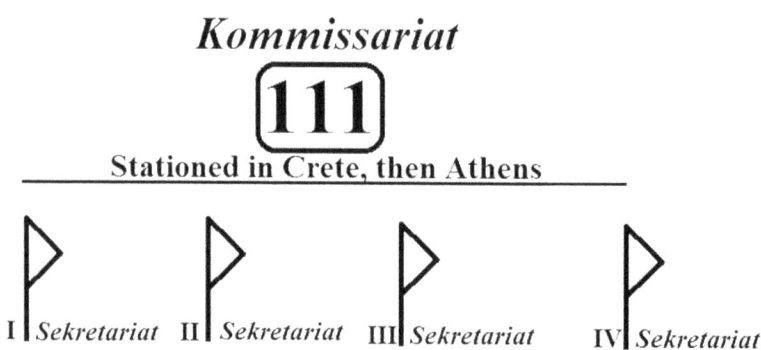

The Secret Field Police Commissariat in Greece (figure by author).

4. Organization of the Secret Field Police in Greece 67

stationed in the town of Heraklion.[82] In 1941 *Feldpolizeikommissar* Ferdinand Friedensbacher accompanied by twelve auxiliary field policemen were sent to establish the *Sekretariat* at Heraklion.[83] When *Kommissariat 110* was shifted to the island of Crete in 1942, its four outer station posts were as follows: *Sekretariat 1* was located at Heraklion, *Sekretariat 2* was at Rethymno, *Sekretariat 3* was in Avgeniki, and *Sekretariat 4* was located in the town of Krousonas. Avgeniki is located some twenty-four kilometers south of Heraklion, roughly halfway to the southern part of the island. Krousonas is about sixteen kilometers' northwest of Avgeniki. Rethymno was located about eighty kilometers west of Heraklion, along the northern coast road. It also lay about sixty-one kilometers east of Chania.

Malasch recalled that at one time *Polizeisekretär* Busse had led *Sekretariat 4* of *Kommissariat 111*. Busse was five feet nine inches tall and had red hair with grey eyes and an oval face. He was originally from Hannover and had a strong build. According to the testimony given by Malasch, Busse was a brutal man and was prone to violence. Malasch avoided him and knew he was not to be trifled with. Malasch believed that in 1942 Busse was about forty years old. He also reported that at times Busse exhibited "a nervous mannerism" that could have been interpreted as either anxiety or frustration. When drunk, Busse would tell his companions how he would beat up prisoners and would slap the soles of their feet with hard blows during interrogation. *Polizeisekretär* Schenk commanded *Sekretariat 2* of *Kommissariat 111*, while *Polizeisekretär* Baar led *Sekretariat 3*. After Busse's tenure, *Polizeisekretär* Murrer was placed in charge of *Sekretariat 4*. Murrer was originally

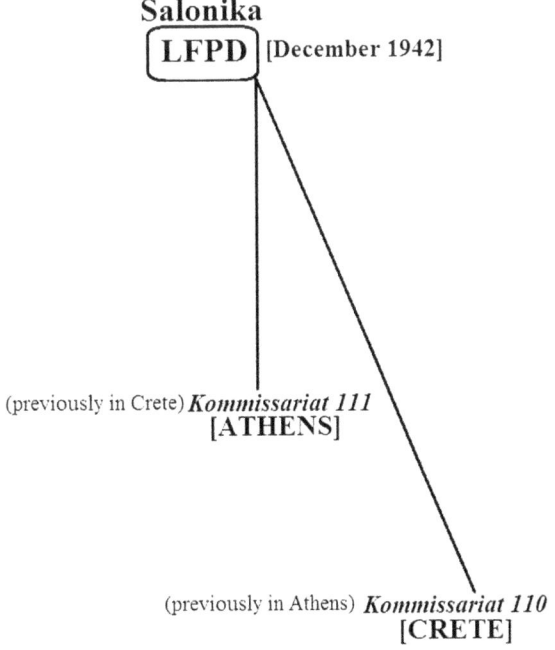

Befehlshaber Griechenland / Abteilung ABWEHR
German Military Commander in Greece / Security Staff of the Army Secret Service
Leitender Feldpolizeidirektor beim Oberfefehlshaber Südost

GFP Südost HQ and its Commissariat Commands, December 1942 (figure by author).

from Munich and had a slight build, with a height of only five feet, six inches. He had black hair and black eyes with an oval face. In 1942, he was forty years old and his distinctive feature were teeth that protruded outward from his mouth. Another member of *Sekretariat 4* was Sergeant Ogrowsky, who was five feet, eight inches in height and was originally from Berlin. He had blond hair with light blue eyes and an oval face. His features however were distorted and he wore spectacles. In 1942, he was thirty-five years old. Malasch also remembers that Ogrowsky was particularly cruel to the Greeks whom he questioned, taking pleasure in the act of interrogating the prisoners.[84]

Atypical Personnel: The Resistance Activities of Malasch and Alfons Hochhauser

According to Corporal Malasch's PW report, he was providing all kinds of information, including photographs of key GFP personnel, to the Greek underground. He was indirectly involved in aiding the Greek resistance to sink a ship in the port of Piraeus in 1942. In spite of this cooperation, Malasch claimed that he found Greeks not to be entirely trustworthy,

GFP Formations in Greece, 1941 (map by author).

4. Organization of the Secret Field Police in Greece

so he tried to limit his cooperation with the Greek resistance.[85] Another GFP member who appeared to be atypical of the type of GFP officers who served in the Balkans was Alfons Franz Emanuel Hochhauser. He turned out to be the interpreter used by GFP-640 and then was employed under the same circumstances for GFP-510. Hochhauser was half Greek on his mother's side and Austrian on his father's side. He would eventually be assigned as a *Dolmetscher* (translator) for GFP-640 and for GFP-510. Hochhauser was born on May 15, 1906, in Judenburg, Austria. His early life proved quite adventurous. He traveled extensively as a young man through the Balkans (Greece and Yugoslavia), the Middle East and even through the newly created state of Turkey. He spoke Greek fluently and virtually had one foot in Austrian society and one foot in Greek life. He was not particularly political and was not an avowed Nazi. After the Nazi Anschluss in 1938 Hochhauser was called up to the military in Styria. After initial training, he was released from military service. After this brief stint in the service, his more adventurous side once again took hold, leading him to be hired as a stoker on a freighter headed for Leningrad in 1940.[86]

In 1941, he was recalled into military service. This time he was called to Berlin and because of his language skills and his extensive Balkan travels, he was assigned to the Secret Field Police. This is when he came into contact with the famous Austrian diving expert, Hans Haas. Hochhauser took part in the Aegean Sea expedition launched by Hans Haas in Greece in 1942, where he employed revolutionary scuba diving equipment. During the expedition, Hochhauser acted as interpreter. In April 1943 Hochhauser was attached to GFP-640 until December 1943 when he was transferred over to GFP-510. In January 1944, he was stationed in Athens. There his actions came to be questioned since (1) he was accused of black market activity by the German command and (2) he was accused of being a Nazi spy by the local Greek community. Nevertheless, post-war testimony by Greek nationals affirmed that he made many attempts to protect Greek civilians from harsh punishment at the hands of the GFP. Thus, he is considered atypical of the type of German member of the GFP in the Balkans. Towards the end of the war, Hochhauser was one of tens of thousands of Germans who withdrew from Greece. However, while stationed in Athens he met a woman that he fell in love with. Knowing the local language allowed Hochhauser to romance this young woman unlike any other German could. He eventually returned after the war and although he did not officially marry her, he had two children from her—a boy and a girl. After the war, Hochhauser involved himself with Hans Haas and expeditions and tours to Greece. Yet, in spite of this, he lived a relatively reclusive life and died in 1981:

> On September 25, 1944, it will be two years since I left with my unit for Athens. On October 30, 1944, we left Salonika and Greek territory. Belgrade was then already occupied by the Russians, so we travelled to Visegrad—by way of Sarajevo and on to Zagreb. At the end of the war I reached my home in Graz. Thanks to God all my relatives survived the war. Since January 10, 1945 I was imprisoned with true politically violent perpetrators—just because of my affiliation to a unit of the Secret Field Police in Greece.[87]

Alfons Hochhauser was assured that he would not be convicted of any war crimes in Greece, yet he understood that he should comport himself with a minimum of notoriety. He behaved throughout the post-war period as a German who had to minimize his foot prints in Greece. This may have been a "knee-jerk" reaction on the part of a soldier who knew he had served an evil regime and needed to keep quiet about that period of his life. He had also witnessed the activities of the GFP directly—thus his reluctance to bring attention to himself and that era. Like millions of Germans from his generation, he didn't brag and avoided speaking at length about that period. Was it a real fear of the realities of having served in the GFP and possibly witnessing crimes? Crimes in which he himself might be implicated? Whatever we may think, it is clear that he made every effort to minimize his impact on Greek history and to keep a low profile after the war.

The GFP in Greece and Its Relationship with the SS

Loos, the top GFP official in the Balkans, has been described as sometimes being in competition with *SS-Standartenführer* Dr. Walter Blume, the head of the SS in Greece. More often than not, this animosity between the army and SS was borne out of ambition by both men and did not interfere with operations:

> At lower levels, and in the mundane business of policing the occupied territories, the Sipo/SD often worked comfortably with the GFP and the regular armed forces. The GFP usually took the lead in the rural areas, where there was a heavy Wehrmacht presence, whilst the SD was based in the cities where they controlled Greek and German police units.[88]

There were some instances of such friction taking place during the war between the Army and SS, but they were mostly created out of personal ambition rather than distaste. One case occurred in France in 1942 where the SD and the Army clashed over the Secret Field

GFP Formations in Greece, 1941–1942 (map by author).

4. Organization of the Secret Field Police in Greece 71

Police. The SD wanted to absorb GFP units in order to help create SD station posts all across France. In the end, the issue was resolved when the SS "disbanded most GFP groups in France. The SS in turn, immediately drafted the demobilized members of the GFP into the Black Corps."[89] This "transfer" was in many ways a mere formality since the a majority of the men who made up the bulk of the Secret Field Police were members of the Nazi Party and had previously served in either the *Sicherheitspolizei, Kriminalpolizei, Gestapo, Sicherheitsdienst, Gemeindepolizei, or Grenzpolizei*—all linked to repression during the Third Reich.[90] In the agreement some GFP units were left intact and continued to operate under the German army in France. In fact, SS/SD and Army cooperation was a regular occurrence throughout the war, although occasionally there was some tension, usually with regard to overlapping jurisdictional matters.

With regard to the GFP, the *Abwehr* and Army shared responsibility for cooperation with the SS and SD.[91] Units of the GFP in the occupied regions, especially in populated areas like cities, were under the command of the *Höherer SS und Polizeiführer*.[92] The GFP therefore, worked quite well under the SS and SD, and cooperated well. The GFP was a vital link between the army and the SS/SD security services. Member of the Secret Field Police in Greece affirmed the close affiliation: "The PW heard from [*Feldpolizeisekretär*]

GFP Formations in Greece, 1942–1943 (map by author).

Busse in a talk he gave to his men, and also from other GFP officers, when they were under the influence of drink, that they were in fact, all members of the *Gestapo*."[93]

Conclusions

In August 1943 Dr. Walter Blume was appointed commander of the Security Police and SD in Athens.[94] Blume was prepared to carry out all of his tasks. The principal mission was the collection and deportation to Nazi death camps, of Greece's Jewish population. Blume's second assignment was to stifle Greek resistance to German rule. In both instances, he would employ not only SS and SD forces, but army elements from the Secret Field Police, the *Feldgendarmerie* (Military Field Police), as well as the *Ordnungspolizei* (Order Police). All of these organizations moved into Greece fully prepared to carry out their assigned operations irrespective of whether those orders were legal or illegal. For the most part, the men who operated in the GFP in Greece were avowed Nazis. A close inspection of the personalities of a good number of the GFP personnel who served in Greece indicates that only one or two cases of exceptionally decent behavior may have occurred. It appears that the overwhelming majority of the GFP personnel in this region of Europe operated with ruthlessness when necessary, and most were committed to their task.

As their biographies affirm, most of the GFP officers who operated in Greece were Nazi Party members who had previously served in either the SS, Security Police, SD, or Order Police. With the exception of one or two men, the overwhelming majority of the officers who served in Greece were dedicated to their tasks. Given their National Socialist background, the GFP in Greece proved to be instrumental as a vital go-between the German Army and the SS/SD. Wilhelm Krichbaum's post-war claim that during the war, the GFP resisted cooperating with the *Sicherheitspolizei* and *Sicherheitsdienst* was a complete falsehood. In fact, the participation of the GFP in the repression of the Greek population and in the Holocaust, was absolutely vital. Given the dedication of its members to the Nazi goals, it's no surprise that GFP units in Greece were culpable of numerous war crimes. In

Members of the Wehrmacht's GFP pose for a photograph near Gniezno, Poland (U.S. Holocaust Memorial Museum, courtesy Instytut Pamieci Narodowej).

4. Organization of the Secret Field Police in Greece

one instance, a GFP member in Greece (Heinrich Deubel) was a former concentration camp commander. The case of Heinrich Deubel is particularly telling with regard to how the GFP was perceived within the Nazi regime. Deubel had fallen out of favor with Himmler while camp commandant of Dachau. Since the late 1930s he had been trying to "rehabilitate" himself in the eyes of the Nazis. That he chose to serve in the Secret Field Police in order to achieve that "rehabilitation" says more about the GFP than it does about Deubel.

5

The Secret Field Police and the Subjugation of the People of Greece

Modus Operandi of the GFP in Greece

The interrogation of Corporal Malasch by the British Army in the summer of 1944 provided invaluable information on the leadership cadre and activities of the GFP in Greece. His testimony gives us an insight into the standard operating procedure of the GFP in Greece. His POW report is filled with minute details regarding the command structure of the GFP in Greece, as well as the character traits and physical features of the principal officials. He also affirmed that besides the repression of the population and murder of the Jews, the "regular" duties of the GFP in the Balkans was to (1) counter sabotage, (2) counter hostile propaganda, (3) search for arms in the possession of the Greek civilian population, (4) suppress anti–Nazi activities, and (5) search for cooperation between the Greek underground and elements in the German Army. In this last instance, the GFP most likely directed their attention to members of *Bewährungstruppe 999* (999th Penal Formation). This was a German military unit that contained a large percentage of anti-war dissenters. The unit eventually reached division level and took part in the final months of the North African campaign. It was then transferred to Greece to serve as a garrison force. Malasch claimed that in 1942 an entire company of the 999th Penal Division, complete with its commander (a captain), were arrested by the GFP and transferred to the prison at Averov. The arrest had occurred on account of suspicions that the captain was about to bring his entire company over to the Greek guerrillas. According to Mark Mazower, the desertion rate of the 999th Penal Division was quite high.[1] The division contained a large number of members from the communist and socialist party, as well as anti-social elements like common thieves, sexual predators, and anti-war draft dodgers and pacifists, like Jehovah's Witnesses.

Malasch stated that in October 1942 some English agents were captured and arrested by the GFP while operating in Greece. They were sent to a prison located along Singrou Avenue, in Athens.[2] He said that German soldiers accused of various crimes were held at a prison in Averov, in another suburb of Athens. Malasch estimated that every year about 350 German soldiers would be arrested for various crimes, then tried and executed in Athens.[3] While this figure appears high, military historians estimate that during the war approximately 25,000 German deserters were executed, while tens of thousands more perished in concentration camps or in "punishment" units like the 999th Penal Division.[4] According to the POW interrogator, Malasch appeared to be sincere in his attempt to aid

5. The Secret Field Police and the Subjugation of the People of Greece

with whatever intelligence information he could provide. He also recounted what measures the GFP would take in case of anti–German activity on the part of the Greek population. A guerrilla attack or an act of sabotage would be met with mass arrests. The GFP, in coordination with available army, SS, and police forces would arrest and apprehend a large and indiscriminate number of men and women from the district where the anti–German action occurred. These people would be left without food or water for several days in order to punish them. The incarceration and denial of food and water was also meant to scare the population into providing information about the partisans or saboteurs. If that didn't produce results, the people were then beaten with dog whips until they collapsed. This punishment appeared to take place on a regular basis and was the "minimum" sentence meted out by the GFP as a form of reprisal. Other measures against the population included withholding food from an entire district. Given the scarcity of food in Greece during the war, this punishment appears harsher since it targeted everyone in the area, and not just a select few hostages.

In addition, the scarcity of food which plagued Greece throughout the German occupation was used to the advantage of the German occupation troops. It was common for German officers, NCOs and enlisted personnel to bring Greek women to the Hotel Majestic in Athens for a sexual liaison, in exchange for the promise of food.[5] Therefore the food shortage and the denial of food were also used as a tool of repression. The physical depredation of having to submit to sex with the enemy in exchange for food was a form of psychological subjugation of the Greek nation. These various German policies were obviously a war crime against the Greek people. In Athens suspected civilians, most of whom were innocent of any crime, were interrogated at the headquarters of *Sekretariat 4*, located at 26 Road, Third of September Street. *Sekretariat 4* belonged to *Kommissariat 111*. The civilian suspects which GFP interrogators deemed guilty, or warranted further scrutiny were taken to the prison at Singrhu, a suburb of Athens. As far as cooperation with other police organizations is concerned, Malasch said he knew of no other police or security forces in Greece at the time (July–December 1942).

He did mention that he was aware of *Sonderstab Hartmann*, a small security section from GFP-611 which was operating on the island of Crete. This squad was apparently under the command of *Feldpolizeisekretär* Hartmann.[6] Malasch stated that the arrest powers of this GFP section appeared to be greater than normal, given the fact that it was operating directly under the orders of Wehrmacht *General der Infanterie* Friedrich-Wilhelm Müller.[7] Müller arrived on Crete to assume command of the island's army garrison in August 1942. He was a hardened veteran of the Russian front who quickly developed a cruel reputation among the Cretan population. Müller would eventually be responsible for numerous atrocities on Crete during his tenure as garrison commander. The principal crimes attributed to Müller included the murders at Viannos, the destruction of the villages of Kedros and Anogia, as well as the execution of civilians in the village of Damasta. The murders at Viannos alone accounted for about twenty villages burned and destroyed and 500 civilians executed. Given the close association between *Sonderstab Hartmann* and the Crete garrison commander, we can assume with almost certainty that this GFP intelligence unit was the eyes and ears of General Müller. At the very least, this implies that *Sonderstab Hartmann* was pointing a finger at specific Cretan villages as possible targets for German reprisals.

Roman Loos employed a network of spies from the very beginning of the occupation of Greece. Post-war reports about the effectiveness of these local collaborators indicate that the GFP at best had mixed results.[8] For example, there were instances when Greek spies working for the GFP would point an accusing finger at an individual who was quite often innocent of anti–German activity. The reason for the claim was most often that they were owed money by the accuser(s) or was somehow at odds with the person or persons making the allegation. In some cases, the spy working for the Germans simply wished to be rid of this person or that person, and turned in the individual knowing that at the very least, he or she would be placed in custody, or perhaps even shot. It is interesting to note that the opposite case was true as well. That is, that quite often Greek citizens would be found dead on the street, with a placard that would say "German spy." That smoke screen was usually good enough to cover up a homicide among the Greek population, but it was easy for the German administration to verify, given that the Nazis knew who their informers were. All the Germans had to do was compare the name of the deceased to their spy list and the truth would be known. If the person who had been killed was not on the list of Greek informers, then that person was either mistakenly killed because the Greek underground thought he/she was a spy, or someone had committed murder and had hidden the fact by accusing the dead person of being a traitor and a spy.

In an infamous case, two Albanian doctors who were moonlighting as spies for the GFP in Tirana, Albania created a mythical anti–German guerrilla organization that was supposedly operating on the island of Corfu. The Germans spent months and much needed personnel and other valuable resources scouring Corfu for this phantom force. The doctors had fabricated the entire story, just so they could continue to receive German funds. Because of this, huge resources were often wasted by the Secret Field Police in chasing down these "partisan ghosts." Like many other German organizations, the GFP offered a monetary reward to anyone for turning in Jews, as well as for denouncing gentiles who were hiding them. Although the price offered was substantial, in general the local population rarely denounced Jews simply because most Greeks were not anti–Semitic.[9] Unfortunately in the Europe of the 1940s this was the exception rather than the norm. Although the standard operating procedure for the Germans was to target for elimination the nearest locality to a Greek partisan ambush or sabotage act, the Secret Field Police were the ones who usually selected which village or town was to be destroyed and its population shot. They were the army military intelligence body that officially pointed an accusing finger at a town or village. In that respect, they were just as guilty of the atrocity as the men who actually carried out the crime.

The Fight Against Partisans and Pacification

From the very beginning of the campaign in the Balkans the GFP was to play an instrumental role in the internal security apparatus of the German occupation forces. That role increased exponentially when the Italian Army surrendered on September 8, 1943. German forces were now forced to cover areas that had previously been defended by their erstwhile ally. As the Germans found themselves with less friends and an increasingly effective partisan threat, they incrementally ratcheted their violence against any resistance to their rule. An order regarding the capture of guerrillas was issued late that summer. It was dated "August 10, 1943" and had been published by the *Befehlshaber Südost*. It was titled *Behandlung der Gefangen und Überläufer im Bandenkampf, Sühne und Evakuierungsmaßnahmen*.[10] In this document, the German Army command in the Balkans spelled out the role of some military groups regarding roundup of partisans, partisan suspects, and even hostages:

> Commanders are to check if established detention centers will suffice before deportations. Transfer to the Reich will occur in accordance with established assembly regulations. An exception to this

rule is only given when the military situation does not allow evacuation. The detection of individual bandits through security sweeps (employing Army Intelligence, the SS Security Service, and Secret Field Police), is still necessary.[11]

The rest of the document dealt with the various repressive measures to be taken if German soldiers were to be ambushed. Not only would hostages be taken, but the village or town in the vicinity of the attack was to be targeted for a reprisal action. The document specifically ordered that any Greek male between the ages of fifteen to sixty was liable for apprehension as suspects or as hostages.[12] This meant that GFP units in the Balkans were tasked (like the *Abwehr*, SS and SD) to help round up partisan suspects as well as civilian hostages. These captives were liable to be shot in reprisal for any guerrilla attacks.[13] Based on the various orders and decrees issued by Adolf Hitler, the SS and the German Armed Forces High Command, Germans in the military, SS or Police were given the legal basis to behave criminally in Greece and elsewhere. Germans were rarely tried and sentenced during the war for committing abuses or atrocities. There are very few cases where a German military or civilian court actually punished someone for crimes against non–Germans. Ten years of rule under the Third Reich had its effect on the average German soldier who was tasked with carrying out an illegal order, like shooting innocent hostages. Quite often Nazi propaganda was sufficient to make the soldier believe that what he was doing was necessary for the survival of the German nation.[14] Even after the war, many men accused of war crimes successfully avoided prosecution by claiming that they were merely following military decrees established by higher authority.[15] In fact, in most cases where the man accused was found not guilty or a case could not be presented for lack of evidence, it was often one where the accused claimed that he was acting in order to safeguard the lives of the men under his command.[16]

The Partisan War in Greece and Atrocities

As the war dragged on and the German military situation worsened, Greek resistance against the Axis occupation forces increased. When Italy surrendered on September 8, 1943, the job of controlling Greece for the German occupation forces increased dramatically. Germany's other existing, though increasingly dubious allies: the Bulgarians, Romanians, and Hungarians, were already beginning to show signs of cracking. In anticipation that the partisan threat would grow and Germany would soon be friendless, the efforts of the GFP were now shifted from combating anti–German elements in the cities to aiding in the hunt for guerrilla forces in the countryside. The Greek countryside was where *Wehrmacht* formations began to conduct increasingly large-scale operations. These anti-partisan drives would yield a terrible cost in human lives, at the center of which was the Greek population of the villages and towns in and around where these *Unternehmen* (operations) took place.

An order originating from the German Army High Command, and dated "9 August 1944," clearly stated that GFP units stationed in Greece were not to be employed on routine military police duties, but were to be utilized as supporting personnel for the German "Ic" (intelligence) sections of the various division and corps commands—especially in the field of counterintelligence.[17] The intensity of this unconventional type of warfare also led to an increased level of brutality that had not been committed by the German Army during its conquest of the West. The Peloponnese and the island of Crete were in such disorder and chaos that by the fall of 1943 the German command declared these regions active combat zones. From the very beginning, the guerrilla war in these areas was greater in intensity than in the rest of the country. The brutal character of the GFP men in Greece now lent themselves fully, as whatever previous restraints the army and SS may have had toward the Greek population, were now withdrawn. The following are the principal massacres in which the GFP took an active role:

1. The Massacres at Mousiotitsa

On July 25, 1943, the 12th Company of the Third Battalion of *Gebirgsjäger Regiment 98* from First Mountain Division murdered one hundred people in Mousiotitsa, claiming that they were partisans. In total the 12th Company burned down about sixty-four homes. This was followed up by German SS troops of the Second Battalion of *SS Polizei Gebirgsjäger Regiment 18* who entered the village on August 27, 1943, and executed another 153 civilians.[18] The attack and resulting massacre was retaliation by German forces against alleged resistance activity in the village. The Germans also claimed that its inhabitants had supported a deadly attack on a German officer in the nearby region of Zitsa. In both instances (the Morfi and Mousiotitsa massacres) the intelligence upon which the German forces acted on were based on reports from the GFP post in Salonika and Ioannina—both of which belonged to GFP-621:

> About the Strength of the enemy it was the Secret Field Police who delivered the analysis. *Feldpolizeiobersekretär* Paul Härtel (GFP-621) was the Secret Field Police liaison with the "Ic" [intelligence officer] for the First Mountain Division: *Oberleutnant* (1st Lieutenant) Karl-Heinz Rothfuchs. The analysis was based mostly on the advice of *Feldpolizeiobersekretär* Härtel who claimed to have received information from prisoners. On the basis of these reports the unit acted. Estimated the enemy strength in the area [of Epirus] to be some 12,000–16,000 men, including supposedly 3,000 Englishmen.[19]

2. The Massacre at Morfi

On August 1, 1943, the village of Morfi was reached by the 54th Reconnaissance Battalion of the First German Mountain Division. The battalion commander of this reconnaissance unit, *Oberleutnant* (1st Lieutenant) Heller, had been directed to this locality by intelligence provided by the Secret Field Police. Heller stated that a gun battle ensued in the village and that "twenty-one bandits were shot." His message further said "one machine gun and a rifle were taken, and the village was set ablaze." One villager, a man named Christos Bosouris was not killed but was taken prisoner. Heller said that the suspect was turned over to the accompanying GFP officer, *Feldpolizeiinspekteur* Paul Härtel of GFP- 621, who questioned him.[20] Although *Oberleutnant* Heller referred to Härtel as a "Lieutenant," his actual GFP rank was *Feldpolizeiinspektor* (given that the rank equivalent of *Feldpolizeiobersekretär* had been eliminated in 1939). What is telling about this massacre is that although only two weapons were found in the village, twenty-one men were executed.

3. The Massacre at Kommeno

On August 16, 1943, the Germans executed 317 inhabitants and torched the village of Kommeno. This massacre was perpetrated principally by members of the 12th Company of the 98th Regiment from the First Mountain Division. The commander of the 12th Company was an officer named *Oberleutnant* Röser. Accompanying the 12th Company was *Feldpolizeisekretär* Leo Eder and a *dolmetscher* (interpreter) named Reinhold Walther from the

Secret Field Police headquarters in Salonika. The German company surrounded the village and then entered in force. After Walther could not get an answer from the village priest regarding the whereabouts of the *Andartes* (Greek guerrillas) that had been reported in the village a few days earlier, 1st Lieutenant Röser lost his patience, took out his revolver and shot the priest.[21] That murder was the signal for the men of his company to start the indiscriminate killing of the inhabitants of the village. Of the 317 people in the village that were killed, seventy-four were little children under the age of ten. A sizable portion of the village's population was able to escape by swimming across the Arachthos River. Although the massacre was instigated by 1st Lieutenant Röser, *Feldpolizeisekretär* Leo Eder made no attempt to stop the slaughter, even though he had the authority as a GFP official, to overrule Röser's actions.[22]

4. The Massacre at Paramythia

From September 19–29, 1943 over two-hundred Greeks were executed and nineteen villages were destroyed in and around the town of Paramythia. The massacre was perpetrated by members of the First Mountain Division and volunteers from the Cham community. The Chams were ethnic Albanians who had lived in northwestern Greece for hundreds of years. When Italy invaded Greece in 1940, the Greek government imprisoned the entire adult male population from the Cham community. This act of mistrust enraged the Cham people of Greece. Many Chams had long ago converted to the Islamic faith, which never sat well with Greeks, who were overwhelmingly Eastern Orthodox Christian. After the Germans defeated Greece, Italy occupied the region where the Chams lived and began to recruit them into a pro–Italian militia. When Italy surrendered on September 8, 1943, the Germans became the benefactors of the Chams.

Feldpolizeisekretär Georg Koch and six other members of GFP-621 were sent from Salonika to Paramythia to try and organize the Chams and make use of them.[23] For their part the Chams had decided to side with the Italians, so they were tainted goods in so far as the Greek guerrillas were concerned. Many had collaborated with the Italians because of the manner in which the Greek government had treated them during the Italian invasion. When Italy surrendered on September Eighth the Chams panicked, rightly assuming that they were now on the losing side of the war. Most were concerned that a Greek victory would cost them their homes and possibly their lives for having collaborated. They were right to be concerned. After the war ended, the newly installed Greek government forcibly expelled the Chams out of northwestern Greece. Most settled in Albania, with a lucky few travelling to the United States and other countries. Abandoned by the Italians, they now threw their lot with the Germans, seeing no other way out of their predicament. The town of Paramythia and the surrounding region was in chaos in early September 1943. Italian units were disbanding, the Greek guerrillas were trying to acquire their military equipment, and the Germans were attempting to prevent that from happening.

In the midst of this bedlam the first thing that the Cham militiamen thought of was to protect their community. One Greek partisan force composed of ELAS fighters attempted to disarm a Cham military unit near the town of Paramythia, but it only resulted in a firefight between the *Andartes* and the Cham militiamen.[24] When the Germans reached Paramythia the town was partly under guerrilla control. Clearing out the town was quick but before it was all over, about forty-nine Greeks had been executed by elements of the *1. Gebirgs-Division*, with the assistance of some very agitated Cham militiamen.[25] *Feldpolizeisekretär* Koch could barely keep the Cham in control, but he eventually managed to reassure the Albanian militiamen that their community was safe.[26] The fear by the Cham community that the Greek partisans would seek retribution was real, but the murder of over two-hundred Greeks (forty-nine in the town of Paramythia alone) proved to be unjustifiable murder. Those Greeks killed in the town had been fingered as possible partisans or partisan supporters by the Cham as the Germans were clearing out the town. They therefore had not died in the fighting, but had been executed.

5. The Massacre at Kalavrita

An incident which occurred in the Peloponnesian peninsula in the fall of 1943 clearly shows the increase in partisan activity in Greece and its rising intensity. The battle had taken place near the town of Kalavrita in October 1943.[27] It began with an intense firefight between members of the *117. Jäger Division* (117th Light Infantry Division) and leftist Greek guerrillas. The Germans eventually surrendered to the communist (ELAS) guerrillas after a prolonged and fierce firefight. Those Germans who surrendered had done so reluctantly and after their ammunition had run out. Seventy-eight to eighty German soldiers were eventually taken prisoner. The Germans had been reluctant to surrender, given that communist units were known to kill their prisoners. The local ELAS commander then made the decision to execute the captured soldiers by throwing them off a high cliff. Three *landsers* miraculously survived the fall, but sustained horrific injuries. They were evacuated to a military hospital in Athens, where they were later able to describe the incident.[28] General Karl von Le Suire, was incensed at the manner in which his soldiers had been treated after surrendering. He wanted repressive measures to be taken in retaliation. He conferred with *Militärbefehlshaber in Griechenland* Wilhelm Speidel, and received approval. This decision for retribution led to a massacre which occurred in the Peloponnesus town of Kalavryta from December 10–13, 1943:

> Toward the end of 1943 Greek guerrillas, striking from mountain hideouts captured eighty German soldiers. They took the captives into the mountains and pushed them over a precipice. Only three of the eighty survived. Nazi retribution was swift and terrible. It was mistakenly directed against the townspeople rather than against the guerrillas.[29]

Speidel was so infuriated at the manner in which the captured German soldiers had been executed, that he agreed with General Le Suire and ordered *repressiven Maßnahmen* ("repressive measures") to be taken against the inhabitants of the region where the killing took place.[30] A *Sonderbefehl* ("special order") sent via telex from Speidel's headquarters and dated "December 31, 1943" ordered that some 758 hostages were to be shot in retaliation for the execution of the German soldiers near Kalavrita. In the Peloponnesus, the ELAS guerrillas had their Third Partisan Division, with perhaps 4,500 men split into five guerrilla regiments. For this reason, the German command took every precaution. The "operation" was considered so important that the leader of GFP-640, *Feldpolizeikommissar* Gottfried Törkler and several other Secret Field Police officials took part in the punitive expedition. The small GFP group was escorted by a battalion of Greek Evzone troops. These pro–Axis forces assisted the *Wehrmacht* troops in surrounding the villages.[31]

Speidel's approval that brutal measures were to be applied, implicitly condoned *Generalmajor* Karl von Le Suire's desire for revenge and set in motion the massacre at Kalavrita. Again, this proved to be standard operating procedure for the Germans in Greece; especially beginning in 1943 when German reprisals increased in tempo. Based on Speidel's consent, Karl von Le Suire ordered his men to "level" Kalavrita and Mazeika and all other villages that had supposedly supported the partisans. The decision to destroy these villages had been made partly on information provided by members of GFP-640, and partly on the nearness to the murder of the captured German soldiers. According to the reports from the *117. Jäger Division*, the two combat groups created for the reprisal: *Kampfgruppe* "Gnass" and *Kampfgruppe* "Ebersberger" killed 696 civilians. The Germans also set ablaze twenty-four towns and villages, and destroyed three monasteries: Roji, Kerpini, Ano Sachlaru, Kato Sachlaru, Suwardo, Vrachni, Kalavrita, Kloster, Meg-Spilaron, Kloster Lawras, A.j. Kiriaki, Avles, Vissoka, Fteri Klapatsuna, Pirgaki, Vallitsa, Melissia, Pangrati, Morochova, Lapanangos, Masi, Mazeika, Pangrati, Morochova, Derveni, Valtos, Planeru, Hütten (west of Mazeika). One document from the *117. Jäger Division* mentioned "600 Greeks shot."[32]

6. The Massacre at Distomo

This massacre was sparked by a Greek partisan attack on June 10, 1944, when a company of *Waffen-SS* troops from the *4. SS Polizei Panzergrenadier Division* under the command of *SS-Hauptsturmführer* (SS Captain) Fritz Lautenbach was ambushed, incurring heavy losses. In retaliation, Lautenbach's unit drove to the closest locality and massacred the Greek inhabitants of the village of Distomo as a 'retaliatory measure' for the partisan attack earlier in the day:

> In total of 218 men, women, and children were killed in Distomo, a small village near Delphi. According to survivors, SS forces bayoneted babies in their cribs, stabbed pregnant women, and beheaded the village priest.[33]

Exactly forty-seven children aged twelve or younger, ninety-one women, sixty men and ten couples were killed. Some of the women who were killed had their breasts cut off. Immediately following the massacre a member of GFP-621 named *Feldpolizeibeamter* Georg Koch did something quite surprising. Sergeant Koch had accompanied the SS troops that day, and had witnessed what transpired.[34] He reported that an illegal killing had taken place by informing the higher German military authorities that, contrary to the account presented by Lautenbach, the SS troops had come under attack several miles from Distomo and had not been fired upon "with mortars, machine-guns and rifles from the direction of Distomo."[35] The regimental commander of the SS company that took part in the massacre (*SS-Obersturmbannführer* Karl Schümer) defended the actions of *SS-Hauptsturmführer* Fritz Lautenbach, but it was clear from what transpired that military order had collapsed and the SS men had behaved like monsters.

In the end, even though Special Envoy Hans Neubacher looked into the matter, no one was prosecuted and Georg Koch's report was buried.[36] Koch was referred to as an *Unteroffizier* ("NCO") or as a *Feldpolizeibeamter*, but in the GFP his rank was *Feldpolizeisekretär*.[37] It's not clear what if anything happened to Georg Koch, but its doubtful he suffered retribution given the involvement of high ranking army officials. Besides, by the summer of 1944 it was clear that a German withdrawal from Greece was inevitable, so the German command had bigger problems to worry about. It should be noted that Koch's actions were atypical to the behavior of the majority of GFP men in Greece.

Operations on the Island of Crete

Crete was one of the principal centers of Greek partisan resistance, and the region was quite active. The island was not only the largest of the Greek islands, but was also the birthplace of Eleftherios Venizelos—the politician that most see today as the father of modern Greece. During the war, the German occupation force lost many troops on account of partisan ambushes on Crete. British commando forces raided the island on many occasions. In one famous incident, English commandos (with the assistance of the local *Andartes*) took captive the commander of *22. Luftlande-Division* (22nd Air Landing Division). The manner in which the Germans replied to this unconventional warfare was quite brutal. Hitler had decreed that for every German soldier killed by partisans, ten hostages should be shot. However, this figure increased as the war progressed and as resistance to German rule rose. For example, when Major-General Franz Krech was murdered in Athens in 1944, the German command executed 300 Greeks in retaliation.[38] Most hostages were to be selected from a pool of suspected partisan suspects, or (if this was lacking), taken at random from the local population—preferably from the area of the partisan attack. In the case of Krech, the Germans claimed that of the 300 hostages executed, one hundred were communist party members and 200 were ordinary citizens.[39] The mathematics of terror was simple: make it extremely costly (in terms of lives) for partisans to operate. It was in this environment that Friedensbacher and the rest of GFP-611 operated.

While GFP-611 was stationed in the West, the formation was led by *Feldpolizeikommissar* Dr. Otto Begus (an Austrian). In late April 1941 Begus was replaced by *Feldpolizeikommissar* Ludwig Albert as commander of GFP-611. That same month GFP-611 was transferred from France to Greece. By June 1941 GFP-611 was operating in the region of Athens and Piraeus. Soon after, it was shifted to the island of Crete. The principal headquarters for GFP-611 while stationed on Crete was in the town of Chania, on the northern coast of western Crete. Due to a heavy Greek partisan presence on the island, two additional GFP branch offices were established: (1) *Sekretariat 1*, at Heraklion and (2) *Sekretariat 2* at Rethymno. Initially *Kommissariat 111* was located on the island, but in 1943 it was replaced by *Kommissariat 110*. While on the island, both *kommissariat* were located in Chania. The principal mission of the Secret Field Police on the island of Crete was as follows:

- Combat sabotage and espionage
- Arrest suspected persons
- Question the prisoners
- After interrogation, all of the prisoners were to be sent to Hania.
- At Hania they would undergo a military court martial that would decide their fate.
- That court martials had three possible outcomes;
    - Guilty Verdict—A term of imprisonment to be determined by the court.
    - Guilty Verdict—Execution by firing squad if the alleged crime was severe enough.
    - Not Guilty Verdict—Release from captivity.

Feldpolizeiinspektor *Ferdinand Friedensbacher*

In 1941, the then twenty-nine-year-old Ferdinand Friedensbacher was assigned *Sekretariat 1* of GFP-611 in Heraklion. *Feldpolizeiinspektor* Friedensbacher was in charge of twelve members in this *Sekretariat*. In September 1943 when Italy left the war, the Italians on the island of Crete were disarmed and mostly withdrawn. A small number of Italian soldiers remained, deciding to continue the war on the side of Germany. It was at this time that Ferdinand Friedensbacher's small GFP force was shifted to the southeastern and eastern region of Crete, in the area of Agios Nikolaos. By then the demands of the partisan war and the occupation in general had diluted his *Sekretariat* to only six members. Out of this small seven-man detachment only the *dolmetscher* (interpreter), who happened to be a local collaborator, could speak Greek. In May 1944 Friedensbacher was responsible for the summary execution of a thirty-year-old pharmacist whom he suspected of being the local leader of the Greek resistance. Standard practice was for the suspect to have been sent to Chania where *Kommissariat 110* would decide whether the case warranted handing the suspect over to be tried by a military tribunal. It was then this Army tribunal that would decide his guilt or innocence. Fearing that he would be acquitted by such a military court, Friedensbacher disobeyed protocol and executed the pharmacist on the spot. The only person who brought this crime to the attention of the Allied authorities was the Greek translator attached to Friedensbacher's *Sekretariat*. This Greek citizen was tried after for collaboration. During his trial the man also claimed that Friedensbacher would regularly torture partisan suspects. Given that this was standard operating procedure for the GFP the story rang true. Unfortunately for this man, he was found guilty of aiding the Germans and shortly thereafter he was executed by the Greek government.

Decades later in 1970, Friedensbacher was eventually brought to trial for the summary execution of the Greek pharmacist on Crete. Friedensbacher vigorously refuted the charge that he tortured Greek prisoners, claiming in his post-war trial that the most he would do with suspects in his custody was to slap them around.[40] Given that the Greek translator had long ago been executed, there was no one in Friedensbacher's 1970 trial to affirm that he had indeed tortured prisoners. His lawyer argued successfully that German forces were the subject of constant guerrilla ambushes and attacks, and that the partisans had also mutilated and shot captured German soldiers. Throughout the trial Friedensbacher swore that he had acted within the existing confines of the guerrilla war on Crete. He echoed his lawyer, swearing that atrocities and unconventional warfare were rampant. He said defiantly that he made the decision to kill the Greek pharmacist in order to protect German lives. The former downhill skier was unapologetic, claiming that he had been morally justified in shooting the man because he believed him to be a "dangerous person." Throughout the trial Friedensbacher remained unrepentant: "I wanted him dead, but I wanted it to be painless. When the pharmacist fell into the sea I probably would have shot him again if he had remained alive!"[41] In 1970, the Austrian courts were apparently not ready to admit the culpability of the army in war crimes, because it acquitted him of the murder. The verdict of the Austrian court read as follows:

Ferdinand FRIEDENSBACHER
Tatvorwurf: Kriegsverbrechen in Agios Nikolaos/Kreta (Griechenland), begangen als Angehöriger der Geheimen Feldpolizei durch Tötung eines mutmaßlichen Angehörigen der griechischen Widerstandsbewegung
Urteil eines Geschworengerichts am Landesgericht Innsbruck am 9. Dezember 1970: Freispruch
Verbrechenskomplex: Kriegsverbrechen
Tatort: Agios Nikolaos/Kreta (Griechenland)
Opfer: Zivilisten (griechische)
Dienststelle: Polizei/Geheime Feldpolizei
Angeklagter/Urteil:
Ferdinand FRIEDENSBACHER (Marschall Nr.: 144): Freispruch (rechtskräftig geworden)
Geschäftszahl des LG Innsbruck: 10 Vr 415/70[42]

It should be noted that the courtroom where this verdict was pronounced contained a sizable number of ex-German soldiers. A local Austrian paper reported: "…the audience, mostly former soldiers, acknowledged the acquittal with applause."[43]

The Massacre at Viannos

Although the Austrian court found Friedensbacher innocent of the murder of the Greek pharmacist, they would have most likely reconsidered their decision had they known that he was also involved in the murder of around five-hundred Cretan villagers in the same month that he assumed command of his GFP post in Agios Nikolaos. From September 14–16, 1943 about twenty villages east of Viannos, Crete were absolutely wiped out and at least 500 villagers were murdered by the Germans. The region lies just southwest of Agios Nikolaos, where *Feldpolizeiinspektor* Friedensbacher's *Sekretariat* was located. The Germans also made sure to ruin the season's harvest in those villages. This was done so that no Greek could harvest the crops. Again, the Germans were using famine as a weapon. This massacre had occurred in retaliation for the supposed support by these villagers for the Cretan guerrillas. Friedensbacher had selected the villages to be destroyed based on intelligence from his *Sekretariat*. This punitive operation became so infamous, that after the war it proved the undoing of *Generalleutnant* Friedrich-Wilhelm Müller, who was executed for his part in the crime. Müller employed elements of the 65th Regiment, accompanied by Friedensbacher and his *Sekretariat*, which was to point out the villages to be targeted. Müller's repressive tactics were so harsh and cruel that he earned the nickname, "the butcher of Crete." While Müller was punished for having given the order to commit this war crime, Friedensbacher's role in this atrocity went unnoticed. As a result, he was never brought to trial for this massacre.

Friedrich Schubert

The placement of GFP-611 on Crete became notorious not only because this unit was involved in the execution of local Greek civilians, but because under its auspices it employed a sergeant named Friedrich Schubert and a collaborationist force which he recruited. Schubert's rank in the GFP was as a *Feldpolizeibeamter* in *Sekretariat 2* of GFP-611. The importance of Schubert to the tragedy that was about to unfold on Crete was belied by his low rank. Not counting the "Butcher of Crete," Schubert would turn out to be the most infamous Nazi on Crete during the occupation.[44] Schubert apparently spoke fluent Greek. He was described as appearing more Greek than German, having an olive-tone complexion more akin to a person from the Mediterranean region rather than a "Nordic Aryan" hailing from the area of western Germany.[45] Locals on Crete also remembered that he spoke with a Greek accent from the region of Anatolia in present-day Turkey. The GFP presence on Crete was so small that *Feldpolizeidirektor* Hartmann (who had assumed command of *Kommissariat 110* when he replaced Dr. Otto Begus) apparently allowed *Feldwebel* Schubert to recruit a band of Greek volunteers to help augment the GFP. Sergeant Schubert recruited a small company of volunteers from the lowest rungs of Greek society: drunkards, malcontents, common criminals released from prison, opportunists, hooligans, low-brow street bullies and toughs, and formed them into what became known on the island of Crete as the "*Schubertiani*."[46] The unit became so infamous that when it was seen approaching a Cretan village or town the cry would ring out, *Schubertiani érchontai* ("the Schubertiani are coming!"), sending the entire local population fleeing in panic.

Unlike his notorious "career" in Greece during the war, Friedrich Schubert's past is vague and nebulous. Schubert's actual birth name was Petros Konstantinidis (Peter Constantine).[47] One source states that he immigrated to Germany at a young age.[48] We know

5. The Secret Field Police and the Subjugation of the People of Greece 85

that he was born in Dortmund, Germany on February 21, 1897, to a Greek father and German mother. The father was apparently a rich tobacco merchant from the city of Smyrna, in what is today western Turkey. The city is ancient and is located along the Ionian coastline of western Anatolia by the Aegean Sea. The foundations of the city date back to the 11th Century BCE when Aeolian Greeks established it as a small settlement. It was later developed during the Archaic Period of Greek history by Ionian Greeks. The city therefore had a lingtime community of Greeks living there. After the First World War the Ottoman Empire collapsed and the map of Europe and the Middle East were redrawn. Greece wished to assert its right to territorial concessions given to her by the Treaty of Sevres as part of the overall Treaty of Versailles. When the western Allies refused to enforce part of those concessions dealing with western Anatolia, the Greeks opted for war against Turkey in order to obtain those territories. The Greco-Turkish War lasted from 1919–1922. During the conflict, around 264,000 Greek civilians were killed.[49] Turks suffered similar losses as well. Greece was the ultimate loser in this bloody conflict. On September 9, 1922, Turkish troops occupied Smyrna. They immediately began to forcibly expel the Greek population from the city. The Greco-Turkish War caused a great deal of suffering on the Greek and Turkish people. As already stated, both Greece and Turkey forcibly exchanged huge numbers of people with each other. Greeks were forced to leave lands that they had lived on for thousands of years. Turks living within Greece's frontier were similarly expelled and sent to Turkey. Before it was all over, close to a million Greeks were expelled from Turkish lands.

It is quite possible that "Peter Constantine," a.k.a. "Fritz Schubert," may have spent some time in Smyrna; perhaps with his father and mother, before the expulsion of the Greek community in 1922. That might be how he obtained his particular Smyrna accent. If his father had indeed moved his family to Smyrna before the First World War, it would not be a stretch of the imagination to assume that his parents may have either been killed or been separated from him during those chaotic months in 1922 when the Turkish Army killed and forcibly expelled the Greek population from Smyrna. Perhaps his parents and Peter himself might have been three among those tens of thousands of Greeks who had to flee the city and Turkish rule in 1922. Nothing is known of his family and events surrounding his life during this time other than that he eventually returned to Germany in the 1920s and became deeply committed to the rising Nazi party beginning in the 1930s.

The separation or divorce of his parents sometime during his youth is another possibility. Perhaps his Greek father may have even abandoned Peter and his mother, and this may have caused the young man to acquire a hatred for the "Greek" side of his heritage. Human nature is a difficult thing to comprehend. Nevertheless, his actions on Crete and on the Greek mainland during the war certainly can attest to his hatred of the Greek people. However, if he grew up in Germany, where did he pick up the "Greek-Smyrna" accent that he had as a 44-year-old? This was the time (1941) when he was assigned to Crete in the service of the GFP. By the time of the Turkish expulsion of Greeks from Smyrna in 1922, Peter would have been about 25 years old—certainly old enough to have picked up the Smyrna accent.

In any event, we know that in 1922 Peter Constantine would have been twenty-five years old. At this time, post–World War I Weimar Germany was politically unstable and in the years 1923–1924 would become an economic basket case—making it a poor choice for a home for someone seeking a better life, especially as a refugee.[50] However, postwar Greece and its recent (disastrous) war with Turkey from 1919–1922 was (most likely) an even worse choice as a destination for Petros Konstantinidis to make. It is quite probable that "Peter Constantine" might have chosen to return to the nation of his birth (Germany), given that he was born there and was therefore a German citizen by birth. He then might have decided to assume his mother's maiden name (Schubert) in order to better blend in. Straddling two worlds and knowing two languages fluently, he had a language skill and was therefore in a unique position for membership in the Secret Field Police as a translator.

Of course, most of the above is mere speculation on my part and is merely an educated guess. What we do know for sure is that he did end up living in Germany in the late 1920s and 1930s and eventually joined the fledgling Nazi Party. Those missing years regarding his early life are an absolute mystery but the conjecture described here is certainly not out of the realm of possibility. Schubert began his reign of terror on August 27, 1941, while stationed in Rethymno (*Sekretariat 2* of *Kommissariat 110*). On that day, he tortured and killed P. Papadakis for hiding an English soldier. When the head of the GFP in Crete [Hartmann] was killed in the late summer of 1943, Friedrich Schubert gained more independence of action. He continued to work with deception and was totally unsympathetic in his actions as shown by this example:

> At the beginning of June (1943) Schubert, the counter-espionage chief who took over from Hartmann, decided to play the role of free-roving stool pigeon himself. He went to Koumaram above Asi Gonia, with four of his renegade Cretans, and pretended to be an English officer newly arrived from Cairo. A trusting boy told them all about the English in the area but at the last moment, when they asked to be led to the English base, he became suspicious; they seized him as he tried to run away and shot him on the spot. Neighbors heard the report and began to appear. Schubert and his accomplices, although armed, went to fetch reinforcements; such was their fear of the villagers' anger.[51]

Anthony Beevor assumes that Schubert had a high rank within the Secret Field Police, when in fact he never went beyond the rank of *Feldpolizeisekretär*. The rank is unimportant, what is important were his actions. The horrific episode described above was but one example of the kinds of horrors which the Cretan people were forced to endure during the occupation. To Schubert and his thugs, the people of Crete were playthings which they could tease, torture, and kill in the same way that a cat plays with a mouse before he kills that mouse. However, Schubert and his thugs weren't just missing their humanity—they were also missing their backbones. Based on who they targeted while they were operating on Crete, it appears from their actions that they were more comfortable abusing and killing defenseless civilians than actually fighting the Andartes on the island.

Schubert's formation was so feared by the Cretan population and had committed such atrocities on the island that Schubert's name had actually made it into the "Allied Central Registry of War Criminals and Security Suspects,"[52] Eventually Fritz Schubert's unit drew such attention that the ELAS Fifth Partisan Division (some 2,000 strong), which was conducting operations on the island, made a pledge that they would hunt down Schubert's unit and destroy it to the last man. Soon after that announcement was made the decision was taken by *Kommissariat 110* to withdraw the 90–100 strong volunteer company and its infamous GFP commander.[53] It was thus that in January 1944 Schubert and his men were sent by air to Salonika. By then Schubert and his ruffians had attained such negative notoriety that *Feldpolizeikommissar* Heinrich Deubel assigned Schubert and his unit to work with a pro–German Greek battalion. This pro–German formation was named after its commander, Colonel George Poulos, and was operating in and around Salonika.[54] During the German withdrawal from Greece, the *Poulos Polizei Verband* was evacuated and made its way to the 18th SS Military District "Alpenland." It appears that most of Schubert's Cretan volunteers were absorbed into this unit. However, Fritz Schubert didn't travel with the *Poulos Polizei Verband* to Austria. It's believed that in late 1944 Schubert was transferred from the GFP into the SD. One unverifiable report states that he joined the SD as an *SD-Obersturmführer* and was posted to the BdS command in Belgrade, Yugoslavia in the fall of 1944.

The Massacre at Chortiatis (Salonika)

Chortiatis is a suburb and a former municipality in the Salonika District. It was here that in early September 1944 Schubert and other accomplices would commit another atrocity against the Greek people. In late August 1944 Greek (communist) ELAS troops apprehended three German soldiers who were eventually executed. Following established (but illegal) protocol, the German military command ordered that a reprisal action be taken against the nearest town or village where the attack occurred. Accordingly, Nazi troops arrived at the village of Chortiatis on September 2, 1944. Units which took part in this attack included the one-hundred-man force led by Fritz Schubert, and elements of the *Poulos Polizei Verband*. The people who happened to be in the town square were immediately arrested, while Schubert's men began to loot and burn local homes. One group of civilians was led into the home of Evangelos Ntinoudis, where they were locked inside while the house was set alight. These poor people burned to death while crying out for help. Another group of civilians were locked in the local bakery. Schubert's men then placed an MG-34 light machine gun on the ledge of a small window and began to shoot the people inside the bakery. The bakery was then set on fire to ensure that there would be no survivors. Many women especially the young were raped and later killed. Schubert's report stated that those killed had been shot trying to escape. In total one hundred forty-six Greek civilians were massacred at Chortiatis on that day. Of the 146-people killed, 109 were women and young girls. By the time the perpetrators left Chortiatis, three hundred homes or businesses were burned to the ground.

The Massacre at Anogeia

The Secret Field Police also took part in other atrocities perpetrated by the German Army. One example occurred in the village of Anogeia. Here elements of the Secret Field Police (GFP-611) and a unit of the Military Field Police from *Feldgendarmerie Abteilung 501* were employed. The exact manner of the atrocity was similar to that which befell the village of Hordaki: it was surrounded by superior German forces, and every male inhabitant was killed.[55] The events leading to the massacre began on August 7, 1944, when *Feldwebel* Josef Olenhauer and ten other Germans went to the village of Anogeia looking for runaway laborers. When the men he chose refused to go willingly, Olenhauer arrested about fifty people from the village and led them back to their station post at Yeni Gave. However, the German squad was ambushed and killed by a unit from the ELAS partisans. A day later Captain William Moss, a British SOE officer led a combined guerrilla force made up of Greek resistance fighters and escaped Russian POWs towards Damasta where the British special operations officer hoped that he could sabotage a bridge to prevent the Germans from reaching Anogeia and exacting punishment for the murder of Sergeant Olenhauer and his men. The expected German attack eventually materialized when a truck and an armored car appeared on the Damasta-Anogeia road. In total, the British commander and his rag-tag guerrilla force killed thirty-five Germans and ten Italians. The German response was swift. The village of Anogeia was surrounded by a large contingent of German troops (including a section from GFP-611) and was wiped out:

> Because the town of Anogia is the center of the English intelligence on Crete, because the people of Anogia committed the murder of the Sergeant from Yeni Gave, as well as of the garrison under his command, because the people of Anogia carried out the sabotage of Damasta, because in Anogia the guerrillas of the various groups of resistance take refuge and find protection and because it was through Anogia that the kidnappers of General Heinrich von Kreipe passed, using Anogia as a transit camp, we order its complete destruction, as well as the execution of every male person from Anogia who would happen to be within the village and around it within a distance of one kilometer. Chanea 13 August 1944, the Commanding General of the Crete Garrison–Friedrich-Wilhelm Müller.[56]

Of the fifteen who were apprehended, the GFP shot eight. The village of Chordaki, located northeast of Chania, in western Crete suffered a similar fate as at Anogeia, although the Germans did not kill every single male. Chordaki was surrounded at dawn on August 22, 1944, by members of GFP-611, accompanied by a platoon from *Feldgendarmerie Abteilung 501*. The *Feldgendarmerie* were the uniformed military police units of the German Army. While the *Feldgendarmerie* stood guard, members of the secret field police began to interrogate the people of the village. A number of men and their next of kin were questioned on the basis of name lists and houses. It appears that the Germans had a list of which civilians lived in each house. After discovering that about fifteen people did not belong in those homes, they were taken by the GFP to the edge of the village for further interrogation. Instead, eight men were shot there by a bullet through the neck. Their bodies were left where they fell. Those villagers who were not selected for execution later told what happened.[57] Based on their testimony and that of other Greeks who witnessed war crimes on Crete, the Greek War Crimes Office on May 26, 1956, issued a request for prosecution to the German judicial authorities for the prosecution of eighty-seven German citizens who were former members of the German *Wehrmacht*. The alleged offenses included:

- The murder of about 3,000 inhabitants on the island of Crete
- Terrorizing the population
- Torture
- Deportations
- Expropriation of private property
- Theft of private property
- The shooting of hostages
- The burning of villages and towns throughout the island

One witness to the massacre in Chordaki (whose last name began with "T") was presented by the Greek War Crimes Office. The witness made a statement to the coroner on May 17, 1960, saying that besides the Secret Field Police and the Military [Field] Police, a certain "Schubert" command also took part in police duties on the island. The witness also confirmed that the actions of the above command did much harm to the reputation of the Germans in the country. More than half of the surviving 87 defendants belonged to the GFP and the *Feldgendarmerie* ("Military Field Police"). Hence, it must be considered that these units had a considerable share in these crimes and violated the laws of war and international laws. German witnesses and Greek nationals confirmed the majority of these acts.[58]

The expansion of the guerrilla war in Greece and the heavy-handed German reaction to it created the conditions for increasing brutality which led to these massacres. The viciousness and intensity of the anti-partisan war was revealed when the commander of Army Group "E" issued a directive, dated "23 July 1944," which specifically forbade GFP personnel from carrying their *Soldbuch* (paybook) during an anti-partisan drive. The logic was that if these GFP personnel were to be captured, their paybook would betray who they were, thus possibly incurring a heavy-handed interrogation by the Andartes and/or immediate execution. Since GFP personnel knew intimately many details about the manner in which the Germans were carrying out their occupation of Greece, it was deemed a national security matter that these men not be identified. Instead, the command ordered that all GFP personnel taking part in anti-partisan operations were to carry an *Ausweis* (ID card), which was to be made and issued by the immediate GFP group.[59] The *Ausweis* was easier to discard or hide if the GFP official was in eminent danger of being captured.

The Infamous "Kommando Befehl" *and Its Consequences*

The *Kommando Befehl* (Commando Order) was personally decreed on October 18, 1942, by Adolf Hitler. In essence it stated that all enemy commando troops who might be captured by German forces in occupied Europe (including in Africa) should be immediately shot without trial. The order expressly stated that it did not matter if (1) the Allied commandos were wearing proper military uniforms, (2) if they were wounded or not, or (3) that they were making an attempt to surrender to German forces. In all instances, no quarter no mercy was to be given to these commando troops and they were to be exterminated. The most important clause was section "3" which read in part:

> From now on all enemies on so-called commando missions in Europe or Africa, challenged by German troops, even if they are to all appearances soldiers in uniform or demolition troops, whether armed or unarmed, in battle or in flight, are to be slaughtered to the last man.[60]

This order also included any individual commando or group of commandos whatever the size; or its agents, and saboteurs not in proper uniforms that fell into the hands of the *Wehrmacht*, either through combat or otherwise. In all instances the commandos were to be handed over immediately to the *Sicherheitsdienst* (S.D., the SS Security Service). The order was issued but was deemed to be secret (not to be made public). The final stipulation of the *Kommando Befehl* made it clear that failure to carry out the Commando Order by any German officer would be considered an act of negligence punishable under German military law.

The *Kommandobefehl* came out of Hitler's frustration over Winston Churchill's idea to "set Europe ablaze" by launching continued commando-style incursions into Nazi occupied Europe. The United Kingdom had initiated this tactic while yet unable to launch an invasion of the European mainland. British commandos became famous for carrying out daring raids all across the continent. They proved to be quite successful and caused untold damage and losses for the Axis. The very success of the commando operations and the frustration in failing to thwart such unorthodox military tactics is what most likely spurred the Nazis to impose such a draconian punishment on any captured commando. British commando operations inside Greek occupied territories were quite common during the war. One of the most famous operations of the war was the British commando kidnapping of General Heinrich Kreipe, the German commander of Crete who had replaced General Friedrich Müller in February 1944.[61] Another successful raid on Crete was reported and investigated by GFP-611. It described how a British commando raid on July 5, 1943, against the German airfield at Heraklion destroyed sixteen Ju-88 bombers and one small reconnaissance plane. These planes all belonged to the *Luftwaffe*'s I. Gruppe / L.G. 1.

Given that British commandos caused so much damage to the enemy, it's no surprise that the Germans wanted to wipe them out, even if this was a breach of the rules of war. From 1942 onwards, if a British commando fell into German hands his fate was grim. R. E. Carpenter was a typical member. He had the misfortune of being captured during a British commando raid on Greek soil on July 5, 1944. He was sent to a prison located on Tsimiski Street in Salonika. There he was interrogated by men of GFP-621. The Germans reported him as having died in a POW camp in Germany. If that had been the case, then the Red Cross would have listed him among their roster of captured Allied servicemen, but no record of this exists. It is more probable that Carpenter never left the GFP jail in Salonika, and was executed there on account of the Commando Order.[62] A similar case occurred regarding the fate of Private Fishwick, another British commando who was also unlucky enough to be taken prisoner during another raid. He was flown to Athens and interrogated in a GFP prison in the Greek capital. The Germans claimed that he reportedly died in a hospital in Athens but again, the Red Cross should have had a record of his death but it did not. This again leads one to conclude that Fishwick, who also happened to be a British Jew, died on account of the infamous *Kommandobefehl*. In Fishwick's case, his religion may have also played a role.

Destruction of Greek Towns, 1941–1944

It appears from this map of German reprisals against Greek towns and villages that half of the communities on the island of Crete were destroyed by the Germans in their attempt to crush the partisan movement there. A good number of Greek communities elsewhere in the countryside were similarly ruined by the Germans. In total the Nazi occupation cost Greece ¼ of the country's forests and other natural resources, including ⅞ of Greece's factories, as well as the destruction of nearly all of the nation's ports, bridges, roads, and railways. When the Germans withdrew, they took with them locomotives and other rolling stock that belonged to Greece. Greece also lost 11 percent of its population at the hands of the Axis forces. Clearly, the German occupation took a heavy toll on Greece. The famine of 1941–1942 alone cost approximately 300,000 Greek lives. Estimates of the number of Greek deaths caused by reprisal actions during the occupation number as high as 30,000 lives.[63]

Numerous war crimes committed by the *Wehrmacht* in Greece that have gone unpunished to this day. In particular, the First Mountain Division, which included many Austrians, took part in numerous massacres. In the Epirus region First Mountain Division was aided in these shootings by the Secret Field Police who often pointed out and targeted villages for reprisals. The 117th Light Infantry Division also took part in numerous atrocities. The GFP aided the *Wehrmacht* in carrying out these war crimes. They also took an active role in the Holocaust in Greece. German repressive measures against the Greek civilian population proved to be considerable. Not only were Greek lives lost but the nation of Greece, already economically weak before the war, came out of World War II with its infrastructure completely ruined. The German government has never fully paid for the destruction that it brought to Greece during the Nazi period.

During the German occupation, a total of about 6,500 Greek towns and villages were destroyed throughout the German occupation. Of that number, 1,600 towns and villages with about 2,000–3,000 civilians were annihilated on the island of Crete alone.[64] To add insult to injury, Greece was forced to pay for the German occupation. In addition, the Central Bank of Greece was coerced into loaning the Third Reich hundreds of millions of *Reichsmarks* that were never repaid. In 1960, West Germany paid Greece 115 million marks,

5. The Secret Field Police and the Subjugation of the People of Greece

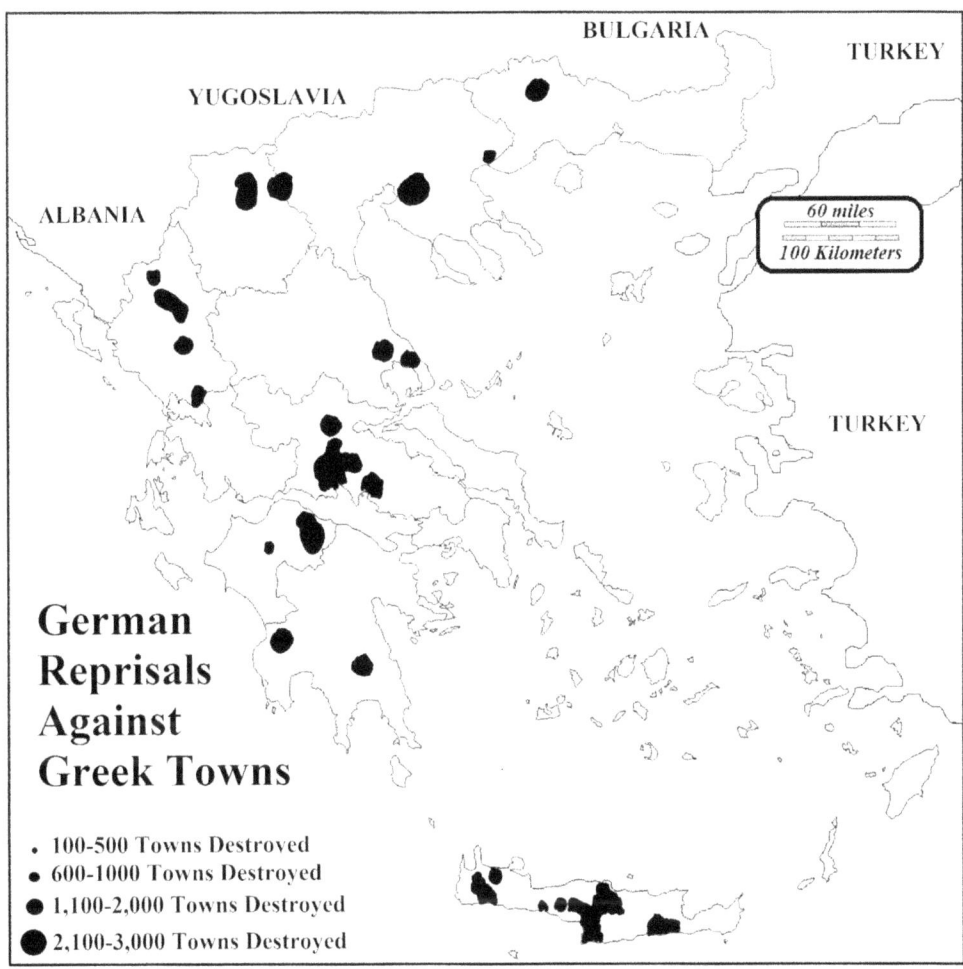

German Reprisals against Greek Towns and Villages (map by author).[65]

claiming the money was payment for war reparations. The Greek government accepted the money, but stated that this amount should merely be a down payment. When Germany was reunited in 1990, the new German government unilaterally demanded that all matters concerning World War II be put to rest. According to the Greek government, Germany still owes Greece war reparations (including interest) equaling some 279,000,000,000 Euros.[66] It is unlikely that Chancellor Angela Merkel will ever agree to repay Greece for all of the destruction human and inanimate, public, and private; as well as for the theft and plunder that Germany perpetrated during the four years of the occupation. The Austrian government has never paid war reparations to Greece.

The GFP and the Withdrawal of the German Army from Greece

In October 1944, Hitler's troops were ordered to withdraw from Greece. This included Army Group "E" in Salonika. The Secret Field Police was ordered to be one of the rear-guard units to stay behind to cover the German withdrawal as well as to aid in the destruction of anything of military value to the enemy. On the orders of *Feldpolizeisekretär* Alois Uch, the leader of GFP-621, a *Sekretariat* on Rhodes supervised demolition squads ordered to destroy the port facilities of Salonika. According a *Tätigkeitsbericht* from this unit dated December 5, 1944, the Secret Field Police officials were to assure that the port at Salonika would be rendered useless after the German withdrawal:

> Along the quay-wall lying where fishing vessels, tugs, and small steamers were docked, many were initially sunk. From October 13–29, 1944, a blocked zone was established. After blowing up the large steamer in the harbor entrance all facilities, cranes and other equipment were rendered useless, blocking the entrance to the harbor with the sunken ships and setting the warehouses on fire.[67]

Similarly, GFP-510 in Athens directed *Pioneer-Bataillon 659* (659th Engineer Battalion) as to which buildings and warehouses were to be dynamited and destroyed.[68] The port of

Map of Major Atrocity Sites in Greece (map by author).

5. *The Secret Field Police and the Subjugation of the People of Greece*   93

Piraeus was also targeted. However, the Germans had virtually destroyed the port when it was bombed on April 7, 1941. Since then, some repairs had been made but the port never operated at full capacity during the German occupation.

Conclusions

It is clear from the behavior of the Secret Field Police in Greece that it was a vital instrument in the Nazi apparatus of repression. The GFP established jails, took part in torture of prisoners on a regular basis, participated in mass shootings of civilians, and even used the denial of food as a form of punishment. In addition, the GFP took part in individual and mass shootings on a regular basis. The overwhelming majority of the personnel making up the Secret Field Police in Greece proved to be totally dedicated to a Nazi victory and all of the consequences that came with such a possibility. With a few exceptions, they behaved cruelly and harshly against the Greek population. The comportment of the Secret Field Police in Greece therefore, proved to be criminal and their actions illegal. Given their close working relationship with the SS it is a surprise that few if any GFP members were ever convicted of war crimes, and the GFP as a whole was never branded a criminal organization.

6

The Participation of the Secret Field Police in the Holocaust in Greece

The Holocaust in Greece

It has already been established that the GFP was complicit in the Holocaust. However, the nature of that participation has not been fully documented. This chapter provides further proof of the actions of the Secret Field Police in helping to perpetrate *ha Shoah* in Greece.[1] Aside from knowing which GFP formations were involved, very little else has been written. Finding which individuals were directly responsible for war crimes will push forward our knowledge of the Holocaust by placing blame on specific perpetrators for a particular offense. By pointing out the individual(s) culpable in a crime, including personnel temporarily assigned to the GFP, we can gain a better insight into how deeply the Secret Field Police was involved in the murder of the Jews of Greece. We can also answer the question just exactly how vital was the support given by the Secret Field Police in the Nazi attempt to wipe out Greece's Jewish population. What GFP unit and which specific men committed these crimes? Which GFP personnel were responsible for rounding up and expelling the Jews of Greece for extermination to Nazi death camps? To answer these questions is to gain a better understanding of the role of the GFP in the Holocaust.

Army Troops Temporarily Assigned to the GFP

Chapter Four established that the average GFP official in Greece was a dedicated Nazi. Chapter Five affirmed their criminal behavior. The importance of the GFP's role as a tool of repression and murder in Greece was also established. But what about the *Wehrmacht* personnel who were often drafted into the Secret Field Police on a temporary basis? Army formations were often tapped for men in order to temporarily augment GFP units. This was especially true shortly before these formations were to perform a major operation. The army personnel were drafted into two basic categories: (1) those serving in the GFP for a one or two year term, considered a "long-term temporary" assignment; (2) and those short-term draftees who were assigned to the GFP for a matter of days, weeks, or months, referred to as a "short-term temporary" duty.[2] Although these men were often chosen to serve in the GFP for a particular talent, such as a foreign language skill, knowledge of communications equipment, or other technical knowledge, they were also often chosen at random simply to increase the manpower of GFP units before going on a mission. Although they did not have a choice whether to serve or not in the GFP, they nevertheless quite often took part in operations under GFP auspices that were criminal. Which unit(s) did these men come from? What were their names and ranks? When were they placed on temporary assignment to the GFP and for what purpose? When did they return to their former commands? Answering these questions will also help us to gain a better understanding of the role the Secret Field Police played in the Holocaust.

Greece's Pre-War Jewish Population

Greece's pre-war Jewish population amounted to some 75,000–77,000 souls. Of that pre-war figure, it appears that only about 11,000–12,000 survived the war. This figure includes about 1,100 who survived the Nazi death camps.[3] The overall survival rate for Greek Jews who were captured by the Nazis in unknown, but we have more detailed figures for the island of Rhodes. Of the 1,100 who managed to live through the horrors of the Holocaust, about 150 came from Rhodes. During the war the Nazis had been able to round up 1,540 out of the estimated 1,700 Greek Jews on Rhodes. Of this number, only about one hundred and fifty survived. Therefore, if you were a Jew living on Rhodes when the Germans began their roundups for transport to the death camps, your chances of returning from the Nazi extermination camps was only 10 percent. The Axis occupation zones which were created to separate Greek territory controlled by German, Italian, and Bulgarian troops, actually aided in extending the lives of some of Greece's Jewish community. This is because the Italians did not have a policy of persecuting Jews.

Bulgaria was ambivalent about the Jews. The Bulgarians who had incorporated a part of Thrace into their nation, inherited somewhere in the neighborhood of 5,000–6,000 Greek Jews. The Italians, who ruled the most Greek territory until September 1943 when they surrendered, controlled about 13,000 Jews. Ironically the Germans, who had initially only occupied Macedonia and most of the Greek islands of the Aegean Sea, had assumed control of the vast majority of Greece's Jewish population. In 1940, anywhere from 53,000 to 55,200 Jews lived in Salonika.[4] This comprised about two-thirds of the Jewish population of Greece. By the end of the Holocaust, only one-fourth (1,950 souls) of the Jewish population remained.[5] Another 2,000 were spread out over the rest of the German occupation zone.[6] While the occupation zones were in existence, Greek Jews did their upmost to cross from the German zone to either the Bulgarian or Italian zone. The Italian zone was preferred as Greek Jews did not trust the Bulgarians. Their fears proved valid when about 4,100 Jews were rounded up by the Bulgarians on March 4, 1943, and turned over to the Germans. The Germans eventually dispatched this group of Greek Jews to Treblinka extermination camp in Poland.[7] Throughout the war, the Italians never persecuted Italian Jews or Jews living under their control. It was only after the Italian surrender in September 1943 that the Germans began the main roundup of Italy's Jews, sending them to death camps in Poland. The same fate awaited those Jews who had managed to hide out under Italian rule in occupied Greece. However, in the German occupation zone, Greek Jews had already experienced persecution on a greater scale. Part of this ill-treatment included the plunder of personal property.

Sonderkommando Rosenberg *and the Plunder of Jewish Property*

The very first action launched against the Greek Jews occurred with the German invasion of that country in April 1941. Alfred Rosenberg the Nazi racial theorist wanted to create a museum and school that would serve as a showpiece of religious and political ideas that were seen as contrary to Nazi ideology (Judaism, Communism, Socialism, Anarchism, Democracy, and even Freemasonry).[8] The Nazis wanted to fill this museum with precious and semi-precious works of art plundered from many nations, but especially from Jews. In order to acquire the necessary books, art pieces, sculptures, torahs and other valuable items for this museum, Rosenberg created a special *Kommando* named after him. The head of the German *Luftwaffe*, Hermann Göring eventually involved himself in this systematic and European-wide plunder of art. Göring eventually selected numerous works of art from the Paris Louvre Museum, as well as from the private collections of prominent French-Jewish citizens for his own personal collection. Nevertheless, by far most of the looted art was earmarked for Adolf Hitler, who envisioned another huge museum that would be named after him once the war ended in a Nazi victory. The museum Hitler wanted would not be composed of "anti–Nazi" art but would include literally the art treasures of Europe. When the Germans entered Greece *Sonderkommando Rosenberg* was to be employed to help plunder Jewish property for the above-mentioned motives.

This Nazi "plunder" formation had already operated in the West. From the very beginning, *Sonderkommando Rosenberg* had been assisted by members of the Secret Field Police. Their tasks were to help the *Rosenberg Sonderkommando* to search archives, libraries, newspaper offices, churches, Jewish synagogues, Masonic lodges, government offices, hospitals, museums, as well as residential and commercial buildings.[9] Jews in Greece and Yugoslavia were targeted, first for their property, then secondly for eventual extermination. In this the GFP was to take part, as attested by the following document:

> Pursuant to an order of the AOK of April 19, 1941 (Abt. Ic/AO No. 103/41 geh.), a Sonderkommando of Reichsleiter Rosenberg is working in the area of the 12th Army with the order to search state libraries, archives, the offices of high-level church authorities, the lodges of freemasons, and Jewish organizations for evidence of political activities directed against the Reich and to seize any pertinent materials. The Sonderkommando Rosenberg ... is attached to the commandant of the army rear area command. In view of the special extent and influence of the local Jewry in Salonika, a permanent work group will be established there within a few days.... To implement these confiscations, the Sonderkommando, upon request, is to be furnished additional personnel from the Geheime Feldpolizei.[10]

Thus, the Secret Field Police took part in and was an active participant in the plunder of personal property from Greece's Jewish population. The theft of Greek Torahs from Jewish synagogues was a particularly heinous act, given that the crime affected an entire Jewish community and not just one single family. In fact, pre-war Salonika was a center for Torah scholarship, bringing students from all across Europe and the world to study. The occupation of Greece and the theft of hundreds of Greek Torahs effectively brought this to an end.[11]

German Reaction to the Greek Famine and Jewish Businesses

The famine winter of 1941–1942 killed about 20,000 Greek Jews nationwide. Tens of thousands of non–Jewish Greek citizens also died during this time. A large percentage of those who died of starvation were the elderly as well as the very young. Very few infants in Greece survived the famine winter.[12] However the Jews and their businesses in Salonika and elsewhere under German rule were initially left untouched. This was not on account of benevolence on the part of the Nazis, but because of the famine that soon developed in Greece. This food shortage, created by the wholesale plunder of the country's foodstuffs at the hands of the Germans, began to show its dire effects as early as the Fall of 1941. It appears that the very nature of the food shortage, which developed in Greece beginning in the summer of 1941 and continued into the fall and winter of 1941–1942, may have proved a factor which played into the German's decision to leave the Jews of Salonika alone.[13] This was on account of the fact that many of Salonika's commercial food stores and associated businesses were owned by Greek Jews. If the Germans had closed those Jewish businesses and expropriated the merchandise, the famine would have reached levels that even the Germans would have been alarmed, not for their concern of the Greek people, but for their anxiety to rule over a restive population.

Early attempts by the Greek exile community to mediate a truce between the Allies and Axis in order to bring food into Greece were met with resistance from both sides. As the civilian food status in Greece became increasingly difficult, the Germans felt it wiser not to disturb an already precarious food situation. In addition, the Germans quickly learned that (with the exception of a microscopic minority of local anti–Semites) Greeks did not consider Jews or the Nazi boogie-man–"International Jewry"–as a threat. An agreement between the Allies and the Axis forces eventually alleviated the Greek suffering, when Canadian grain began to arrive via the International Red Cross during the spring of 1942. The first shipment to arrive via neutral Turkey aboard Swedish ships was about 15,000 tons of Canadian wheat.[14] However, the problem of food shortages in Greece was still an issue late in the war, as described in various German correspondences from the period 1943–1944.[15] Later reports even spoke of how prices for various items had dramatically risen. One dated "July 7, 1943" listed the current price of a ½ liter of beer at a whopping 120 Drachmas.[16] The Secret Field Police used this artificially created disaster for their own ends by creating a policy in Greece of denying a region or district vital food supplies, in order to punish the Greeks for any acts of resistance. Starvation therefore, became a tool of repression employed by the Secret Field Police on a regular basis.

Repressive Measures Against the Jewish Population

The fear that the famine in Greece would reach proportions that might cause a widespread uprising or an uncontrolled plague had forced the Germans to delay their persecution of the Jews until the summer of 1942. Since many businesses in Salonika were Jewish-owned, particularly stores that sold food, the Germans were unwilling to close them down for fear of exacerbating the food shortage.[17] However by the summer of 1942 the Red Cross was beginning to bring in some food supplies and the number of deaths from starvation dropped to "acceptable levels" by Nazi standards. With the threat of a widespread revolt or an out of control plague over, the Nazis began to undertake repressive measures against Greece's Jewish population. On July 8, 1942, the Germans ordered that 9,000 Jewish men and boys register for "labor service" in Salonika.[18] On February 6, 1943 the chief rabbi of Salonika was told that henceforth all Jews would be required to wear the Star of David on their clothing. Jews were responsible for paying and supplying these cloth stars. The penalty for a Jew who was caught not wearing the Star of David was instant arrest and transport to a Nazi death camp (if they were not killed outright).

Once the Germans began to register and isolate Greece's Jewish population, the process which they had perfected in other regions of Europe was employed. The expropriation of Jewish property as well as personal effects proceeded in Greece as elsewhere. The Jewish section of Salonika was turned into a Ghetto, and Jews living outside this section of the city were forced to move there. All of this was done in preparation for the Jews of Greece to be sent to their deaths in Nazi extermination camps. As soon as the Greek Jewish community was expelled the Germans were on the scene, ready to distribute their property. The theft of Jewish property was supposed to be organized in a manner that would benefit the German people, but quite often Nazis on the scene absconded with a portion of the booty. In this the Secret Field Police played an active role, as testified by a former member of GFP-621 in Greece:

> German authorities appropriated part of the deportees' property. As a former soldier of the GFP in Ioannina testified during a police interrogation in 1966, "every member of our unit received a special allotment from the assets of Jewish business 'estates.'"[19]

The "Final Solution" was played out in Salonika throughout the spring and summer of 1943. Between March and June most of Salonika's Jewish population was deported to Nazi death camps. One final batch of transports left Salonika in August 1943. In all, around 46,000 Jews were deported.[20] During this time men of GFP-510 (led by *Feldpolizeidirektor* Alois Uch), and from GFP-621 (led by *Feldpolizeikommissar* Rhode) took part in the roundup and arrest of Salonika's Jewish population. According to one source, the elimination of Jewish life in Salonika at the hands of the Germans had been so severe, that in 1947 less than 2,000 Greek Jews could be found in the city.[21] The participation of the GFP in these roundups was essential in allowing for a smooth operation to occur between SS and Army forces.

Italian Surrender and the Expansion of the Holocaust in Greece

Even before the Germans began to identify and concentrate Greece's Jewish population for eventual transfer to the Nazi death camps, the GFP had been involved in helping to restrict the movement of Jews and in apprehending any who attempted to flee from the clutches of the Nazis. A report from GFP-621, dated "27 April 1943" describes how even before the Italian surrender, this German Secret Field Police unit was expressing its frustration over Italian General Consul Zamboni's apparent attempts to aid Jews to flee from German control in Salonika. The message sent by GFP-621 was addressed to the German General Consulate in Salonika, warning of the complicity of Consul Zamboni in attempting to give Greek Jews safe passage to Italian territory. The report, dated Tuesday, April 27, 1943, stated that at 11:45 an Italian "holiday train" was at the Salonika train station with twenty Greek Jews. The GFP men realized that these Jews were attempting to escape German control by taking this holiday train into Italian-held territory.

Corroborating reports were given by the Salonika Station Officer, as well as by the Salonika Transport Command (*Hauptmann* Hahn). Consul Guelfo Zamboni soon called the German command and complained that "Italian citizens" were being detained illegally even though they possessed all proper paperwork. The law provided that Italian citizens be equipped with an Italian transit permit and were not required to posses the special German permit (*Erlaubnisschein*). The GFP unit went out of their way to counter Zamboni's argument by contacting *SS-Hauptsturmführer* Alois Brunner, who traveled personally to the Salonika Central Train Station. Brunner established that thirteen of the twenty Jews had proper paperwork and were allowed to leave. However, the other Jews were detained. In two instances, where family members were going to be separated, a few spouses chose to stay with their loved ones instead of fleeing to temporary safety in Italian held territory. In this way, the Nazis were able to retain even those Jews who had proper documentation:

> Permission to leave the area for Athens was immediately granted to these thirteen Jews. The following Jews were prohibited from leaving: a certain Daniel Modiano, who was in fact able to prove his Italian nationality but against whom legal proceedings were initiated by GFP-621 because—and this has already been proven—he had accepted gold from Greek Jews, believing that he would be able to evade German authorities in this way.
>
> It has been repeatedly been pointed out that this kind of behavior is considered a punishable offense.... Modiano's wife stayed here of her own free will when she learned that her husband was not allowed to leave. Furthermore, permission to leave was denied to a Jew named Sam Navarro, as well as to his wife and her mother, who was allegedly ill and had first tried to hide in another part of the holiday train. Navarro is an alleged Italian who obviously was made into an Italian national following measures against Jews....
>
> Further information will be given about the progress of this affair.
>
> On behalf of the Commander of Salonika—Aegean
> [signed] Schönberg[22]

This document clearly indicates that the Germans were doing their best to apprehend or at the very least, restrict the movement of Jews living in the Italian occupation zone. By curtailing movement and the possible escape of Jews from their area of control, the Germans were already preparing the way for the eventual assembly of Greece's Jewish population and their removal to Nazi death camps. The document is also an example of the involvement of the Secret Field Police in this repression.

Mussolini was overthrown my members of his own Fascist High Council in July 1943. The new head of the Italian government now became Marshal Badoglio who initially feigned continued allegiance to an Axis victory. However, the Germans were not surprised when on September 8, 1943, Italy surrendered. In total, there were some 13,000 Jews living under Italian control in the areas of the Greek mainland, and the Ionian and Dodecanese Islands.[23] If you count the regions of Albania and Montenegro, which the Germans now also had to occupy, then this figure rises to 16,000. With the Italian collapse the *Wehrmacht* and the SS Security Service began the search for those Jews who were in hiding—especially on what used to be Italian controlled Greece. On the mainland, about 2,000 Jews saved themselves by fleeing to the mountains. Some 200 joined the leftist ELAS partisan army and fought bravely during the war. Unfortunately, most of the Jews of Greece would not be as lucky. The German preparations for the deportation of the Jews from the many islands making up Greece began even before the Italian surrender in September 1943. In February 1943, a *Sekretariat* of GFP-611 located in the town of Chania (western Crete) asked the mayor to provide a list of all Jews living in the town.[24] All of this was in preparation for the eventual collection of the Jews living on the Greek islands.

SS/SD and Police Apparatus in Greece

GFP participation in the Holocaust in Greece fit into the larger plans of the SS and Army. When the Italian war effort collapsed in September 1943 the Germans had to quickly fill in the gaps left by its erstwhile Fascist ally. The mission of the GFP was now expanded to operations into the countryside and was no longer relegated to the major cities. Before 1943, it had been the German Army in the form of the *Befehlshaber Saloniki-Agäis* (Commander "Salonika Aegean") headquarters that had controlled the countryside. After the Italian surrender in September 1943, the Germans felt it was necessary for the SS/SD apparatus be employed in order to get a better handle on the growing guerrilla war. The SS and SD would also be the principle tool in helping to roundup Greece's Jewish population in preparation for their transport and eventual extermination in the death camps. On September 8, 1943, the very day in which Italy surrendered, the Germans demanded that Rabbi Eliahu Barzilai provide a list of all the Jews living in Athens. With the aid of the Greek resistance, Barzilai was able to escape to the relative safety of partisan controlled mountains. With this show of resistance, most of the Jewish community in Athens went underground.

September 8 was also the day that *Reichsführer-SS* Heinrich Himmler appointed SS General Jürgen Stroop to the new post of *Höherer SS und Polizeiführer Griechenland* (Higher SS & Police Leader "Greece"). All Higher SS & Police headquarters answered directly to the chief of the SS (Himmler). On September 13, 1943, the position of Higher SS & Police Leader "Greece" was changed to *Höherer SS und Polizeiführer beim Militärbefehlshaber in Griechenland* ("Higher SS & Police Leader under the Military Commander for Greece").[25] This meant that Stroop would be in a subordinate position to the German Military Commander in Greece. This was an unusual situation given that SS officers, especially high ranking officers, never liked having to answer directly to the Army. The decision to assign this new SS headquarters under the tutelage of the Army Commander in Greece was likely a means to assuage matters of overlapping jurisdiction between the SS and the Army. It is an example of how the SS and Army could work with one another.

Stroop's first order upon arriving in Athens was ordering that all Jews be registered. He had arrived in Greece fresh from the destruction of the Warsaw ghetto.[26] As Stroop set about making preparations for the collection and deportation of Greece's Jewish population, his reputation for ruthlessness worked against him. His actions in crushing the Jewish uprising in Warsaw had followed him to Greece. Although it was a serious crime to listen to Allied radio reports, many people living in occupied Europe would risk listening to the banned radio stations. Many Greeks heard about the atrocities committed in Warsaw by Stroop's command. The crimes perpetrated by Stroop were so serious and troubling that even the collaborationists in Greece were shocked. Ioannis Rallis, the new leader of the puppet Greek government, gave Stroop the cold shoulder by refusing to visit him on his arrival in Athens.[27]

Stroop himself did nothing to assuage the fears on the part of the Greeks that what he had done in Warsaw would not be repeated in Athens. For example, when Stroop learned that the Greek Orthodox Archbishop Damaskinos had signed a letter addressed to the collaborationist Greek government, protesting German treatment of Greek Jews, he threatened to shoot the Archbishop personally. This was a direct attack on the head of the Greek Orthodox Church and therefore, a slap in the face to most Greeks. Damaskinos actually stood up to Stroop, penning a defiant reply: "According to the traditions of the Greek Orthodox Church, our prelates are hung and not shot. Please respect our traditions!"[28] This proved to be the final straw, since even the puppet Greek government could not support someone who openly attacked the Eastern Orthodox Church in Greece. Ioannis Rallis now found Stroop so detestable that he ordered the Greek police not to cooperate with the SS in any way while Stroop was in command.[29] Stroop even managed to piss off the supreme German Army commander in Greece, General Alexander Löhr.[30]

6. The Participation of the Secret Field Police in the Holocaust in Greece

Within a month, Himmler realized that Stroop was *persona non grata* in Greece, so he reluctantly transferred him to the Reich where he held various positions within the SS until the end of the war. As his replacement, Himmler appointed 45-year old *SS Brigadeführer der Waffen-SS und Polizei* Walter Otto Schimana on October 6, 1943. Like Stroop, Schimana remained under Army control, but cooperation between the SS and Army was smooth under his tutelage. In this Schimana reached out to Roman Loos, the head of the Secret Field Police in the Balkans as a go-between the SS and Army.[31] Loos was able to smooth any hurt feelings or conflicts regarding overlapping jurisdictional issues between the SS and Army. Relations between the SS and Army were so quickly mended that on February 20, 1944, Schimana's SS command was made independent of the Army.[32] During his tenure in Greece as head of the SS, Schimana was able to work closely together with the Greek collaborationist government and was prominent in helping to raise additional pro–Axis Greek troops.[33] He remained in Greece until October 5, 1944, when he was reassigned to the post of Higher SS & Police Leader "Hungary." Schimana was replaced by Hermann Franz, a police colonel who had been the former commander of *Polizei-Gebirgsjäger-Regiment 18*.

Records show that the headquarters for the Higher SS & Police Leader "Greece" was located on K. Sophia Street No.11 (in Athens). Schimana's staff on April 10, 1944, consisted of seven officers, fifteen NCOs, eight enlisted personnel and three vehicles. The head of the Order Police in Greece—the *Befehlshaber der Ordnungspolizei Griechenland* (abbreviated as "BdO"), was also located in Athens. The headquarters of the BdO was Othonos Street No.5, and its staff consisted of nineteen officers, three *Beamte* (civilian officials acting as officers), thirty-two NCOs, and eighteen enlisted men, of which sixteen were pro–German Italians.[34] The principal SS & Police officers and their respective commands in Athens were as follows:

- *Höhere SS-und Polizeiführer Griechenland beim Militärbefehlshaber in Griechenland*[35]
    - *SS-Brigadeführer und Generalmajor der Polizei* Jürgen Stroop[36]
      September 8, 1943—October 4, 1943
    - *SS-Gruppenführer und Generalleutnant der Polizei* Walter Schimana[37]
      November 9, 1943—February 20, 1944
- *Höhere SS-und Polizeiführer Griechenland*[38]
    - *SS-Gruppenführer und Generalleutnant der Polizei* Walter Schimana
      February 20, 1944—October 5, 1944
    - *SS-Brigadeführer und Generalmajor der Polizei* Hermann Franz
      September 26, 1944—November 18, 1944
- *Befehlshaber der Sicherheitspolizei und des Sicherheitsdienst Griechenland*[39]
    - *Kriminalrat* Hans Dörhage[40]
      May 1941—March 1942
    - *SS-Standartenführer und Ministerialrat* Walter Blume[41]
      August 1943—December 1944
- *Befehlshaber der Ordnungspolizei Griechenland*[42]
    - *SS-Oberführer und Oberst der Schützpolizei* Friedrich Hermann Franz[43]
      November 23, 1943—September 23, 1944
- *Kommandeur der Ordnungspolizei Athen*[44]
    - *Oberstleutnant der Schützpolizei* Gottlieb Nagel[45]

It would be these men in the SS and SD headquarters that would direct the Holocaust in Greece. In addition, the Secret Field Police would provide additional manpower and coordination with the Army that would be needed to round up the Jews of Greece. The collection of Greece's Jews would not have been as effective as it turned out to be without the assistance of the German Army and the GFP. In this the Secret Field Police proved vital as a link between the Army and the SS. From the very beginning of the German occupation of the Balkans, cooperation between the Army and SS was good:

> The Army Ic (intelligence officer) was responsible for coordinating the tasks of the *Sonderkommando* with military intelligence, the activities of the GFP [Geheime Feldpolizei, Wehrmacht secret field police], and the necessities of the various operations.[46]

Complicity of the Militärbefehlshaber in Griechenland in the Jewish Roundups

After Italy's surrender, the Germans extended their plan to collect and send Greece's Jewish population to death camps in the entire country. On October 3, 1943, the *Höherer SS und Polizeiführer Griechenland* ordered that all Jews be registered. This was done in anticipation of collection and deportation to the death camps. Only a very small number of Jews complied with the order, most likely fearing (quite correctly) that it would lead to their imprisonment and perhaps their death. As a result, *Luftwaffe General der Flieger* [Air Force General] Wilhelm Speidel decreed that all Jews who did not register were to be expropriated immediately. Speidel had been in charge of the German Military Mission to Romania when, on June 15, 1942, he was transferred to Greece to become *Kommandierenden General und Befehlshaber Südgriechenland* (Commanding General and Commander-in-Chief of Southern Greece). He held this post until September 8, 1943. After the war, Wilhelm Speidel was sentenced to twenty years' imprisonment on February 19, 1948. However, he was pardoned and released from Landsberg Prison on February 3, 1951.[47]

On September 10, 1943, Speidel's authority in Greece was expanded due to the Italian collapse, and became *Militärbefehlshaber in Griechenland* (Military Commander in Greece). During this time, the Germans committed numerous war crimes in Greece for which Speidel was ultimately responsible. In fact, General Speidel was not in Greece long before he executed his first civilians. On July 5, 1943, he ordered the execution of ten random Greek civilians in retaliation for the mining by guerrillas, of the Italian steamer "Citta di Savonna" in the port of Piraeus.[48] The explosion had killed 69 horses but no Italians or Germans had been killed. Nevertheless, Speidel ordered the executions to proceed. Five days later, on July 10, 1943, he reported to the Commander-In-Chief Southeast that he had ordered the execution of fifteen hostages in Athens and three on the island of Salamis in retaliation for a partisan attack on the search lights stationed on Salamis.[49] Again, no German lives had been lost, and yet Speidel ordered the executions of innocent civilians.

Deportations of Jews from the Greek Mainland

Although ordered to register, most Jews in Athens had been smart enough to distrust the Germans and as a result, had failed to do so. As Passover 1944 was approaching, the Germans tried a ploy that appeared to partially work. They announced that Matzos would be distributed at the Athens synagogue. Based on this promise, by Passover (March 24/25) about eight hundred Jews had registered in Athens.[50] These were mostly hungry and despondent people who were near their breaking point. The Nazis had cynically chosen Passover as the start of the Jewish roundups in Athens and elsewhere around the country. The SS and SD in Athens, supported by *Feldpolizeikommissar* Hans Behan and GFP-510, were able to apprehend 1,690 Jews who were living in the Greek capital. Also, assisting in the roundups in Athens were soldiers of the German 11th Air Force Infantry Division and men of the First Evzone Regiment, which was a unit of the puppet government of Ioannis Rallis.[51] The Nazis soon deported this group from Athens to Auschwitz-Birkenau, where most would die before the war came to an end. A good number of the Jews apprehended in Athens from March 24–25 were refugees from Salonika. The overwhelming majority of the Jews who lived in Athens went into hiding and was protected by ordinary citizens or the Greek underground. Very few were ever betrayed to the Germans by collaborators or black mailers.

In the region of Thessaly, many Jews had taken to the hills after ELAS partisan forces had warned the Jews of Volos, Karditsa, Larissa, Trikkala, and Katerini that the Germans were preparing a major roundup for Passover. In Thessaly, the collaborationist Greek police was more sympathetic to the plight of the Greek-Jewish community. Many Greek *Gendarmes* actually turned a blind eye or even assisted Jews in fleeing the clutches of the Nazis. In Epirus, the situation was different. Here the right-wing EDES partisan group operated. Support and aid to the beleaguered Jewish communities was minimal. The deportation of the Jews of Ioannina also began in earnest on March 25, and was coordinated between the Army Intelligence Section (Ic) of *XXII. Gebirgs Armeekorps,* pro–Axis Greek police of the Ioannis Rallis government, as well as members of GFP-621. As a result, around 1,725 Greek Jews were rounded up and deported. Another figure given for the deportation in Ioannina was 1,860 people.[52] However, this discrepancy in numbers is because an additional one hundred thirty-five Jews were rounded up subsequent to the arrests made on March 25, 1944. These additional Jews were mostly young men who had fled to the mountains, but had been recalled back to their homes in Ioannina by their mothers at the insistence of Sabetai Kabelli, the interim leader of the Ioannina Jewish community.

Feldpolizeisekretär Wilhelm Pranz, one of six to eight [GFP] men stationed in Ioannina from GFP- 621, confirmed that virtual cooperation existed between the intelligence officers (Ic) of the 22nd Mountain Army Corps in Ioannina, and the GFP. That is, that the GFP in Ioannina would share information with the intelligence section of the headquarters for the 22nd Mountain Army Corps *vis-à-vis* as it related to the arrest of the Jews and the fight against the partisans. It was made clear however, that GFP-621 was to be responsible for intelligence in Salonika itself.[53] In the town of Kastoria where *Wehrmacht* troops were in the minority, most of the 763 Jews were apprehended by a *Sekretariat* of GFP-621 supported by the Fifth Macedonian Security Battalion, and First IMRO Battalion: both of whom were collaborationist units.[54] During the sweeps of the countryside in the region of Epirus the Germans actually apprehended a good number of Jews from Yugoslavia. In southwest Greece, the headquarters for the 104th Light Division was located in the town of Agrinion. The second battalion of *SS Polizei Gebirgsjäger Regiment 18* was located northeast of Agrinion, at Karpenisi. These two German military units would take part in the roundup of Jews in this region of the country. *Feldpolizeikommissar* Hans Behan of GFP-510, at the time was stationed in Athens, ordered a *Sekretariat* to assist in the arrests. In spite of this the forty or so Jews of Agrinion were able to avoid capture because they had taken to the hills surrounding the town as soon as the Italians had surrendered back in September 1943.

Background to the Deportation of Jews from the Greeks Islands

The island of Rhodes had belonged to Italy since 1912 when it had been taken from the Turks. Its Sephardic Jewish community was small in 1943—perhaps numbering some

2,000 Jews at most. Anti-Semitism was non-existent except for a rare case which had occurred in 1840 when the Jews on the island were falsely accused of killing an Orthodox Christian boy. This became known as the "Rhodes Blood Libel." This incident may have been spurred by another "blood libel" allegation, which happened earlier in the year in Damascus, Syria when a Jewish barber was accused of killing a monk in order to use his blood for Passover.[55] The community of Judeo-Spanish Ladino speaking Jews on Rhodes was so isolated that they had no idea of the fate of the rest of European Jewry. This made them ideal victims since many were easily rounded up like lambs to the slaughter.[56] Another "Blood Libel" incident occurred on another island populated by Jews and Christians. This turned out to be the Ionian island of Corfu. The accusation occurred in 1891 and did however sour relations between the Orthodox Christians and the Jews on that Ionian island:

> The island of Corfu in the Ionian Sea had been home to Jews for over 800 years. When the Venetians annexed the island in the fourteenth century, they enclosed the Jewish community in a ghetto. The island's Jewish population was a mix of Greek-speaking Romaniotes, Ladino-speaking Sephardim, and Italian-speaking Jews from Apulia and Sicily. The relationship between Jews and Christians on the island had been soured by a notorious "Blood Libel" investigation conducted in 1891. The story of the Holocaust in Corfu is especially unfortunate, in part because it occurred late in the war. The Germans took control of the island in 1943 after the fall of Italy and promulgated anti–Semitic laws. Corfu's Mayor Kollas was a known collaborator.[57]

Italian Surrender in September 1943

After the departure of the Italians, GFP-611 which was currently stationed on the island of Crete was assigned to also cover the Ionian island chain. The area of operations for GFP-621 was also extended from Salonika to as far south as Rhodes. Rhodes is the largest of the twelve Dodecanese islands on the Aegean Sea's eastern edge. Around 2,000 Italian speaking Jews lived on the Ionian island of Corfu. About three hundred lived on the Ionian island of Zante, while over three hundred Jews lived on the island of Crete. Finally, about 2,200 Jews lived on the East Aegean islands of Rhodes and Kos.[58] With the Italians out of the war, elements of the German 999th Africa Division were assigned to protect Rhodes and its surrounding smaller islands from Allied invasion. Originally a good portion of the core personnel for this division had come from parts of the German 22nd Infantry Division and Fortress Division "Crete."[59] The unit was not in any sense of the word an elite German formation. In fact, it was composed of "fortress" brigades: the 939th (stationed in Rhodes), the 967th (located on the island of Cos), and the 938th (posted on the island of Leros).[60] The commander of this division was *Generalleutnant* Ulrich Kleemann.[61] Of the approximately 28,000 German soldiers that served in the 999th Division, about ⅓ of them were political prisoners who had been given a choice of either lingering in a concentration camp, or serving in the German Army. Some were socialists or social democrats, but the overwhelming majority were members of the German communist party.

It's no surprise then that many of these Germans deserted to the partisans while serving in Greece, and the Secret Field Police had a full-time job keeping an eye on them and investigating cases of desertion or sabotage. The German command attempted to limit desertions by placing the various brigades of this division on Greek islands. Although the 999th Division had operated in Tunisia and surrendered to Allied forces in May 1943, a good number of its component units didn't arrive in time to serve in North Africa. Instead they were used to help form a German division that would help garrison Greece. It was thus that in

6. The Participation of the Secret Field Police in the Holocaust in Greece   105

June 1943 *Sturm Division Rhodes* ("Assault Division Rhodes") was created, employing parts of the 999th Division as well as remnants of the 164th Light Division. The unit was designated as the garrison division for Rhodes and the surrounding islands. Eventually, several GFP *Sekretariat* were posted to the island from GFP-510 (Athens) and GFP-621 (Salonika). These GFP station posts would be assigned a three-fold mission while stationed on Rhodes and the surrounding Dodecanese islands: (1) investigating Greek partisan attacks, (2) keeping a watchful eye on the German penal troops, and (3) helping to arrest and deport the Jewish population.

At best these punitive troops were politically unreliable and quite often desired the demise of the Third Reich. As a result, they proved ineffective in taking part in the Holocaust. For example, in 1944 *VII Bataillon / 999 Division* (Seventh Battalion of the 999th Division) was stationed on the Ionian island of Zakynthos ("Zante" in German).[62] The two hundred and seventy Jews who lived on the island were able to avoid capture because the Austrian commander of *VII Bataillon / 999*–a former Socialist, had no interest in rounding up Jews to be sent to their deaths. He simply claimed that he couldn't find them. The Greek

GFP Formations in Greece, 1944. While the headquarters of GFP-621 remained in Salonika, elements of this Secret Field Police unit were sent to operate in Epirus and Thessaly. Similarly, a "Sekretariat" from GFP-611 was dispatched to the Ionian Islands (including Corfu), while GFP-621 and GFP-510 both contributed sections for employment on Rhodes and the surrounding islands (map by author).

guerrillas were thus able to extract the Jews and take them to safety without the interference of the German garrison. In effect, the Jewish community of Zakynthos escaped the Holocaust because the troops on the island were not politically reliable.

A *Sekretariat* of GFP-611 had been sent to Corfu & Cephalonia, but no GFP or SS officials were on Zakynthos which could have forced this battalion to perform the unsavory task of rounding up the Jews. Corfu in particular, had been chosen by the Germans as an island to concentrate their efforts at combing for partisans and Jews. This decision had been made partly based on the large numbers of Jews living there, and on GFP intelligence information provided by two Albanian physicians working for the Germans in Tirana (see chapter five). The Germans concentrated their security forces on Corfu based on this tip. It was later discovered that these doctors had made up the story of a vast partisan network on Corfu, and had fed this false information simply in order to continue to receive funds from the Germans. However, their story of a large partisan force on Corfu most likely helped to divert SS and Secret Field Police forces from Zakynthos, inadvertently saving the lives of the Jewish population on that island.

Preparations to Deport the Jews from the Greek Islands

From March 23–25, 1944 GFP-621 was suddenly ordered to assist GFP-510 in the transfer of Jews from the Dodecanese islands to the mainland.[63] Although already undermanned for the task assigned it in Ioannina and Salonika, GFP-621 had to send an additional *Sekretariat* (section) to the Dodecanese to assist GFP-510 in this operation. The Secret Field Police units directly involved in the deportation of Greece's Jews would be principally GFP-510, GFP-611, and GFP-621. Shortly after the Greek surrender, GFP-611 had initially been posted to Athens. It was then shifted to Salonica in 1942 where it remained throughout 1943. Beginning March 25, 1944, and continuing through the week, the Jewish Community of Ioannina, Greece was rounded up and deported to Auschwitz-Birkenau. Of the estimated 1,725 to 1,960 Jews which were deported, most would never return.[64] A Secret Field Police report from GFP-621 which was sent to *SS-Standartenführer* Hafranek at the SD office in Athens, regarding the supervision and evacuation of the Jews of Ioannina, stated that the operation would include trucks from the army employing *Waffen-SS* guards and drivers, as well as the employment of units of the GFP augmented by the collaborationist Greek police. The GFP also oversaw the acquisition of Jewish property.[65]

In April 1944, the roundup of the Greek Jews on the islands of Corfu and Crete began. The GFP was deeply involved in these roundups.[66] On the islands of Corfu and Crete the Secret Field Police unit that took part in these roundups was GFP-611. On Corfu, the Germans were anxious to deport the island's Jewish population, claiming that they were "useless mouths" that needed to be gotten rid of:

> Next higher in the reporting chain, Department Ic of the Corps Group Ioannina, agreed with the point of view of the Geheime Feldpolizei and the Ic branch office, and in a report about the island of Corfu informed Department Ic/AO at Army Group E headquarters that "2,000 Jews are still present, most of them inhabiting the city's outskirts." The deportation of these people, in the opinion of this officer, "would provide a not insignificant relief of the shortage of food supplies. At this time, the SD and the GFP are busy preparing the deportation of these Jews."[67]

Thus, the intelligence officer of Army Group "E" ordered that all Jews living on the island of Corfu were to be deported as soon as possible.

6. The Participation of the Secret Field Police in the Holocaust in Greece

This operation had to be coordinated with the German Navy—given that ships needed to be made available. On April 28, 1944, Colonel Emil Jäger, who was the intelligence officer of "Corps Group Ioannina," requested that preparations for the expulsion of the island's Jews were to start.[68] Jäger explained that food shortages on the island would be alleviated by a rapid deportation of the island's Jewish population. He said that this could assuage the food situation on Corfu by doing away with "worthless mouths." After the Navy agreed to supply ships, the deportation could commence. In mid–May 1944, an official request from the SS office in Athens to the German headquarters of Army Group "E" directed the arrest of all Jews across the nation. Army Group "E" responded immediately by in a telex to their lower echelon commands, including the army commander of fortress Crete: the German navy was also to "provision space on cargo ships for the accelerated transport of 350 Jews from Crete and 1,600 Jews of Corfu."[69]

Sadly, on June 17, 1944, through a concerted effort on the part of [1] the Commander of the Security Police on Corfu, [2] a *Sekretariat* from GFP-611, and [3] *Festung-Brigade 1017* (which was the garrison unit on Corfu under *XXII. Gebirgs Armeekorps*), one-thousand-seven-hundred-ninety-five Jews were arrested and shipped out from the island. The ships carrying the Greek and Italian Jews were bound for the port of Patras. From there they traveled in railway cars to Salonika, and then through Belgrade on to extermination camps in Poland.[70] During the spring and summer of 1944, GFP-611 took part in the roundup of Jews on numerous Greek islands.[71] In Corfu a *Sekretariat* of GFP-621 was also brought in to assist a *Sekretariat* from GFP-611, which was already stationed on the island, to round up the Jews who lived there:

> The deportation operation started on June 8 [1944] and was completed around a week later. The delay in the implementation of the plan was due to difficulties related to sea-transportation, while concerns over an eventual reaction of the non–Jewish population of the island had been quickly dispelled. A situation report issued by the Corfu branch of the Secret Field Police (*Geheime Feldpolizei 621–GFP*), on April 27, 1944, stated: "As is well known, the expulsion of Jews from mainland Greece has been accepted by the Greek population. Difficulties are only to be expected due to lack of shipping material." On the evening of May 29, 1944, after consulting with *SS-Obersturmführer* [Anton] Burger and Sergeant Günter, a member of the Secret Field Police, the Island's Commander determined that the Jews would be concentrated and detained in the old Citadel prior to deportation.[72]

In this way about 1,800 of Corfu's 2,000 Jewish residents were rounded up. In 1943, the area of operations for GFP-621 had been extended from Salonika to the island of Rhodes. By 1944 this GFP unit was also taking part in operations in Epirus, Thessaly, and the Ionian islands.

In the Dodecanese, the expulsion of the Greek Jews proved to be a logistical nightmare given the fact that there were so many islands in the region and the Jews were dispersed and living on many of them. The initial stage of the Nazi campaign to round up and deport the Jews in this region of Greece was to concentrate them on the island of Rhodes before sending them off to Nazi death camps. The GFP on Rhodes was to help organize the roundups, supported by Army elements stationed there. A document dated "July 12, 1944" clearly places *Sekretariat 4* from GFP-510 on the island of Rhodes at the time:

Secret Field Police Group 510
12 July 1944
Section (Secretariat) IV (Rhodes)
Reference Nr. IV/751/44.

Note:

According to a phone call from Lieutenant Mölter (IV Battery / Artillery Regiment 999), for a discussion of the last time the telephone cable was sabotaged in the region Psito–Afando–Calitea

occurred, with a view to terminating and reducing the same, I went today in the morning hours on the orders of inspector Manshausen, towards the direction of Psito to check the sabotaged local cable that since then no messages had yet to be sent.
Signed
Eisele
Corporal and Auxiliary Police Recruit
Viewed: Manshausen, Military Police Inspector & Group Leader[73]

The text referred to a sabotage incident that was reported by 1st Lieutenant Mölter from the headquarters' battery of the Fourth Battalion of Artillery Regiment 999. The lieutenant requested that men from *Sekretariat 4* go out and investigate an apparent telephone cable sabotage that was disrupting communication between the villages of Psito, Afando and Calitea.

The corporal who wrote the report (Eisele) said that he was directed by *Feldpolizei-inspektor* Karl Manshausen to investigate the matter. He reported that the cable had been cut near Psito but as of yet no one had repaired the line. Karl Manshausen had been born on October 31, 1911. In July 1944 he was almost 33 years old. By then he had already established a brutal reputation on Rhodes. In April 1944 he had been implicated in the torture of three Greek civilians and a captured British commando officer. The incident began on April 7, 1944, when three Greeks and several British commando troops were captured in Alimia, a small island just off the western coast of Rhodes. The captured men were numerous enough that both *Sekretariat 4* (GFP-510) and *Sekretariat 6* (GFP-621) were needed to interrogate them. According to testimony Manshausen was instrumental in applying torture to obtain information from four of these men.[74] These Allied soldiers knew that they were liable to be shot after being tortured during questioning. Instead they were sent to a GFP jail in Salonika for further interrogation.[75]

After the Italian surrender in September 1943 the British made every effort to occupy those Greek islands where Italian soldiers wished to switch sides. For the most part, this job was left to the British Navy, and its commando and Marine forces. Given this increased Allied military activity in the eastern Aegean Sea, it's no surprise that the GFP found itself interrogating more and more Andartes and captured British commandos. In the fall of 1943 and spring and summer of 1944 the Germans launched a concerted effort to recapture many of the Greek islands which had fallen into Allied control. The Germans also employed special forces, using their famous "Brandenburger" commando units as well as other *Wehrmacht* forces. Sizable forces from the German Navy and Air Force were also assigned to support this effort. Those British soldiers captured were usually commando and special forces troops, which meant that these men fell under the *Kommandobefehl* which Adolf Hitler issued on October 18, 1942. In essence, the order stated that all commandos caught by German forces, even those dressed in enemy uniform, were to be killed immediately. *Feldpolizeiinspektor* Karl Manshausen's actions in using torture as a weapon was perhaps the minimum pressure that GFP officials would apply to captured prisoners. Based on the increased Allied activity in the region, the organization of *Sekretariat 4* was expanded to cover not only the principle island of Rhodes, but the surrounding islands of Cos, Leros, and Samos. In addition, the GFP was deployed in order to assist in the collection of the Jews of the Dodecanese islands. The Jews were to be collected from the surrounding islands and gathered on Rhodes before being transported by boat to the Greek mainland. A telex dated August 24, 1944, shows how the *Sekretariat* was distributed:

1. In the Southern Defense Region: (1) Secretariat 4 (Secret Field Police Group 510).

6. The Participation of the Secret Field Police in the Holocaust in Greece   109

    2. In the Northern Defense Region: (1) Secretariat 4 & (2) Outer Station Post on Cos Island (Secret Field Police Group 510).
    3. For the rest of the Italian islands of the Northern Defense Region: (1) Outer Station Post on the island of Leros (Secret Field Police Group 510).
    4. For the Greek islands of the Northern Defense Region: (1) Outer Station Post on the island of Samos (Secret Field Police Group 510).
    5. These regional defense areas were to notify GFP-510 in Athens (Tracking and Search Department).
    6. Secret Field Police Group 510 is in communication with:
- the senior police Commander Director Southeast,
- the army patrols of the OKH,[76]
- the Commander of the Army Patrol Service "Southeast" for Passenger Traffic

Signed: Commander Eastern Aegean[77]

In addition to reorganizing itself in response to an increase in Allied activity and in preparation for collecting the region's Jewish population, the GFP (and German forces in general) were given a freer hand to operate when on August 28, 1944, Hitler issued another diktat. It decreed that court-martial proceedings were to come to an end. The order eliminated the legal process that would adjudicate whether a civilian suspect was guilty or not guilty of anti–German activities. Henceforth and all suspects, without due process, were to be handed over to the Security Police and SD in Athens:

> The *Führer* has ordered that effective immediately court-martial proceedings against the civilian population in the occupied territories are not to be carried out due to acts of terrorism against the German occupation forces and sabotage acts. Terrorism and acts of sabotage within the meaning of this order are all acts of violence by non–German civilians in the occupied territories against the German *Wehrmacht*, SS, police, and against institutions that serve their purposes. Those that have been found guilty of such terror and sabotage are to be handed over directly to the Commander of the Security Police and the SD in Athens, Greece.[78]

Those civilians accused of aiding the Allied cause were not to be tried but handed over to the Sipo/SD in Athens. The implication of this order was simple. The most serious implication was that the Sipo/SD command in Athens would have the sole responsibility over the guilt or innocence of a Greek civilian. In effect, it would become the judge, jury and executioner.

Augmenting the GFP in the Dodecanese in Anticipation of the Jewish Expulsion

In anticipation of the expenditure of time, equipment, and men which would take to assist in the deportation of the Jews living on the Dodecanese islands, it appears that *Sekretariat 4* on Rhodes was augmented in early April 1944. A document typed by Manshausen, dated "August 22, 1944," listed the strength of his command prior to and after April 1, 1944. Out of the thirteen men prior in the unit April 1, two (*Unteroffizier Naumann*, and *Obergefreiter Wenniger*) were stationed on the island of Cos. In addition, two other men were also not present on Rhodes: *Gefreiter Willstorfer*, who was in a hospital in Vienna as a patient with an unspecified illness, and *Unteroffizier Korn*, who it appears had been permanently transferred back to the main *Sekretariat* of GFP-510 in Athens. Thus, Manshausen only had nine men (including himself) on Rhodes. The document seems to affirm that a sizable increase occurred in the size of *Sekretariat 4* after April 1, 1944:

Secret Field Police Group 510
Secretariat IV (Rhodes)
August 22, 1944

Employment of the Secretariat before and after April 1, 1944

Before April 1, 1944
- Staff Sergeant Stollberg
- Staff Sergeant Brosig
- Sergeant Korn
- Sergeant Naumann
- Senior Lance Corporal Hager
- Senior Lance Corporal Linder
- Senior Lance Corporal Kohl
- Senior Lance Corporal Palzenberger
- Private 1st Class Willstorfer
- Specialist Officer Wieland
- Sub-Sergeant Bolies

After April 1, 1944
- Sergeant 1st Class Ruschmeyer
- Staff Sergeant Wienns
- Sergeant Naumann (on Cos island)
- Senior Lance Corporal Rach
- Senior Lance Corporal Linder
- Senior Lance Corporal Palzenberger
- Senior Lance Corporal Lechner
- Senior Lance Corporal Wenniger (on the island of Cos)
- Senior Lance Corporal Stelzmann
- Private 1st Class Eisele
- Specialist Officer Wieland
- Sub-Sergeant Korn (on vacation)
- Private 1st Class Willstorfer (on vacation)

Addendum:
Sergeant Korn is transferred to Athens
Corporal Willstorfer is located in Vienna in the hospital.
Access:
Senior Lance Corporal Bilchmeier of the group [GFP-510]

Signed: *Manshausen*
Field Police Inspector[79]

Notice that after April 1 *Feldpolizeiinspektor* Manshausen could count on eleven men stationed on Rhodes (including Bilchmeier and himself), plus two men on the island of Cos. He also had two additional men (Private Willsdorfer and Sergeant Korn) on vacation. Therefore, his command now comprised fifteen men. Some of these men had been drawn on a temporary basis from Army formations stationed on the island. These soldiers had been assigned in anticipation of additional expulsions of the Jewish population on Rhodes and the surrounding islands. Additional reinforcements were later ordered and agreed upon by Army Group "E" on June 28, 1944. Army Group "E" requested that further Secret Field Police forces be sent to Rhodes and the islands of Cos, Halki, Symi, Tilos, and Karpathos:

> Temporary reassignment for GFP-621, *Sekretariat 6* (Rhodes); by order, the following members of the *Wehrmacht* soldiers are considered suitable for final transfer to the Secret Field Police:
> [1] Sergeant William Ruschmeyer (Second Company / Armored Reconnaissance Battalion 999); [2] Sergeant Wienns (Third Company / Fortress Infantry Battalion 1002); [3] Corporal Stelzmann (Sixth Company / Grenadier Regiment "Rhodes"); [4] Corporal Less (Third Company / Grenadier Regiment "Rhodes"); [5] Corporal Eisele (Third Company / Fortress Infantry Battalion 1002 / Assault Division "Rhodes").
> Section III has by Army Group "E" Division IIb Command, the simultaneous application for permanent transfer to the GFP under the command of Army Group "E"–Section IIb No.85/44. Submitted from January 23, 1944, Group GFP-510, Athens, and GFP-510 *Sekretariat 4* (Rhodes) agree with these transfers.
>
> Signed: *Manshausen*
> Feldpolizeiinspektor[80]

Again, we see that both *Sekretariat 4* (GFP-510) and *Sekretariat 6* (GFP-621) stationed on Rhodes were augmented from Army units on the island:

The command staff has transferred Master Sergeant Ruschmeyer [who speaks Greek] and therefore can meet the requirements [of the GFP]. His assignment to the Secret Field Police is therefore desirable because of a lack of soldiers who meet these [GFP] requirements in the interest of the command's area of control. The "Ic" [intelligence officer] of Assault Division "Rhodes" therefore, has requested and advocates this transfer to the "IIb" [personnel] department. *Sonderführer* Wieland of the Secret Field Police, who himself had been reassigned to *Secretariat 6* (Rhodes) of GFP-621 since October 1943, from the Staff of Assault Division "Rhodes," has gained [these] six men for GFP-621. This decision was taken because of the requirements [of the GFP] and lack of Greek interpreters.[81]

This last example of the Army augmenting the strength of the GFP also shows the close cooperation extended to the GFP by the Army command.

Expulsion of the Jews from the Dodecanese and Ionian Islands

The order to apprehend the Jews of the Dodecanese islands appears to have been delayed somewhat depending on the island in question, the availability of sea transport to evacuate the Jews, and the military situation. For example, on the island of Rhodes, it wasn't until July 13, 1944, that *Generalleutnant* Kleemann directed that the city of Rhodes, as well as the towns of Cremastro, Villanovo and Trianda be made collecting points for the island's Jewish population.[82] Military units on belonging to the 939th Fortress Brigade stationed on Rhodes were alerted, and prepared to be employed to follow this order. German plans were temporarily short-circuited when resistance groups on Rhodes disrupted these preparations. The Andartes on Rhodes were composed of local Greeks, but also contained former Italian soldiers who had evaded capture when the Italian garrison there had been disarmed by the Germans. Bridges were blown up, telegraph lines were cut, German patrols were attacked, and even German forces in the principal towns were not safe. For example, on June 27, 1944, an explosive charge was attached below a window of the building housing the headquarters of the GFP detachment from which was stationed in the city of Rhodes.[83] This increased partisan activity made the concentration of Jews on the island of Rhodes all the more difficult.

Nevertheless, the Germans were finding some success in rounding up the Jews from the islands of Greece. The new head of the SD in Athens, *SS-Obersturmführer* Anton (Toni) Burger, whom Adolf Eichmann had sent to Greece in February 1944 to replace Dieter Wisliceny, had arrived on Corfu on May 15, 1944.[84] The principal German garrison unit on Corfu was Fortress Brigade 1017. The principal Army intelligence officer involved with the expulsion of the Jews of Corfu was Colonel Jäger. Colonel Jäger had initially been successful at delaying the withdrawal of the island's Jewish population, citing numerous logical reasons why it was inadvisable. He had done this not because he felt any sympathy for the plight of the Jews. On the contrary, he had no love for them. Although the Jews of Corfu had been registered as early as April 25, 1944, Colonel Jäger advised that transports sent to pick up the Jews of Corfu should first pick up demobilized Italians. He considered the former Italian soldiers a greater threat to the safety of the German garrison than the Greek Jews. He also cited that there was a Red Cross ship in the harbor that was bringing in food supplies to ease the famine. He claimed that the sailors and Red Cross agents onboard the ship could act as possible witnesses to the German arrest and deportation of the Jews of Corfu. This he argued, would provide more anti–German propaganda for the Allies who were already claiming that Germany was committing atrocities. After some delay, the arrival of *SS-Obersturmführer* Anton Burger on Corfu pushed all political and military considerations aside. On June 9, 1944 1,650 Jews were ordered to gather near an old Venetian fort in the city on the island of Corfu. *Obersturmführer* Burger was assisted by units from the Corfu garrison, a company from Military Field Police Battalion 501, a *Sekretariat* from GFP-611, and another *Sekretariat* from GFP-510. From June 11–17, 1944 1,795 Jews from Corfu were apprehended, On the island of Zante, some 257–270 Jews managed to escape the Nazi roundup because they were hidden with the assistance of the island's mayor. These Jews were later able to reach Allied controlled southern Italy in boats provided by the island's non–Jewish population.[85] By August 17, 1944 the last Greek rail transports reached Auschwitz-Birkenau in southern Poland.[86] At the end of the war, only about 10,000 Greek Jews could be accounted for. It appears then, that during the entire occupation the Germans were able to eliminate about 45,000 Jews, plus an additional 20,000 killed through the starvation winter of 1941–1942. The final count is therefore around 65,000 Greek Jews killed through Nazi aggression, although other sources state that a little over 59,000 died.[87]

The Haidari Prison Camp

The GFP was also connected with the Haidari prison camp. When the GFP prisons in Athens became overcrowded in the summer of 1944, the GFP shipped off a number of their prisoners to Haidari. Established by the Italian Army on what was a former Greek Army barracks, the camp was located several kilometers outside of Athens, near the Byzantine church at Daphni. The Germans took it over from the Italians on September 10, 1943, and used the camp until September 1944. During the thirteen months in which it was run by the Nazis approximately 21,000 prisoners went through its gates. Of that number, around 2,000 were killed in the camp. Haidari also served as a transit camp for Greek Jews. Jews were sent from there to the Auschwitz-Birkenau extermination camp. A sizable number of non–Jewish prisoners were also sent to forced labor camps in Germany. Initially the camp was run by the German Order Police. On November 28, 1943, the SS assumed control of the camp when *SS-Sturmbannführer* Paul Radomski became the camp commandant. Radomski was an *alter Kämpfer* ("old fighter") from the early days of the Nazi Party. A sadist at heart and in action, he began to brutalize the inmates, even personally shooting some prisoners. Radomski's brutality eventually got him fired as camp commandant. In February 1944 while celebrating his birthday he got into a drunken rage with his subordinate when the SS officer could not locate his room keys.[88]

He was replaced by *SS-Obersturmführer* Karl Josef Fischer who had previously served in Auschwitz and Oranienburg (Sachsenhausen) Concentration Camp. Karl Fischer was a bit subtler, using mendacity and employing spies and informants in the camp. However, he was not opposed to violence. For example, when a new batch of Greek Jews arrived at the camp early in 1944 he was seen whipping small Jewish children with one hand, while caressing his dog with the other.[89] Although the SS controlled the camp beginning in late November 1943, the camp's guards were all part of the German *Ordnungspolizei* ("Order Police"). Records indicate that on April 10, 1944, the camp's guard company contained twenty-three NCOs and 126 men and was led by *Leutnant der Schützpolizei* Stubenbeck— all members of the German police.[90] Throughout its use prisoners who had been arrested by the Security Police, SS Security Service, State Secret Police, Order Police and Secret Field Police, were sent to Haidari Prison. There they were interrogated, tortured, and abused. The lucky ones were forced to perform hard labor, and served various terms of imprisonment. The unlucky ones were either murdered in the camp, or shipped off to extermination camps. Haidari was not the only prison where GFP prisoners ended up.

6. The Participation of the Secret Field Police in the Holocaust in Greece 113

Wherever the Secret Field Police operated they established a prison, and in the case of Salonika, several prisons.[91]

Conclusions

The Secret Field Police was directly involved in the Holocaust in Greece inasmuch as they took part in the roundup and assembly of Jews for transport to Nazi extermination camps. Every GFP unit which served in Greece and almost all of its personnel took part in this crime. Again, and again, GFP participation proved critical in Nazi attempts to apprehend the Jewish population. The deportations which occurred in Greece needed the absolute compliance of the German military and in particular, the Secret Field Police which worked as a conduit and liaison between the SS/SD and the Army. The use of GFP forces in a particular area of Greece increased the probability that Jews would be apprehended in that area. In regions where no GFP units were employed, and where the SS/SD presence was also lacking, the roundup of Jews proved less effective. The employment of forces from the German Army was also crucial for the successful apprehension of Greece's Jewish population to Nazi death camps. In this respect, the GFP was employed by the SS/SD to help muster that Army support. Because the GFP had one foot in the Army and another in the SS, it allowed for smooth cooperation between the Army and SS. In addition, it is interesting to note that for the most part, GFP units were usually under the command of the local Higher SS & Police Leader. In the case of Greece, it was under the Commander of the SS Security Police.[92] The conclusion must be that the Holocaust in Greece would have been all the more difficult had the GFP not been employed for that purpose. The GFP was therefore an important and vital tool of the Nazi Holocaust in Greece.

Officers of the Wehrmacht GFP. Left to right: Büttner, Wiese, Pätzke, Fenske, Gernert, Baucke, Göde, Klatt, Sowa, Grieger, Albrecht, Rüskriem, Gawehns, and Luecke (U.S. Holocaust Memorial Museum, courtesy Instytut Pamieci Narodowej).

7

The Secret Field Police in Yugoslavia, Romania and Bulgaria

Mission of the GFP in Yugoslavia, Romania and Bulgaria

By the beginning of the Balkan campaign in April 1941 GFP units had already taken part in all of the major battles except the invasion of the USSR. Initially around three to four GFP groups were employed during the German invasion of Yugoslavia and Greece.[1] Along with German rear area security forces, GFP units were to secure the conquered territories, investigate acts against the German Army, and interrogate captured enemy soldiers and guerrillas. Men of the GFP were also tasked with performing such "mundane" jobs as stopping Black Market activities and tracking down deserters. The nefarious mission of hunting down Jews and deporting them to concentration camps was also a task of the GFP. In the satellite states of Romania and Bulgaria, only one GFP unit was assigned per country: GFP-171 (Romania), and GFP-640 (Bulgaria). Because these nations were either Axis allies (Romania) or nominally allied to Germany (Bulgaria), the GFP could not operate with a free hand. In Romania, GFP-171 was given the surreptitious job of establishing lists of Jews in every Romanian community, in anticipation of their apprehension and deportation to Nazi death camps. The same mission was applied to GFP-640 in Bulgaria, however its late arrival to Sofia in the second half of 1943, coupled with Bulgaria's defection to the Soviet camp in the summer of 1944 prevented GFP-640 from performing the same mission. In addition, King Boris of Bulgaria, as well as leaders from the Bulgarian Orthodox Church refused repeated German demands to give up the 48,000 Jews that lived in Bulgaria. Unfortunately, the above rule did not apply for Jews living in occupied territories held by Bulgaria, such as Yugoslav Macedonia or Greek Thrace. In those regions, Bulgarian forces turned over Jews who did not possess a Bulgarian passport to the Germans.

GFP Units in Yugoslavia, Romania and Bulgaria

The employment of the Secret Field Police in Yugoslavia, Romania and Bulgaria would be small compared to the number of GFP units employed elsewhere.[2] Nevertheless their actions in this region of Europe would prove instrumental and important when it came to the Holocaust and in the repression of the local population. GFP-20 would be employed in the region of Slovenia, while GFP-9 was stationed in Serbia and Croatia several times

7. The Secret Field Police in Yugoslavia, Romania and Bulgaria

during the war. GFP-171 would end up serving in Romania. GFP-639 which took part in the invasion of Yugoslavia, was eventually transferred to the Soviet Union in 1941. It returned to Yugoslavia (Montenegro) in August 1943 where it operated until 1944. GFP-640, which served most of the war in Greece, was eventually withdrawn and sent to Bulgaria sometime in 1943 under the German military attaché. In late summer 1944, it withdrew from Bulgaria into Yugoslavia. By 1945 GFP-640 was operating in Croatia. Although relatively small in numbers, the GFP proved to be a vital cooperative link between the German Army and the SS killing apparatus in the Balkans.

GFP-9

GFP-9 was established on August 26, 1939, in *Wehrkreis VI* (6th Military District). It was assigned to *Grenzschutz Abschnitt Kommando 9* (Ninth Border Guard Sector Command), which was located in Aachen. The unit was initially placed on border guard duty along the Dutch frontier. It remained there until 1941 when it was moved to Scheveningen in Holland, and operated from this Dutch town until mid–1944. However, a captured German document, dealing with the occupation of Belgrade, Yugoslavia in the summer of 1941 contradicts this. The captured document lists a "*Sonder Kompanie der Geheime Feldpolizei Gruppe 9*" (Special Company of the Ninth Secret Field Police Group) as being assigned to the Belgrade garrison commander in August 1941.[3] Since each GFP unit was perhaps no more than 70–90 men, it is not possible that two companies of the same unit existed. Therefore, it is most likely that GFP-9 was temporarily split up.

Most of GFP-9 traveled from Yugoslavia by rail and arrived in northern France in January 1942. It had been sent to northern France to strengthen GFP-3, which was then stationed in Lille. GFP-9 had its headquarters in Wimereux, near Boulogne-sur-Mer. It had two *Sekretariat* located in (1) Calais and (2) Dunkirk. In addition to other duties, GFP-9 was entrusted with monitoring the coastal region between both towns. The confusion over the issue of whether GFP-9 was kept in Yugoslavia or sent to France comes from the fact that a part of GFP-9 remained behind in Yugoslavia. This turned out to be the above-quoted *Sonder Kompanie der Geheime Feldpolizei Gruppe 9*. This unit was not a company at all, but a *Sekretariat* which remained behind and was posted in Belgrade in 1941 and Zagreb in June 1942. Notice that when GFP-9 was posted to northern France in January 1942, it only created two *Sekretariat* posts, when its T/OE strength should have allowed it to create 3–4 such sub-commands. The commander of this "*Sonder Kompanie*" for GFP-9 was *Feldpolizeiinspektor* Paul Schmidt-Zabierow.[4] In June 1942 he was the senior GFP official in Zagreb, Croatia. Paul Schmidt-Zabierow had been born on December 18, 1903. His Nazi Party membership number was 2 382 392, and his SS number was 83 132. He had served in the SD before the war, and had been transferred into the GFP when war broke out. By all accounts he was a dedicated Nazi Party and SS member.

Unlike Serbia, which was occupied territory, Croatia was a sovereign Axis nation allied to Nazi Germany. The Germans could not operate there with a free hand. *Feldpolizeiinspektor* Schmidt-Zabierow kept himself busy by assisting the German Plenipotentiary headquarters in Zagreb with various duties. For example, in June 1942 he accompanied Dr. Petersen who was a representative of the Reich Labor Ministry, to the town of Stara Gradiska (located SE of Zagreb and north of Banja Luka) to help in the recruitment of 2,500 workers for employment in the Reich. The demands of the war had forced Germany to recruit more of its workers into the armed forces. This required that the Third Reich recruit more foreign workers for its armaments industry to make up for the manpower losses in the factories.

In February 1943 GFP-9 was transferred to Croatia where it finally incorporated the temporarily detached *Sekretariat* under *Feldpolizeiinspektor* Paul Schmidt-Zabierow. GFP-737 which was located at Arras, was now moved and assumed the tasks of GFP-9 in Wimereux, Calais, and Dunkirk. GFP-9 did not return to the West until May 1944. This time it was stationed in The Netherlands, under the *Wehrmacht Befehlshaber Niederlande* (W.B.N.). When the Allied invasion of the European continent occurred on June 6, 1944, this GFP unit was made subordinate to *LXXXVIII Armeekorps* in Utrecht. It was finally withdrawn from Holland in the late summer of 1944 and was returned to Zagreb, Croatia. It served as part of the forces under the *Befehlshaber der deutschen Truppen in Kroatien* (German Military Commander in Croatia). In 1945, it was still operating under this command and ended the war there.

GFP-20

This secret field police formation was established on August 26, 1939, in *Wehrkreis XVIII* (southern Austria). GFP-20 was stationed in Klagenfurt under *Grenzschutz-Abschnitt-Kommando 20* (20th Border Guard Command).[5] When Yugoslavia was invaded in the spring of 1941 the unit moved into the country and initially took part in the occupation of the region of Slovenia. There it assisted in the roundup of Jews in Slovenian territory annexed into the Reich. In 1942 GFP-20 was disbanded and its members were absorbed into the *Sicherheitspolizei* in those regions of Slovenia that were brought into the Reich. Therefore, its personnel remained in those annexed lands throughout the war. In 1945 Sipo and SD units left Slovenia as part of a general German withdrawal. Most of these men ended the war in Vienna, Austria.

GFP-171

This GFP unit was established on August 26, 1939, in East Prussia (*Wehrkreis I*). GFP-171 was attached to the German Army command which controlled the various frontier guard units employed as a blocking force during the Polish campaign. The bulk of these German border guard units were centered in the East Prussian towns of Johannesburg and Lyck. In the beginning of 1941, GFP-171 was operating under the German Commander in Copenhagen, Denmark. It then served from the middle of 1941 until 1944 as part of the German Army Military Mission to Romania. After the German withdrawal from Romania in August 1944, GFP-171 served under Army Group "F" (Southeast Europe–Balkans) until the end of the war.

GFP-639

GFP-639 had been established on September 10, 1940 in *Wehrkreis V*. The formation was employed in Poland and then was earmarked for the planned invasion of the Soviet Union. Throughout most of its history it served under the Second Panzer Army, where it operated in the central sector of the Russian front from 1941–1943. In September 1941, GFP-639 was in the region of Bobruisk. Together with *Polizeiregiment "Mitte"* (Police Regiment "Center"), an army infantry regiment, and a troop from *Einsatzkommando 8* it took part in a "cleansing" operation which netted twenty-two partisans killed.[6] At this time, the leader of GFP-639 was *Feldpolizeikommissar* Benno Kukawka.[7] On a regular basis this unit took part in the shooting of captured Red Army political commissars. For example, one document states that on April 25, 1942, GFP-639 travelled to *Gefangenen-Sammelstelle 20* (Prisoner

Collection Camp No.20) in the city of Orel and interrogated Red Army POWs suspected of being political commissars. Those they deemed to be Red Army commissars were segregated and then shot.[8] When the headquarters of Second Panzer Army was shifted from the USSR to Yugoslavia in August 1943, GFP-639 was also transferred as part of the intrinsic forces of the headquarters command of Second Panzer Army. When it arrived in Yugoslavia, GFP-639 was ordered stationed in Cetinje (in Montenegro).[9] Sometime after its transfer to the Balkans, *Feldpolizeikommissar* Karl-Heinz Meissner became the unit's commander.[10]

The Holocaust in Slovenia and Croatia

The roundup and eventual extermination of those people labeled as "undesirables" by the Nazis began in Yugoslavia almost as soon as the Germans occupied and broke up what had been known up until 1929 as the "Kingdom of Serbs, Croats, and Slovenes." The first anti–Jewish laws were enacted by the Croatian government on April 30, 1941—just twenty-one days after that state was established under German and Italian auspices. More than half of these Croatian Jews (about 19,800) were killed by the Croatians in labor and death camps from 1941–1945.[11] In 1941 approximately 35,000 Jews lived in what would become the Independent State of Croatia. Of that number, about 12,315 were living in Zagreb, the Croatian capital.[12] A further 8,000 Croatian Jews were living in the countryside. In the autumn of 1941 3,600 Jews were interned in the Croatian camps of Jasenovac, Laborgrad, Stara Gradisca, and Gredjarn, while 2,400 were sent to a camp on Pag Island, which also housed some 4,500 Serbians. Upon hearing that the Italian Army was about to occupy the island, the Croatian *Ustashe* killed about 4,500 of the estimated 6,900 Serbian Eastern Orthodox Christians and Croatian Jews.[13]

By 1942 the Jewish community in Zagreb had been reduced to around 4–5,000 Jews, given that about 6–7,000 Jews had fled to the relative safety of the Italian occupation zone. Another 4,927 Croatian Jews were transported to death camps in Germany and Poland during the summer of 1942.[14] The only area in Croatia which offered temporary safety for Jews was the Italian zone of operation, where the Italian Army absolutely refused to enforce any anti–Jewish measure. Of course, once Italy left the war in early September 1943 that protection disappeared. Once Italy surrendered 2,662 of the approximately 6–7,000 Jews in the former Italian zone in Croatia were caught in German sweeps. The lucky ones were several thousand Jews who had been concentrated on the island of Rab when the Italian surrender occurred. Those Jews managed to escape into partisan held territory, although some were later caught in German anti-partisan drives. In total, only about 7,000 of Croatia's pre-war Jewish population survived the war. The elimination of the Croatian Jews seems to have been perpetrated mostly by the Croatians themselves with the help of the German police and SS/SD apparatus in Croatia. No secret field police unit appears to have taken part in the murders or deportations.

In Slovenia, the prewar Jewish community amounted to less than a thousand. Most did not survive the roundups and deportations, especially in light of the fact that when the German and Italian occupation of Slovenia began, most of the Slovenian Jews were located in the German zone. They suffered the same fate as the Hungarian Jews. The deportations of the Slovenian Jews were carried out by the Gestapo and SS, with the aid of the local ethnic-German *Wehrmannschaft* (Self-Defense Militia).[15] The only secret field police unit to serve in Slovenia during the occupation period when the Jews were sent to their deaths (1941–1944) was GFP-20. As stated earlier, this unit was disbanded in 1942 and its men

The Annexed Areas of Slovenia. When Yugoslavia was partitioned, the Germans annexed Upper Carnolia and Lower Styria (from Slovenia) and incorporated those lands into the Reich. These regions returned to Slovenia as part of Yugoslavia when the war ended (map by author).

used to create SD and Gestapo posts in Slovenia. Its men were employed by both the German Military Commander in northern Slovenia and the local SD and Gestapo office in Marburg (Maribor). Like the German police forces in the region, GFP-20 took part in the expulsion of the Slovenian Jews in the spring of 1941 in the areas that had been incorporated into the Reich. In the regions of Slovenia occupied by the Italians, the roundup of Jews occurred in the fall of 1943.[16] After the German conquest of Yugoslavia the region of Prekmurje (North-Eastern Slovenia) was handed over to the Hungarian state. Jews living there remained relatively safe until the spring of 1944 when the Germans overthrew Admiral Horthy, occupied Hungary and eventually installed a Fascist, Count Ferenc Szálasi, as the new head of the Hungarian government. In April 1944, the Jews from the Prekmurje region of Slovenia were rounded up and sent to Nazi death camps.[17]

Organizing the Holocaust and Nazi Occupation of Serbia

The German occupation of Serbia was much like the German occupation of the Soviet Union, in that no actual Serbian government was allowed to exist—rather, a puppet government under Serbian General Milan Nedic was tolerated in order for the country to continue to run on a day-to-day basis. Therefore, no diplomatic embassies from foreign countries were allowed to communicate directly with the Nedic administration. All palavers and contacts had to be made through the German Army occupation command that was established shortly after the collapse of Yugoslavia. This military administration would soon be responsible for physically apprehending Serbians as hostages and for providing the firing squads that would execute them as retribution for guerrilla attacks. These rear-area army commands would work hand in hand with the SS and GFP.[18] The city garrison commander (*Standortkommandantur Belgrad*) was also under the control of *Feldkommandantur 599*. Throughout its existence, the Belgrade garrison commander had an attached motorized field police platoon under the command of *Leutnant* Gerhardt Bloose. This unit was *Feldgendarmerietrupp (mot.) 616*. Within the context of procuring civilians for the firing squads GFP-9 actively took part in sweeps where random Serbian civilians were picked off the streets of Belgrade to be shot in retaliation for partisan attacks against the Germans.[19] Hitler had decreed that for every German killed, one hundred Serbians were to be shot, and for every German wounded, fifty civilians would be killed. Serbian nationals living in Belgrade as well as throughout the countryside quickly learned to avoid the streets after it became known that a partisan attack had occurred.

The Holocaust in Serbia was, as elsewhere, primarily in the hands of the SS. Another military field police unit, *Feldgendarmerie Ersatz Kompanie 1*, under the command of *Hauptmann der Feldgendarmerie* Geisler, worked with the special company of GFP-9 as part of the Belgrade garrison commander.[20] This turned out to be the *Sekretariat* from GFP-9 which remained in the Balkans when the bulk of this Secret Field Police unit was transferred to northern France. In September 1941 *General* Franz Böhme was appointed as the *Kommandierender General in Serbien* (Commanding General in Serbia).[21] The actual post of *Höhere SS und Polizeiführer Serbien* (Higher SS & Police Leader "Serbia") was not established until January 22, 1942, when *SS Gruppenführer und Generalleutnant der Polizei* August Meyszner assumed command. That same month the position of *Befehlshaber der Ordnungspolizei Serbien* (Supreme Commander of the Order Police for "Serbia") was created, although the post and staff were not actually established until February 17, 1942.[22] Meyszner's Higher SS & Police Leader staff in Belgrade would be responsible for the deaths of the remaining Jews of Serbia.[23] The German Order Police was another security organ that was employed in the repression of the Jewish and non–Jewish population. The headquarters of the *Befehlshaber der Ordnungspolizei Serbien (BdO Serbien)* was established in early 1942 to support the SS in Serbia.[24] This German Order Police command would also be employed to oppress the local Serbian population.[25] The head of the *SD/Sipo* command in Serbia was *SS Standartenführer* Dr. Wilhelm Fuchs. Fuchs was in charge of an SS killing unit from the RSHA.[26] This *Einsatzgruppe* would lead the actual "actions" against the Serbian Jews. Dr. Wilhelm Fuchs also assumed command of the *Kommandeur der Sicherheitspolizei und SD Belgrad* (Commander of the Security Police & Security Service for "Belgrade"). According to one source, about 200 *SD/Sipo* officers, NCOs, and men were available for operations in Serbia in August 1941.[27]

During this month alone, *Standartenführer* Fuchs's SD office reported shooting 1,000 "communists and Jews." The death of these Jewish and non–Jewish Serbians was supposedly in retaliation for partisan attacks against the German occupation force. During the summer and fall of 1941 Fuchs employed the 200 men from his *SD* command, and the only German

Order Police battalion stationed in Serbia: *Polizei Bataillon 64*.[28] In 1942 Fuchs would be transferred to Russia where he would temporarily assume command of the *SS und Polizeiführer Lettland* (SS & Police Leader Latvia).[29] Fuchs's transfer from Serbia would occur in the beginning of February 1942—just a matter of days after the infamous Wannsee conference.[30] In his place *SS Oberführer und Oberst der Polizei* Dr. Emanuel Schäfer assumed command. Schäfer was one of Reinhard Heydrich's most trusted officers, having served with the State Police in Oppeln and the Gestapo office in Cologne. Upon taking over in Serbia, Schäfer's command had eleven principal officers.[31] These were organized and stationed in Belgrade.[32]

Bruno Sattler was a late-comer to the SD command in Serbia. Promoted at the beginning of 1942 to *SS-Sturmbannführer und Kriminaldirektor* of Department IV (Gestapo), he was assigned to the *Befehlshaber der Sicherheitspolizei und SD Serbien* ("Commander of the Security Police and the Security Service in Serbia"). This headquarters was now led by *SS Oberführer und Oberst der Polizei* Dr. Emanuel Schäfer. Sattler held the "Department IV" position until October 1944 when the Yugoslav capital was abandoned and German forces in Serbia began a general withdrawal. Even though Fuchs had been busy eliminating "communists and Jews" since the summer of 1941 until he was relieved, Schäfer found that there were still 6,280 Jews (mostly women and children) in the Semlin concentration camp when he assumed command of the Belgrade Sipo & SD.[33]

Around 16,000 Jews lived in Serbia at the time of the German invasion of Yugoslavia in April 1941.[34] It appears then that Schäfer's predecessor (Fuchs) had only been partially successful at eliminating the Jews of Serbia. Schäfer reacted by eliminating the remaining Jewish population, and did it so quickly that by July 1942 *SS Gruppenführer* Dr. Harald Turner declared that Serbia was *Judenfrei* ("free of Jews").[35] Not having any further "work" the Belgrade Jewish Bureau was finally closed in October 1943. Through the efforts of the German SS security and police forces, by the late summer of 1942 the Jews of Serbia had been wiped out. At the end of the war, about thirty principal Germans involved in the elimination were singled out by the Yugoslav government for prosecution:

> In Serbia, the defendants numbered under thirty employees who were made up of members of the Gestapo, the police and the Secret Field Police. For the duration of their membership in the Abteilung IV [Department IV] also members of the police and the Secret Field Police were considered equivalent Gestapo officials. Each member of Abteilung IV constantly stood a national German interpreter. As head of this department the defendants served in Serbia, where the central police repression was against "communists," "White Russians" and "Jews."[36]

As for which German units took part in the Holocaust in Serbia, we know that they included the SS security forces. We also know the formations, based on the order of battle for German units and commands deployed in Serbia, that were present during the specific time period when the murders took place. The forces which took part in the murder of the Serbian Jewish population were members of the following commands:

1. Elements of the Gestapo, Sipo and SD stationed in Belgrade
2. *Polizei Reserve Bataillon 64* (of SS Polizeiregiment 5)[37]
3. *Feldgendarmerie Ersatz Kompanie 1*[38]
4. *Sonder Kompanie der Geheime Feldpolizei Gruppe 9* (GFP-9)[39]

No other GFP unit was located on Serbian territory from late 1941 to the summer of 1942. Notice that the transfer of *Sonder Kompanie der Geheime Feldpolizei Gruppe 9* (actually just one *Sekretariat*, as the rest of GFP-9 was in northern France) from Serbia to the "quieter" territories of Croatia occurred in June 1942, when the Germans had completed the murder of all of the Serbian Jews in their control. It's no coincidence that once the killings were completed, this *Sekretariat* from GFP-9 was shifted to "other duties"—in this case, Croatia.

The GFP in Yugoslavia worked not only to assist in the repression of the Yugoslav people, but in the rounding up and murder of the Jews. They were also active in confiscation of Jewish property. In addition, the SS, SD, Order Police, and Secret Field Police would be employed in the murder of hostages as reprisal shootings. This was all done under the pretext of combating the partisans.[40] As early as the summer of 1941 the German Army practice of randomly rounding up people in Serbia and shooting them after a guerrilla attack in retaliation, was rampant.[41] With the exception of one or two relatively minor members of the GFP, most senior Secret Field Police members seem to have been what was termed "hard men"—ruthless and totally dedicated to a Nazi victory.

Table 2. Secret Field Police Units Operating in Balkans, 1941–1945

#	GFP Unit	Unit	Higher Command
79	510	Transferred to 12th Army (the Balkans) in March 1941. Took part in the German invasion of Yugoslavia & Greece. It was stationed in Salonika in 1941. From 1942–1943, it was located in Salonika and Rhodes. In 1944 it operated on Rhodes, Leros, and Samos before it moved to Kalamaki (by Athens). In 1945, the unit was shifted to Croatia.	*Oberkommando des Heers and Oberkommando der Wehrmacht* then *Heeresgruppe E/F*
80	611	Transferred in March 1941 to 12th Army in the Balkans. It took part in the German invasion of Yugoslavia and Greece. The unit passed through Belgrade, Serbia but by late 1941 had been shifted to Salonika in Greece. From 1941–1942 it operated in Athens and Crete. The unit's Field Post Number was 10448. From 1943–1944 it operated mainly on Crete but also had men on the island of Corfu. GFP-611 withdrew from Greece in October 1944. By 1945 it was operating in Croatia.	*Oberkommando des Heers and Oberkommando der Wehrmacht* then *Heeresgruppe E/F*
81	612	Transferred to 12th Army (the Balkans) in February 1941. Took part in invasion of Yugoslavia. Shifted east for the upcoming Russian campaign in May 1941.	*Oberkommando des Heers and Oberkommando der Wehrmacht*
82	621	Transferred to the Balkans under 12th Army in March 1941. It was stationed in Salonika from 1941–1944. In 1944, it extended its area of operations throughout Epirus and Thessaly. It Withdrew from Greece in October 1944. By 1945 it was operating on Croatian soil.	*Oberkommando des Heers and Oberkommando der Wehrmacht* then *Heeresgruppe E/F*
83	640	The unit was transferred to Greece in 1942. Sometime in 1943 it was transferred to Sofia, Bulgaria.[42] It remained in Bulgaria until the late summer of 1944 when it was withdrawn into Bosnia. In 1945, it was under Second Army in Croatia.	*Oberkommando der Wehrmacht*, then *Heeresgruppe E/F*

The Holocaust in Romania and Bulgaria

As for other countries in the Balkans, the German Military attaché in Romania kept one GFP group until the summer of 1944 when all German forces were withdrawn because of the advancing Red Army, and because Romania switched sides and declared war on Germany on August 23, 1944. Technically, GFP-171 was under the command of the German *Polizeiattache* (police attaché) that was part of the German military presence in Romania. The same was true of GFP-640 in Bulgaria. GFP-171 was attached to the German Army mission in Romania from 1941–1944. The duties of GFP-171 included monitoring Romanian political and military affairs, to protect the German attaché as well as leading German officers of the German mission to Romania, and to monitor the activities of Jews entering or leaving the country. They were also to try and establish the size and distribution of the Jewish community in Romania in preparation for their apprehension. Of course, wherever possible the GFP (like the SS) was to encourage anti–Jewish pogroms in these pro–Axis nations, but their status in an unoccupied country limited that activity. The anti–Jewish efforts depended on the cooperation of the Romanian and Bulgarian governments.

The support which the Romanian and Bulgarian governments extended to the Germans in aiding in the deportation of "their Jews" to the Nazi death camps depended on various factors. Bulgaria refused to turn over their Jewish nationals, but had no qualms about turning over Jews who did not hold Bulgarian citizenship. Romania which had closer ties with Nazi Germany and was more strongly anti–Semitic, had no qualms whatsoever. This was especially true while the Germans were winning the war. Romania supported the expulsion and handover of their Jews, but as the war turned against the Third Reich this assistance weakened, fearing Allied retribution.[43] Although it was under the control of the German Police Attaché, the *Geheime Feldpolizei* answered to *SS-Sturmbannführer* Gustav Richter, Adolf Eichmann's man in Romania from the RSHA.[44] Gustav Richter was supposed to make a census of the Jews in Romania, which at the time numbered around 300,000.[45] Once the census was completed, he was to obtain permission to place Romania's Jews in ghettos in anticipation of deporting them to Belzec extermination camp in Poland. Secret Field Police Group 171 was to assist in the census and in identifying areas around the countryside where Jews were living.

When the Germans launched their invasion of the Soviet Union on June 22, 1941, the areas of eastern Romania (Bessarabia and Transnistria), which had been taken from Romania by the USSR in 1940, were re-occupied by Romanian troops and German forces. In the town of Iasi (Jassy) an anti–Jewish *pogrom* occurred from June 27–28, 1941. This *Aktion* eventually cost 13,266 Jewish lives. The massacre was perpetrated by a combined Romanian and German force. Units from the 11th German Army that took part in this shooting spree included GFP-626, GFP-647, GFP-720 as well as the 683rd Motorized Field Police Battalion.[46] Elements of *Einsatzgruppe D* were also used in the two-day operation.[47] The GFP units separated the Jews from the non–Jewish population, while the military policemen provided a cordon preventing any escape. Members from *Einsatzgruppe D* provided the firing squads. The Romanian contribution was composed of elements from the 14th Infantry Division, police and *Gendarmerie* forces, and members of the *Serviciul Special de Informatii* (Special Information Service). The Romanian army element as well as the *Gendarmerie* served to cordon the area and prevent escape, while the SSI officers performed the job of making sure no Jews managed to melt into the general population. The SSI was the intelligence arm of Marshal Ion Antonescu's military dictatorship in Romania. Those officers from the SSI implicated in the Jassy *pogrom* were Lieutenant-Colonel Gheorghe Balotescu, Lieutenant-Colonel Petrescu, Colonel Radu Dinulescu, Grigore Petrovici, Junius Lecca, and Emil Tulbure.[48] After the war the Chief of the SSI was interrogated. He said that members of the SSI took part in this massacre, but he also implicated members of the German *Geheime Feldpolizei*.[49]

The Secret Field Police presence in Romania before the German invasion of the Soviet Union was also instrumental in assisting anti–Jewish elements. For example, when the Romanian right-wing movement, the Iron Guard, attempted a *coup d'état* against Marshal Antonescu's government in early 1941, most of the members of this pro–Nazi group were rounded up and imprisoned. The Gestapo and SD representatives in Romania were completely implicated in the *putsch*, and were forced to leave the country. The head of the Gestapo in Romania was Kurt Geisler. In order to avoid having to leave Romania, Geisler was quickly transferred to GFP-171. Since the GFP were not required to leave Romania like the Gestapo and SD elements, Geisler was allowed to remain. In 1942 Geisler's efforts were critical in allowing Horia Sima, a leading member of the Romanian Iron Guard, to escape to Nazi Germany.[50]

Conclusions

The conduct of the Secret Field Police in Yugoslavia, Romania, and Bulgaria depended on the relationship of that nation to the Third Reich. A Secret Field Police unit was stationed in both Romania and Bulgaria. However, their role was limited due to the military and political situation and the fact that these were sovereign nations. In Romania, which had closer ties to Nazi Germany and where Anti-Semitism was more pronounced, the GFP took part in preparing for the expulsion of the Jews and even participated in some anti–Jewish actions, like the Jassy *pogrom* in late June 1941. In Bulgaria, the GFP could not achieve the same "success" as in Romania, given that the government of King Boris III protected Jews with Bulgarian passports. Jews in Bulgarian controlled regions of Greece and Yugoslavia however, were readily handed over to the Nazis. Even after the king's death in August 1943 his son and successor, King Simeon II continued his father's policy of protecting Jews who were Bulgarian citizens.[51] In Slovenia and Serbia by contrast, the GFP had a free hand. In April 1941, the Nazis annexed certain border regions of Slovenia and absorbed them into the Reich. Once that occurred, GFP-20 took part in regular roundups of what few Jews lived in those areas. In 1942, this Secret Field Police unit was disbanded and its men absorbed into the Sipo and SD command in the region. When Italy surrendered in September 1943 Jews still living on Slovenian lands were rounded up.

In Serbia and Montenegro, the Germans ran rampant from the very start of the occupation. In Serbia, where the Germans had a military government and a token puppet regime under General Milan Nedic, the Jews were completely wiped out through German Army and SS efforts. Mass executions, the roundup of Serbian Jews and their elimination occurred so effectively that by the summer of 1942 SS *Gruppenführer* Dr. Harald Turner boasted that Serbia was *Judenfrei* ("free of Jews").[52] GFP-9 as well as regular German army units proved indispensable in rounding up not only the Jewish community, but also in accosting people from the streets and executing them as a reprisal for anti–German attacks. Hundreds of innocent Serbian civilians would be executed based on Adolf Hitler's mathematical calculation that for every German wounded, fifty civilians would be shot and for every German killed, 100 civilians would be executed. While initially the GFP and other Army forces selected known Jews and communists for the reprisal shootings, by 1942 Serbian civilians were being grabbed off the streets randomly.

The creation of the Independent State of Croatia under Ante Pavelic and the [Fascist]

Ustashe fanatics guaranteed that the job of rounding up the region's Jews would be accomplished by the Croatians themselves with a minimum of German support. The only problem lay with the areas under Italian Army control where Jews were able to hide out successfully until the Italian surrender in September 1943. The GFP in Serbia featured prominently in the attempt to wipe out these Jews. In Greece, the comportment of the GFP appears to have been increased incrementally as the German military situation worsened. By late 1943 the Germans in Greece were behaving as harshly as in Serbia and in the Eastern campaign. The only drawback which the Germans encountered in Greece was the almost total lack of Anti-Semitism which prevented locally instigated *pogroms* the likes of which had occurred in Lithuania, Ukraine, Estonia, and Latvia when the Germans occupied those countries. For the most part, the puppet Greek government of Ioannis Rallis was loath to support anti-Jewish activities until forced to by the Germans.

8

The GFP in the West and Scandinavia

It has already been established that the GFP in the West behaved better than elsewhere. Was there a difference however, in the manner in which the Secret Field Police behaved in western European countries as opposed to its actions in the Balkans? What about its behavior in Poland, the Baltic States and the Soviet Union? Was the Secret Field Police molded in only one fashion and made to fit all molds, or did their performance vary according to national boundaries or political and military goals? Was the comportment of the GFP in the West as proper as has been claimed? By comparing the behavior of the Secret Field Police in the West and in the USSR, we can gain a better understanding of the differences or similarities of their actions in Greece. This chapter will cover the organization and history of the GFP in the West and Scandinavia as a comparison to GFP actions in Greece and the Balkans.

Organization of the GFP in France

When the Wehrmacht was planning for the conquest of France and the Low Countries, the GFP featured as part of the German occupation force. Once France was conquered, it was divided into two principal sections: occupied and unoccupied France. The GFP would serve in all regions of occupied France where German military forces operated—both in frontline areas such as along the coastline and in the rear areas of the occupied territories. Un-occupied France would be the domain of a new regime—Vichy France under Marshal Henri Philippe Petain who now became its Prime Minister. This regime was pro–German in character, and eventually aided in the roundup of Jews on Vichy French territory.[1] German forces would occupy the other half, which faced the English Channel and Atlantic Ocean. Within the German occupied areas of France several distinct regions were created. For example, those areas along the coastline and immediately behind the coast were designated as military front lines and troops were positioned there to garrison the shoreline in case of Allied invasion. The regions behind the military coastline comprised the hinterland of the German occupation area where German garrison forces and administrative garrison commands were established. While the provinces of Alsace and Lorraine were re-absorbed into the German Reich, a "closed zone" existed west of these two border provinces that were earmarked for German colonization. In this area, the return of French refugees was forbidden.[2] Finally, the area of northern France as well as Belgium was made a separate military administration and was to be governed in that manner.

On November 8, 1942, the American and British military launched "Operation Torch"—the Allied landings on Vichy French territories in North Africa. While some Vichy French units initially resisted, many began to surrender en-masse to the Allied troops and soon joined as part of the Free-French forces that were now being led by General Charles de Gaulle. Because of a growing fear that more Vichy French forces would join the Allies, that same month the Germans decided to invade the unoccupied part of France, bringing an end to the Vichy government. This began on November 11, 1942, and was code-named *Unternehmen Anton* ("Operation Anton"). After the German occupation of metropolitan Vichy France, the government of Petain remained as mere "window dressing" for the real rulers—the Germans.

The manner in which the rear area of the German forces was organized in World War II was through administrative commands. The *Oberfeldkommandantur* (administrative area headquarters) was the highest military administrative body. This type of headquarters in all theatres of operation came under the control of the commander of an Army or Army

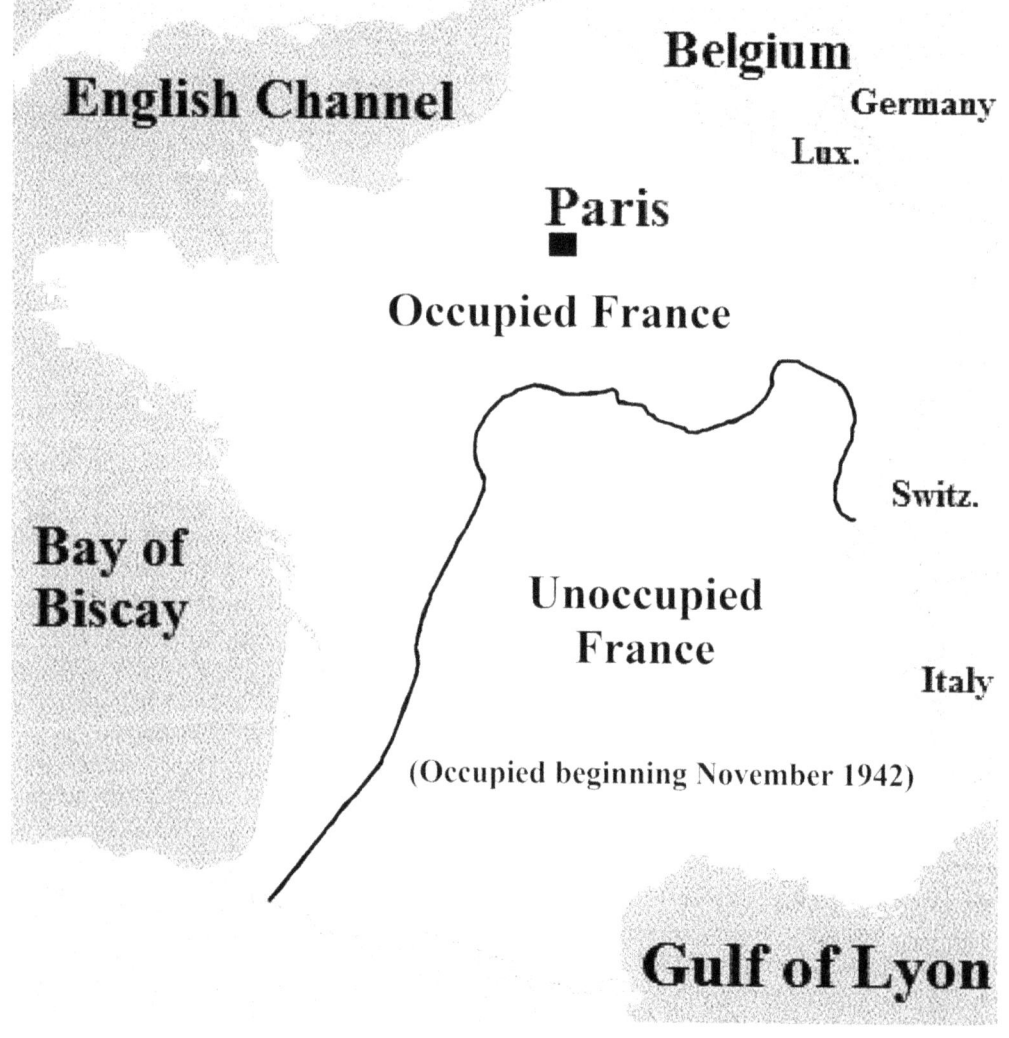

Occupied and unoccupied France (map by author).

8. The GFP in the West and Scandinavia

Group Rear Area. In occupied territories outside the theatre of operations they came under the military commander in charge of the military administration for that country. Subordinate administrative headquarters were the *Feldkommandantur* (administrative sub-area headquarters), usually led by an *Oberst* ("Colonel") or *Generalmajor* ("Major General"). The *Ortskommandantur* (Town headquarters) was normally officered by a Major. The *Kreiskommandantur* (District headquarters) was a rural district also usually led by a Major. The *Stadtkommandantur* (City headquarters) were found in the major cities.

During the initial occupation of France and Belgium from 1940–1942 the GFP was divided into five districts (or "territories"), named "A," "B," "C," "Paris," and "Belgien-Nordfrankreich." In Belgium, an initial number of eleven GFP groups were eventually reduced to three by 1943. Five GFP units were initially assigned to The Netherlands. Norway and Finland each had a single GFP group at any one time. Paris was so large and important that at any one time the city held somewhere between five and seven GFP groups. In the spring of 1942 the Sipo and SD assumed control of some of the personnel in these GFP units. Many GFP commands were disbanded and their men were now transferred into the Sipo & SD. In many cases the men being reassigned into the Sipo/SD were returning to the parent organization, which they had served before being posted to the Secret Field Police. In total the SD disbanded an initial batch of seventeen GFP units in France.[3] This increase in Sipo/SD strength allowed the SS Security Service to create sufficient station posts within France, Belgium and the Netherlands. This had been done before by the SD in Poland and in the USSR. There the SS killing units organized for both the Polish and Russian campaign were eventually disbanded and their personnel were used to create the various Sipo/SD commands and station posts. In the West, the Sipo/SD had not employed any SS killing units so they resorted to disbanding numerous GFP formations.[4]

In addition, one more GFP formation (GFP-20) was disbanded in 1942. This unit however, was stationed on the constituency of northeastern Slovenia. This region was absorbed into the Reich in 1942. The members of GFP-20 were used to flesh out the Sipo and SD commands in this area (see chapter seven). Those GFP units disbanded in France in the fall of 1942 included: GFP-2, GFP-7, GFP-11, GFP-14, GFP-30, GFP-550, GFP-603, GFP-627, GFP-632, GFP-633, GFP-649, GFP-701, GFP-731, GFP-732, GFP-733, GFP-734, and GFP-736. A further eight GFP units were disbanded throughout 1944, and their personnel reabsorbed into the Sipo/SD. The units that were disbanded were: GFP-718 in February, GFP-711, and GFP-712 in April, GFP-730 in August, and GFP-722, GFP-724, GFP-739, and GFP-740 in September. These final eight GFP units added a boost in strength to the Sipo/SD commands in the Reich.

The various SD station posts that were created throughout France in late 1942 therefore, included a good number of men who had seen service in the GFP. After the war many senior GFP officials were debriefed. One of these was *Feldpolizeidirektor* Philip Greiner. According to Philip Greiner's testimony, the operational forces of the GFP under the various army commands in France were not under his control, but directly subordinate to *Feldpolizeidirektor* Erich Vogel, as *Leitender Geheime Feldpolizei West* (Senior Secret Field Police Superintendent "West"). In addition, Greiner affirmed that the intelligence officer (referred to in German military terms as the "Ic") for each German army headquarters had direct control over the employment of the various GFP units assigned to the Army. Greiner insisted that the GFP units assigned to the "territorial" regions ("A," "B," "C" and "Paris") were under his control and were separate from the GFP units assigned directly to the various German armies in occupied France. The region of *Belgien-Nordfrankreich* ("Belgium–Northern France") was assigned to a separate senior Secret Field Police superintendent:

Leitender Feldpolizeidirektor beim Militärbefehlshaber Nord-Frankreich, stationed in Brussels.[5] The principal consequence of this decision was that the Franco-Belgian border would be the monitored by the GFP headquarters in Brussels (i.e.–the *Leitender Feldpolizeidirektor beim Militärbefehlshaber Nord-Frankreich*).

Philip Greiner's position as *Leitender Feldpolizeidirektor beim Militärbefehlshaber Frankreich* was basically administrative. His duties included the following:

1. To maintain liaison between the *Militär Befehlshaber Frankreich* and the staffs of the GFP headquarters under his command (see below).
2. To maintain liaison between the *Militär Befehlshaber Frankreich* and the staffs of the GFP groups in Paris.
3. To maintain liaison between his HQ and the *Stadtkommandantur* of Paris.
4. To maintain liaison between the Paris Police and his HQ.
5. To attend military conferences of the *Militär Befehlshaber Frankreich* whenever GFP matters were on the agenda, and to follow up on any resultant decisions regarding the GFP groups.
6. To supervise and inspect GFP groups in France, and to guarantee the training and equipping of the various GFP groups, as well as to submit regular reports to both the *Militär Befehlshaber Frankreich* and *Leitender Geheime Feldpolizei West*.
7. To advise the military on criminal police matters.
8. To check the work of the lower echelon *Leitender Feldpolizeidirektoren* of the various military administrative districts.
9. To supervise the overall organization of the GFP in France.[6]

Feldpolizeidirektor Dräger replaced Greiner sometime in late 1941. Dräger held this post even after the absorption of most of the GFP groups in the West by the SD in 1942. As for Philip Greiner, he returned to the *Kriminalpolizei* in Nuremberg where he was promoted to *Regierungs und Kriminalrat* in the beginning of 1942.[7] The GFP "territorial" organization in France from July 1940 until 1942 was as follows:

Senior Secret Field Police Superintendent "West"

Leitender Geheime Feldpolizei West–Feldpolizeidirektor Erich Vogel was assigned in 1941. The regions included the *Leitender Feldpolizeidirektor beim Militärbefehlshaber Frankreich* in *Paris* post led by Philip Greiner, then *Feldpolizeidirektor* Friedrich Sowa. From 1940–1941 this GFP headquarters was located in the Hotel Lutetia. In 1941, it was moved within Paris to Rue-de-la-Faisanderie. The HQ was composed of the following men: *Feldpolizeidirektor* Greiner, *Feldpolizeikommissar* Hochgrabe and Retzeck, *Feldpolizeisekretär* Rudi Engel, plus three NCOs, two orderlies and one driver.[8] Rudi Engel had previously served on the staff of GFP-603 and GFP-610 in Paris. Under the *Leitender Geheime Feldpolizei West* Engel was in charge of the unit registry.[9] The lower GFP commands under the *Leitender Feldpolizeidirektor beim Militärbefehlshaber Frankreich* included the following:

Leitender Feldpolizeidirektor beim Chef des Militarverwaltungsbezirks A (Leading Field Police Director by the Chief of Military District "A"), stationed in Saint Germain and led by *Feldpolizeidirektor* Ernst Rassow until May 1941,[10] then *Feldpolizeidirektor* Hans-Jochen Bartsch beginning in June.

Leitender Feldpolizeidirektor beim Chef des Militarverwaltungsbezirks B (Leading Field

Police Director by the Chief of Military District "B"), stationed in Bordeaux und Angers and led by *Feldpolizeidirektor* Tesenfitz. Later *Feldpolizeidirektor* Zucklic assumed command. *Leitender Feldpolizeidirektor beim Chef des Militarverwaltungsbezirks C* (Leading Field Police Director by the Chief of Military District "C"), stationed in Dijon and led by *Feldpolizeidirektor* Dr. Hermann Herold.[11]

Leitender Feldpolizeidirektor beim Paris (Leading Field Police Director in Paris).[12]– According to Greiner's U.S. Army interrogation report, the position of the Paris GFP command was to be left under the command of *Feldpolizeidirektor* Vogel. However, in the same report Greiner listed *SS-Sturmbannführer* Karl Dräger as the *Feldpolizeidirektor* for Paris. Karl Dräger was born on June 21, 1896. He was married and spoke French. He had served in the Berlin Kripo (Criminal Police). He was said to have left Paris in the autumn of 1942.

Leitender Feldpolizeidirektor beim Militärbefehlshaber Nord-Frankreich (Senior Field Superintendent for the Military Commander Northern France) stationed in Brussels and led by *Feldpolizeidirektor* Kurt Kletzke.

Paris GFP Garrison Command

Paris, as the capital and largest city in France, was considered so important that it was assigned a large force of GFP units. In total five to seven Secret Field Police formations were stationed in the French capital at any given time. Paris was the heart of the French nation, and a center of resistance activity. Because of this, a substantial number of GFP units were assigned to the city. One of the missions of the GFP in Paris before 1942 was to seek out the French underground and attack it. From August 1941 until June 1942, a total of 471 French hostages were executed on account of anti–German activity in the French capital.[13] The GFP in Paris was also responsible for performing the mission of vetting the prostitutes who worked at the Sphinx. The Sphinx was a Parisian luxury brothel that was opened in 1931 and operated until it was closed in 1946. It was located at 31, boulevard Edgar-Quinet. During the war, it was frequented by high-ranking German officers. The principal units assigned to this mission were numerous and included the following formations:

GFP-11

GFP-11 was led by *Feldpolizeikommissar* Dr. Bohlsen. From July 1940 until November 1941 the headquarters for this unit was at the Hotel Chatham 18, intersecting rue Volney and rue Daunou in Paris. Beginning in December 1941 it was located at the Hotel Sport along Avenue Duquesne and Avenue Tourville.[14] On May 12, 1942, *Feldpolizeikommissar* Dr. Theodore Mommsen assumed command of GFP-11. Other officials in GFP-11 included *Feldpolizeikommissar* Josef Sonka, *Feldpolizeikommissar* Christian Hemmer (born January 10, 1899), *Feldpolizeikommissar* Hans Jessen (born February 26, 1895), *Feldpolizeisekretär* Peter Zimmer, *Feldpolizeisekretär* Heinrich Vögler, and *Feldpolizeibeamter* Albert Schneuer (born January 24, 1905).

Dr. Zaimig was also a member of GFP-11. He was transferred into the Sipo/SD in 1942 when GFP-11 was disbanded and given the rank of *SS Hauptsturmführer*. It was said that Wilhelm Krichbaum held Dr. Zaimig in high esteem. In June 1942, this GFP unit was dissolved and its men were incorporated into the Sipo and SD. In April 1941 Peter Zimmer, who had earlier served in the *SS Verfügungstruppe*, was posted to the GFP replacement battalion located in Altenburg (*Infanterie Ersatz Bataillon 600*) before being reassigned to a GFP unit on the Eastern Front. The same fate awaited *Feldpolizeikommissar* Josef Sonka. He was posted to Altenburg in August 1941 before being assigned as commander of a brand new GFP unit on the Russian Front.

GFP-550

GFP-550 was led by *Feldpolizeikommissar* Dr. Bernhard Niggemeyer (later to be replaced by *Feldpolizeikommissar* Bernhard Hannig). Hannig was the average middle-class man with a family. He was in many respects a typical example of the generation who witnessed the First World War as a young man, and had tasted the bitterness of defeat during the inter-war years. He was also a typical GFP official. He was born in 1907, eventually married and fathered three children. During the Second World War his family lived in Hannover, where he had grown up. Before the start of World War II he had served in the *Kriminalpolizei* (Criminal Police) in Hannover. In the beginning of the war he had been drafted into GFP-550. At the start of 1941 GFP-550 was located at Avenue de la Grande Armee in Paris. In 1942 when his GFP unit was disbanded, he joined the *Befehlshaber der Sicherheitspolizei Paris*.

GFP-603

GFP-603 was led by *Feldpolizeikommissar* von Ostrowski who was later replaced by *Feldpolizeikommissar* Joachim Kaintzik (born December 13, 1905). This unit was stationed at the Hotel Matignon. GFP-603 was disbanded sometime during the fall of 1942.

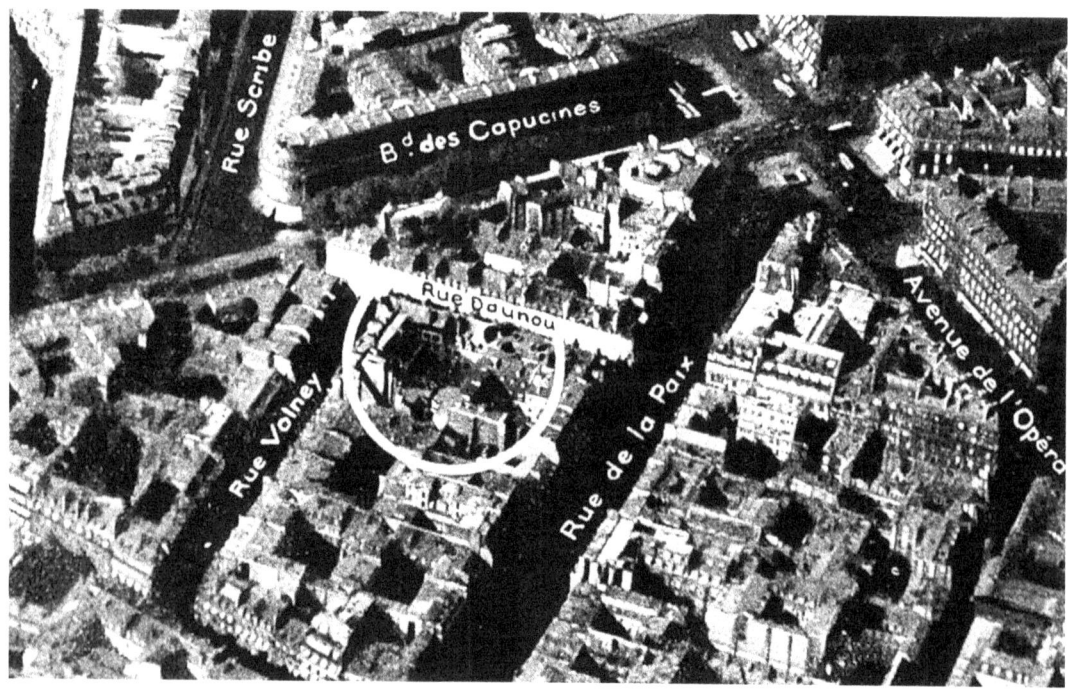

Location of Hotel Chatham in Paris, where GFP-11 was stationed. Photo was originally taken from a partial scan of a 1924 French poster advertising the Hotel (author's collection).

GFP-610

GFP-610 was led by *Feldpolizeikommissar* Hargard; later to be replaced by *Feldpolizeikommissar* Arthur Kallenborn (or Kallenbonn?). Its HQs was located in Hotel Edward III, somewhere along the Avenue de l'Opera. In 1940/41 Dr. Theodore Mommsen was the adjutant to GFP-610 before being posted as commander of GFP-11 in May 1942. At the end of 1942 this unit was transferred to Army Group "A" in southern Russia. In 1944, it was serving under 14th Army in Italy.

GFP-649

GFP-649 was led by *Feldpolizeikommissar* Jetzinger.[15] It was disbanded in 1942 and its personnel drafted into the Sipo/SD. Two other formations were eventually posted (temporarily) to the French capital and employed on various missions. These were *Geheime Feldpolizei Gruppe 625 (L)* and *626* respectively:

GFP-625 (L)

GFP-625 (L) was led by *Feldpolizeikommissar* Kühn while his adjutant was *Feldpolizeikommissar* Jellositz. Other members of this Air Force GFP unit included *Feldpolizeisekretär* Knaus and Hoppe; *Feldpolizeiinspektor* Koch, Distel, and Sensenbrenner. The unit was created in Paris because the headquarters of *Luftflotte Kommando 3* was located there from June 1940 to August 1944. It was eventually stationed in Falaise, but later located in Deauville, Rennes, Cherbourg, and Rambouillet. Secret Field Police units were also needed for service in the German Air Force. For this reason, several GFP formations were created completely staffed with *Luftwaffe* personnel.[16] It remained in the Paris region until the German withdrawal from the French capital in July 1944. In 1945, it was at the disposal of *Oberkommando West*.

GFP-626

GFP-626—Transferred to Poland in March 1941.[17] In the summer of 1941 it was attached to *Panzer Gruppe 1* (later re-designated as First Panzer Army) in Russia. In 1945, it was still operating under this army in Slovakia.

Final Note on the GFP Garrison Command

GFP-625 (L) was nominally under the *Feldpolizeidirektor bei der Luftflotte 3* command. The officer in charge of this post was *Feldpolizeidirektor* Hergt. Hergt would eventually be responsible for another Air Force GFP unit: GFP-743 (L). This unit was created in 1943 and would not belong to the Paris GFP garrison. It was led by *Feldpolizeikommissar* Keithahn, whose adjutant was *Feldpolizeikommissar* Denibir. In 1943 GFP-743 (L) was stationed in Brussels, Belgium. The number of GFP units assigned to Paris changed from time to time. One captured document, dated "22 March 1942" listed the following six GFP units under the *Leitender Feldpolizeidirektor beim Paris* post: GFP-11, GFP-550, GFP-603, GFP-649, GFP-733, and GFP-734.[18] Although the Paris garrison command held numerous GFP formations, many more were distributed in the countryside. What follows next is a roster of the GFP units attached to the various *Militarverwaltungsbezirks* (military administrative districts) that were created by the Germans for garrison purposes. These military administrative districts held specific German occupation forces, including particular GFP units which had been assigned to them.

GFP Garrison Command in Northwest France

The *Leitender Feldpolizeidirektor beim Chef des Militarverwaltungsbezirks A* included the following formations:

GFP-633

GFP-633 was led by *Feldpolizeidirektor* Kollath, later *Feldpolizeikommissar* Retzeck. Stationed in the Chateau-des-Spoir area, but later transferred to Orléans. On November 15, 1942, it was disbanded and its personnel absorbed into the SD.

GFP-644

GFP-644 was led by *Feldpolizeidirektor* Dr. Paulat, and stationed in Le Mans, with outer station posts in Redon, Quimper, St. Lo, St. Brieuc, Auray, Brest, Cherbourg, and Rennes.

GFP-701

GFP-701 was stationed in Rouen. On November 15, 1942, it was disbanded and its personnel handed over to the SD.

GFP-731

GFP-731 was stationed in Maisons-Lafitte. On November 15, 1942, it was disbanded and its personnel handed over to the SD. Like the other disbanded Secret Field Police units, the more physically fit members were earmarked for the Russian Front, while the lesser qualified members were earmarked to help staff the SD station posts in France.

GFP Garrison Command in Southwest France

The *Leitender Feldpolizeidirektor beim Chef des Militarverwaltungsbezirks B* included the following formations:

GFP-2

This GFP unit was stationed in Rennes. On November 15, 1942, it was disbanded and its personnel were handed over to the SD. With this and other disbanded GFP units, the SD station posts in France were established.

GFP-14

GFP-14 was Led by *Feldpolizeidirektor* Kurt Arlt, and later in 1941 by *Feldpolizeikommissar* Reighe. It was stationed in Bordeaux. Kurt Arlt was born on September 26, 1908, in

8. The GFP in the West and Scandinavia

Breslau, Silesia although according to Philip Greiner, Arlt was born in 1910. Greiner's report stated that Arlt was five feet-five inches in height, of stocky build, with blond hair, and a fair complexion. Greiner also said that Arlt was married and spoke French. According to his service record, in 1938 he was an *SS-Untersturmführer* (SS 2nd Lieutenant) with SS No.290380 in the *SD-Hauptamt*. From 1935 to 1939 he served as a *Kriminalrat* in the Breslau Gestapo.

From 1939, he served as the leader of a GFP unit in the Polish campaign. He served in this capacity during the French campaign in 1940 as leader of GFP-14. His unit was stationed in Bordeaux from 1940–1941. From June 1941 until 1944 he served as Field Police Director under the 213th Security Division in southern Russia. He was also affiliated with GFP-725 (also under the same security division). From 1944 until 1945 he served as a liaison officer for the GFP in the OKH (German Army High Command).[19] Kurt Arlt in many ways exemplified the interrelationship between the SS and the GFP, and therefore the intertwining of the SS with the Wehrmacht. He is also an example of the link between the GFP and the Gestapo. On November 15, 1942, GFP-14 was disbanded and its personnel handed over to the SD.

GFP-520

GFP-520 was led by *Feldpolizeikommissar* Dr. Ernst Wagner. In July 1940 Wagner was promoted to *Feldpolizeidirektor*. The unit was stationed in southwest France, under 18th Army. In the spring of 1941 it was transferred with 18th Army to Prussia in anticipation of the planned German invasion of the Soviet Union.

GFP-590

GFP-590 was led by *Feldpolizeidirektor* Benhard Schulze, and was stationed in Bordeaux, with outer station posts in Biarritz, Genevieve, Niort, Avignon, Paris, Royan, and Soulac-sur-Mer.

GFP-632

GFP-632 was stationed in La Rochelle. On November 15, 1942, it was disbanded and its personnel handed over to the SD.

GFP-732

GFP-732 was led by *Feldpolizeikommissar* Adrian and was stationed in Angers. On November 15, 1942, it was disbanded and its personnel handed over to the SD.

GFP Garrison Command in Northeast France

The *Leitender Feldpolizeidirektor beim Chef des Militarverwaltungsbezirks C* included the following formations:

GFP-7

GFP-7 was stationed in Dijon. It remained intact throughout the German occupation. It surrendered in 1945 as part of a bypassed German garrison in Lorient (*Festung Lorient*). One report claims that on November 15, 1942, it was disbanded & its personnel handed over to the SD.

GFP-30

GFP-30 was led by *Feldpolizeidirektor* Max Häuserer and stationed in Nancy. Häuserer was said to have been born in 1890 in Vienna. It was known that he was married but not known if he had children. The unit was located in Nancy with an outer station post in Chalons-sur-Marne. On November 15, 1942, it was disbanded and its personnel handed over to the SD.

GFP-611

GFP-611 was led by *Feldpolizeikommissar* Dr. Otto Begus. Stationed in Neufchâteau. Transferred to the Balkans under 12th Army in March 1941.

GFP-612

GFP-612 was transferred in February 1941 to the Balkans under the Second Army. Later served under Army Group "Center."

GFP-627

GFP-627 was led by *Feldpolizeidirektor* Cuno Schmidt, and later by *Feldpolizeikommissar* Jessen. This unit was stationed in Troyes. On November 15, 1942, it was disbanded and its personnel handed over to the SD.

GFP-639

GFP-639 was led by *Feldpolizeikommissar* Benno Kukawka. It was located in Nancy under the First Army. In the spring of 1941 it was transferred to Poland in anticipation of the German invasion of the USSR. It served under Second Panzer Army. In 1943, it was transferred to Montenegro. In 1944, it was located in Bosnia, and in 1945 it was stationed in Croatia.

GFP-647

GFP-647 was led by *Feldpolizeikommissar* Dr. Adalbert Hermann. This unit was stationed in Bordeaux under Seventh Army. In April 1941, it was transferred to Romania in anticipation of the Russian campaign.

GFP-736

GFP-736 was stationed in Besancon. On November 15, 1942, it was disbanded and its personnel handed over to the SD.

GFP Garrison Command in Northern France

Leitender Feldpolizeidirektor beim Militärbefehlshaber Nord-Frankreich was responsible not only for northern France, but for Belgium as well. Here the GFP possessed the following units[20]:

GFP-3

From 1941–1943 GFP-3 was led by *Feldpolizeikommissar* Paul Härtel and stationed in Lille, Boulevard de Liberte 49 in Pas-de-Calais. The unit was also responsible for the Belgian province of Hennegau. In 1944, it was shifted to the Netherlands. By 1945 it was located in Zwolle.

GFP-8

GFP-8 was led by *Feldpolizeikommissar* Schletitzki and stationed in Couter 23, Ghent. It was for employment in both eastern and western Flanders. In 1944, it was located in Holland, but may have been shifted to Copenhagen, Denmark in 1945.

GFP-530

GFP-530 was led by *Feldpolizeikommissar* Dunker and was stationed in Rue de Traversiere 6, in Brussels. It was earmarked for employment in the provinces of Antwerp, Brabant, and Limburg. It served in the West from 1940–1944.

GFP-540

GFP-540 was led by *Feldpolizeikommissar* Thoss and stationed initially in Paris, but in the beginning of 1941 was located in Laon, with outer station posts in Amiens, Rouen, St. Quentin, Lyon, Mailly-le Camp, Grasse, and Hyeres.

GFP-648

GFP-648 was led by *Feldpolizeikommissar* Eube and stationed in Emilie Dupont 18, in Lűttich, for service in the provinces of Lűttich and Namur. During the fall of 1944 the unit was dissolved.[21]

GFP-716

GFP-716 was led by *Feldpolizeikommissar* Jentsch. This unit was stationed in Arras, and had outer station posts in St. Lo, St. Martin, Forges-les-eaux, Canchy and Fruges.

The GFP groups who were attached to the various German army groups and army commands in France included the following formations: in the region of Army Group "D"—part of GFP-1, stationed in Dijon; Army Group "A"—part of GFP-1, stationed in Saint-Germaine; First Army—GFP-590 and GFP-639,[22] both stationed in Nancy; Sixth Army—GFP-560, stationed in Dinard; Seventh Army—GFP-644, stationed in Bordeaux; Ninth Army—GFP-580, stationed in Rouen; and 15th Army—GFP-131, was stationed in Dinard but later transferred to Torcoing, NE of Lille. GFP-131 was led by *Feldpolizeikommissar* Brosius. Its HQ was located at Rue de Lille 47, Tourcoing.

As for the fate of these units, GFP-1 left on April 25, 1941, towards Köslin, in Western Pomerania. Today this town is known as Koszalin and is part of Poland. GFP-1 was reorganized at Köslin before being assigned to serve under the 207th Security Division in the planned invasion of the Soviet Union. On July 26, 1942, it was stationed in Konotop, in the Ukraine. It was later transferred to Trieste, Italy in 1944. It operated from that city until the end of the war. GFP-590 served in the West from 1940 until the end of the war, while

GFP-639 later served in Russia from 1941–1943, and the Balkans from 1943–1945. GFP-560 served under Sixth Army in the region of Army Group "South." Sometime in 1943 it operated in and around Kharkov. GFP-644 served in the West throughout the war. Beginning June 1941 GFP-580 served under Ninth Army in central Russia. GFP-131 served in France until 1944. In 1945, it was located in the Netherlands.

In addition, three GFP units were listed as "reserve" formations under the *OKW-Amt Ausland/Abwehr* ("Armed Forces High Command–Foreign Department / Army Intelligence Office"). These units were: (1) GFP-312,[23] (2) GFP-540,[24] and (3) GFP-610.[25] These three formations were labeled "for special employment" so they were considered a sort of strategic reserve.[26] GFP-312 and GFP-610 were transferred to Army Group "A" in late 1942 or early 1943. GFP-312 ended up serving in the 17th Army in Russia, ending the war under the control of the German Commander in Hungary; while GFP-610 was transferred to the 14th Army in Italy in 1944. GFP-540 continued to serve in the West until the end of the war.

From 1940–1941, about thirty-five separate GFP groups served in France, Belgium, and the Netherlands. One unit (GFP-629) operated out of Oslo, Norway from 1940–1944. GFP-171 was stationed in Denmark beginning in April 1940. It remained stationed in Copenhagen until 1941 when it was transferred to Romania. Another unit, GFP-735, served in northern Finland from 1941–1944. By 1945 GFP-735 was located in northern Norway. All GFP units in The Netherlands were withdrawn immediately after the conquest of that country, with the exception of a small detail which was tasked with protecting Kaiser Wilhelm II. This was the former head of Imperial Germany from 1888–1918:

> An inspection trip to Holland was refrained from since the OKH had already ordered the GFP to withdraw from Holland immediately after the cessation of hostilities. Only one detail comprising one Field Police Secretary and 3–4 soldiers remained in Holland, and this, upon Hitler's request, was stationed in "Huis Doorn," the home of former Kaiser Wilhelm II. They were to protect him from undue inquisitiveness on the part of members of the Armed Forces, especially since several unpleasant incidents had already occurred. This "Huis Doorn" detail was charged only with this protective mission and had no other authority. They were frequently invited to dine with the Kaiser and were recalled after his death to be employed elsewhere.[27]

The detail to "protect" the former German Imperial ruler ended on June 4, 1941, when Wilhelm II passed away. During the German invasion of the Netherlands, Winston Churchill who was First Lord of the Admiralty and had yet to become Prime Minister, had offered "asylum and protection" in the United Kingdom for the former German monarch.[28] Wilhelm II rebuffed Churchill's offer and remained in The Netherlands. His refusal did not stem from a fear that he would be tried for crimes against humanity for his role in World War I. Although the French had requested that The Netherlands hand over the Kaiser in 1919, he was never formally tried or convicted of any war crimes by the Allies. His refusal to take advantage of Churchill's offer was purely out of nationalism and to prevent the English from reaping a political propaganda coup.

Many of the GFP units that had been stationed in France and Belgium in 1940 were either transferred to the Russian Front shortly before the eastern campaign began on June 22, 1941, or were disbanded in 1942 and their personnel mainly absorbed into the SD.[29] When the SD disbanded about seventeen GFP groups and absorbed their personnel, only 12–13 GFP formations remained active in France and Belgium. About 1,300 members of the GFP in France were transferred *en masse* into the *Sicherheitspolizei* and *Sicherheitsdienst* by an executive order dated April 25, 1942, which reassigned these men from the *Militärbefehlshaber Frankreich* into the Sipo/SD.[30] One source puts the transfer at 2,000 GFP men, most of whom had been former *Kriminalpolizei* members.[31] The difference in these two figures can be explained by the decision to send the more physically fit members of the GFP to the Russian Front. When most of the GFP units were disbanded in France, seven hundred of the younger and more able-bodied members were immediately sent to serve in GFP units in Russia. The older GFP members remained to staff the numerous Sipo and SD station posts. It should be noted that these older members had more criminal police experience:

> Keitel supported Canaris's general strategy but did not dare to flagrantly oppose Himmler [the head of the SS]. He eventually negotiated an agreement with the SS that disbanded most GFP groups in France. The SS, in turn, immediately drafted the demobilized members of the GFP into the Black Corps. Younger agents were sent to the eastern front while older policemen returned to France for service in the Sipo and SD under the command of Helmut Knochen.[32]

On the face, it appears that this transfer of the younger members of the GFP for service on the Russian Front might have been done with three possible motives in mind. First, service on the Eastern Front was harsh and brutal. Even so-called "rear-area" security, or service immediately behind the front lines was physically and mentally exhausting as there was a huge guerrilla uprising which the Germans had to deal with. Therefore, service in Russia was considered extremely dangerous. Things were so chaotic behind the front lines that Germans serving there would often recite a ditty: *vorne Russen, hinter Russen, und dazwischen schueßen* ("Russians in front, Russians behind, and in between shooting"). Therefore, older-age GFP personnel were less desirable on the Russian Front than younger and more physically fit men who could handle the fierce fighting.

Secondly, most of the older GFP personnel who remained in France and were absorbed into the Sipo/SD had seen extensive service in various police organizations like the Criminal Police, State Secret Police, and even beat detectives from the regular German Police. Therefore, their experience would come in handy combating resistance activities in occupied France. Finally, the type of "work" which the GFP was assigned in the East did not require much guile or deductive reasoning as would be required from a police detective. It appears by their "exploits," that the mission of the GFP in the USSR was much akin to the job of the SS *Einsatzgruppen*—the SS killing units. The men of the GFP formations in Russia often took part in murderous drives and operations. On a regular basis, their actions included shooting all captured Jews, partisan suspects and political commissars that fell into their hands. This all indicates that there was intent behind the decision on the part of the SS to assign those 700 younger age GFP men for the Russian Front.

Organization of the GFP in Belgium and Northern France

A total of seven GFP groups were posted to operate in both Belgium and northern France during the German occupation. Four of these GFP units were under the command of the *Leitender Feldpolizeidirektor beim Militärbefehlshaber Nord-Frankreich*. Their *Aussenstelle* (branch offices) were as follows:

GFP-3

Main Headquarters–Brussels, assigned to guard the Belgian King. It was then transferred to Lille, with outer station branch offices in Valenciennes, Cassel, Arras, and Wimereux.

GFP-8

Main Headquarters–Ghent, with outer station branch offices in Brügge and Kortrijk.

GFP-131

Main Headquarters–Tourcoing, just across the Belgium border in France, with outer station branch offices in Aire and Antwerp. *Feldpolizeikommissar* Brosius led this unit.

GFP-501

Main Headquarters–Tourcoing (near Lille). Moved to Prussia in the spring of 1941 when the German 16th Army left Belgium and northern France in anticipation of the German invasion of the USSR.

GFP-530

Main Headquarters–Brussels, with no outer station branch offices given that the entire unit was devoted to working within the city of Brussels. It was then stationed in Lille under 16th Army but moved to Poland in the spring of 1941.

GFP-621

Main Headquarters–Brussels. It was transferred to the Balkans under 12th Army in March 1941.

GFP-637 (L)

Main Headquarters–Brussels, with outer station posts in Lille and Noailles. There it operated under the command of *Luftflotte 2*.

GFP-648

Main Headquarters–Luttich, with outer station branch offices in Huy, Arel, and Ferrieres.

Other GFP formations in Belgium included:

GFP-712

Main Headquarters–Antwerp, with outer station branch offices in Brussels and Hasselt. *Feldpolizeikommissar* Salaw led this unit. It was later transferred to Namur.

GFP-738

Main Headquarters–Mons, with outer station branch offices in Loveral, Namur, and Tournai. *Feldpolizeikommissar* Esser led this unit. It was created on June 21, 1941.

GFP-739

Main Headquarters–Namur, Belgium. It was created on June 21, 1941.

GFP-740

Main Headquarters–Brussels. It was created on June 21, 1941.

The GFP, the Command Staff and the Military Administrative Staff in France

The *Militärbefehlshaber in Frankreich* was divided into two parts: (1) the *Kommandostab* (Command Staff) and (2) the *Militärverwaltungsstab* (Military Administrative Staff). In 1941, it was Major Dernbach who was in charge of the GFP office under the *Militärbefehlshaber in Frankreich*. The *Kommandostab* directed the various *Landesschützen Bataillonen* (Regional Defense Battalions) which the German Army had stationed in occupied France. On occasion, it also controlled the numerous GFP units. Until 1942 the GFP was administered and controlled by the *Militärverwaltungsstab*.[33] The GFP involvement in stolen French art occurred during the German occupation and under orders of the Military Administrative Staff, who in turn was asked by the German embassy in Paris to provide GFP personnel to help confiscate works of art. The GFP was active in many seizures, especially for *Reichsmarschall* Herman Göring who considered himself an "art connoisseur." The head of the GFP in Paris was Major Greiner. After the war Greiner claimed that he was personally opposed to the illegal seizure of French artworks by the Nazis. Nevertheless, he agreed to subordinate GFP officers to the Paris embassy as long as confiscation operations were approved by the *Militärverwaltungsstab*.

As far as confiscation of Jewish property in occupied France is concerned an "accord" between the German Army and SS was reached on October 4, 1941. It allowed GFP units to seize Jewish property in the occupied regions of France, but it also denied the SS the same rights, thus weakening SS authority (at least temporarily) on French soil as German Army resistance to SS "encroachment" of occupied France increased.[34] Of course once the SD was able to absorb a good number of their former personnel from the GFP formations stationed there, and use them to create the various SD station posts throughout the countryside, the German Army began to lose the fight over who would be responsible for combating resistance in France, as well as who would be ultimately responsible for "Jewish matters." This was a clear victory for the SS over the Army, and was one case where the Army resisted the SS and did not initially wish to cooperate.

Comportment of the GFP in the West vs. the East

While the men of the GFP conducted themselves quite ruthlessly in the USSR, taking direct part in the Holocaust, their behavior in the West was less direct. The GFP in the West participated in apprehending Jews, confiscating works of art and all manner of Jewish property. They also established GFP jails that held people suspected of pro–Allied activities for interrogation. The GFP selected hostages for executions performed in reprisal of partisan activities. The GFP was responsible for tracking down opponents of the German occupation. Fighting the partisans ended officially in the fall of 1942 for GFP units assigned to the German Army. GFP formations under Army command were now relegated to more conventional assignments like chasing deserters, Black Marketers, and counterintelligence work. In essence, the Sipo and SD removed the task of hunting down members of the French underground from the Secret Field Police in the West.

The absorption of 1,300 former GFP men into the SD however, meant that ex–GFP men would still hunt down partisans and partisan supporters under Sipo/SD auspices. Their participation in the arrest of Jews for transport to the extermination camps in Poland,

and the expropriation of stolen Jewish property made the GFP culpable in the Holocaust, even if these men did it while serving in the Sipo and SD. However, the Nazi agenda in the West was different than in the East. While the Soviet Union was to be "cleansed" of the *Untermenschen* (subhumans), to make way for future German colonization, the population in the West would "only" be cleansed of Jews, communists, and anyone offering resistance to Nazi hegemony. The war in the Soviet Union was literally a slaughter characterized by the term *vernichtungskrieg* (war of annihilation). This is clearly seen by the fact that of the estimated twenty-five million people which the USSR lost, only twelve million were soldiers, while thirteen million were non-combatants. This figure indicates that the civilian population was targeted for extermination.

A case in point depicting the differences in the manner in which the GFP in the West behaved as opposed to their actions in the East, was the capture and interrogation of a British bomber crewmember, Sergeant Harry Levy, by a Secret Field Police unit stationed in Brussels, Belgium. The key factor in this episode is that this British airman was Jewish:

> At the *Feldpolizei* headquarters we passed queues of men and women waiting for documents and all the other paraphernalia necessary for citizens living in an occupied city. As we entered the building, the two Germans on either side of me, people looked at us out of the corner of an eye, not turning their heads. Inside the building there were no screams, no frightening sounds. Soldiers and civilians went about their business. I was struck by the normality of the place. The officer, who interrogated me, just typed the answers. Despite my obvious lies he made no comment—seemingly, a clerk in soldier's uniform.[35]

In spite of the obvious fact that Levy was Jewish, he was nonetheless treated well by the members of the GFP. As a sergeant of the Royal Air Force, Levy eventually made it to a German run POW camp for Allied soldiers. What this episode shows is the difference in the manner in which GFP units operated in the West, as opposed to their actions in the East. Had the place of Levy's capture been the Soviet Union instead of Belgium, it is almost certain that he would have been executed immediately after questioning. This would be more so if his interrogators had known that he was Jewish. Yet, because he was captured in the West, and was a member of the British military, he survived interrogation by the Secret Field Police, incarceration in a German POW camp, and was eventually liberated when the war ended.

There were three GFP operatives in Brussels who oversaw Sergeant Levy's arrest and interrogation. The first was *Oberfeldwebel* Frithjof Kleinpaul.[36] Before the war, Kleinpaul had been a professor in a commercial school in Leipzig. Kleinpaul had a good working knowledge of French. There was also *Feldpolizeiinspektor* Paul Brosan, who lived in Berlin where he had worked for the Criminal Police before the war.[37] Then there was *Feldwebel* Alois Pederzani, who was living in Lubeck in 1940.[38] Pederzani was fluent in English and was an interpreter working at the GFP office at Rue Traversiere, in Brussels. A special GFP prison was established at Fort De Huy, in Belgium. Between May 1940 and September 5, 1944, the Secret Field Police used the fort as a detention center. In total 1,240 French citizens and about 6,000 Belgian, English, Czech, Polish, Italian, Hungarian, Austrian, and German citizens were also housed in this fort as prisoners of the GFP.

Although the behavior of the GFP in France and Belgium was far better than how they operated in Russia, it can be said that the French and Belgians were treated much harsher than the people of The Netherlands, Denmark, and Norway. In these occupied countries, the Nazis saw the people as Nordic so their comportment there was to be "more considerate." The actions of the GFP units operating in Scandinavia were quite different from the actions of the GFP elsewhere. In the Netherlands, Denmark and Norway Secret Field Police units were restricted to making investigations which only dealt with the protection of the German Armed Forces. Those powers were extended substantially in France and Belgium, where the GFP forces were allowed (until 1942) to directly combat all resistance networks, allied espionage and sabotage efforts. In particular, and in contrast to Scandinavia, the GFP was allowed to conduct individual and mass arrests. Those civilians that were apprehended were interrogated or used as hostages. In case of any underground activity, the hostages would be shot. In this way the behavior of the GFP in France and Belgium mimicked the actions of the SS. This was something that the GFP was completely forbidden to do in the Netherlands, Denmark and Norway.

It is true that the life of a German soldier performing occupation duty in the West was far better than the brutal and violent life and death struggle of the German *landser* on the Russian Front. But Germans garrisoning the western countries of Europe could not expect a completely peaceful tour of duty. According to reports listed by the Secret Field Police in Belgium-North France, between 1941 and 1945 French and Belgium resistance forces assassinated around 500 German soldiers. In addition, from September 1942 until August 1944 around 1,000 Belgian and French collaborators were also executed by the resistance.[39] Interrogations by GFP officials in Scandinavian countries did not involve torture. In France and Belgium, it was possible that a GFP official might rough up a suspect, but this all depended on what evidence they had on the suspect or lack thereof. What was the overall behavior of the Secret Field Police in the West? The answer lies mostly in the manner in which these GFP units conducted themselves from 1940–1944.

Suppression of Resistance in France

The GFP played a central role in suppressing resistance and dissent in France from 1940–1942. We know for example, that the first major operation which the Secret Field Police undertook in large numbers happened in June 1941. This was the mass arrest of six hundred well-known and prominent communist activists in France.[40] This roundup coincided with the German invasion of the Soviet Union that same month, and was most likely launched in order to prevent these communist leaders from organizing a resistance to that invasion. The rest of 1941 was spent fighting the French *Maquisard* (the French underground) in the region of Paris. The various GFP formations tasked with this mission were led by *Feldpolizeidirektor* Kurt Moritz. Another action worthy of mention in 1941 in which numerous GFP units took part, was the apprehension of eighty suspected resistance fighters in Caen during a roundup which was organized by the Gestapo office in that French city.[41] An operation employing the GFP was also prepared and coordinated by the *Abwehr* between June and October 1941. The *Abwehrleitstelle Paris*—the German Army Counterespionage Section stationed in Paris was able to penetrate a French resistance cell that was finally cracked in the fall of 1941. During the subsequent arrests, every single GFP unit on French soil took part in the apprehension of the identifiable operatives:

> The German infiltrators, who were controlling the communication with London, managed to minimize what London learned and stall any significant sabotage, intending to delay action against the network as long as possible in order to learn as much as they could about its capacities and intentions. But after attacks on German officers in Paris on 10 and 15 September, Reile became concerned that the network might already be passing to action and persuaded Colonel Rudolph that the time for arrests had come. On 9 October [1941], they launched a crackdown of unprecedented scale,

engaging all the units of the Geheime Feldpolizei in France and Belgium. Within a few days, 962 individuals were behind bars.[42]

As far as Vichy France was concerned, the GFP in France worked in close unison with the newly created *Brigades spéciales des Renseignements généraux* ("General Intelligence Special Brigades"). These pro–Axis units searched for French partisans whether they were communist or not, and also assisted in rounding up Jews for deportation from France to extermination camps in the East. Apparently, the Germans found the *Seconde Brigades Spéciale* (Second Special Service Brigade) to be a particularly trustworthy and aggressive French unit, which they employed frequently. In practice and from the very beginning, the Secret Field Police in France exercised suppression of resistance activities and functioned much like the Gestapo. Early on the Secret Field Police realized that operating without the assistance of the French police would prove problematic:

> From a numerical point of view, it is obvious that a couple of hundred men of the GFP could not conduct any large-scale operations. Its limited strength forced the GFP to collaborate very closely with the French police and led to the creation of a so-called *Kommission auf Kapitalverbrechen Bekämpfung* ("Commission to Combat Capital Crimes"), which consisted of GFP and French criminal police. Up to 1942, that is, up to the time when the Senior SS and Police Leader appeared in France in May 1942, the collaboration between the GFP and the French police was absolutely loyal, correct, and legal.[43]

Until the middle 1942 the GFP also investigated the French civilian population in conjunction with the local *Gendarmerie* (rural constabulary). In retaliation for a *Maquisard* attack on German forces, 95–98 hostages were rounded up and shot by the GFP and SD in the French cities of Nantes and Bordeaux.[44] The execution of these hostages occurred on December 15, 1941. The hostages selected to be shot were members of the French communist party.[45] Although three-quarters of the victims were close to communist circles, over half of them were Jewish. This suggests that perhaps their selection for elimination may not have simply been for their communist affiliation but because they also happened to be Jewish.

On March 9, 1942, a decree from the *Führer* gave the Sipo and SD control of the main repressive powers in France. A further *Führerbefehl* ("Leader Decree") dated "25 April 1942" transferred all executive powers regarding the GFP from the OKW to the RSHA, or *Reichssicherheitshauptamt* (the Reich Main Security Office).[46] After 1942, GFP units which remained under Army control did not take any further active role against the *Maquisards*. German Army commands only kept very weak GFP units of about 50–60 men each, which were employed (as stated previously) against actual criminals, deserters, investigating cut phone lines, as well as individuals operating on the black markets in occupied France.[47] The closest that these GFP units came to fighting the *Maquis* was to investigate the thousands of cut telephone lines that would occur within occupied France, Belgium, and the Netherlands, as well as cases of theft of military property. Thus in 1942 the SS expanded their powers in occupied France at the expense of Army intelligence (the *Abwehr*). At the beginning of 1942 the *Abwehr* and GFP in France were limited to protecting the German Armed Forces and its military installations from foreign saboteurs and agents. About twelve to thirteen GFP units remained intact in France after the SD absorbed seventeen GFP formations. These 12–13 were employed by the German Army in France. The GFP personnel absorbed into the SD took the war to the French *Maquisards*. In spring 1941, just shortly before the start of the Russian campaign in June, GFP forces in France & Belgium were comprised fifty-one units. For a detailed listing of the posting of these units, please refer to Appendix VI.

Cases Studies of GFP Units in the West, 1941–1945

The following are some additional examples of GFP comportment in the West, by way of unit histories from some of those GFP formations and the operations which they took part in. By listing these and comparing them with the behavior of GFP formations elsewhere, we can come to an honest evaluation of the overall attitude of the GFP in the West, as compared to their behavior in the East and in the Balkans. From all accounts, it appears that the principal reason for the difference in their actions by region, was mostly based on racial and political matters. While serving in the West under the German Army, the GFP was to limit indiscriminate torture and murder. This was especially true in the initial occupation period from 1940–1941. However, once these former GFP men were absorbed into the Sipo and SD the same men had no qualms in applying such heavy-handed tactics. As the French and Belgian underground expanded their attacks, the German security forces began to apply greater pressure and harsher tactics.

GFP-2

This unit was established on August 26, 1939, in the city of Stralsund, in *Wehrkreis II* (Military District II), whose headquarters was the city of Stettin.[48] Stralsund lies on the North Sea coast, northeast of Rostock. As a point of reference, the old German city of Stettin lies to the southeast of Stralsund. Stettin is now on Polish territory and is called "Szcezecin." The city of Stettin lies near the mouth of the Oder River. At the beginning of the war, GFP-2 was serving as a frontier-guard unit by Deutsche Krone under *Abschnitt-Kommando II*. On October 26, 1939, it was transferred to *Wehrkreis VI*, whose headquarters was Münster. *Wehrkreis VI* bordered the Netherlands. On March 4, 1940, GFP-2 was operating directly under the command of Army Group "A." It was this army group, composed of one hundred and thirty-six divisions (grouped into three armies, the 4th, 12th and 16th) which would attack through Luxembourg and Belgium and outflank the French Maginot line when the campaign in France began on May 10, 1940.[49] By June 18, 1940, the unit had been assigned to the *Militärbefehlshaber in Frankreich* (German Army Military Commander "France"). At the beginning of 1941, GFP-2 was still operating under the *Militärbefehlshaber in Frankreich*. At this time, the unit's headquarters was located in Rennes, with two *Kommissariate* (commissariats): (1) in Rennes, and (2) in Brest.[50] The unit was disbanded sometime in the second half of 1942. Its personnel were returned to the SS/SD.

Corporal Willy (Wilhelm) Drechsler. was a perfect example of one GFP member who was absorbed back into the Sipo/SD in 1942. Drechsler was born in the region of Hamburg-Bergstedt on August 3, 1903. From April 26, 1942, to November 11, 1942, he was assigned to GFP-2. After GFP-2 was disbanded in the second half of 1942, Drechsler was returned to Germany and temporarily assigned to the GFP replacement battalion which supplied personnel to the GFP units in the field.[51] He remained with the 600th Training & Replacement Battalion for twelve days in November 1942 before being reassigned to the SD. He eventually ended the war serving in the Gestapo. His career is indicative of the apparent connections between the Wehrmacht/GFP and the SS. Corporal Willy Drechsler appears to have remained with the Gestapo for the remainder of the war, given that his discharge paper from an Allied military internment camp indicated that he was a member of the Gestapo when he was released.

GFP-3

This unit was established on August 25, 1939, in *Wehrkreis VIII* in Leobschütz for service with Border Command 3 in Oppeln. On October 26, 1940, it was sent to the West Wall under Army Group "B." On June 27, 1940, the unit was transferred to the *Militärbefehlshaber Belgien-Nordfrankreich*. In March 1943 GFP-3 reported on the espionage activity of the "Belo" resistance group in Belgium. The report included notes on the discovery of weapons in the previous month. The report also mentioned that during the search of a local house, an English infantry rifle and other objects were found inside a fertilizer container. It was requested that more attention be brought to investigating areas that were seen as unpleasant (such as latrines, dung piles, etc.), because it appeared that resistance cells were hiding weapons in these places. In 1944 GFP-3 was responsible for arresting 134 Belgian and French citizens involved in resistance activities. In addition, fifteen of the twenty-nine Allied aviators who were being hidden by Belgian civilians and caught in April 1944 in Belgium were apprehended by GFP-3. The unit also took prisoner numerous French and Belgian civilians who were ignoring the German draft call for workers. This group was also responsible for bringing down the Belgian *Voix du Nord* ("Voice of the North") resistance cell.[52] GFP-3 operated in Belgium until the fall of 1944 when it was moved to the Netherlands. The unit was shifted to the town of Zwolle, in the Dutch province of Overijssel. There they continued to work at digging up Dutch resistance to German rule until the end of the war.

GFP-7

This unit was established on August 28, 1939, in *Wehrkreis V* in the town of Donauschingen, which is located in the Black Forest, southwest of the federal state of Baden-Württemberg in the Schwarzwald-Baar district.[53] The headquarters for *Wehrkreis V* was the city of Stuttgart. *Geheime Feldpolizei Gruppe 7* was attached to *Generalkommando der Grenztruppen Oberrhein* (Corps Command for Frontier Troops "Upper Rhine"), which itself had only been created two days earlier (on August 26, 1939). *Generalkommando der Grenztruppen Oberrhein* was renamed *25 Armeekorps* less than a month later, on September 17, 1939. On December 13, 1940, GFP-7 was attached to the Seventh Army and was made a part of the German occupation of France. Its headquarters was located in the city of Dijon under Administrative District "C" (*Verwaltungsbezirk "C"*), of *Militärbefehlshaber in Frankreich*. Between October 1939 and June 1940 GFP-7 was attached to the German Seventh Army in the Upper Rhine region of southwest Germany. The unit was briefly under the command of the German 12th Army in July and August of 1940, and was then shifted to Sixth Army between December 1940 and April 1941. In May 1941, *25 Armeekorps* was transferred to the German Seventh Army—and stationed in Brittany. GFP-7 however, remained for a time in Eastern France, since it had been established that Eastern France contained a large number of French partisans at this time. Although the headquarters for GFP-7 was the French city of Dijon, it was also partly located in Besancon.[54]

In July 1944, following the U.S. breakout at St. Lo, the bulk of the German 265th Infantry Division became cut off and was eventually trapped in the port city of Lorient (in Brittany).[55] The city was quickly designated a "fortress" by Hitler. One of the units which ended up with the trapped garrison was GFP-7.[56] *Festung Lorient* held out until the end of the war, surrendering on May 10, 1945. The French citizens trapped in the city were actually allowed to mail letters to relatives in Allied occupied France. It is the rare instance where

Vichy French stamps were permitted to be circulated in liberated France. The Germans stamped the "Petain" stamps with the words *"Festung Lorient"* in order for the Free French postal system to permit the French letters (with Vichy French stamps) to travel through their postal system.[57] GFP-7 remained intact as a formation and continued to perform its various missions, to which was now added the inspection of civilian mail going out of and coming into the city. Obviously, censorship and counter-espionage played a role in this scrutiny of civilian mail.

GFP-8

This unit was formed on August 26, 1939, in *Wehrkreis VI* for initial operations in the Eifel region. It took part in the campaign against France in the summer of 1940. From June 20, 1940, until the German withdrawal from France, the unit was under the command of the *Militärbefehlshaber Belgien-Nord Frankreich*. It was led by *Feldpolizeikommissar* Schletitzki and was stationed in Ghent, Belgium. By the fall of 1944 the formation was under Army Group "B" in the Lower Rhine region. In 1945, the unit was transferred to Denmark and stationed in Copenhagen. While operating in France and Belgium GFP-8 cooperated with *Abwehrtrupp 364*,[58] making an arrest of over twenty members of the Belgian-French "Zero" espionage network.[59] This was affirmed by corroborating documents.[60] For example, a report from the spring of 1943 stated that on March 24 two Belgian citizens were apprehended by members of *Reserve Grenadier Bataillon 350* at a local checkpoint. They were caught carrying about 2,000 anti–German flyers.[61] This reserve battalion belonged to the German *189 Reserve Division*, which at this time was stationed in Montluçon in central *France* (on the banks of the Cher River).[62] The German report from this unit stated that the two Belgians were eventually turned over to GFP-8, for further interrogation.

This indicates that GFP-8 was located in central France in the spring of 1943. During the course of the investigation begun by the apprehension of the two Belgians carrying the anti–German propaganda flyers, this secret field police unit apprehended an additional twenty-nine French and Belgian citizens and confiscated forty-two knives, eleven pistols and two rifles.[63] Additional reports indicate that in the spring of 1944 GFP-8 was no longer operating in central France, but was transferred to the region of Belgium and Northern France. In January 1944 GFP-8 captured a former Belgian Army lieutenant, named Bruyninckx, who was caught with arms and a radio. This former lieutenant turned out to be a member of the Belgian pro–Allied espionage group "Zero." Unfortunately, the report did not state "how" GFP-8 was able to gather this information—that is—whether they employed coercive tactics in obtaining this information or if lieutenant Bruyninckx willingly gave up this critical bit of information. However, it was standard practice by the Security Police, the Criminal Police and the Secret Field Police to employ *verschärfte Vernehmung* ("intensified interrogation") if a suspect refused to speak.[64] In April 1944 GFP-8 (again cooperating with *Abwehrtrupp 364*), was able to apprehend and arrest twenty-one members of the Belgian espionage group "Voice of the North."[65] In 1945 the unit ended the war stationed in Copenhagen, Denmark.

GFP-11

This formation was probably created in August 1939, and attached to *Generalkommando der Grenztruppen Saarpfalz* (General Commander of Border Troops "Saar-Palatinate").

From July 1940 through the fall of 1942, this GFP unit remained stationed in Paris, France. On August 21, 1941 a French national, Pierre Georges, who was later to be known in the French underground as "Colonel Fabien," killed a German midshipman named Moser at the Barbès Metro Station in Paris. Enraged, the head of the *Militär Befehlshaber in Frankreich* ("German Military Commander in France") announced that immediately French citizens detained by the Germans would be considered hostages, and therefore liable to be shot.[66] According to General Hans Speidel (who in August 1940 had become Chief of Staff to the *Militär Befehlshaber in Frankreich*),[67] it was his commanding officer that had personally directed that GFP-610 be tasked with investigating the case, while GFP-11 was to be charged with selecting the victims that would be shot in reprisal.[68] Initially (at least until about late 1942), the Germans would choose either French communists or Jews for retaliation shootings. In the fall of 1942 GFP-11 was disbanded and its personnel were transferred into the SD.

GFP-14

This unit was established on August 26, 1939, in *Wehrkreis VIII* (Breslau, Silesia). It was raised in Breslau and was immediately attached to *Grenzschutz-Abschnitt-Kommando 14* (Frontier Guard Command 14). The unit served in the Polish campaign under *"Korps Gienanth"*—a formation led by *General der Kavallerie* (Cavalry General) Curt Ludwig Freiherr von Gienanth. *Korps Gienanth* was established from *Grenzschutz-Abschnittskommando 14* on September 8, 1939. It was re-titled *Höheres Kommando XXXVI* on October 19, 1939. Gienanth had been in charge of Fortress Command "Breslau" to which *Grenzschutz-Abschnitt-Kommando 14* was a part.[69] *"Korps Gienanth"* operated in Poland from September 8 to October 19, 1939, when the unit was disbanded and General von Gienanth was assigned to lead the 36th Mountain Corps.[70] On July 5, 1940, GFP-14 was serving under *Militärbefehlshaber in Frankreich* with its headquarters located in the French city of Bordeaux. It also operated in Biarritz and Hendaye, on the Franco-Spanish frontier. On October 1, 1942, it was still located in Bordeaux, Biarritz and Hendaye, under *Militärverwaltungsbezirk "B"* of *Militärbefehlshaber in Frankreich*.[71]

The French and Belgian underground had established an escape route for runaway Allied soldiers. This escape route was eventually nicknamed the "Comet Line." Hundreds of Allied POWs and downed airmen were brought back to England through the "Comet Line." One of the greatest successes of the secret field police in the West was the eventual disruption of this important Allied escape network and the capture of most of its French and Belgian underground members. This had been accomplished through the employment of collaborators who betrayed the network to the Secret Field Police. A very unusual case occurred in Belgium towards the end of the war in which the Secret Field Police was involved. In 1945, the Secret Field Police arrested a German national, Albert Dykers, who had married a local girl in the Belgian town of Sint-Niklaas. He had served there as a German policeman. His crime was that he had been working as an operative in the Belgian resistance. Perhaps marriage to his Belgium wife might have influenced him to betray his country, although it is equally possible that hatred of the Nazi regime might have served as the catalyst.[72]

GFP-30

This formation was established on August 26, 1939, in *Wehrkreis XVII* under *Abschnitt Kommando Wien* in Austria. It was led by *Feldpolizeidirektor* Häuserer and was engaged in

The Comet and Shelburne Route of Escape for Allied Servicemen Behind Enemy Lines, 1941–1944 (map by author).

Poland from the start of the campaign on September 1, 1939, until shortly before the start of the French campaign on May 10, 1940. Häuserer was said to have been born in 1890 in Vienna. It was known that he was married but not known if he had children. GFP-30 was employed in the West from 1941–1942 as part of the German occupation forces under the command of the *Militärbefehlshaber in Frankreich*. In France, it was stationed in the city of Nancy, with a branch office in Chalons-sur-Marne. On November 15, 1942, it was disbanded and its personnel handed over to the SD. The men then served in numerous SD offices all across France. Although very little is known about GFP-30 it was listed here as an example of one of many GFP units that were disbanded and their personnel reabsorbed into the RSHA (the Reich SS Main Security Office).

GFP-131

This unit was established on August 26, 1939, in East Prussia (*Wehrkreis I*) under *"Gruppe Brand"* which was attached to the commander of *Festung Königsberg* (Fortress Königsberg). The 15th Army was established in France on January 15, 1941 under General Curt Hasse. At this time, GFP-131 was assigned directly to this Germany army command. The formation was located in the French town of Dinard.[73] This secret field police group remained under the command of the 15th Army well into 1945. In 1944, during the retreat from France, GFP-131 withdrew north with 15th Army towards Holland. In September, it took part in the German defense of "Operation Market Garden." During "Market Garden" the unit helped to interrogate captured British paratroopers. GFP-131 was eventually stationed in Cologne, Germany in December 1944. At the beginning of 1945 it was still located in Cologne. In April 1945, as 15th Army formed a part of the German forces trapped in the Ruhr pocket, GFP-131 was still under its command.[74] Very little data has been forthcoming regarding this unit but it was included here as an example of a GFP formation that was not disbanded in 1942. It appears that it performed intelligence missions of a military nature.

GFP-161

Secret Field Police Group 161 was established on August 26, 1939, in East Prussia. That same year the unit was located in Greifswald as a replacement force for the Secret Field Police. From 1941 to 1944 GFP-161 was stationed in France under the Seventh Army. It remained trapped in the Channel Islands of Guernsey and Jersey until the end of the war. It spent most of its history reporting on cut communications caused by French resistance, chasing black marketers, German deserters, and other military intelligence tasks.[75] The HQ of this unit was located in the Pareme district of St. Malo, a coastal city in Brittany. The unit had outer station posts in Granville, Havelot, and on the islands of Jersey and Guernsey. This GFP formation served as the intelligence unit for the 319th Static Infantry Division, which garrisoned both English islands throughout the war.

GFP-550 and Philip Greiner

This unit was created on August 26, 1939 in *Wehrkreis V*. According to the files of the former commander of this unit, Philip Greiner, when created, GFP-550 was composed of thirty men: one field police director, about eight field police commissioners, approximately twelve field police secretaries, and nine clerks, drivers and orderlies.[76] Greiner was assigned to head GFP-550. For the French campaign, Secret Field Police Group 550, together with GFP-7 were assigned to the Seventh German Army. Greiner's post-war interrogation report stated that he was almost five feet eight inches tall and had sunken, gray eyes. His face was round and he had what was considered a medium build. At the time (1945) he weighed about 170 pounds.

Greiner was born on December 27, 1895 in Ingolstadt (Bavaria). He received his education in Nuefchen[77] until, when in December 1914, he joined the Bavarian army as a

Fahnenjunker (officer candidate). In January 1916, he was commissioned a lieutenant, but was captured six months later. He remained in a French prisoner of war camp for the rest of the First World War. In February 1920 Greiner was released from captivity and returned home. That same year, Greiner embarked on a police career, when he began studying Criminal Investigation at the University of Berlin.

In 1923, he was appointed Criminal Commissioner in Berlin. In order to understand what this man was all about we need to see what his actions had been throughout his life. When Nazi Germany collapsed, his interrogators stated (during the interview of March 16, 1946) that he was very keen to cooperate with the U.S. Army, and gave up valuable intelligence willingly. He also volunteered for service in the post-war (Americans-sponsored) German police force.[78] Greiner had been a member of the Catholic "Centre Party" since 1929; however he joined the NSDAP on March 1, 1933. He stated during his interview that he had become convinced in 1932 that his party could not bring about change in Germany; and that had been the reason why in 1933 he joined the Nazi Party. Another interpretation would be that Greiner saw the star of the Nazi Party rising, and he latched on to this like an opportunist. Based on his post-war interrogation and his actions during his career in the *Gestapo/SD* and *Geheime Feldpolizei*, it is most likely that Philip Greiner was motivated, not by political conviction, as much as by opportunism.

On May 1, 1933 Greiner was promoted to "*Kriminal Rat*."[79] However, because of differences of opinion with other criminal police officials, he was sent away to Königsberg (East Prussia) in November 1934. In May 1937 Greiner was transferred to Karlsruhe as chief of the criminal police, with the rank of criminal director. A year later he was promoted to the rank of *Regierungs und Kriminal Rat* (equivalent to the rank of an army major). In 1938 Greiner was given the SS rank of *SS-Hauptsturmführer*, which was raised to *SS-Obersturmbannführer* in March 1942.[80] In his U.S. Army interview, Greiner attempted to explain these SS promotions by stating that *Reichsführer-SS* Heinrich Himmler had gained control of the German Police in 1938 and wanted to assimilate these police forces into his SS Empire. At least, that is what he claimed in 1946.[81]

In August 1939 Philip Greiner was assigned to the *Geheime Feldpolizei* and became commander of GFP-550. After the war, Greiner claimed that he disliked his service in the GFP and only wished to serve in the criminal police. Obviously, this was a self-serving and disingenuous statement. The headquarters of GFP-550 was at Freudenstadt (in Württemberg), while GFP-7 had its headquarters in Freiburg. The duties of GFP-550 were as follows: (1) control of foreigners in the Seventh German Army area of operations; (2) control of all railroad facilities in the operational areas; (3) apprehension of deserters and AWOL (absent without leave personnel) at the forward collecting point at Pforzheim (Baden); (4) spot checks of military offices for violations of security regulations; (5) investigation of cases of violation of security by army personnel; (6) execution of special missions from *Ic AO* (Army Intelligence) e.g.–investigation of flash signals from German positions to the enemy or of unauthorized use of carrier pigeons; (7) Investigations of suspicious persons; (8) Investigations of instances of lack of morale and defeatism within the Army, when especially ordered by the Army CIC; (9) Investigation of Army Courts Martials, when especially requested by the Seventh German Army.

In January 1940 fifteen members of GFP-550 were removed and, together with *Feldpolizeidirektor* Hergt and thirty additional replacements (mostly lawyers, merchants and trade correspondents with a working knowledge of French), were used to form a brand new GFP formation; to be under the supervision of the *Luftwaffe* (Air Force).[82] This turned out to be *GFP-625 (L)* which was established on February 15, 1940 and which was assigned to *Luftflotte-Kommando 3* in France.⁸³ Training of the new GFP recruits for GFP-625 was given *by Feldpolizeikommissar* Dr. Higgeneyer, although Greiner insinuated that the criminal police training was rudimentary.

When the Germans launched their invasion of France on May 10, 1940, Greiner's unit remained under Seventh German Army (*Generaloberst* Friedrich Dollmann), which was holding the front lines against the Maginot Line from Bitche/Strasbourg to the Swiss frontier. When France surrendered, and requested an armistice on June 24 the Germans began to move their Seventh Army to the region of Paris.⁸⁴ Towards the end of June 1940 Secret Field Police Group "550" and "7" were moved to the region of Paris. *Geheime Feldpolizei Gruppe 550* travelled to Paris by way of Brussels. The initial mission of GFP-550 was to organize a successful occupation by:

1. Organize a bureau of wanted persons in France with a central office in Paris with *Feldpolizeidirektor von Weiland* in charge of this office.
2. Establish licensed brothels for the *Wehrmacht*.
3. Investigate French resistance activities.⁸⁵

After these initial tasks were accomplished (under the overall supervision of *Heeresfeldpolizeichef* Cuno Schmidt) Greiner was once again promoted. This occurred three weeks later, in July 1940, when he was promoted to *Leitender Feldpolizeidirektor Militärbefehlshaber in Frankreich* ("leading field police director military commander in France"). Greiner's liaison officers in Seventh German Army were *Hauptmann i.G.* de Ondarza and *Major* Meyer who were both listed as "Ic" (intelligence) officers. Greiner served in the GFP until March 1942 when a good portion of the GFP forces in France were absorbed into the SD. As for who assumed command of GFP-550 when Greiner was promoted in July 1940, it turned out to be *Feldpolizei Kommissar* Dr. Niggemeyer, and later by *Feldpolizeikommissar* Bernhard Hannig. According to Greiner, supervision of the various GFP formations wrested under the intelligence officer of the local army command, although disciplinary matters were the jurisdiction of *Heeresfeldpolizeichef der Wehrmacht* Wilhelm Krichbaum, in *Abwehr III* of the *Wehrmacht*⁸⁶; however this chain of command had to go through the "middle" office of the *Feldpolizei Chef beim OKH* ("Field Police Chief of the Army").

GFP-712

This unit was established on April 26, 1941, in *Wehrkreis IV*. While stationed in Belgium and France, GFP units tried to uncover underground agents whenever possible. One such example was the Belgian, Charles Melotte, born in 1886 in Liege. In September 1942 he was recruited by Maurice Guillaume, a Brussels hairdresser by day and Allied spy by night. Guillaume's real name was Sidney Webb, a British agent. On July 6, 1943 officials of GFP-712 stopped and questioned Melotte in Hoeilaart, a suburb which lay southeast and just outside of the Brussels city limits. Under interrogation the GFP found probable cause to detain Melotte.

On July 17, 1943, Melotte was turned over to GFP-530 and transferred into GFP custody in St. Gilles Prison, arriving there on July 24, 1943. There he remained for seven months while he was interrogated and tortured by members of GFP-530. On February 12, 1944, he was transferred to Essen in Germany. From there he eventually ended up in Buchenwald and later, Flossenburg Concentration Camp.⁸⁷ Melotte's case was a perfect example of Nazi Germany's "Nacht und Nebel" ("Night and Fog") decree. "Nacht und Nebel" was a category instituted by Adolf Hitler on December 7, 1941, against "anyone endangering German security" (*deutsche Sicherheit gefährden*). If a person was categorized as a *Nacht und Nebel* ("Night and Fog") class of prisoner, they were to be interrogated, tortured, and if they had survived at least eight days in custody, they were to be transported to a concentration camp in Nazi Germany where their fate would inevitably later be decided. In 1944 GFP-712 arrested fifty-five persons under suspicion of being members of the "M.N.B." espionage group. Eventually thirty-five of the fifty-five were found guilty after their trials. Later in the year twenty-three Belgians were arrested by this GFP group. In total, in the region of Northern France and Belgium 2,396 arrests were made, while a further 1,490 were held in detention.[88] Sometime in the fall of 1944 this secret field police unit was absorbed into the SS.[89]

GFP-735 in Finland / Norway

GFP-735 was created on June 21, 1941 in *Wehrkreis IV* (4th Military District). In the second half of 1941 it was sent to serve under the *Militärbefehlshaber in Frankreich*. This Secret Field Police unit served briefly in France from 1941–1942 before being transferred to Finland where it operated from 1942–1944. In 1942 GFP-735 was transferred to Lapland in northern Finland to serve under the German 20th Mountain Army.[90] Finland was an Axis allied nation, so GFP-735 could only operate within the framework of intelligence duties in the rear and front-lines of German military units operating in that country. The Commissar Order was also active in this northernmost region of the Russian Front. *Armeeoberkommando Norwegen* (as the 20th Mountain Army was initially referred to) observed this order. The unit followed the Commissar Order as well as Operational Order Nr. 8 issued in August 1941.[91] The order demanded that Communist functionaries caught in battle were to be interrogated and then immediately killed. The employment of GFP-735 in enforcing the Commissar Order appears to have taken place:

> In the 1960s and 1970s German legal representatives of the government instituted multiple investigative proceedings on account of the suspicion of the murder of defenseless prisoners of war in Finland on the basis of Operative Order No. 8. Indeed, no more perpetrators could be investigated after the long period of time; however, the clear result of the proceedings was that up until the summer of 1942, on several occasions SS officers or members of the Geheime Feldpolizei (Secret Military Police) had stayed in Stalag 309 and 322, as had Finnish officers. Interrogations and deportations of prisoners were tied to their presence; several witnesses testified that they remembered this presence had to do with "commissars" and "Jews." These people were later shot in bomb craters in the vicinity of the camp. One soldier secretly photographed such a crater; the photos left such an effect on his comrades that several sent for prints of them.[92]

From late 1944–1945 the unit served in Norway. By 1945 GFP-735 was still operating under the 20th Mountain Army, which was serving in northern Norway. No cases of abuse of captured prisoners or any criminal activity have surfaced regarding GFP-735 while it was serving on Norwegian soil. However, its actions in northern Finland while fighting the Russians appears to have been the typical murderous behavior exhibited by the GFP in the USSR. Yet again we see a difference in behavior by the same men and the same GFP unit (in this case, GFP-735), depending on where it was operating (Norway or the USSR). We do not know who led this unit but we know that one of its members was Fritz Röhler. Röhler was trained under the 600th Infantry Training and Replacement Battalion at Altenburg—the unit which trained all GFP members. After training, he and other newly-qualified members were assigned to GFP-735. Röhler served in the unit from March 31, 1942, until May 8, 1945.

GFP-743 (L)

This Secret Field Police unit was established in 1943 using *Luftwaffe* personnel stationed in *Wehrkreis XXI* (21st Military District) in the western Polish territories which the Germans called *Wartheland,* and had been incorporated into the *Reich* in 1940. The unit was sent to the Netherlands where it remained stationed until the end of the war. In November 1944 seven members of GFP-743 were stationed in Dordrecht. The Dutch underground stated that these men wore *Luftwaffe* uniforms. In mid–December, this GFP *Kommissariat* (station post) was moved to Utrecht. The Dutch underground also identified GFP-743 as operating in Rotterdam in December 1944 and January 1945.[93] In January GFP-743 was involved in investigating food hoarding and black marketeering in Rotterdam. According to one Dutch source, this unit was composed of *Luftwaffe* personnel. The leader of the group was *Feldpolizeikommissar* Keithahn, while *Feldpolizeikommissar* Denibir was the group *Vertreter* (representative). Alwin Hitzeroth was said to have served in this unit, as well as *Feldpolizeikommissar* Denibir, and *Feldpolizeisekretär* Dreier. GFP-743 (L) was initially located in Brussels. The group was divided into two *Kommissariate* and two *Sekretariate*:

1. *Kommissariat Brussels*
   Leader: *Feldpolizeikommissar* Denibir
   Representative: *Feldpolizeisekretär* Dreier
2. *Kommissariat Lille*
   Leader: *Feldpolizeikommissar* Eger
   Representative: *Feldpolizeisekretär* Shipper
3. *Sekretariat Oriel*
   Leader: *Feldpolizeisekretär* Gersonde
   Representative: no one was assigned
4. *Sekretariat Reims*
   Leader: *Feldpolizeisekretär* Hunecke
   Representative: *Stabsfeldwebel* Jungmann[94]

Conclusions

The GFPs role in the Holocaust in the West appears to have been limited to assisting with the round-up of Jews and their deportation to the Nazi death camps. A good portion of the men from the GFP units stationed in the West were transferred over to the SD in 1942 and retained in these regions of Europe. Some GFP units were not disbanded and absorbed into the SD station posts in the West but were retained by the Wehrmacht. Those GFP units under Army or Air Force control performed counter-intelligence operations, sought out spies, saboteurs, Black Market operators and military deserters. Evidently these particular GFP units didn't play much of a role in the Holocaust or in the repression of the French and Belgian population. However, given that the SD was deeply involved in the removal of Jewish property and the expulsion of the Jews to the concentration camps, as well as combating the French and Belgian underground, members of the GFP who were absorbed into the SD in 1942 played a significant role in that Nazi mission in the West. It may seem like splitting hairs, but overall the GFP in France and Belgium behaved in an honorable manner while serving in the German Army. That comportment disappeared however, once many of these former GFP men were transferred into the Sipo and SD.

8. The GFP in the West and Scandinavia

In spite of committing individual atrocities and as a general practice, shooting hostages, the behavior of the GFP, even while serving in the Sipo/SD, was far less severe than their behavior in the East, where the mission of the GFP was not merely the apprehension of Jews and their expulsion to extermination camps. In the East, the GFP quite often operated as a branch of the SS killing units. Members of the GFP operating in the East regularly shot captured Jews, as well as partisan suspects and political commissars day in and day out. Even civilians suspected of partisan activity were not given a just trial as was the case in the West. What would happen is that a decision would be made by the GFP official on the spot. If the GFP officer felt that the civilian was likely a partisan or partisan supporter, he or she would be shot. This did not happen in the West. The execution of Jews did not occur in the West *en masse*. Excuses were used. For example, when the French underground began their attacks in late 1940, the Germans would arrest known communists. However, they would make sure that those arrested were communists who happened to be Jews. When the supply of communist Jews ran out for the firing squads, the Germans resorted to communists and later still to indiscriminate apprehensions of people from the streets of French towns and cities.

Like elsewhere in Europe, the GFP appears to have operated as a vital link between the Wehrmacht and the SS, linking both of these powerful institutions together in a solid bond of cooperation. Although tensions appeared in early 1942 over the issue of the GFP in France, the problem appeared to have been quickly resolved. Thus, the transfer of GFP personnel from the Wehrmacht into the SS appears to have been a relatively easy process. The mass transfer that occurred in France in 1942 indicates this all too well. Cases of temporary and permanent transfers of personnel from the GFP/Wehrmacht into the SS/SD and back have been documented not only in the West, but in the East as well as in the Balkans. In essence then, the movement of personnel from these various branches was institutionalized and ran without problems. The fact that many of the men who eventually served in the GFP came from the pre-war Kriminalpolizei, Geheimstaatspolizei, and even detectives from the Gemeindepolizei of the German Order Police (Ordnungspolizei) organization meant that these transfers were often fast and the paperwork required was minimal given that the men transferring back to the SS/SD already had files and were already "vetted."

9

The Secret Field Police in the Soviet Union

Introduction

Adolf Hitler's Russian adventure has gone down in history as the most titanic struggle between two of the worst totalitarian regimes in world history. The campaign in the East was unique in many other ways. For one thing, the sheer size and scope of the territory in which the war was waged and the size and number of the combatants made all other human wars and campaigns seem Lilliputian by comparison. For the initial invasion in June 1941, Adolf Hitler was able to muster a staggering assault force that, including his Axis allies, amounted to some 3,800,000 troops, 3,350 tanks, 2,770 aircraft of all types, and 7,200 artillery pieces! After having to delay the planned invasion by more than a month, the Führer set the new invasion date at June 22, 1941.[1] This date is significant given that this was the date back in 1812, when Napoleon Bonaparte chose to make his ill-fated invasion of Russia some one hundred and twenty-nine years earlier. Hitler appears to have been tempting fate here, given that Napoleon ultimately failed to topple the Czar, even though he managed to capture Moscow. Of the 650,000 men which Napoleon Bonaparte sent into Russia, only about 200,000 made it back to Lithuania in the spring of 1813. That same year he lost the Battle of Leipzig and he was forced into his first exile. It is interesting to note that the winter of 1941/42 would prove to be as cold and bitter as the winter of 1812/13.

Hitler's Russian campaign had basically the same goal as Napoleon Bonaparte's invasion: destroy the Russian nation, topple its government, and bring its leader to his knees. However, Hitler's invasion differed greatly from Napoleon's earlier endeavor in many ways. For one thing, it had been launched partly to convince the United Kingdom of the futility of continued resistance against Nazi Germany. Another reason was for *Lebensraum* ("living space"), where the populations living in the East would be "culled" in anticipation of German colonization. Hitler had written clearly about this intention in his rambling political manifesto *Mein Kampf*. The resources of the USSR were also to be seized and employed for the benefit of Germany and her war machine. Finally, and most important to the history of the Secret Field Police, the manner in which Hitler and the Nazis would conduct this war against the Soviet Union would be completely lacking in any sort of chivalric conduct, or conventions of war. From the very beginning the campaign in the East was to be a life and death struggle that was to be waged in a brutal and uncompromising manner. In effect, the German adventure in the USSR would be fought as a *Vernichtungskrieg* ("war of annihilation").

9. *The Secret Field Police in the Soviet Union* 155

Two GFP secret military field police auxiliaries, being observed by a GFP official, interrogate two Red Army prisoners in occupied Soviet territory in the summer of 1942 (U.S. Holocaust Memorial Museum, courtesy Paul Brown).

The German SS and its underlying agencies, as well as the Wehrmacht would engage in this titanic war of extermination. Members of the SS as well as German Army forces would be knee-deep in blood fighting in the East. This carnage would not merely target the Jews in the East, but the general population as a whole. The Slavic peoples of the Soviet Union would experience the full fury of the Nazi killing machine. During the war, the German military in the Soviet Union managed to kill about twelve million Red Army soldiers, while sustaining just over one million one hundred thousand dead. However, the Soviet civilian population killed from 1941–1944 on account of the German invasion, amounted to some thirteen million people! That figure alone tells us that something different was occurring in the USSR during the Second World War. It indicates that the manner in which the German military waged their campaign in the East did not delineate in any way between combatants and non-combatants. This was in stark contrast to the comportment of the German military during the conquest of Western Europe, where civilians were not usually targeted.

Within this gigantic life and death struggle, the GFP played its role. What exactly was that role? What duties were assigned to the Secret Field Police during the campaign in Russia? What was the relationship between the Holocaust in the USSR and the racial/ideological war waged against all Soviet citizens? What was the role of the various services and particularly the GFP with relation to the Einsatzgruppen in the Holocaust, and in the war of annihilation? Did the GFP take an active role in the killing of Jews and in the killing of the general Soviet civilian population? Was the GFP a vital lynchpin of cooperation between the Wehrmacht and SS in the Holocaust? Was it also a valuable tool of repression that was also employed in murdering the Soviet civilian population as part of this "war of annihilation"? From all accounts and sources gathered, it appears that the answer to all these questions is an undeniable "yes."

But why wage such a horrible campaign of extermination in the East? It is beyond the scope of this study to ponder a full and complete answer to this question, but certainly we can surmise that the Nazis, with their racial theories, considered the Slavic and Turkic peoples making up the majority population of the USSR in 1941 as *lebensunwerten lebens* ("life unworthy of life"). When they came to power in January 1933, the Nazi Party had about eight years to indoctrinate the German nation before the Russian Campaign was launched. This racial hatred and contempt for the peoples living in the East, coupled with several murderous commands emanating from Hitler, the SS, and even the German Army High Command, combined with the ferocity and intensity of the Russian Front, proved a sufficiently strong "cocktail" to create the nihilistic conditions which were so pervasive during the campaign.

A Pattern of Brutal Comportment in the East

The GFP, like the rest of the German military, soon established a pattern of brutal behavior in the East. For example, a German rear area command, *Ortskommandantur I/882* noted in a report dated "April 9, 1942," that in the region of Melitopol, its army troops with the aid of GFP personnel had discovered forty Gypsies in the Beloserka Kolkhoz. The report causally stated that all forty Gypsies were shot.[2] In June 1941 approximately 100,000 Red Army soldiers and 40,000 civilians were being held at a large POW camp near Minsk. The camp had been established in that month by the Army and was administered by the rear area commander. because the camp held too many prisoners, conditions were terrible. There was not enough food to go around and most of the POWs had to sleep out in the open. When winter would come, large numbers would die from exposure and malnutrition.

In an attempt to relieve the huge numbers of prisoners, the Germans resorted to employing the GFP to help cull the camp population. GFP officials would interrogate the prisoners there on a regular basis in order to ascertain if any were Jews or political commissars. If they discovered any, they were taken out of the camp and executed.[3] Although the GFP became a part of the mass murder going on behind the German lines, their duties were many. The conduct of the GFP in the USSR was not merely relegated to the hunting of Russian partisans and Jews. By June 1944 in the area of Army Group "Center" alone, the GFP was searching for approximately 3,142 members of the German Armed Forces who had deserted from their front-line units. Many of these men had simply taken to the forests to hide out the remainder of the war. A few had the nerve to hide in the larger occupied cities. Some would hide out in the military bases of the rear areas, and because conditions were becoming more chaotic by the day, often times these men were listed AWOL by their units and could hide in plain sight immediately behind the lines of another formation or unit.

The German wholesale exploitation of Russian resources had an impact on the rise in the activities of the Black Market, as well as in desperation on the part of the local population. A section from GFP-501, operating under the 18th Army (in the Leningrad region) was temporarily attached to the headquarters of the German 121st Infantry Division in December 1941 to investigate some ghastly murders. The unit reported apprehending a Russian near the town of Pavlosk who was later accused of cannibalism.[4] Another mission that was eventually assigned to the GFP in Russia was to judge the political competency of teachers in the few schools the Germans allowed to remain open behind the German lines. Those teachers found to be unreliable were arrested and sent to a POW camp. In this mission, the GFP was to be assisted by the SD.[5] In an attempt to "downsize" this huge number of prisoners, the SD, together with units of the Secret Field Police began a screening process in July. The method selected 20,000 people for release from the camp and 10,000 (mostly Jews) for immediate execution.[6] This episode is a perfect example of SD-Secret Field Police cooperation, as well as the power over life and death which the GFP held— much like the SD and the SS killing units. In fact, the death toll caused by GFP units was in the thousands as depicted clearly in the following table:

Table 3. Partisans Killed or Captured by GFP Units, 1941–1942

Formation	Date	Partisans Taken Prisoner and/or Killed	Total
GFP in A.G. "North"	10–12/1941[7]	6,550	
GFP in A.G. "South"	05/1942[8]	2,729	
	07/1942[9]	5,599	
	07/41–07/42	5,000 in Zhitomir	
	08/42–12/43	3,000 in Zhitomir	
GFP in A.G. "B"	08/1942[10]	291	
	09/1942[11]	693	
GFP in A.G. "Center"	10/1942[12]	1,001[13]	
			21,683
GFP in the entire USSR	07/01/42–03/31/1943[14]		21,000

Organization of the GFP for the Russian Campaign

By far the region which contained the greatest number of deployed Secret Field Police units was the Soviet Union. GFP groups were attached to rear-area security divisions, as well as to the three Rear Area Security HQ's which were to control the various rear area and security forces tasked with maintaining order immediately behind the three German Army Groups in the USSR: Rear Area Commander "North," "Center" and "South." These three rear area headquarters corresponded to the three principle German army group commands: *Heeresgruppe Nord, Mitte* and *Süd* (Army Group "North," "Center" and "South"). In addition to being an integral part of the security divisions as well as the rear area headquarters, GFP units were also assigned directly to the front-line armies and army groups. They were attached to Armies in frontline regions and *Militär Verwaltungs* (Military

Administrations) in the occupied areas. GFP units were also attached directly to army commands.

Thus, the GFP was to serve not only in the rear areas under the German military administration, but also on the front lines. The German rear-area commands such as the *Feldkommandantur* and *Ortskommandantur*—the German military government immediately behind the front lines, were supported first by the Secret Field Police, and the *Feldgendarmerie* (Military Field Police) in the maintenance of order and security.[15] The backbone of the rear area commands, however, were the security and regional defense battalions. While GFP units were distributed behind the lines, other GFP formations operated along the front lines. These were the GFP units attached to various Army commands. The German security divisions which were to operate immediately behind the front lines of the advancing German armies were also assigned several GFP units as an integral part of each security division. Securing the rear area of the German armies immediately behind the front lines was the mission of the rear area military commander under the title *Befehlshaber des Rückwärtigen Heeresgebietes* ("Commander of the Rear Army area"). The German rear areas were organized as follows:

- *Befehlshaber des Rückwärtigen Heeresgebietes*
  - *Oberfeldkommandantur* (divisional level)
  - *Feldkommandantur* (regimental level)
  - *Ortskommandantur* (battalion level and locally stationed)

Numerous rear area commands were established for the Russian campaign. As for the issue of whether SS formations would operate alongside the Secret Field Police in the combat zones, that question remained to be determined between *Reichsführer-SS* Heinrich Himmler and the Armed Forces High Command.[16] As it turned out, the need to determine this became a moot point, given that very quickly the operations of the GFP and the SS killing units became almost indiscernible from one another. Cooperation between the Army and the SS in the East was very cordial, and close. Only in rare instances was there a dispute as to the employment of GFP units alongside security forces of the SS, and then only as a matter of overlapping jurisdiction. Because the GFP was an integral part of combating Soviet resistance from the very beginning of the campaign, the employment of Secret Field Police forces alongside army security, front-line army formations, and SS killing units, was not given further thought.

The principle GFP groups assigned to the region of central Russia were: *GFP-Gruppen 570, 580, 612, 639, 703, 706, 707, 709, 710, 716,*[17] *717, 718, 723, 724, and 729*. The principle GFP groups assigned to the region of northern Russia and the Baltic States were: *GFP-Gruppen 1,*[18] *501, 520, 704, 713, 714, 715, and 722*. The principle GFP groups assigned to the region of southern Russia and the Crimea were: *GFP-Gruppen 1,*[19] *626, 647, 706, 708, 719, 720, 721, 725, 730, and 739*.[20] All of the GFP units which served in southern Russia and the Crimea except GFP-626 and GFP-647 served under the *Befehlshaber der rückwärtigen Heeresgebiet Süd* (Commander of the Rear Area Army Group "South") between January and August 1942.[21] Between September and December 1942, *Befehlshaber der rückwärtigen Heeresgebiet Süd* employed the following units: GFP-1, GFP-708, GFP-719, GFP-721, GFP-725, GFP-730, and GFP-739.[22] As the duties of the GFP increased and the conflict widened, so did the need for more units. Therefore, the GFP forces employed in World War II increased in number as the war progressed. The initial batch of GFP units that were used to invade the USSR was soon augmented by newly created formations. These included the following secret field police units:

Table 4. Units Created for the Russian Campaign in Spring & Summer 1941

#	GFP	Parent Organization & Initial Employment in 1941
1	702	Formed April 26, 1941. Employed under 18th Army, Army Group North.
2	703	Formed April 26, 1941. Employed under *Panzer Gruppe 3*
3	704	Created from parts of GFP-530. Established on April 26, 1941. Employed under *Panzer Gruppe 4*.
4	705	Formed April 26, 1941. Employed under 281st Security Division of 16th Army, Army Group North.
5	706	Formed April 26, 1941. Employed under 403rd Security Division of Ninth Army, Army Group Center.
6	707	Formed April 26, 1941. Employed under 221st Security Division, Army Group Center.
7	708	Formed April 26, 1941. Employed under 454th Security Division of the *Befehlshaber Rückwartig Heeresgebiet Süd*. (Commander of Rear Area Forces South).
8	709	Formed April 26, 1941. Employed under 286th Security Division, Army Group Center.
9	710	Formed April 26, 1941. Employed under 403rd Security Division, Army Group Center.
10	711	Formed April 26, 1941. Employed initially under 454th Security Division of the *Befehlshaber Rückwartig Heeresgebiet Süd*. (Commander of Rear Area Forces South).
11	713	Formed May 21, 1941. Employed under 207th Security Division of Army Group North.
12	714	Formed May 21, 1941. Employed under 281st Security Division of Army Group North.
13	715	Formed May 21, 1941. Employed under 285th Security Division, Army Group North.
14	716	Formed May 21, 1941. Employed under 286th Security Division, Army Group Center.
15	717	Formed May 21, 1941. Employed under 403rd Security Division, Army Group Center.
16	718	Formed May 21, 1941. Employed under 221st Security Division, Army Group Center.
17	719	Formed May 21, 1941. Employed under 221st Security Division of the *Befehlshaber Rückwartig Heeresgebiet Süd*. (Commander of Rear Area Forces South).
18	720	Formed May 21, 1941. Employed under 444th Security Division of the *Befehlshaber Rückwartig Heeresgebiet Süd*. (Commander of Rear Area Forces South).
19	721	Formed April 26, 1941. Employed under 454th Security Division of the *Befehlshaber Rückwartig Heeresgebiet Süd*. (Commander of Rear Area Forces South).
20	722	Formed May 21, 1941. Employed under 207th Security Division of Army Group North.
21	723	Formed May 21, 1941. Employed under 286th Security Division, Army Group Center.
22	724	Formed May 21, 1941. Employed under 403rd Security Division, Army Group Center.
23	725	Formed May 21, 1941. Employed under Sixth Army, Army Group South.
24	726	Formed May 21, 1941. Employed under 444th Security Division, as part of the *Befehlshaber Rückwartig Heeresgebiet Süd*
25	727	Formed June 21, 1941. Employed by 281st Security Division of 16th Army, Army Group North.
26	728	Formed June 21, 1941. Employed under 285th Security Division, Army Group North.
27	729	Formed June 21, 1941. Employed under 221st Security Division, Army Group Center.[23]
28 total	730	Formed June 21, 1941. Employed under 454th Security Division, Sixth Army; then as part of 454th Security Division under the *Befehlshaber Rückwartig Heeresgebiet Süd*.

In general, and in practice, the GFP units assigned to the Russian campaign numbered about a hundred men (the authorized complement was ninety-five). The official figure was 54 field police officials (drawn from the German civilian detective force, the *Kriminalpolizei* and/or *Sicherheitspolizei*), one chief Field Police Official, and the remaining forty personnel taken from the German Army, whose assigned tasks within each unit would be as drivers, clerks, mechanics, etc. In addition, a unique feature of the Russian Campaign which was not witnessed in GFP units operating in the West was the employment of auxiliary volunteers drawn up from the local population. This did not merely include locals acting as *übersetzer und dolmetscher* ("translators and interpreters"), but so-called *hilfswilliger* ("auxiliary volunteers") who would be tasked with the shooting of captured Jews, Red Army commissars, Gypsies, and partisan suspects.

This was in stark contrast to the manner in which GFP units operated in Greece, where the translators and interpreters were supplied by the GFP replacement system or came from the Wehrmacht as men temporarily assigned to a particular GFP unit for a limited amount of time. Usually this would be done in anticipation of a large-scale operation. These attached army personnel often times were present at interrogations, anti-partisan drives, SS killing sweeps, and as a result were often ordered to perform "other" tasks not normally assigned to them. Those tasks included shooting captured prisoners—regardless of whether they were soldiers, partisans, or civilians. They had to take an oath of secrecy when assigned to a GFP unit, and when they were transferred out of the Secret Field Police and returned to their parent army formation, they were sworn to silence on pain of death.

Leading Members of GFP Units in the East

For the campaign in the Soviet Union the title and position of *Leiter der Geheimen Feldpolizei Ost* (Chief of the Secret Field Police "East") was created. This new GFP post was initially assigned to Ernst Rassow. Rassow was responsible to Cuno Schmidt who held the post of *Heerespolizeichef der Armee*, or [Secret] Field Police Chief of the Army.[24] *Oberfeldpolizeidirektor und SS-Sturmbannführer* Ernst Erich Viktor Rassow held this post from June 22, 1941 until January 1942.[25] After attending school and belonging to a right-wing *Freikorps* unit, Rassow began a career in the police. In the 1930s, he was inducted into the *Reichskriminalpolizeiamt*. After the founding of the RSHA (Reich Main Security Office) Rassow served as a *Kriminaldirektor* in the *Reichskriminalpolizeiamt*. He held this rank and high position within the GFP on the staff of the Secret Field Police in Berlin. Rassow is another perfect example of the close connection and cooperation between the GFP and the SS/SD. From June 1941 to January 1942 Rassow, as Chief of the GFP in the East, was responsible for about forty-one GFP units comprising around 4,000 men. This averaged out to about 97–98 men per GFP group. However, this number does not include Wehrmacht personnel on short-term assignments to GFP formations, as well as local volunteers attached as scouts, interpreters, soldiers, and local informers.

The position of *Leiter der Geheimen Feldpolizei Ost* was held initially by *Feldpolizeidirektor* Joachim Kaintzik. From January 1942 until July 1944 the position of *Leiter der Geheimen Feldpolizei Ost* was held by *Oberfeldpolizeidirektor* Max Häußerer.[26] Before the war Kaintzik had served in the Gestapo department tasked with locating and arresting homosexuals. When war broke out he was assigned as the head of GFP-603. Häußerer was a German civil servant from 1907 until 1912 when he joined the Police. He worked as police official in the city of Mainz from 1912–1934, when he joined the State Secret Police. Max Häußerer actually played an important role in providing political "ammunition" against both Werner von Fritsch who was accused of homosexuality, and Werner von Blomberg who was accused of marrying a former prostitute. Both men were part of the German Army High Command and were in Hitler's way. They were blocking Hitler's plans for military aggression and according to the Nazis, they had to go. The whole event came to be known as the Blomberg-Fritsch Affair. Again, Häußerer's history and service in a high position within the GFP indicates the closeness of the Nazi Party and SS to the Secret Field Police.

The Russian front was dived into three principle groups: "North," "Center," and "South." Below the position of *Leiter der Geheimen Feldpolizei Ost* were the GFP staffs in charge of certain regions of the Russian Front. These GFP posts were: *Leitender Feldpolizeidirektor beim Befehlshaber Heeresgebiet Nord, Leitender Feldpolizeidirektor beim Befehlshaber Heeresgebiet Mitte,* and *Leitender Feldpolizeidirektor beim Befehlshaber Heeresgebiet Süd*. For example, for Army Group South the senior GFP official (beginning in March 1943) was Hans

Stephainski. Stephainski had previously served as commander of GFP-13 and later still, of GFP-530.

In February 1943, the position of Leitender *Feldpolizeidirektor im rückwärtigen Heeresgebiet Mitte* was held by Bernhard Niggemeyer. Niggemeyer was yet another example of the close association between the SD and the GFP. In 1939 Bernhard Niggemeyer had been serving in the *Kriminalpolizei* in the city of Karlsruhe. Since 1940 he was head of GFP-550. Beginning in February 1942 he was promoted to *Feldpolizeidirektor bei der Sicherungsdivision 201*–[principal] Field Police Director for the 201st Security Division. After serving as the head of GFP units in the region of Army Group Center, he was transferred back to the RSHA in Department IV (Gestapo). This occurred in September 1943.[27] In the region of Army Group North, the position of *Leitender Feldpolizeidirektor beim Befehlshaber Heeresgebiet Nord* was held by *Oberfeldpolizeidirektor* Zugnig.

Relations Between the GFP and SS/SD During the Russian Campaign

Relations between the German Army intelligence group, the rear area army commands, the attached GFP forces, as well as the local SD command was, on the whole, usually *reibungslos* ("*smooth*"). Therefore, the atmosphere was cordial and accommodating. The GFP also worked as a vital link between the SS/SD and the Wehrmacht.[28] This was in stark contrast to postwar statements made by former GFP members, who stated that resistance to SD "methods" existed within the membership of the GFP. These postwar reports were full of similar anti–SD comments, to the point that one would believe that friction existed between the GFP and SD. It is obvious that these post-war reports were most likely generated in order to help distance the GFP and its members from the activities attributed to the SS and SD:

> Another tactic was to portray the Sipo-SD and the GFP as rival organizations. Such assertions undoubtedly were made to distance the GFP from the "Nazi character" of the Sipo-SD, while simultaneously bolstering the GFP's image as an army formation independent of Sipo-SD influence.[29]

In fact, the manner in which the GFP would operate in the USSR was far different than the way they would perform their duties while stationed in west European countries. Secret Field Police units would behave much like the mobile SS killing units (the *SS-Einsatzgruppen*) that would operate in Poland and the USSR—earning it the applicable nickname: "Gestapo of the German Army." This was in stark contrast to the almost courtly manners which the GFP would comport themselves in Western Europe. An example of the behavior of the GFP in Russia was given by the testimony of a captured GFP official, Reinhard Retzlaff. He had been assigned to GFP-725 serving with the German Sixth Army. He was one of the approximately 91,000 German soldiers taken prisoner after the surrender of the German Sixth Army at Stalingrad on February 3, 1943. He was eventually put on trial as a war criminal in Kharkov in December 1943. Whether forced to confess, or by free will, he stated during the trial that GFP units killed civilians on a large scale—much like the infamous SS killing units. He stated that in Zhitomir alone, the GFP was responsible for the murder of 5,000–8,000 civilians.[30] It was not solely Russian Jews who were persecuted by the Germans. In general, Jews and Gypsies were equally targeted by the Germans in the East. For example, on June 23, 1942, the commander of the 281st Security Division noted that the Secret Field Police had executed 128 Gypsies in Novorshev.[31]

Deployment During the Russian Campaign: The GFP in Army Group North

The operational area of Army Group North would contain the shortest frontage for the German forces operating there than the length of the front lines in the region Army Group Center and Army Group South. However, this part of the Russian Front would experience the largest concentration of Soviet partisan forces second to the region of Army Group Center. It would also encompass the German civilian administrative region for the Baltic states (Lithuania, Latvia, and Estonia) the so-called *Reichskommissariat Ostland*.[32] The principal headquarters for the GFP for the region of Army Group North (*Leitender Feldpolizeidirektor beim Befehlshaber Heeresgebiet Nord*) would actually be located in the Baltic states of Estonia and Latvia. As the campaign in Russia dragged on, and the Germans began to withdraw, the location of this HQ changed:

Table 5. Location of the H.Q. for the GFP Chief Army Group North[33]

From	To	Town Posting	Country
Feb 1941	Feb 1944	Voru (Verro)	Estonia
Feb 1944	Sept 1944	Cesis (Venden)	Latvia
Sept 1944	Nov 1944	Edola (Courland)	Latvia
Nov 1944	Jan 1945	Goldingen (Courland)	Latvia

The following territorial groups were directly subordinated to the Chief of the GFP of Army Group North (later, Army Group "Kurland"):

Table 6. Units Directly Under the Command of the GFP Chief of Army Group North

Unit	From / To	Town Posting	Country
GFP-705	1941–1943	Opochka,	Russia
	1943–1944	Ventspils (Windau)	Latvia
	10/1944	Courland	Latvia
GFP-713	12/41–2/17/44	Pskov	Russia
	2/1944–9/1944	Cesis (Venden) in the TB Institute	Latvia
	9/1944–10/1944	Edole, in *Kurland* (Courland)	Latvia
	10/1944–01/18/1945	Danzig, Niedersiegen	Germany
	01/1945–May 1945	Neubrandenburg	Germany
GFP-714	1941–1942	Ostrov	Russia
	1944	Courland	Latvia
	1945	West Prussia	Germany
GFP-715	1941–1942	Strugie-Krasnye (Pskov District)	Russia
	1943–07/1944	Parnu (northern tip of Riga Gulf)	Estonia
	08/1944–01/1945	Warsaw	Poland
	02/1945–04/1945	H.Q. OKH	Germany
GFP-722	07/1941–09/1944	Gdov (by Lake Peipus)	Russia
GFP-727[34]	1944	Novgorod (Lake Ilmen)	Russia
	10/1944–05/1945	Courland	Latvia
GFP-728	1944	Luga	Russia

In the case of GFP-713, several *Aussenkommando* (external commands) were created during the war. These were located and existed as follows:

Table 7. *Aussenkommando* Created by GFP-713

Unit	Aussenkommando	Date Formed and Date Dissolved	Country
GFP-713	*Dorpat (Tartu)*	1942–Dec 1943	Estonia
	Karamishevo	1942–Dec 1943	Russia

Unit	Aussenkommando	Date Formed and Date Dissolved	Country
	Seredka	1942–Jan 1944	Russia
	Reval (Tallinn)	1942–Dec 1943	Estonia
	Kresti (Pskov suburb)	08/1943–02/1944	Russia
	Slavkovichi (SE Pskov)	11/1943–02/1944	Russia
	Volmar (Valmiera)	03/1944–09/1944	Latvia
	Lemsal (Limbazi)	03/1944–09/1944	Latvia
	Heeresgruppe Nord Sonderrat "R"[35]	06/1943 (in the Pskov prison)	Russia
		02/1944 (Valka, then Wenden)	Latvia
		09/1944 (Edole, Courland)	Latvia
		11/1944 (in the Petri School in Danzig)	Germany

Note: In September 1944 *Aussenkommando Sonderrat "R"* absorbed almost all of the personnel of GFP-713. In essence, GFP-713 became a full-time interrogation company for returning German POWs.

In addition to the above-named formations, two additional GFP groups were operating directly under army command: GFP-520 (under 16th Army), and GFP-501 (under 18th Army). One additional unit, GFP-744(L)—a GFP formation created from German Air Force personnel—was operating and was at the disposal of the commander of Army Group North.[36] These were the GFP forces that were available to the army commander as security troops behind the lines.[37]

The Russian Campaign: The GFP in Army Group Center

The region of Army Group Center would see the deployment of the largest number of Secret Field Police units. This is most likely because the region with the greatest number of Soviet guerrillas was located in the area of Belorussia and the central region of the Russian Front. As the guerrilla war intensified, the demand for the employment of the GFP would increase. Therefore, the number of GFP units would only grow as the campaign in the East would drag on. By April 1944 there were a total of 3,142 members of the *Wehrmacht* in the GFP units operating in the region of Army Group Center alone! This number did not even include the 25–30 or so additional *östlichen Freiwilligen* (eastern volunteers) attached to each of these GFP units. In July 1944, the number of Germans assigned to the entire GFP organization stood at around 16,000 men. From June 22, 1941, until the end of November 1941 GFP units in the East were responsible for taking into custody some 5,193 people, and shooting 737 of them outright. What these figures do not say is that of the number taken into custody, the overwhelming majority were not released, but were instead forwarded to the SD for *sonder behandlung* ("special treatment"—a euphemism that meant elimination). The GFP in the area of Army Group Center was initially employed under the following headquarters:

Table 9. Secret Field Police Units in the Region of Army Group Center

Geheime Feldpolizei Gruppen	Befehlshaber Rückwartig Heeresgebiet Mitte 102
Geheime Feldpolizei Gruppe 707	221.Sicherungs Division
Geheime Feldpolizei Gruppe 718	221.Sicherungs Division
Geheime Feldpolizei Gruppe 729	221.Sicherungs Division
Geheime Feldpolizei Gruppe 709[38]	286.Sicherungs Division
Geheime Feldpolizei Gruppe 716	286.Sicherungs Division
Geheime Feldpolizei Gruppe 723	286.Sicherungs Division
Geheime Feldpolizei Gruppe 706	403.Sicherungs Division[39]
Geheime Feldpolizei Gruppe 710	403.Sicherungs Division

Geheime Feldpolizei Gruppe 717	*403.Sicherungs Division*
Geheime Feldpolizei Gruppe 724	*403.Sicherungs Division*
Geheime Feldpolizei Gruppe 709	*339.Bodenständige Division*[40, 41]
Geheime Feldpolizei Gruppe 639	*Panzergruppe 2*
Geheime Feldpolizei Gruppe 703	*Panzergruppe 3*
Geheime Feldpolizei Gruppe 704	*Panzergruppe 4*[42]
Geheime Feldpolizei Gruppe 580	*9. Armee*
Geheime Feldpolizei Gruppe 612	*2. Armee*
Geheime Feldpolizei Gruppe 570	*4. Armee*

Some GFP units did not actually begin operations until 1942. For example, when the *201. Sicherungs Division* (201st Security Division) was activated in the Polotsk region of White Russia in July 1942 it received the newly formed GFP-804. In addition, many of these Secret Field Police units saw active service in various regions of the Eastern Front. For example, GFP-707 and GFP-729 began the Russian campaign under the 221st Security Division (Bialystok & Bobruisk areas), but were later posted to the 286th Security Division (Orsha region). GFP-707 was shifted to the 286th Security Division on December 14, 1941, while GFP-729 was transferred a month earlier in November. In March 1942, when the 221st Security Division was shifted to the region of Army Group South, GFP-729 followed this security division to its new posting in the area of Orel. GFP-709 remained in the region of Army Group Center and was reassigned to the area of Rogachev under the newly established 203rd Security Division in June 1942.[43]

One particularly active GFP unit was GFP-723, operating in the region of Army Group Center under the 286th Security Division. Between July 1941 and September 1943 this GFP unit shot 3,137 people! Another was GFP-707. From 1941–1942 GFP-707 was stationed in Bobruisk (in White Russia). In August and September 1942 GFP-707 took part in a mass shooting of captured Jews who had been hiding in a forest camp located near the town of Bobruisk.[44] On January 5, 1943, GFP-707 was once again transferred—this time to the 201st Security Division. In 1944 GFP-707 was operating under the Ninth Army of Army Group "Center." Since the beginning of 1945 the formation was in the West under the 1st Parachute Army near Wesel in The Netherlands. After the war, many of the members of GFP-707 were brought to trial.

The importance of the Secret Field Police and its assistance to the SS in the elimination of "undesirables" (Jews, Gypsies, Communists, etc.) is highlighted by the fact that in 1944 the entire GFP organization was absorbed into the RSHA. This had occurred after the German Armed Forces Secret Service (the *Abwehr*) fell into disgrace following the July 20, 1944, attempt on Hitler's life, and the discovery that one of the conspirators was Admiral Canaris (the head of the *Abwehr*). The fact that many members of the GFP had come from the RSHA was also another factor in the decision to simply absorb the GFP into the RSHA.

Like elsewhere in Europe, the GFP units employed in the Soviet Union were fully motorized and had tremendous police powers. The leader of these groups was only fully responsible to the Army Group commander to which his unit was attached. All other *Wehrmacht* commanders had only a minor hand in the actions and control of these units. What made the units of the GFP in the East different from all other GFP units employed elsewhere is that on a regular basis each unit recruited a sizable number *östlichen hilfswilliger* (eastern auxiliary volunteers). The structure of the average Secret Field Police group in the East was as follows:

- One Field Police Director
- Eight Field Police Commissioners

- Twenty-Two Field Police Secretaries
- 18-25 Field Police NCOs and Men
- Twenty-Five to Thirty Eastern auxiliary volunteers

In the USSR, the average amount of territory that the German rear area security forces had to cover was enormous. The task assigned to the German rear area forces was simply overwhelming. For example, in July 1941 the 221st Security Division was responsible for the "pacification" of an area approximately 23,333 square miles![45] The 221st Security Division had been created on March 15, 1941, from elements of the 221st Infantry Division. The 221st Security Division initially had a small complement of men, containing only the First, Second and Third Infantry Battalions of the 350th Infantry Regiment (Reinforced), as well as the 701st Guard Battalion. The divisional administrative troops included the 350th Divisional Signals Company, as well as the Staff Headquarters of the 45th Regional Defense Regiment. To these four battalions were added the three Secret Field Police units of roughly small company size: *Geheime Feldpolizei Gruppe 707, 718,* and *729.* Therefore, this security division, which in July 1941 had to cover an area of 23,333 square miles, only had roughly about 4½ battalions of men with which to do it.

The vast amount of territory which the Germans had to secure was another factor which likely led the *Wehrmacht* to behave in a harsh manner towards the subject population—believing like Nicolo Machiavelli that in order to have unchallenged control it was preferable to be feared than to be loved.[46] This tactic however (cruel and brutal treatment of the local population) had the effect of creating more partisan cadres and inspiring further resistance. In fact, the manner in which the Germans were operating in the East was so repressive and cruel that Aleksander Sergueyevich Shcherbakov, who was a member of the *Politburo* (executive committee) under Stalin, as well as a founding member of the Soviet Writers' Union (alongside Maxim Gorky), was famously quoted as saying "We should thank the Germans for their policies which has enabled us to fan the flames of the guerrilla movement."[47]

Nevertheless, the Germans persisted in this tactic throughout the war. This was likely borne out partly out of fear of having to be operating in vast territories where enemy guerrilla bands could appear at anytime from anywhere. Faced with the impossible task of safeguarding tens of thousands of square miles, comprising large numbers of potentially hostile locals, the German reaction was to resort to repressive measures. Throughout the three-year German occupation of the USSR, these killings began to take a toll on the Soviet population. For example, GFP-709 had been involved in the murder of approximately 7,000–8,000 Jews in Mogilev in the beginning of October 1941; providing security at the murder site while the SS and SD provided the killing units. During this *Aktion,* the 339th Static Division had cordoned off the Mogilev ghetto. From October 20–21, 1941 GFP-709 and the 339th Static Division also took part in a mass shooting by Borisov.[48] This also occurred in cooperation with Latvian and Russian auxiliary policemen. In total, about 7,000 Jews were killed in Borisov.[49]

On October 25, 1941 the Jewish population of Tatarsk and Starodub resisted the German attempts to kill them. The Germans had to bring in units from their Army Rear Area security forces in order to quell both revolts. This included elements of the 221st Security Division, which at the time was operating in the area of Bobruisk. In this operation *Wach Bataillon 701* (701st Guard Battalion), which was a part of the 221st Security Division, was employed against the Jewish defenders of Tatarsk and Starodub. Artillery as well as aerial bombardment had to be used before the rebellions were crushed in both towns.[50] GFP-707, 718, and 729 were also brought in by the division to help quell the revolt. As resistance behind the German lines increased many German rear area formations, including the 221st Security Division would have to be reinforced as the Soviet partisan war escalated.[51]

The GFP in Army Group South

In the region of Army Group South, the GFP initially employed eleven formations. However, the need for further GFP units eventually forced the deployment of more substantial Secret Field Police formations. Like elsewhere along the Eastern Front, security measures had been divided between the *Wehrmacht* rear area forces, the Police and the SS. However, after a few months of combat and occupation this division of command began to blur as these three services began to take on more and more of the tasks which had originally been assigned individually to each organization.[52] What this meant was that it did not matter if you were a German Army soldier, SS/SD trooper, or a member of the German Order Police when it came down to (1) killing Jews and other "undesirables," (2) fighting the growing partisan threat, or (3) subjugating and persecuting the Soviet civilian population. As if affirming this point about the overlapping mission of these three branches of Nazi government in the USSR and the general "mission" of the Nazis in the East, Hitler appointed individuals to high ranking posts that would follow these brutal policies to their end. For example, in Ukraine (the former *Gauleiter* for East Prussia) Erich Koch was appointed as *Reichskommissar*. Koch would treat the conquered peoples of the Ukraine quite brutally while exploiting the resources of the region for Germany. Another example was *Generalkommissar für Weissruthenien* (General Commissioner for White Russia) Wilhelm Kube. Kube's rule would be fraught with excesses and abuses. While holding this position Kube personally amassed a great fortune.[53] One expert on the topic described it this way when explaining the type of individuals tasked with running Byelorussia:

> Kube took with him Nazi waiters and dairly men, yesterday's clerks and superintendents, graduates of quick training courses, or, at best, of the famous Nazi Ordensburgen, they now found themselves dizzy with power, self assured yet utterly unfit for their jobs.[54]

Therefore, from the very beginning of the campaign in the East in 1941 the Germans operated in a manner that treated the peoples of the East as *lebensunwerten lebens* (life unworthy of life). This infectious attitude also contributed to the general feeling that one less Russian would benefit Germany and that the war in the USSR was in many respects a "culling" of the Slavic population in the East. The actions not only of the SS and SD, but of the Secret Field Police and the *Wehrmacht* as a whole, ascribed to this idea of reducing the Slavic population in the USSR. It was a mission that may have not been written down on any orders that we can point to and affirm, but the actions of the Germans in the Russian campaign testify all too well to their desire to achieve this goal. The following table lists the initial batch of Secret Field Police formations that were assigned to the area of Army Group South at the start of the Russian campaign on June 22, 1941:

Table 10. German GFP Formations in the Region of Army Group South, 1941

Geheime Feldpolizei Gruppe 560	6. Armee, Heeresgruppe Süd
Geheime Feldpolizei Gruppe 626	11. Armee, Heeresgruppe Süd
Geheime Feldpolizei Gruppe 647	11. Armee, Heeresgruppe Süd
Geheime Feldpolizei Gruppe 708[55]	Befehlshaber Rückwartig Heeresgebiet Süd 103[56]
Geheime Feldpolizei Gruppe 711[57]	Befehlshaber Rückwartig Heeresgebiet Süd 103
Geheime Feldpolizei Gruppe 719	Befehlshaber Rückwartig Heeresgebiet Süd 103
Geheime Feldpolizei Gruppe 720	11. Armee, Heeresgruppe Süd

Geheime Feldpolizei Gruppe 721[58]	Befehlshaber Rückwartig Heeresgebiet Süd 103[59]
Geheime Feldpolizei Gruppe 725	6. Armee, Heeresgruppe Süd
Geheime Feldpolizei Gruppe 726	Befehlshaber Rückwartig Heeresgebiet Süd 103
Geheime Feldpolizei Gruppe 730[60]	6. Armee, Heeresgruppe Süd then under the control of the 105th Hungarian Light Infantry Division which was attached to the Befehlshaber Rückwartig Heeresgebiet Süd 103 command.

The GFP forces deployed in the region of Army Group South altered and changed commands often. Initially beginning the Russian campaign under specific German armies, GFP units were quickly transferred to the rear area security command titled the *Befehlshaber Rückwartig Heeresgebiet Süd 103*. This was the case with the German 444th and 454th Security Divisions, which were originally attached to the 17th Army, while the 213th Security Division would serve under the Sixth Army at the start of the invasion of the Soviet Union.[61] However, by 27 June 1941 the 444th and 454th Security Divisions were listed under the *Befehlshaber Heeresgebiet Süd 103* (Commander of Rear Area South 103).[62] The 213th was later attached to the *Befehlshaber Heeresgebiet Süd 103* command, beginning in August 1941.[63] The 403rd Security Division, which up until August 1941 had been serving in the region of Army Group Center, was transferred to Army Group South that same month and attached to the *Heeresgebiet Süd* command. So by September 1941, the Germans were employing a total of four security divisions in the Ukraine and southern Russia. Adolf Hitler expected to destroy the Soviet Union within this time frame, so he had apparently allocated enough security forces to safeguard the rear of his advancing armies for this time period. The campaign was expected to last only six months. Accordingly, German estimates of the number of rear area forces allotted for the period was, in theory, sufficient for the length of time the campaign was estimated to last. It appears however, that even that calculation was too low. That the Russian campaign would last three years was never anticipated. This problem of an insufficient number of rear area security forces was worse in the area of operation of Army Group South—that is, the region of the Ukraine and southern Russia. In 1942, as the German Army was planning the summer campaign to capture the oil fields of the Caucasus Mountains, the Germans expanded the number of GFP units in the area of the Ukraine and southern Russia.

The GFP in the Region of Army Group South

GFP-725 would see initial employment under the Sixth German Army. It would operate in the region of Army Group South well into 1944 when it would be attached to the Eighth German Army. The initial officer in charge of GFP-725 was *Feldpolizeikommissar* Ignatz Roisel. Roisel fell in battle on April 18, 1942, fighting Red Army parachutists who had landed behind German lines to help organize another partisan group. On June 14, 1942, Kurt Arlt was the Field Police Director (with the army equivalent rank of "major") and head of all GFP units in the region of Army Group South. Previously he had been in charge of the Secret Field Police units assigned to the 213th Security Division.[64] From February to April 1942 Secret Field Police Superintendent Richard Sithof was in charge of GFP-708, GFP-721, and GFP-730–all of which were currently performing security duties in the operational area of the 105th Hungarian Light Infantry Division (in the region of Army Group South). From May 8, 1942, Sithof's successor was *Feldpolizeikommissar* Karl Eschweiler. Eschweiler would end the war with the rank of *Leitender Feldpolizeidirektor*. The *Leitender Feldpolizeidirektor* in the 444th Security Division was named Schmidt.[65] From September

1941 until October 1942 *Feldpolizeidirektor* Hans Stephainski was *Leitender Feldpolizeidirektor beim Heeresgruppe Süd* (Senior Field Police Director by Army Group South). From 1943–1945 this position was taken by *Feldpolizeidirektor* Joachim Kaintzik. The leader of GFP-730 in June 1943 was *Feldpolizeikommissar* Moll. The leader of GFP-708 in April 1943 was *Feldpolizeikommissar* Forejtnik. Some GFP officials were made responsible for several GFP units within a higher divisional or army/rear area headquarters. These posts often had a large turnover of commanders as seen by the following listings:

Leitender Feldpolizeidirektor für die Gruppen in den Ung. 105. Division (GFP-708, 721 & 730)
April 2, 1942, *Leitender Feldpolizeidirektor* Sithoff
May to July 1942 *Feldpolizeikommissar* Dr. Heinrichs
August 27, 1942, *Feldpolizeidirektor* Karl Eschweiler[66]

Leitender Feldpolizeidirektor für die Gruppen GFP 706, 719 u. 725
February to July 1942 *Feldpolizeidirektor* Kurt Arlt

Leitender Feldpolizeidirektor bei der 213. Sicherungs Division (GFP-706, 719, & 725)
From August 30, 1942, *Feldpolizeidirektor* Kurt Arlt

Leitender Feldpolizeidirektor bei Befehlshaber Heeresgebiet Süd 103
From January 4, 1943 *Feldpolizeidirektor* Friedrich Walz.

Leitender Feldpolizeidirektor bei der 444. Sicherungs Division (GFP-711, 720, & 726)
Feldpolizeidirektor Schmidt

Leitender Feldpolizeidirektor bei der 454. Sicherungs Division (GFP-708, 721, 726, & 740)
Feldpolizeidirektor Sithoff, then *Feldpolizeidirektor* Hochgräbe

In July 1942, the 403rd Security Division was transferred to the region of Army Group South. GFP-706 which was operating under the 403rd Security Division was also transferred. The leader of GFP-706 from March to April 1942 was *Feldpolizeikommissar* Jakobs; from May 1942, it was *Feldpolizeikommissar* Beuys.

GFP-708 was employed under 454th Security Division of the *Befehlshaber Rückwartig Heeresgebiet Süd*. Its Secret Field Police commanders were as follows:

January 25, 1942, *Feldpolizeikommissar*? [illegible]
February to April 1942 *Feldpolizeikommissar* Haimann
March to June 1942 *Feldpolizeikommissar* Gerhahn
July to August 1942 *Feldpolizeikommissar* Haimann
October to November 1942 *Feldpolizeikommissar* Lamy
December 25, 1942, *Feldpolizeikommissar* Haimann[67]

From January until November/December 1942 GFP-719 was led by *Feldpolizeikommissar* Schöffler. From November or December 1942 *Leitender Feldpolizeidirektor* Kurt Arlt temporarily led this unit. GFP-720 had been created on May 21, 1941. It was employed under 444th Security Division of the *Befehlshaber Rückwartig Heeresgebiet Süd 103* (Commander of Rear Area Forces South 103). The commander of this GFP unit on August 25, 1942, was *Feldpolizeikommissar* Steng. GFP-721 had been Formed April 26, 1941. It was employed under 454th Security Division of the *Befehlshaber Rückwartig Heeresgebiet Süd 103*. Between January and September 1942 *Feldpolizeikommissar* Müller led this GFP formation. In October 1942, it was taken over *Feldpolizeikommissar* Karl-Heinz Meissner. GFP-725 had been formed May 21, 1941 for employment under the German Sixth Army of Army Group South. The leaders of this GFP unit were as follows:

1. From January to February 1942 *Feldpolizeikommissar* Reisl (or Roisl?);
2. In March 1942 *Feldpolizeikommissar* Schweitzer;

3. From April to August 1942 *Feldpolizeikommissar* Schweitzer;
4. From October to November 1942 *Feldpolizeikommissar* Karhan, and
5. In December 1942 *Feldpolizeikommissar* Schweitzer.

GFP-730 had been created on June 21, 1941, and was employed in late summer 1941 as part of the *Befehlshaber Rückwartig Heeresgebiet Süd 103* command. From January 1942 until June of the same year its leader was *Feldpolizeikommissar* Kunze. Kunze went on vacation in June 1942. From July until August 1942 *Feldpolizeikommissar* Pudewell led this Secret Field Police Group, given that Kunze was claiming to be suffering from an old eye ailment and refused to return until it was taken care of. In September 1942 Kunze returned from vacation and once again assumed command of GFP-730.[68] The unit later operated under the newly reestablished Sixth German Army in the region of Army Group South Ukraine, but was disbanded in late July or early August 1944 and its personnel absorbed into the RSHA.

GFP Participation in the Holocaust

Although the Germans experienced shortages of rear area security forces in the regions of the Baltic States as well as north and central Russia and Belorussia, these deficiencies were not as great simply because the areas taken and covered by Army Group South were larger. In spite of these shortages of rear area forces in the summer and fall of 1941, the destruction of the Russian-Jewish population proceeded quickly. A possible factor in this may have been the "criminal orders" which labeled all Jews as partisans—thus allowing any front line or rear area formation, whether it was an SS, GFP, police, or army unit, to murder them on sight. It goes a long way to explain how these GFP units, as well as police, army security and garrison formations assigned to control the rear areas of the advancing German armies and to combat the partisans, were again and again used to directly and indirectly assist in the policy of extermination which the *SS Einsatzgruppen* murder commandos were principally charged with from 1941 to 1943.

As can be seen, Army Group South was to have comparatively fewer security divisions than in the areas controlled by Army Group North and Center. This was simply because of the larger territories that made up the Ukraine and southern Russia. However, it appears that the murder of the Jewish population in the Ukraine and southern Russia was actually greater than all other areas. One reason for this was the fact that two entire SS killing units had been assigned to this region. Another reason has to be the policy of shooting all Jews on sight which, as we shall see, *Wehrmacht* forces appear to have followed. From 22 June 1941 until December 1942 the various *SS Einsatzgruppe* totals for the murder of the Jewish population in the USSR stood as follows:

- Region of Army Group North [Einsatzgruppe A]—363,337 Jews killed.
- Region of Army Group Center [Einsatzgruppe B]—134,000 Jews killed.
- Region of Army Group South [Einsatzgruppe C]—118,341 Jews killed.
- Region of Army Group South [Einsatzgruppe D]—91,728 Jews killed.
- Forces Directly Under the Higher-SS & Police Leaders—82,114 Jews killed.
- Higher-SS & Police Leader South—363,211 Jews killed.[69]

As the figures above indicate, the region of Army Group South experienced a total number of 573,280 Jews killed. This is quite a significant number of victims. The German

Army operating in this southern region of the USSR was, like the rest of the regions of the Russian front, not free of implication in the murder of the Jewish population or, for that matter, in the murder of innocent Ukrainian and Russian civilians or captured Red Army soldiers. Killing of civilians is illegal and immoral, but the murder of captured soldiers who have surrendered is equally reprehensible and is considered a war crime. This was also true of the behavior of most armies, especially European armies in the 1940s. It matters not that the Germans were operating "under orders," since it is up to individuals to decide if an act is moral or immoral. Most Germans serving in the *Wehrmacht* had lived in pre-Nazi times and knew what was morally right and what was morally wrong. Christopher Browning has already pointed to the fact that men, who refused to take part in these killings, were ostracized but not really punished. Browning instead blames peer pressure from what he terms the "immediate community," which was the particular unit which the German soldier was attached to, and the "society at large," which was anti-Semitic and anti-communist Nazi Germany.[70]

The war diary of army Corporal Rudolf Lange is an example of this unity of purpose regarding the murder of Jews which pervaded the German armed forces on the Eastern Front. On July 1, 1941, he wrote that sixty prisoners were shot at the regimental headquarters. The entry for the next day simply read: "Jews shot."[71] Thus the ideological struggle which was waged in the USSR pervaded the manner in which the Germans' thought processes worked regarding the war in the East and in particular, the way they viewed and treated the Jews:

> A striking example of how the theory invaded German thinking is furnished in the format of portions of two reports by the army's Secret Field Police in occupied Russia:
>
> Punishable Offenses by Members of the Population—
>   Espionage—1
>   Theft of Ammunition—1
>   Suspected Jews (Judenverdacht)—3
> Punishable Offenses by Members of the Population—
>   Moving About with Arms—11
>   Theft—2
>   Jews—2
>
> In the culmination of this theory, to be a Jew was a punishable offense (*strafbare Handlung*). Thus, it was the function of the rationalization of criminality to turn the destruction process into a kind of judicial proceeding.[72]

Within this framework of murder, the GFP formations charged headlong and with full vigor to eliminate the perceived "Judeo-Bolshevist" threat. The following are numerous sample unit histories of these GFP formations detailing their actions and comportment while operating in the USSR. By assessing these we can come to a base judgment of their overall behavior in the East.

Cases Studies of Secret Field Police Units in the East, 1941–1945

This section contains case studies on the activities of numerous GFP units which operated in the USSR. When taken together, a general pattern of criminal activity emerges—regardless of whether the GFP units operated in the northern, central, or southern sector of the Russian Front. This comportment was fostered for several reasons. Nazi racial theories had been force-fed to the German nation even before the Nazi Party takeover of the German government in 1933. This not merely included a hatred of Jews, but also of Gypsies and Slavic people as a whole. Numerous illegal and immoral commands and orders, such as the infamous Commissar Order, were established shortly before the start of the Russian campaign that allowed the German military to act criminally without fear of ramifications. Anti-communism and a tradition of conservative and/or reactionary views within the German military was another factor that propelled such brutal behavior. The intensity and size of the conflict also worked to dehumanize its participants, thus making them more susceptible to killing without forethought of right vs. wrong.[73]

Under the Nazis, Germans had a general attitude that Slavic people were inferior to Aryans, believing that they were not worthy of life. Since the Soviet Union was the home of the majority of the Slavic people, German actions there would be an expression of this sentiment. This too, contributed to the brutalization and murder that occurred in the East. The genocide of the Jews dehumanized and cheapened life even further. There was also a psychological factor that may have played a role in the brutal and repressive manner in which the German Secret Field Police (as well as the German military as a whole) operated in the USSR. This was the sheer size and scope of the territories captured by the Germans and the relatively few rear area formations that were initially assigned to cover these vast tracks of land. Under these circumstances the Germans developed a "cowboys and Indians" mentality, where fear of the indigenous population rising up and overwhelming the numerically inferior occupation force was etched into the minds of the German rear area security forces. The growing partisan threat threatened German rear area forces from every direction. German security troops were subject to attack at any given time. The relentless fear that civilians living around them could be part of the resistance movement must have had psychological effects on the German occupation forces. The stress of not knowing where the next attack would come certainly would have hardened and brutalized most German soldiers and may have worked to unhinge many of them. In order to mitigate this threat, the Germans decided to resort to terror, brutality and genocide. Given who the Nazis were, who could imagine that their response would have been different?

GFP-520

This unit was created in Vienna on August 15, 1939, under *Wehrkreis VII*. During the Polish campaign, this formation operated in the region of Third German Army, which was attacking south, out of Prussia and in the direction of Warsaw, Brest-Litovsk and Lublin. During this campaign GFP-520 was attached to one of numerous *SS-Einsatzkommandos* which swept into Poland immediately behind the German Army. Their mission was to locate, apprehend and in most instances, eliminate important Polish intellectuals, leaders, educators and military commanders in order to head off any possible resistance. GFP-520 was assigned to *Einsatzkommando 5/II* which had the task of securing Polish leaders in Lublin.[74] This *Einsatzkommando* was led by *SS-Sturmbannführer* Dr. Robert Schefe.[75] Before being selected to lead *Einsatzkommando 5/II*, Dr. Schefe had been director of the State Police Station in Allenstein since 1938. After the Polish campaign, he would work in the *Reichssicherheitshauptamt Amt* (RSHA)—the Reich Main Security Office.[76]

On September 12, 1939, and working under the orders of Einsatzkommando 5/II, GFP-520, as well as two companies of *Feldgendarmerie Bataillon 652 [mot.]* (652nd Motorized Military Police Battalion) fanned out across all villages throughout the region of Lublin, seeking prominent persons on a Nazi "hit list." Jewish villages were targeted and many houses were plundered. During this time 102 Polish mayors were arrested by this secret field police unit. Those men were later executed.[77] GFP-520 later went on to form the cadre for the Criminal Police office in Kielce (west and south of Lublin). In this they were also assisted by ethnic Germans in Poland who had been quickly recruited as *Hilfspolizei* (Auxiliary Police).[78] In 1940, Field Police Director Ernst Wagner was assigned command of GFP-520.[79]

Like the other GFP units earmarked for the Russian campaign GFP-520 was expanded and its staff doubled in size, going from fifty to ninety-five members. It operated behind the lines of 18th German Army as it moved through the Baltic States in the summer and fall of 1941 and was said to have collaborated closely with *SS-Einsatzgruppe A* against both the partisans and the Jewish population. Personnel documents from one former member of GFP-520 told the following story of this single GFP individual:

> Josef Deschmer a WWI veteran who joined Geheime Feldpolizei Gruppe 520 in August 1939 when this unit was created in Vienna. He wasn't a police officer but a chauffeur/mechanic. In 1939, a GFP unit had only 50 members, 33 police officers and 17 soldiers in support such as chauffeurs & clerks. In June 1941, he was promoted to Feldwebel and most likely acted as the unit's motor-pool NCO. GFP units expanded for their big task in the east from 50 to 95 members, 55 police agents, 40 soldiers in support. GFP 520 was a part of the 18th Army and thus they followed the path of the 18th Army. In the Baltic States and North Russia, they collaborated closely with Einsatzgruppe A in their actions against partisans and the Jewish population. In April 1942, he left his unit most likely because of health problems and he was transferred to a motor pool unit and spent a lot of time in convalescent units until his discharge in January 1943.[80]

GFP-520 continued to serve under 16th Army throughout the war. It ended the conflict serving under Army Group "Courland."

GFP-570

This GFP unit was created on August 26, 1939 in *Wehrkreis XI* (11th Military District) in Nuremberg. Quite often GFP-570 has been erroneously labeled as GFP-507 (but no such GFP formation with the numerical designation "507th" ever existed in the ranks of the Secret Field Police). In September/October 1939, during the Polish Campaign, the unit served under Fourth German Army. It continued to serve under this army while stationed in France from 1940 until the spring of 1941, when it was shifted east for the coming invasion of the Soviet Union. It took part in *Operation Barbarossa* from 1941–1942—serving in the region of Army Group Center. During this time period (1941–1942) the commander was *Feldpolizeikommissar* Jochum. However it would be *Feldpolizeikommissar* Hans Gerhard Günther Riedel who would lead GFP-570 throughout most of its operational employment in the Soviet Union.[81] Although one unconfirmed source states that *Oberstleutnant* (Lieutenant-Colonel) Hinterseer led this formation from July 1942 to July 1943. This same source states that *Feldpolizeikommissar* Wertel was the deputy director of the unit in July 1943.[82]

In the spring of 1943 the *Geheime Feldpolizei* assisted in the discovery of Polish Army officers who had been executed by the NKVD at Katyn on March 5, 1940. A report from March 27, 1943, states that GFP personnel from GFP-570 forced 35 local Russians into digging up part of the mass grave that eventually uncovered about twenty-two thousand Polish Army officers shot by the Red Army at the end of the Polish campaign in 1939. This massacre of approximately 22,000 Polish officers of various ranks was prompted by NKVD Chief Lavrentiy Beria's proposal to shoot all captive members of the Polish Officer Corps. The

9. The Secret Field Police in the Soviet Union

order was dated March 5, 1940, and was approved by Joseph Stalin and the Soviet *Politburo*. The discovery of the bodies was a great propaganda coup for the Germans, although the Soviets blamed the murder on the Nazis:

Gruppe Geheime Feldpolizei 570
Außenkdo. bei Heeresgruppe Mitte
Tgb.-Nr. 56/43

O.-U., den 27. März 1943

Vorbericht über den Beginn der Ausgrabungen.

Vom OKH. ist die Freilegung des Massengrabes angeordnet worden.

Zur Durchführung der erforderlichen Erdarbeiten sind aus den benachbarten Dörfern 35 Zivilrussen befohlen worden, die am 29. 3. die Arbeit aufnehmen. Ferner ist das notwendige Material wie Tragbahren, Wasserwagen und ein Sezierraum beschafft bzw. in unmittelbarer Nähe aufgebaut.

Zur Sicherung des Geländes, insbesondere um Leichenplünderungen zu unterbinden, ist eine Nachtwache—gestellt vom russ. Ordnungsdienst in Stärke von 1/6—eingerichtet.

Die Abtragung des Hügels wird etwa 5 Tage in Anspruch nehmen.

gez. Voß
Feldpolizeisekretär[83]

Under Reidel's command, GFP-570 operated in the Russian city of Mogilev from 1943–1944. This GFP unit was involved in the gassing of at least seven partisans by means of "*Gaswagen*," or trucks outfitted to kill the intended victims by pumping carbon monoxide fumes from the truck's engine exhaust system (Court decisions: LG Kiel 740614 / BGH 750415).[84] The principal party tried in this case was Heinz Gerhard Günther, who was eventually acquitted.[85] GFP-570 is one of the more notable units of the GFP because there were post-war war crimes trials in both the DDR (*Deutsches Demokratische Republik*—East Germany) as well as in West Germany. Strangely, in the case of the West German trial, the unit was mislabeled—calling the formation GFP-507, instead of GFP-570. This is a mistake as the Germans never raised a "507th Secret Field Police Unit."

This unit was accused of illegal arrest, misuse of statements, extortion and shooting men, women and children that stood as "suspected partisans" or "partisan supporters." In addition, the unit was accused of forcibly deporting Soviet citizens to work in Germany. GFP-570 was also guilty of shooting five partisans which had been arrested shortly after an anti-guerrilla operation. As stated earlier, it was also accused of the murder of prisoners by means of "Gas Wagons" [see also JuNSV Nr. 809].[86] In this case Herbert Hugo Paland was given a life sentence.[87] The region of the USSR where GFP-570 operated was quite varied. During the campaign in the USSR, GFP-570 served in the Ukraine, White Russia and central Russia. The principal towns in which the unit's activities were recorded included: Tolochin, Smolensk, Orscha, Mogilev, Pazyn, Spass-Demensk, Wschody, Juchnow, Kislowo, Nowy Bychow–Rogatschew, and Wschody.[88] The 570th Secret Field Police Group was, in many ways, a typical GFP formation. Standard operating procedure for these units was to assign a certain number of its men to the various towns and cities in the region where the secret field police group was operating. An example would be the order of battle for GFP-570 for its entry into the city of Orscha (dated July 14, 1941) located just west of Smolensk.

Order of Battle, GFP-570, 14 July 1941

14 July 1941–*Einsatzkommando Orscha*:

1. *Kommandeur—Feldpolizeikommissar Müller*
   Sonderführer Ebert
   Hilfsfeldpolizeibeamte: Corporal Dornhecker.
   Fahrer (Driver): Soldat Früngel

2. *Feldpolizeisekretär* Engel
   Hilfsdolmetscher: Nizienko
   Hilfsfeldpolizeibeamte: Corporal Droste and *Soldat* Kurzhals
   Fahrer: Feldwebel Mohr
3. *Feldpolizeisekretär* Rostalski
   Sonderführer Torinus
   Unteroffizier Paland
   Gefreiter Hartung
   Soldaten Mau, and Ermark,
   Fahrer: Feldwebel Dukat and *Soldat* Rangk
4. *Feldpolizeisekretär* Isensee
   Hilfsfeldpolizeibeamte Feldwebel Eisenblätter
   Gefreiter Hartung
   Soldaten Stentzel and Hennemann

The 570th Secret Field Police Group was reorganized for its entry into Tolochin and Smolensk from July 20–21, 1941. The organization of the unit was divided into two, then three *Sekretariat* and now looked as follows[89]:

Order of Battle, GFP-570, 20–21 July 1941

July 20, 1941–*Einsatzkommando Tolotschin* (Tolochin, also spelled Talachin, in Belorussia):

1. *Kommandeur–Feldpolizeisekretär* Rostalski
   Hilfsdolmetscher: Soldat Torgler
Fahrer: Feldwebel Dukat
2. *Kommandeur–Feldpolizeisekretär* Engel
   Sonderführer Torinus
   Hilfsfeldpolizeibeamte Müller
   Hilfsfeldpolizeibeamte Kurzhals
   Fahrer: Horstmann
   Fahrer: Mäcker

21 July 1941–*Einsatzkommando* Smolensk:

1. *Kommandeur–Feldpolizeikommissar:* Jochum
   Hilfsfeldpolizeibeamte: Feldwebel Dornhecker
   Fahrer: Sergeant Mohr
2. *Kommandeur–Feldpolizeisekretär:* Rostalski
   Sonderführer Torinus
   Hilfsfeldpolizeibeamte: Feldwebel Strottmann
   Hilfsfeldpolizeibeamte: Gefreiter Sakowitz
   Hilfsfeldpolizeibeamte: Gefreiter Müller
   Hilfsfeldpolizeibeamte: Soldat Mau
   Fahrer: Corporal Dukat
   Fahrer: Soldat Rangk
3. *Kommandeur–Feldpolizeisekretär:* Czinczel
   Hilfsdolmetscher: Soldat Torgler
   Hilfsfeldpolizeibeamte: Wachtmeister (Sergeant) Wenk
   Hilfsfeldpolizeibeamte: Wachtmeister Wengenroth
   Hilfsfeldpolizeibeamte: Wachtmeister Dossmann
   Hilfsfeldpolizeibeamte: Soldat Bürger
   Fahrer: Unteroffizier Grosche
   Fahrer: Soldat Gebhart[90]

From July 21–26, 1941, GFP-570 continued to examine the civilian population of the city district of Smolensk. It was at this time the Germans began advertising for V-personnel within the city.[91] However on July 27, 1941 GFP-570 was shifted west from Smolensk to the forest region east of Krasny Rog—near Chochlowo (Chochlow), in the Zamosc region of Eastern Poland.[92] A year later (July 27, 1942) GFP-570 was operating in central Russia. Through the investigation of *Feldpolizeisekretär* Michaelis (a member of GFP-570), it was ascertained that Maria Savkina, since the winter of 1941/42, had eventually been swayed by the recruitment efforts of a local partisan band; and had voluntarily joined this guerrilla unit in the spring. After being interrogated by Michaelis on July 26, 1942, Savkina was ordered shot.

On this same day Michaelis interrogated Nikolai Karpov, a twenty-two-year-old volunteer partisan who had been recently captured by the Germans. During the interview, it was disclosed that in February 1942 Karpov had killed two German soldiers. After the questioning, he was promptly shot by the GFP.[93] On August 3, 1942, *Feldpolizeisekretär* Michaelis reported on the interrogation and execution of Daniel Ossipov, who had been appointed mayor of a town by the Germans in October 1941. According to the Germans, Ossipov had switched sides in May 1942 and had even joined the Communist Party. How they came to find this was not explained in the report.[94] That same day *Hilfsfeldpolizeibeamter Feldwebel* Droste interrogated two suspected partisan members: Xenia Suyeva and Piotr (Peter) Tiyanienkov. While Suyeva was eventually released, Tiyanienkov was ordered shot.[95] On July 18, 1942, two members from GFP-570, *Gefreiter* Kurzhals and *Sonderführer* Liebus took part in an anti-partisan sweep with a *Jagdkommando* from the 268th Infantry Division. Every partisan that was captured were shot.[96]

On August 4 *Feldpolizeisekretär* Michaelis, *Unteroffizier* Prokscha and a group of Russians serving in the pro–German *Wachmannschafte* (Local Defense Guard Units)[97] performed an operation in the region of Bolschaye–Lochovo which netted the arrest of fifteen partisan suspects. Thirteen were men and two were women. Also seized were a sizable number of weapons. After their interrogation ten men and one woman were shot, while the rest were sent to an SD prison camp. On August 7, 1942, *Feldpolizeisekretär* Michaelis interrogated Kusma Ivanov from Vyasovez. In the course of questioning, it was discovered that Ivanov was a member of the NKVD and working as a part of the local partisan support services. The suspect was shot after interrogation.[98]

On August 9 *Feldpolizeisekretär* Isensee and *Sonderführer* Torgler interrogated Peter Yaroschevskiy, a Jew who was believed by the Germans to be a principal leader of the partisan bands operating in the district of Dorogobusch (in the Smolensk *Oblast*). Yaroschevskiy had been caught with messages from Moscow. After interrogation, he was shot.[99] The significance of the messages found on his person was most likely what convinced the Germans of the importance of Yaroschevskiy to the Smolensk Oblast partisan movement. In fact, in August and September 1942 Joseph Stalin had summoned leading personnel from the Party underground and commanders and commissars of large guerrilla formations operating in Belorussia, the Ukraine, and the Orel and Smolensk Oblast to attend a conference to improve partisan unit efficiency[100]; as well as to formulate a common strategy for the estimated 608 separate guerrilla units behind the German lines. According to one source, only 69 out these 608 guerrilla bands possessed radios and therefore,[101] the ability to communicate and take orders directly from the Central Staff of the Partisan Movement located in Moscow.[102]

On August 11, 1942, *Feldpolizeisekretär* Michaelis delivered three prisoners to the commander of security forces for the rear area of the 263rd Infantry Division. These included the Russians, Anna Bolrova, Yegor Kupriyanov and Dimitriy Borissov.[103] Anna Bolrova maintained connections with the partisans and supported them. Kupriyanov had betrayed a German reconnaissance troop (which numbered thirty men) to the partisans. Subsequently twenty-seven men from that force were killed. Dimitriy Borisov belonged to a partisan group and had shot a German soldier and the Russian woman who had his child. All three prisoners were executed. That same day thirteen Russians were apprehended in and around the town of Chvatov-Savod who appeared to have Partisan connections. After interrogation, members of GFP-570 ordered five of these Russians shot; four were placed in prison, and the rest were released.

That same day *Feldpolizeikommissar* Stockmann and *Hilfsfeldpolizeibeamte* Märthesheimer interrogated Otto Hammer, a gunner who was serving in the Eighth Company of 260th Artillery Regiment. Suspicion about Hammer's loyalty had begun in 1940. While stationed in France, Hammer had tried to join the French Foreign Legion. However suspicious his behavior had been, the GFP came to the conclusion that the risk that Hammer would engage in anti–German espionage activity did not exist. On August 12th *Hilfsfeldpolizeibeamter* Sergeant Dossmann and *Sonderführer* Plath interrogated two Russians whose surnames were "Kusmezov" and "Gavrin," who were serving in the German sponsored *Ordnungsdienst*. The *Ordnungsdienst* was the Russian indigenous police force that had been established in 1941 as part of the German rear area security force.[104] They were employed by the Germans because they knew the local region, but they were never completely trusted. For example, the force was armed with Russian weapons and the Germans purposely limited the number of bullets which this force could carry. After the interrogation both men were released for lack of evidence.

On August 13, 1942, *Feldpolizeisekretär* Isensee and *Sonderführer* Torgler interrogated and then shot two Russians, Henia Yekaterina and Yelena Tarakanova, for being *Flintenweiber* (female gunmen).[105] On August 15, 1942, *Feldpolizeikommissar* Lamy and *Feldpolizeisekretär* Hansen were sent to investigate the murder of Senior Lance-Corporal Robert Meyer. Meyer had been found dead at his *Kubelwagen* (jeep). The contents of the trunk of the vehicle were missing, and murder was deemed to have been a simple robbery.[106] Four days later, on August 17 *Hilfsfeldpolizeibeamter* Sergeant Droste reported that a member of the "*Shabo*" partisan band named Losutschenkov was apprehended. Losutschenkov had been identified by locals as having assassinated the town mayor and three German soldiers who happened to be present. Sergeant Droste reported that Losutschenkov was executed soon after his capture.[107] A day later, on August 18 *Feldpolizeisekretär* Isensee and *Sonderführer* Torgler reported that Eugen Danilov, a Russian defector who had crossed through the defense lines of the German 263rd Infantry Division,[108] had been interrogated and found to be a spy. Danilov was shot after the interrogation.[109] On August 21, 1942, *Hilfsfeldpolizeibeamter* Sergeant Prokscha reported that Nikolai Procherov and Aleksandra Radionova had been apprehended.[110] Both had been living in the town of Deminka. Procherov was accused of destroying a bakery, a bridge and killing a mule in the town of Chvadov Savod. With the aid of Radionova, Nikolai Procherov was also charged with the assassination the town's pro–German mayor.

After killing the mayor, both had fled to the forest. However, they were apprehended and soon after were ordered shot. A day later (August 22) *Hilfspolizeibeamter* Corporal Laubert reported that on August 4 Ivan Kulakov, a known *Komsomol* member, had been apprehended in the town of Koptevo.[111] After interrogation by GFP-570, Kulakov was sent to an SD prison camp for further interrogation.[112] That same day *Feldpolizeikommissar* Stockmann and *Sonderführer* Torgler apprehended and interrogated Uyana Mytinkova. She had betrayed three German soldiers and the district mayor of Vschody to the guerrillas, who were subsequently apprehended by the partisans and killed. During the interrogation, she confessed to being a close colleague of the partisan leader, Charitonov. After interrogation Mytinkova was handed over to the SD for *Besondere Behandlung* ("Special Treatment").

On August 24, 1942, *Hilfsfeldpolizeibeamter* Sergeant Dossmann and *Sonderführer* Plath from GFP-570 interrogated a Russian named Schura Kondaurova who was working for *Luftwaffen-Bau-Regiment 6/XIII*.[113] This female was brought to the attention of the Secret Field Police because she was not registered and was working without proper documentation. The suspicion of espionage was confirmed, not because she readily admitted to it, but because (1) she had requested to work in the headquarters of the regiment and (2) she gave contradictory statements when interrogated. The Russian was turned over to the SD for "Special Treatment." A day later, *Feldpolizeisekretär* Hansen wrote a report about an ambush that occurred on August 5, 1942, by Russian partisans, of a German veterinary company by the village of Rshavez, near Yasveno. The German unit ambushed was the Second Platoon of the 592nd Army Veterinary Hospital. This German platoon consisted of one officer and 45 NCOs and enlisted men. It had under its supervision 80 horses and a large supply of veterinary medicine and equipment—all of which were being transported to Terenino by way of Talishkino.[114] During the ambush, two German soldiers were killed and six were wounded. The partisans also killed ten horses and absconded with the remaining seventy. *Feldpolizeisekretär* Hansen concluded that the reason for the guerrilla attack was to acquire horses. The Germans had responded by sending the 555th Security Battalion after the partisan force. One Russian was captured: Vasiliy Filtschenkov, who claimed that he had been forcibly recruited by the partisans. Hansen reported that in spite of Filtschenkov's claim, this seventeen year old was executed.[115] On August 26, 1942, *Hilfsfeldpolizeibeamter Unteroffizier* Wagner and *Sonderführer* Schroeter reported killing Aleksey Schurikov, who had been identified as the commander of a partisan battalion operating around the town of Klutschi.[116]

The actions of several *Sekretariat* from GFP-570 between August 31 and September 30, 1942, are a perfect example of the "regular" behavior of the unit while it operated in the Soviet Union. On September 13, a weekly report for GFP-570 related that on August 31, 1942, a *Sekretariat* of GFP-570, led by *Hilfsfeldpolizeibeamte* Sergeant Menzel, was operating behind the rear area of the 267th Infantry Division in search of partisans.[117] The area of operations was the region west of Milyatino. The German 267th Infantry Division spent all of 1942 fighting defensive battles in and around the towns of Gzhatsk, northeast of Vyazma, on the motor highway to Moscow, Yuchnov and Spass-Demensk. During 1942, the 267th Infantry Division served in the first half of the year under the Fourth Panzer Army; and the second half under the Fourth Army mainly in the region of Spass-Demensk.[118] Sergeant Menzel and his *Sekretariat* entered Milyatino with firm intent to neutralize the partisan threat in that town.

The local Mayor of Milyatino, as well as policemen from the town were asked to assist in the apprehension of suspected Soviet agents. The week was spent combing the town and the surrounding area. Three uniformed Russians living in the woods outside of the town as well as an agent operating inside the town were eventually apprehended by the *Sekretariat*.[119] Menzel's detachment from GFP-570 also interrogated a Russian woman by the name of Kristina Guryev, whose son Alexander Guryev, relayed that the Russians Vasili Filtchenko, Yegor Filtchenko and Michail Filtchenko, were part of a secret Russian signals unit operating in the villages of Asovaya and Bolschaya. At the end of this investigation, *Hilfsfeldpolizeibeamter* Paland wrote in an after-action report that Kristina Guryev, Vasili and Michail Filtschenkov were ordered shot by Menzel.[120] On September 15, 1942, the unit further reported shooting Maria Anayeva, on suspicion of being a *"Partisanhelfer"* ("partisan helper").¹²¹ Between September 7–8 two Russians, Michail Yakovlev and Alexander Orlov who were suspected of being spies, were also ordered shot. During that same time period a man by the name of Yacob Petrakov from the locality of Polnyschevo was caught with a pistol on his person. Although Petrakov pleaded that he was only armed to protect himself from the partisans, he was immediately executed.¹²² On September 3, 1942, a *Sekretariat* from GFP-570, led by *Feldpolizeikommissar* Stockmann and Corporal Paland, reported encountering a small partisan unit. During the firefight four partisans were killed while the rest managed to get away. During the engagement, Corporal Mäcker and a Cossack volunteer were wounded.¹²³

On September 9, 1942, a *Sekretariat* led by Sergeant Droste of GFP-570, accompanied the pro–German "Volga" Battalion of the *"Graukopf"* experimental brigade of Russian volunteers on a partisan hunt near the town of Kamenka. Pro-Nazi Russian policemen from the town of Istopki also tagged along. The operation reported capturing and executing Feodor Szisov, who was identified as a partisan organizer. The report also declared in a matter-of-fact manner that more Russian civilians were shot during this anti-partisan sweep.¹²⁴ The report of the operations of GFP-570 near Kamenka, dated "14 September 1942" also mentioned that a *Selbstschutzkompanie der Geheime Feldpolizei 570* ("Self Defense Company of the 570th Secret Field Police Group") existed. This might have been however, *Ost-Kompanie 612*, since this unit was known to have made anti-partisan sweeps alongside GFP-570. *Ost-Kompanie 612* operated as an attached formation of this secret field police unit from 1942–1945. This volunteer company was composed of Russian nationals. The report listed a Russian, Peter Andreyenkov, as joining the volunteer company.¹²⁵ However, other pro–German formations were used.

During the summer of 1942 GFP-570 also employed a Tartar Volunteer Company, which was led by a Russian officer, Oberleutnant Sorov.¹²⁶ On July 15, 1942, this Tartar Company alongside a GFP group led by Corporal Paland led a anti-partisan operation in the region of 12th Army Corps. During the operation two partisans were shot and three were apprehended.¹²⁷ A report dated "12 September 1942" written by *Feldpolizeisekretär* Karich, investigated two attempted desertions from the Second Company, First Battalion, of the 359th Infantry Regiment.¹²⁸ The soldiers in question were Private Josef Butta who was eventually convicted and shot; and Private First Class Julius Reitzner. GFP-570's investigation concluded that Russian flyers, encouraging German soldiers to desert, were the apparent reason for the desertion attempt. What is fascinating about this report is not so much the desertion itself, since the German Army experienced them on a regular basis, but that throughout 1942 the 359th Infantry Regiment (of the 181st Division) was supposed to have been stationed in Drontheim, Norway and *not* in central Russia!¹²⁹ Either the report was incorrect regarding the numerical designation of the regiment, or perhaps the First Battalion of the 359th Infantry Regiment was temporarily transferred to central Russia sometime in 1942.¹³⁰ In fact, the 181st Infantry Division was only transferred from Norway in October 1943, when it was sent to Yugoslavia. When the 181st Division left Norway, it left behind the 349th Infantry Regiment (which was then attached to the 230th Infantry Division), replacing it with the 363rd Infantry Regiment. The 359th Infantry Regiment however, was retained by the 181st Division and operated in Yugoslavia until the end of the war.¹³¹

From September 1942–July 1943 GFP-570 was operationally under the orders of Lieutenant-Colonel Hinterseer, the Intelligence Officer of the Fourth German Army. During this time period GFP-570's main office was located in the Russian city of Roslavl. The records examined consist of the unit's weekly activity reports for this period which describe who was interrogated, why, the results, and who conducted the interrogation. For example, during the month of September 1942 (consisting of four weekly reports) a total of approximately one hundred alleged Soviet agents, Partisans, Communists, Jews, deserters and Soviet citizens were interrogated. Of these, about eighteen were shot (agents, Partisans, and Jews determined to be "fanatical" communists). The rest were either released or put in prison camps. All of those found to be "partisan-helpers" were shot or put in camps.

Red Army deserters were turned over to the *Abwehr* for interrogation by military intelligence. Many of the interrogations in these reports, perhaps 30 percent, were routine counterintelligence screenings of Russian civilians requested by various *Heer* (Army) and *Luftwaffe* (Air Force) units employing them in the Roslavl area. The order to execute the detainees that were interrogated came directly and exclusively from Lieutenant-Colonel Hinterseer. We know from captured German documents that in 1941 *Feldpolizeikommissar* Jochum served as the leader of GFP-570. In January 1942, he was still in command. However, by September 1942, *Feldpolizeikommissar* Stockmann had taken over. Stockmann's tenure lasted until May 1943, when Jochum once again assumed command. Then in July 1943 it was the turn of *Feldpolizeikommissar* Riedel. *Feldpolizeikommissar* Wertel was Deputy Director in July 1943. Between 1942 and 1945 *Ost-Kompanie 612*—a Russian volunteer company, served under *Geheime Feldpolizei Gruppe 570*. By 1945 GFP-570 was serving in East Prussia.[132]

An interesting report appears in the Wartime Journal for GFP-570 in the third week of July 1942. On July 21, 1942, *Feldpolizeisekretär* Michaelis and *Sonderführer* Dr. Quiring reported that after an extensive search in Roslavl by *Abwehrtrupp von Tarbuk*, the Soviet agent, Ivan Makarov, was apprehended.[133] The current *Heeresfeldpolizeichef Ost*, Max Häuserer—the former commander of *Gestapo-Stelle Wien* (Secret State Police Post "Vienna"), took a special interest in this case. The reason was that Haußerer had known Makarov while the Russian agent had been a member of the Soviet delegation to Belgium in 1939. In January 1942 Haußerer had taken over as *Heeresfeldpolizeichef Ost* from Ernst Rassow, who had held the post since June 1941.[134] On the orders of the *Heeresfeldpolizeichef*, Makarov was brought to Germany. The German Army intelligence unit which had helped the GFP to locate Makarov in the city of Roslavl (*Abwehrtrupp von Tarbuk*) was led by Major Felix von Tarbuk Sensenhorst. What is interesting is that all biographical data on this *Abwehr* officer says that he only served in Italy from 1942–1944.[135] Yet here he is, serving behind the lines of Army Group Center in the third week of July 1942. *Abwehrtrupp von Tarbuk* was later re-designated *Abwehrtrupp 150*, the unit which he led while on the Italian peninsula.[136] The most likely scenario is that *von Tarbuk* served in Russia and sometime in the second half of 1942 he and his Abwehr formation were transferred to Italy.

GFP-580

In 1940 and 1941 this unit was stationed in Rouen, France under Ninth Army. At the end of July 1943, between Bryansk and Orel, as the German army was in the process of withdrawing, GFP-580 shot 450 Russian prisoners.[137] Members of GFP-580 were tried for war crimes after the war. Hans Julius Kraus was accused of the following acts: participation in shootings of civilians labeled "partisan suspects"; and involvement in "prison clearance" [shooting prisoners to empty the jails] in Orel and Bryansk shortly before the entry of the Red Army. The number of prisoners ordered shot in the GFP prison at Orel had been 350, while the number of prisoners shot in the GFP jail at Bryansk was 450.[138] Scouring of villages whereby partisan "suspects" were arrested and some subsequently were shot [see also procedure Nr. 1022 and Nr. 1034]. GFP-580 took part in these crimes while operating in the following localities: Sytschovka, Serkovo, Merzalovo, Michailovka, Grabovo, Orel, Bryansk, and Rogachev. Hans Kraus was found guilty of crimes against humanity and was given a life sentence by an East German court. Another member of this GFP unit, Karl Gorny, was given the death sentence by an East German court for the following crimes against GFP-580:

> War crimes directed against Jews, the mentally ill, prisoners of war and other groups of victims, in concentration and forced labor camps, in East European ghettos and other killing centers. It covers cases involving the SS, the police, the Task groups (Einsatzgruppen), police battalions and regiments, medical personnel involved in the euthanasia program and judicial representatives, such as judges or state attorneys and staff members of camps and ghettos. Also among the cases are a number of trials against German army units, such as the Army police (Feldgendarmerie) and the Secret Field Police (Geheime Feldpolizei), which took part in anti-partisan actions and the mass killing of Jews in Poland, the former Soviet Union and former Czechoslovakia.[139]

The specific charge against Karl Gorny was the combing of villages, arrest, detention, and shooting of suspects in the area of the High Command of Ninth Army against guerrilla attacks. Participation in ten execution commandos, of which at least 113 people were killed. He was also accused of taking part in at least forty-two *Erschiessungskommandos* (shooting commandos). Finally, Karl Gorny was accused of taking part in the shooting of inmates in the Secret Field Police prison located in the city of Orel shortly before the liberation of the city by the Red Army.[140]

GFP-626

This secret field police unit was established in *Wehrkreis VI* (Münster) in February 1940. In July 1940 the unit was assigned to the *Militär Befehlshaber Frankreich* (Military Commander "France") until sent to *Panzergruppe 1* in March 1941. *Panzergruppe 1* was designated to operate in the region of the Ukraine for the upcoming Russian campaign (launched on June 22, 1941).[141] A report from GFP-626 from the latter half of 1943 (dated September 25, 1943) indicated that the unit was operating under 57th Panzer Korps of *1. Panzerarmee*. What is shocking about the report is what happened to a twelve year old boy arrested by GFP-626. The text of both reports said the following:

> In the vicinity of Lichovka, near the Dnjepr, the 12-year-old school-boy Derechenko was arrested; when detained, he started to contradict himself and was turned over to the Secret Field Police Secretariat of the LVIIth Panzer Corps. It was proved by interrogation, that, in spite of his youth, Derechenko had already twice successfully acted as agent for the Soviets. He received instructions from a Lieutenant Ivan Brusenko who lived in the house of his parents in Poltava. It was Derechenko's task to carry out the usual military reconnaissance and above all to watch the traffic on the roads. Within two to four days he had to return to a certain spot on the Dnjepr, where he was met by members of the Red Army who took him back in a boat. Until his arrest during his third crossing of the enemy lines Derechenko was able to move freely behind the main defensive line. He preferred to approach the German soldiers by begging for bread and on these occasions did his spying. His employer rewarded the boy with bread, cigarettes and sweets. After fulfilling his third mission he was to get a suit. Derechenko was shot.[142]

Even more appalling is the fact that this incident of a child being shot by GFP-626 was not uncommon. Just one month later, on October 25, 1943, another report from the same secret field police unit stated the following:

> A boy of 12 was proved guilty of espionage. He had been enlisted by the commander of a cavalry unit and trained near Belgorod together with thirty more boys and girls. He had already carried out

a reconnaissance mission in the Charkow district together with ten boys. He was now-together with another two boys whom he lost en route-given the task by the above-mentioned commander Verotzk, Ivan, to locate airfields, tank units, and details of the protection provided for guarding bridges in the Poltawa-Lesewaja district. Each of them carried a red star for identification. He was instructed to say, if arrested, that he had no home and earned his living by begging. The suspect was shot.[143]

Another example was given from the same source, but the end result was the same, the GFP shot a young boy:

A boy of 14 had already carried out four espionage missions. He had left with the Russians in February 1943, and was trained as an agent by a Lieutenant Beloussou, Nikolai, for whom he had first worked as a shoeblack. His first four missions referred to general military observations in Charzisak near Stalino. His fifth mission was to be carried out in the Losowaja district with the same task; in the Charzisak district, he was shepherded through the front line, afterwards using the railway without encountering any controls. He was always sent out on his own and issued with money and food. He had been promised the Order of the Red Star and an easy life after carrying out his tenth mission. When arrested he told the usual fairy story.[144]

The shooting of children, even those who actually performed espionage for the Red Army, was a clear violation of the Geneva Convention. German arguments that because the USSR was not a signatory to the Geneva Convention, it was therefore not subject to its rules of conduct fall on deaf ears when one considers the gravity of killing a child. GFP-626 would continue to operate under *Panzergruppe 1* (redesignated First Panzer Army on October 5, 1941) until the end of the war.[145] GFP-626 would end World War II while operating in Slovakia in 1945.[146]

GFP-639

This GFP formation was created on September 10, 1940 in *Wehrkreis V*. Throughout most of its history it served in central Russia under the Second Panzer Army.[147] In September 1941, in the region of Bobruisk, *Polizeiregiment Mitte* (Police Regiment "Center"), together with an army infantry regiment, a section of the Secret Field Police and a troop of *Einsatzkommando 8* took part in a "cleansing" operation which netted a measly 22 partisans.[148] The Secret Field Police unit which took part in this action was GFP-639.[149] At this time, the leader of this GFP unit was *Feldpolizeikommissar* Benno Kukawka.[150] Sometime during the history of GFP-639, *Feldpolizeikommissar* Karl-Heinz Meissner served as the unit's commander.[151] This unit took part (on a regular basis) in the shooting of captured Red Army political commissars. For example, one *Bundesarchiv* file states that on April 25, 1942, GFP-639 travelled to *Gefangenen-Sammelstelle 20* (Prisoner Collection Camp No.20) in the city of Orel and interrogated Red Army POWs suspected of being political commissars. Those they deemed to be Red Army commissars were segregated and then shot.[152]

GFP-647

This unit was created on September 10, 1940, in *Wehrkreis VII*. At the beginning of 1941 it was stationed in France under the *Militärbefehlshaber in Frankreich*. This unit was led by *Feldpolizeikommissar* Dr. Adalbert Hermann. Five members of this unit had taken part in an SD extermination operation in the Crimea (Ukraine) in the autumn of 1941. In November 1972, the Munich District I court failed to prosecute these men "for lack of sufficient evidence"—even though one of the accused had made the following statement:

Some of the victims fell into the pit immediately; while others remained on its edge.... The children stood between the adults and were killed just like them.... I can't give you any figure about the number of Jews shot in this operation.... In any event, the shooting went on without break the whole day, like on a conveyer belt.[153]

On August 2, 1941, at Kamenets-Podolsk, *SS-Sonderkommando 11a*, together with a unit of Geheime Feldpolizei Gruppe 647, were ordered to supervise the mass of persons streaming back westward and to prevent Jews from being expelled to the east.[154] The massacre of the Jews of Kharkov in early January 1942 was carried in cooperation between *SS-Sonderkommando 4a* and the 314th Police Battalion, which was in charge of cordoning off the murder site. In addition, *SS-Sonderkommando 4a* was reinforced by policemen from two police reserve battalions as well as members of *Feldgendarmerie Abteilung 683* and GFP-647.

In January 1942, Red Army agents landed a sizable enemy force dressed partially in civilian clothes near the town of Evpatoria in the Crimea and melted into the city. According to German intelligence reports, the local civilian population of Evpatoria had prepared the landing site, and some civilians from the city had taken part in the fighting that ensued. Major Hans Riesen, the intelligence officer or "Ic/AO" was informed by his superior, Major Werner Ranck (the chief intelligence officer of 11th German Army) that the commander in chief, Field Marshal von Manstein "orders an action in Evpatoria." Major Ranck then said that "We must decide on the spot whether houses should be demolished or people should be shot." Further instructions would have to be obtained from Colonel Müller, the garrison commander of Evpatoria. Major Riesen next informed the head of GFP-647, *Feldpolizeikommissar* Dr. Adalbert Hermann, and *SS-Brigadeführer* Otto Ohlendorf (the head of *Einsatzgruppe D*) of the upcoming operation in Evpatoria.[155] Between 1942 and 1944 GFP-647 operated in the Crimea. GFP-720 was said to have operated alongside GFP-647 during the years 1941–1943.

GFP-703

GFP-703 was established on April 26, 1941, in *Wehrkreis IV*. This GFP unit was attached to Third Panzer Army, which in 1941 was known as *"Panzergruppe 3."* It served under this army command throughout the war. In June 1942 GFP-703 handed over to *SS-Einsatzkommando 9* not only Jews and communists for the killing unit to exterminate, but they also made it a practice to hand over every crippled person that they could find in the region of Third Panzer Army. The logic behind the murder of handicapped people was that they were "useless mouths" which produced nothing and therefore were considered a waste of resources. By eliminating them, the Germans were saving food for those civilians who were useful to the war effort.[156] From February 22 to March 8, 1943, GFP-703 was employed in an anti-partisan operation called *"Kugelblitz"* ("Lightning Ball") in the region of Vitebsk, Surash, and Nevel. During the operation this GFP-703 assisted in shooting 1,204 people while operating under the 201st Security Division. This was a joint operation with an SS unit, *Einsatzkommando 9* which GFP-703 had cooperated previously.[157]

GFP-707

The unit was established on April 26, 1941, in *Wehrkreis IV* (Military District No.4). It was assigned to the 221st Security Division in the rear of Army Group "Center." This GFP unit was led by *Feldpolizeikommissar* Paul Lose.[158] It was transferred to the 286th Security Division on December 14, 1941. From 1941–1942 GFP-707 was stationed in Bobruisk

9. The Secret Field Police in the Soviet Union

(in White Russia). In August and September 1942 GFP-707 took part in a mass shooting of captured Jews who had been hiding in a forest camp located near the town of Bobruisk.[159] On January 5, 1943, GFP-707 was once again transferred—this time to the 201st Security Brigade (later re-designated as the 201st Security Division). In 1944 GFP-707 was operating under the Ninth Army of Army Group "Center." Since the beginning of 1945 the formation was operating in the West under the First Parachute Army near Wesel in The Netherlands. After the war, many of the members of GFP-707 were brought to trial. The principal individual members accused of crimes against humanity were as follows:

Table 11. Legal Proceedings Against Members of GFP-707

GFP-707 Member	Trial No. After 1945 (1964)
Johann Weitschacher	LG Wien 27a Vr 4763/64
Franz Kögl	LG Wien 27a Vr 4763/64
Friedrich Kasper	LG Wien 27a Vr 4763/64
Peter Wilhelm	LG Wien 27a Vr 4763/64
Oswald Hrabal	LG Wien 27a Vr 4763/64
Josef Schmatzberger	LG Wien 27a Vr 4763/64
Richard Strausz	LG Wien 27a Vr 4763/64
Franz Chmel	LG Wien 27a Vr 4763/64
Walter Nedwed	LG Wien 27a Vr 4763/64
Wilhelm Wonisch	LG Wien 27a Vr 4763/64
Franz Rechenauer	LG Wien 27a Vr 4763/64

GFP-715

While GFP-631 had been guarding the headquarters of the OKH for most of the war (since April 29, 1940), GFP-715 had operated under the 285th Security Division in the region of Army Group North throughout the Russian campaign. In April 1944 GFP-715 was operating under the 18th Army and in that year, it was inducted into the SS (like the rest of the GFP units). Sometime in August 1944 it was sent to Warsaw to help put down the Polish uprising. In the beginning of 1945, GFP-715 was assigned to help GFP-631 protect OKH—the *Oberkommando des Heeres* headquarters. A document dated April 1, 1945 states that GFP-715 was assigned to guard the OKH headquarters, alongside GFP-631. In fact, the document listed the strengths of both units on that date:[160]

Dienststellen	Jststärken:						Fehlstellen:					
	Offz.	Beamte	Uffz.	Mann.	Gesamt	St. H.	Offz.	Beamte	Uffz.	Mann.	Gesamt	St. H.
O-Sicherungstruppen:												
1. Wachkompanie 631	2	—	34	224	260	—	2	—	1	8	11	—
2. Wachkompanie 631	2	—	31	248	281	—	2	—	7	1	10	—
Gr. G.F.P. 631	—	8	39	42	89	—	8	—	—	—	8	—
Gr. G.F.P. 715	—	10	26	34	70	—	—	—	—	—	—	—
Gesamt C:	4	18	130	548	700	—	12	—	8	9	29	—

Photograph taken by author, of a NARA document listing the strengths of GFP-631 and GFP-715 while serving as security for the *Kommandoamt des Hauptquartiers* (author's collection).

Based on the document shown in the figure above, the following were the strengths of both GFP-631 and GFP-715 on April 1, 1945:

Table 12. GFP Units Guarding the OKH, April 1, 1945

GFP-715	GFP-631	Strength
—	—	Officers
10	8	Officials
26	39	NCOs
34	42	Enlisted
70	89	Total

GFP-717

This GFP group was established on May 21, 1941 in *Wehrkreis IV*. For the Russian campaign, GFP-717 was attached to the 403rd Security Division (of Ninth German Army). In June and July 1941, it operated out of the White Russian town of Bialystok, but between August and December 1941 (while still attached to the 403rd Division) it moved further east, operating immediately behind the advance of the German Army. In June 1942 GFP-717 was transferred to the newly upgraded 201st Security Division (of Third Panzer Army). Previously, the 201st Security Division had been designated as the 201st Security Brigade (*Sicherungs Brigade 201*), but was enlarged by the addition of several units.[161] GFP-724 was also included in the new table of organization of the 201st Security Division.

For the rest of the year (July to December 1942) and into March 1943, GFP-717 remained in and around the town of Polotsk.[162] However in March 1943 the worsening military situation necessitated that the 201st Security Division be sent to the front lines in the region of Nevel. GFP-717 and GFP-724 acted as the intelligence gathering units in the field for the division. It was in the region of Nevel in October 1943 that GFP-717 was involved in the illegal seizure of local inhabitants for shipment to Germany to work as forced laborers. Those deemed too old and too young were not sent to Germany to work, but created a problem for the Germans. This "problem" was often settled by liquidation. A report dated "19 October 1943" and presented during the Nuremberg War Crimes trial of Field Marshal Wilhelm von Leeb, indicated the complicity of GFP-717 in forced imprisonment of Soviet citizens:

> Visit of the Secret Field Group 717 concerning the question as to which camp civilian prisoners can be sent to, who are old and infirm and who have small children, and whose kin have been executed as bandit supporters, or have been handed over to the SD to be transported to Lublin. It seems intolerable to settle these persons anywhere in the army area because they spread an extremely poisoned atmosphere against Germans.[163]

Throughout the remainder of 1943 GFP-717 operated in the region of Vitebsk under Third Panzer Army. It remained in Vitebsk until January 1944. In December 1943, the Soviets broke the German defense line just south of Nevel, requiring the 201st Security Division to be sent to the area once again. GFP-717 remained in the Nevel region 201st Security Division (now attached to 16th Army) in February and March 1944. Still under the 201st Security Division, it continued to serve in the northern fringes of Army Group "Center." From April to June 201st Security Division was assigned anti-partisan duty around Minsk, in Belorussia. In July as a result of the Soviet summer offensive, the 201st Security Division (with GFP-717 in tow) withdrew westward as the Soviets pressed their attack.

After the destruction of Army Group Center and the subsequent expulsion of the

German Army from Belorussia in the late summer of 1944, GFP-717 remained with Third Panzer Army, but in early 1945 it was transferred to Army Group "G," which comprised two armies: 1st and 19th Army. GFP-717 was sent to the Upper Rhine region and was therefore attached to the 19th Army. It remained under the 19th Army for the remainder of the war.[164]

GFP-721

This formation was created on May 21, 1941, in *Wehrkreis IV*. It was employed under 454th Security Division of the *Befehlshaber Rückwartig Heeresgebiet Süd 103* (Commander of Rear Area Forces South 103). Beginning in March 1942 this secret field police unit was led by Field Police Secretary Alfred Dittmann. Sometime later, Field Police Director Karl-Heinz Meissner served as this unit's leader.[165] In 1943 GFP-721 was operating under the Sixth Army. It remained under this army command until 1945 when it ended the war fighting in Hunary by the city of Raab. After World War II, men who served in GFP-721 were tried for crimes against humanity. One such case was that of Arnold Kostrowski who became a member of GFP-721. He was accused of taking part in an illegal shooting while serving in GFP-721. He was an ethnic German Soviet citizen who had offered his services to the Secret Field Police as an interpreter after the entry of the German Wehrmacht in the USSR. He was accused of abuse of detainees, as well as in the participation in the shooting of arrested Jews (Soviet citizens and non–Soviet citizens), Soviet civilians and resistance fighters and prisoners of war of the POW camp at Khorol. There he was accused of the torture and murder of 326 victims by shooting. Kostrowski was sentenced to life in prison.[166]

GFP-723

GFP-723 was established on May 21, 1941, in *Wehrkreis IV* (Dresden). It took part in the occupation of central Russia during the Russian campaign but later became a part of the rear area security forces of Army Group "South." At the end of October 1941, it took part in the murder of fifty-six Russian Jewish civilians in the region of Chernevka. The Seventh Company of the 354th Infantry Regiment took part in these murders.[167] In the fall of 1941 GFP-723 took part in the murder of 4,000 Jews in Nievish. Later it also took part in the killing of another 250 Jews who were murdered at Voronovo and 750 at Lida.[168] From March 1941 until July 1944 GFP-723 was assigned to the 286th Security Division, which operated in the region of Army Group "Center" during the same time period. Throughout this time, the 286th Security Division operated in the region of Orscha. Records for the GFP-723 stated that up until December 1941 the unit had shot a total of 487 men.[169] GFP-723 served under the Second German Army until September 1944.[170] In the autumn of 1944 the unit was disbanded and any remaining personnel were sent back to serve in the Sipo and SD.

GFP-725

This group was raised on May 21, 1941, in *Wehrkreis IV*. It was posted to the German Sixth Army which was to make up a part of *Heeresgruppe Süd* (Army Group "South") during the upcoming Russian campaign. On October 30, 1941, the unit was under the command of *Kommissar* (Commissar) Jakobs. It took part in a *Säuberungsaktion* ("cleansing operation") west of the Ukrainian town of Cherkassy. The operation ran through the villages of Olschanka (Olshana), Beloserye, Mleyovo Moschny, and Gorodischtsche (Gorodische) and Smela.[171] Other German forces taking part in this mission included the following units: First and Second Companies of the 637th Regional Defense Battalion; Staff Company, plus the Third and Fourth Companies of 703rd Guard Battalion[172]; 13th Company of 318th Infantry Regiment; Third Company of 24th Engineer Battalion. This engineer unit was part of the German 24th Infantry Division, which had been withdrawn from frontline action and in October and November 1941 was placed directly under the command of 17th Army.[173] It was listed "for special employment."[174] For operational reasons, the headquarters of GFP-725 was located in the village of Gorodische.[175] Another *Wehrmacht* formation included *I. Bataillon / 375. Infanterie Regiment* which also took part in this *Säuberungsaktion*. At this time, the 375th Infantry Regiment was a part of the German 454th Security Division.[176]

Another German unit used in this operation included 57th Regional Defense Regiment of the 213th Security Division.[177] The reserve formation for this operation was a German armored train, which was stationed in Gorodische. This armored train unit was *Panzerzug 7*. The drive took place from October 10–30, 1941, southwest of Cherkassy, and centering in the region of Gorodische. The object of the operation was to destroy the Soviet Schvedov Partisan Group: about fifty men and seventeen so-called "partisan liaisons" (which could mean women, old people, and children). In total the partisan force lost twelve dead and sixteen captured. The sixteen captured were all wounded. Two of the wounded subsequently died of their wounds. The remaining fourteen partisans were brought back to the command post of 637th Regional Defense Battalion and turned over to officials of GFP-725. An after-action report from this operation listed the following statement in a matter-of-fact manner:

> Sixteen partisans were shot, of which fourteen were taken prisoner. The wounded prisoners were handed over to the Secret Field Police. Statements gathered from the prisoners contributed quite substantially to the clarification of the strength of the enemy in the region as well as their escape routes. The prisoners were shot after interrogation.[178]

What this shows is that shooting of captured partisans and partisan suspects was a common procedure right after interrogation. On November 4, 1941, GFP-725 was attached to First battalion of the 375th Infantry Regiment that was operating west of Cherkassy.[179] A final report on the operations of First battalion of the 375th Infantry Regiment and GFP-725 in October 1941 stated the following grim statistic in a matter-of-fact way:

A. 42 partisans were killed in battle.
B. 27 partisans were captured and later executed.
C. 60 partisans and 7 partisan helpers were apprehended with the help of the local [Ukrainian] militia and were handed over to the Secret Field Police and later shot.[180]

In the winter of 1941–1942 *GFP-725* was operating under the 213th Security Division. The senior GFP official in the 213th Security Division, *Feldpolizeidirektor* Kurt Arlt, gave the members of GFP-725 numerous political indoctrination lectures geared to maintain "proper National Socialist attitudes."[181]

In 1944 GFP-725 was assigned to the German Eighth Army, which was still operating in the region of the Ukraine under Army Group "South." Beginning in April 1944, it was under Army Group "Southern Ukraine." By 1945 this secret field police unit was attached to "Army Group Center" in the southeastern German region of Silesia.[182]

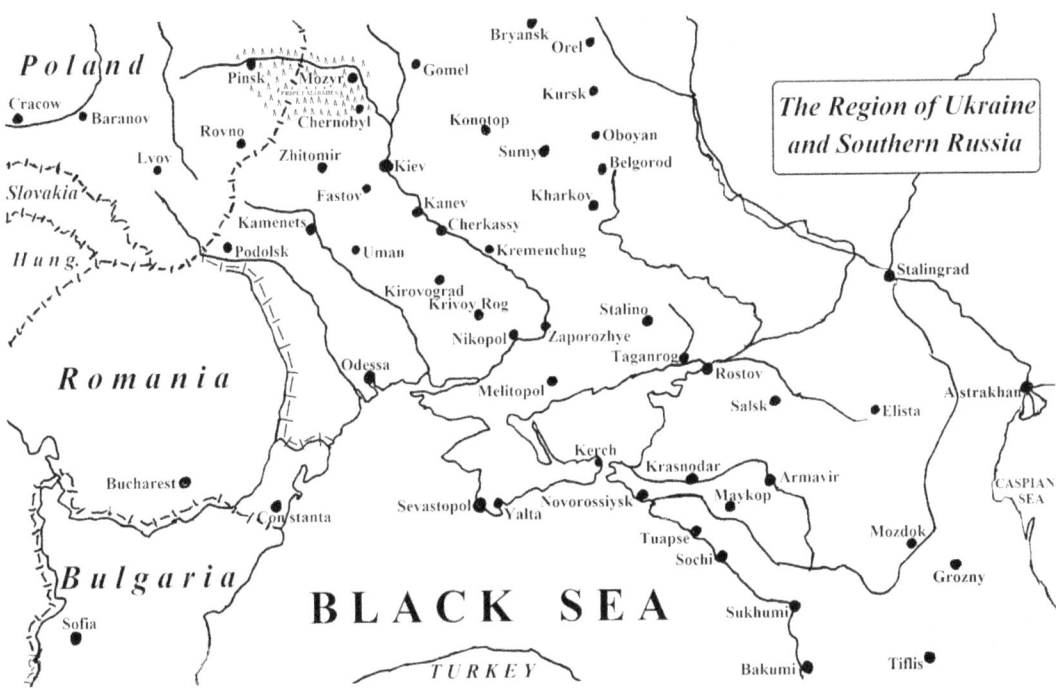

The Region of Ukraine and Southern Russia. Map depicts the areas under German control in November 1942 (map by author).

Conclusions

The worst excesses committed by the Secret Field Police occurred in the Soviet Union. Their behavior was not unlike the actions of the men who served in the SS mobile killing units. The murder of thousands of lives was directly attributed to the Secret Field Police on the Eastern Front. This incorporated not only suspected partisans, but Jews as being a Jew was made synonymous with being a guerrilla. These murders also included suspected "partisan helpers" which in many instances meant women, old folks and even children. All of them were killed directly by members of the GFP or were handed over to the SS/SD for *Sonderbehandlung* ("special treatment," i.e.–execution). The rear areas of the Eastern Front became a veritable killing field where all normal rules of civilized behavior were ignored and mass killings was the normal operating procedure for German forces. When it was all over, the USSR not only lost 12,000,000 soldiers in the war, but an additional 13,000,000 civilians. This huge number of civilians killed cannot simply be attributed to "collateral damage." Clearly the Germans targeted the civilian population, and the GFP in the East proved to be deeply involved these murders.

10

Towards a Reckoning

The SS Killing Units and the Secret Field Police

Considering the role of the GFP with regard to Hitler's goals towards the occupied territories and Nazi goals with regard to the elimination of "undesirables," the GFP obeyed all orders and commands fully. The relationship of the GFP to the mobile SS killing units was based on a stringent division of authority. All matters which would affect the security of the German forces in the occupied territories was to be handled exclusively by the GFP. However, the GFP and the SS mobile killing units were to cooperate with each other by a prompt exchange of information. This also included the exchange of prisoners and on occasion, the elimination of prisoners on the spot. The *SS-Einsatzgruppen* were to report to the GFP all issues that concerned it. In turn the GFP was to turn over to the *SS-Einsatzgruppen* all information pertaining to their sphere of influence. Given this security guideline, it was just a matter of moving this "policy" towards the assistance of the *SS-Einsatzgruppen* by the GFP:

> The first consequence of army "security" policy was the practice of handling over Jews to the *Einsatzgruppen* for shooting. In Minsk, the army commander established a civilian internment camp for almost all the men in the city. Secret Field Police units and *Einsatzgruppe B* personnel together "combed out" the camp. Thousands of "Jews, criminals, [Communist Party] functionaries, and Asiatics" were caught in the roundup.[1]

This appears to indicate that simply being a Jew was itself a punishable offense. To further elaborate on this theme, an example of how being Jewish was quantified as being an enemy of the state (and by extension, being a "guerrilla") by quoting two reports from Secret Field Police Group 722, which in the spring of 1943 was attached to the 207th Security Division in the region of Army Group North. The reports, dated February 23, 1943, and March 25, 1943, provided the following format:

> Punishable Offenses by Members of the Population: 23 February 1943
> Espionage—1
> Theft of Ammunition—1
> Suspected Jews—3
> Punishable Offenses by Members of the Population: 25 March 1943[2]
> Moving About with Arms—11
> Theft—2
> Jews—2

Therefore, in the eyes of the Nazi regime, to be a Jew was a punishable offense. By abiding by all of the orders and commands of the Third Reich the GFP operated in a manner that enforced the goals of the Nazi government. During World War II the German Army's Secret Field Police operated as one of numerous military organizations which not only helped to sustain the Nazi regime, but also actively implemented Nazi policy. It involved itself in suppressing the occupied peoples of Europe and was directly and indirectly involved in the Holocaust. Immediately after the war, the International Military Tribunal established that members of the GFP had committed war crimes. Nevertheless, it judged that the Secret Field Police was not a criminal organization:

> The third organization was the so-called Secret Field Police which was originally under the Army but which in 1942 was transferred by military order to the Security Police. The Secret Field Police was concerned with security matters within the Army in occupied territory, and also with the prevention of attacks by civilians on military installations or units, and committed war crimes and crimes against humanity on a wide scale. It has not been proved, however, that it was a part of the Gestapo and the Tribunal does not consider it as coming within the charge of criminality contained in the Indictment, except such members as may have been transferred to Amt IV of the RSHA or were members of organizations declared criminal by this Judgment.[3]

Not having a fuller understanding of the GFP in 1946, the International Military Tribunal failed to comprehend the complicity of the Secret Field Police in Hitler's murderous plans. It thus failed to label the GFP correctly as a criminal organization.

Empowering the GFP to Commit Crimes

There were several orders, commands, and decrees that were issued by the Germans during the Second World War which aided in criminalizing those organizations and individuals who complied with these commands. The Nazi fanatics were expected to follow these decrees blindly, but the majority of the German Armed Forces also followed the commands. In all instances, the Secret Field Police obeyed these orders just as blindly as the rest of the Nazi military, SS and police apparatus. The first of these commands was actually a secret order issued on the same day in which the Empire of Japan launched their attack against the U.S. Pacific Fleet based on the islands of Hawaii:

The "Night and Fog" Decree

On December 7, 1941, as the German armies were reeling back from the first Soviet counter-offensive in front of Moscow, and Hitler was considering declaring war against the United States, the Third Reich was beginning to feel the pressures of total war. In effect, a nation of eighty million Germans was fighting the world! The Nazi regime resolved to arrest and imprison anyone they deemed was a danger to their rule. Although the order had originated with Adolf Hitler, it was *Reichsführer-SS* Heinrich Himmler who was tasked with writing out the decree:

> After lengthy consideration, it is the will of the Führer that the measures taken against those who are guilty of offenses against the Reich or against the occupation forces in occupied areas should be altered. The *Führer* is of the opinion that in such cases penal servitude or even a hard labor sentence for life will be regarded as a sign of weakness. An effective and lasting deterrent can be achieved only by the death penalty or by taking measures which will leave the family and the population uncertain as to the fate of the offender. Deportation to Germany serves this purpose.[4]

Like the rest of the Nazi war machine, the German Secret Field Police had a role to play in this decree as witnessed during the Nuremberg War Crimes Military Tribunal:

Nacht und Nebel Befehl (Night and Fog Decree): A further point in the indictment of the SD deals with participation in the execution of the *Nacht und Nebel* Decree. Competence for the execution of the *Nacht und Nebel* Decree was divided between the *Wehrmacht* offices and the Gestapo, as is shown by Document L-90. The *Wehrmacht* offices had received instructions to impose the death penalty for criminal acts against the *Reich* and the occupation army, undertaken by non–German civilians. However, if no such punishment was to be expected, these, civilians were, according to Paragraph IV of the first supplementary regulations to the instructions contained in Document Number 91, to be taken to Germany by the Secret Field Police, there to be turned over to a *Stapo* [*Staatspolizei*—State Police] office.[5]

The Barbarossa Jurisdiction Order of May 13, 1941

This order, issued about a month before the invasion of the Soviet Union gave the German military a virtual *"carte blanche"* to commit any crime against captured soldiers and the subject population of the occupied Soviet territories. In essence, all German personnel had complete freedom to action with little or no regard to human life. Numerous cases have been documented where members of the Secret Field Police shot partisans and even suspected *Partisanenhelfer* (partisan helpers) and justified it under the Barbarossa Jurisdiction Order.[6] The standard operating procedure was to label someone as a guerrilla or supporter of the partisan movement. Even moving about outside of your locality could get a Russian *Krestyanin* (peasant) shot.

The "Commissar Order" of June 6, 1941

The Commissar Order which was personally issued by Adolf Hitler on June 6, 1941, was a decree that demanded that all Communist Political Commissars be shot immediately after interrogation, or barring that possibility, then to be shot as soon as captured. The official title was *Richtlinien für die Behandlung politischer Kommissare* ("Guidelines for the Treatment of Political Commissars"). The logic of the order was that the war in the East was not merely a military conflict but a war of ideologies. This order empowered all members of the German military during the Russian campaign, including the GFP, to eliminate all captured political commissars once they surrendered or after interrogation. Once the Red Army discovered the decree sometime in 1942, most political commissars were loath to surrender to the Germans in any way, shape, or form. Since Red Army units were often led not only by regular officers but by political commissars, the *Kommissarbefehl* actually worked against the Germans because it increased the possibility that a Red Army formation would fight to the last man rather than surrender.

The "Commando Order" of October 18, 1942

This order, dated October 18, 1942, stated that all Allied commandos caught by German troops either in continental Europe or North Africa would be instantly shot without trial, even if caught in Allied uniform. It showed the growing frustration on the part of Adolf Hitler, for the "hit and run" tactics of Winston Churchill's commando troops. The order also held sway for any commando attempting to evade capture. Any Allied or pro-allied member not in proper uniforms, who happened to fall into Axis hands were to be immediately handed over to the SD. The order, which was issued in secret, made it clear that failure to carry out this command by any officer would be considered an act of disregard to orders punishable under current German military justice. As before, the Secret Field Police complied with this order, although there were exemptions where individual members of the GFP took it upon themselves to shoot these partisans and/or commandos instead of transferring them directly to the SD. In fact, two GFP units in Greece (GFP-510 & GFP-621) were responsible for either killing or handing over to the SD numerous Allied commandoes from 1943–1944. The "Commando Order" was also used to establish the shooting of hostages by the Germans.

The final judgment of the Secret Field Police by the Nuremberg Court was quite lenient, given its activities, especially in the Soviet Union. Its commander Wilhelm Krichbaum and the top leadership cadre of the GFP made every effort to portray the Secret Field Police as just another German Army intelligence unit. The "darker missions" of Secret Field Police during the war were successfully covered up. This allowed the GFP as a whole to be absolved of the crimes of the Nazi regime:

> The *Gestapo* and SD were used for purposes which were criminal under the Charter, involving the persecution and extermination of the Jews, brutalities and killings in concentration camps, excesses in the administration of occupied territories, the administration of the slave labor program and the mistreatment and murder of prisoners of war. The defendant Kaltenbrunner, who was a member of this organization, was among those who used it for these purposes. In dealing with the *Gestapo* the Tribunal includes all executive and administrative officials of Amt IV of the RSHA, or concerned with *Gestapo* administration in other departments of the RSHA, and all local Gestapo officials serving both inside and outside of Germany, including the members of the Frontier Police, but not including the members of the Border and Customs Protection or the Secret Field Police, except such members as have been specified above. At the suggestion of the Prosecution the Tribunal does not include persons employed by the *Gestapo* for purely clerical, steno- graphic, janitorial, or similar unofficial routine tasks. In dealing with the SD the Tribunal includes *Abteilung III, VI*, and *VII* of the RSHA and all other members of the SD, including all local representatives and agents, honorary or otherwise, whether they were technically members of the SS or not.[7]

It has already been established that in the eastern territories, the GFP took a more "hands-on" approach towards the murder of so-called undesirables such as Jews, Gypsies, political commissars, and partisans which the Germans simply labeled as "bandits." Even civilians whom the Germans suspected were aiding the guerrillas were wantonly shot on the slightest pretext.[8] Therefore the judgment at Nuremberg was (most likely) incorrect and based on the limited knowledge and a deliberate misinformation campaign which its former commander, Wilhelm Krichbaum and his senior leadership cadre, put forth at the end of the war. The exculpation of the GFP from being labeled a criminal organization (like the SS) was all the more surprising given that Allied intelligence had a clear understanding of the connection between the Secret Field Police and the SS during the war:

> Most of the executive personnel and officers of the GFP are furnished by the *Gestapo*, although some have been drawn from the *Kripo* [*Kriminalpolizei*, or Criminal Police] and even from various branches of the *Orpo* [*Ordnungspolizei*, or Order Police]. The remainder of the Secret Field Police personnel, however, is recruited to some extent on a less selective basis from regular Army and Air Force units. Theoretically all members of the GFP are chosen for special qualifications such as knowledge of languages and travel experience abroad and for ability to deal with people. In practice however, it is reported that GFP personnel is of rather poor caliber.
>
> Originally co-operation between the *Gestapo* and GFP was strongly emphasized, but importance of the GFP has gradually dwindled in proportion to the growth of power of the combined *Sipo* and SD. Since the GFP was dependent for its funds, equipment and facilities on the Military Intelligence Department of the OKW it was never able to compete with the vastly superior resources of the RSHA.
>
> The original clause denying the GFP jurisdiction over matters within the field of the Sipo and SD, and the remaining units of the GFP were reduced to a small field security corps of the Armed Forces. Personnel of the GFP transferred to the Sipo and SD who had previously been members of the SS, received SS ranks equivalent to their former position and the GFP insignia worn on the shoulder straps were removed.

Thus, like most of the other agencies and functions of military intelligence, the Geheime Feldpolizei is now largely controlled by Himmler's police system. Not only are the Armed Forces now dependent on the Sipo and SD for their intelligence information, but at the same time Himmler is enabled to keep a close watch over activities of Army personnel.[9]

Yet, in spite of this apparent connection and close relationship between the GFP with the Sipo/Kripo/SD/Gestapo and SS, Krichbaum and his men were allowed to avoid the stigma of being associated with the criminal excesses committed by the Nazi regime and its various organizations. In 1947 at the behest of American military intelligence, but ostensibly at the request of the U.S. Army Historical Division, Wilhelm Krichbaum was asked to write a detailed monograph about the activities of the Secret Field Police during World War II.[10] The Cold War was beginning to heat up and the OSS (the forerunner of the CIA) needed to know as much as possible about anti–Soviet sentiments behind the growing "Iron Curtain." Relations between the German Army Abwehr, the GFP, as well as the SD was on the whole usually smooth. Throughout the war, these three services worked well with one another.[11] This was in stark contrast to postwar statements made by former GFP members, who said that resistance to SD "methods" existed within the membership of the GFP. These postwar reports were full of similar anti–SD comments—most likely generated to distance the GFP member from the activities attributed to the SD:

> Another tactic was to portray the Sipo-SD and the GFP as rival organizations. Such assertions undoubtedly were made to distance the GFP from the "Nazi character" of the Sipo-SD, while simultaneously bolstering the GFP's image as an army formation independent of Sipo-SD influence.[12]

Therefore, we can agree with almost 100 percent certainty that the GFP should have been labeled a criminal organization at Nuremberg but because of various reasons it was able to avoid prosecution. What were these reasons which caused the Secret Field Police to be exempted? In essence there were five important factors that aided in the deception regarding the criminality of the Secret Field Police:

First, the personnel of the GFP served as members of the *Wehrmacht* and were classified as *Wehrmachtsbeamten* ("military officials"). Accordingly, the men of the GFP wore the uniform of an Army Administration Official, with the addition of a stamped aluminum insignia attached to the shoulder boards bearing the initials "GFP" and a black cuff band on their left jacket sleeve with the words *Geheime Feldpolizei* sewn in silver thread. Light blue piping was added to the collar tabs, shoulder boards, and caps. Not wearing the SS or SD uniform worked to distance the GFP from the crimes attributed to the SS. Second, most of the documents of the GFP were "lost" or destroyed at the end of the war, so a full study of the actions of the organization cannot be properly performed. Third, those members who were captured and interrogated by the Allies immediately after the war made every effort to portray the GFP as just another typical army counterintelligence agency, emphasizing that the GFP was virtually devoid of Nazi ideological penetration.

Fourth, shortly after the war ended Wilhelm Krichbaum, who had been head of the *Secret Field Police*, was asked by the U.S. Army's historical division to write a detailed report regarding the activities of his organization. This gave the former leader of the GFP the opportunity to misinform the Allies about the true nature of some of the "less honorable" missions of the GFP during the war. Fifth, the rising East-West tensions that soon turned into the Cold War created a need on the part of the West, especially the American military and CIA (the ex-OSS), for former German intelligence officers with knowledge of the Soviet Union and counterintelligence work. A person with intimate knowledge of the Soviet Union, especially for those who had served in the USSR and "knew the region and its people," was greatly prized. Ex-GFP members therefore, were seen as a valuable asset to the West. This is not so hard to believe, given that it has already been established that after the war, American intelligence used former *Gestapo* and *SD* officers to fight the communist threat during the Cold War. *Klaus Barbie*, the former *Gestapo* Chief of Lyon, France immediately comes to mind, as one of the most notorious examples.

The Military Career of Wilhelm Krichbaum

Wilhelm Krichbaum was the head of the Secret Field Police during the Nazi period. The man eventually turned out to be a very controversial figure. This was not merely because he served during a time when the GFP was involved with the excesses of the Nazi regime, but because his behavior even *after* the war, showed that he was (in essence) an opportunist by nature. He was born on May 7, 1896, in Wiesbaden. His parents were Adam Krichbaum (born in 1871) and Johannette Caroline (born in 1875). From his youth, it appears that Krichbaum grew up in a conservative household. On August 28, 1914, he volunteered for service in the 87th Infantry Regiment. A month later he was serving in the 223rd "Royal" Reserve Infantry Regiment. He initially served in Northern France before being transferred to the Eastern Front in the region of Poland.[13] In December 1914 while serving in Poland, he was wounded and temporarily reported missing.

In February 1915 Krichbaum was released from a hospital where he was recuperating and was assigned to the 87th Infantry Regiment, which was serving on the western front. In May 1915, a new regiment was created employing the cadre of the 87th Infantry Regiment. This turned out to be the 186th Infantry Regiment. Krichbaum served in this unit from 1916 until the end of the war. He served in this new regiment as a messenger, like Corporal Adolf Hitler had done during the war in a different unit. In 1916 Krichbaum was promoted to the rank of Sergeant, and for a time was posted to the Secret Field Police. In the fall of 1917, Krichbaum was promoted to *Stoßtruppführer* (assault troop leader), and was transferred to one of dozens of special assault battalions (*Stoßtrupp bataillonen*) that the Imperial German Army was creating in preparation for their last offensive on the western front. He took part in this final German drive of the war, the "St. Michael" offensive, which was launched in the spring of 1918. Krichbaum was later assigned to the region of Flanders, in Belgium. He remained there until the war ended. After the war Krichbaum

Feldpolizeichef Wilhelm Krichbaum, seen here wearing the uniform of an *SS-Untersturmführer*, ca. 1925 (Bundesarchiv, Berlin-Lichterfelde).

became involved in right-wing politics. In 1920 he joined the *Freikorps*, and served under *Brigade Erhardt,* taking part in the so-called "Kapp Putsch" which sought to overthrow the newly created Weimar Republic.

From 1921–1923 he was active in the *Organisation Consul* that operated in the Rhineland region. The *Organisation Consul* was an ultra-nationalist force operating in Germany from 1921 and 1922. It was responsible for the assassinations of the Weimar Republic's Minister of Finance, Matthias Erzberger in August 1921. They were also responsible for the murder of Foreign Minister Walter Rathenau in June 1922. In 1923 while living in Dresden, Krichbaum joined the *Nationalsozialistische Deutsche Arbeiterpartei* (the Nazi Party, abbreviated to "NSDAP"). Until 1925 he was the adjutant to *SA-Obergruppenführer* Manfred von Killinger. In 1926, he was leader of the *Feldjägerkorps Dresden.* In 1934 Krichbaum became an *SS-Oberführer* and inspector of the German frontier police, with the title of *Grenzinspekteur Südost "Dresden."* He held this post until 1938.

In addition to his Nazi Party position, Krichbaum also served in the German Army. Between 1926 and 1928 he served as company, battalion and eventually regimental commander of the Dresden Infantry School. In 1928, he was put in charge of a Saxon border guard unit. Krichbaum entered the military police in the Saxon government after the *Feldjägerkorps* was disbanded in 1932. Krichbaum oversaw the total overhaul of the field police force in Saxony. After the incorporation of the *Gestapo* (*Geheime Staatspolizei*) in the *Reich* Security Main Office as *Amt IV*, Krichbaum became the representative of the Gestapo chief, Heinrich Müller. From 1933–1934 Krichbaum served in Department 3. In 1938 during the Czechoslovak crisis, Krichbaum served as *Heeresfeldpolizeichef im Oberkommando der Wehrmacht* (Army Field Police Chief of the Armed Forces High Command).[14] From 1940 until the end of the war, he became *Heeresfeldpolizeichef der Wehrmacht* (Field Police Chief of the Armed Forces).[15]

Krichbaum's post-war work for the U.S. Army purported to be an honest and detailed account of the operations and functions of the GFP during the war. Krichbaum devoted the initial pages of the study to portraying the group as just another army intelligence formation, similar to the Abwehr. In addition, he used seven whole pages to list every conceivable duty—some of it mundane, some of it interesting but all of a police nature—which the GFP was involved in. However, he conveniently failed to list the "additional duties" assigned to the GFP; that being to treat all captured Jews and political commissars as partisans—which meant elimination after interrogation. His pamphlet worked to reinforce the testimony of captured members who painted the GFP as a regular army police unit. Krichbaum's efforts initially succeeded in duping his U.S. Army and OSS interrogators until the 1950's. What is amazing about all of this is that as early as 1946, U.S. military personnel were aware of at least some deception that was taking place by members of the GFP. The document shown on the next page from the Security Review Board, dated "March 26, 1946" succinctly summarizes what was happening[16]:

U.S. Army requirements for information on the Soviet Union and the Red Army was becoming essential as early as 1946. As the growing "Cold War" was increasing it was requiring American intelligence to provide greater resources. There seemed to be a rush in the intelligence sector to prepare for a future possible confrontation with the Soviet Union. This in turn led the Americans to recruit men from the German Armed Forces, such as Reinhard Gehlen, who was the former head of German Army intelligence in the USSR. It didn't take too long before the Allies were reaching out to former SS members who were deemed "knowledgeable" about all things dealing with the Soviet Union. One extreme example of this rush to recruit was the employment of Klaus Barbie, a former member of the Gestapo in Lyon, France:

10. Towards a Reckoning

```
                    HEADQUARTERS              MJJ/RES/kpk
              OFFICE OF MILITARY GOVERNMENT
                   WUERTTEMBERG-BADEN
                  SECURITY REVIEW BOARD

                                              APO     154
                                              26 March 1946

    SUBJECT: Request for Information on Geheime Feldpol-
             izei.

    TO     : Assistant Chief of Staff, G-2, United States
             Forces, European Theater, APO 757, US Army.

             ATTN: Captain Allen, Counter Intelligence
                   Branch.

         1. It is urgently requested that this office be
    forwarded all available information on the organization,
    employment and personalities of the Geheime Feldpolizei.

         2. Information is also desired concerning the
    following points:

              a. Connections between the Geheime Feld-
                 polizei and other intelligence agencies.

              b. To what extent the Geheime Feldpolizei
                 was involved in partisan liquidation.

              c. Numbers of various gruppen and per-
                 tinent "order of battle" data.

         3. This office has, at present, numerous ap-
    plications for the release of members of the Geheime
    Feldpolizei, all of whom claim to be innocent mechan-
    ics and chauffeurs. Without adequate information it is
    impossible to separate the wolves from the sheep.

                        For the Director:


                                    MATTHEW J. JASEN
                                    Capt              CAC
                                         President
                                    Security Review Board

    TELEPHONE: Stuttgart Switch 93 221 Ext 626 or 637.
```

Letter from the Security Review Board dated March 26, 1946. This document can be found in: Geheime Feldpolizei—EI (GFP) [Secret Field Police] G-2 Department of the Army, Volume II, XE 019650 (author's collection).

After the war, United States intelligence services employed him for their anti–Marxist efforts and also helped him escape to South America. The *Bundesnachrichtendienst*—the West German intelligence agency, recruited him, and he may have helped the CIA capture Argentine revolutionary Che Guevara in 1967. Barbie is also suspected of having a hand in the Bolivian *coup d'état* orchestrated by Luis García Meza Tejada in 1980. After the fall of the dictatorship, Barbie no longer had the protection of the Bolivian government and in 1983 was extradited to France, where he was convicted of war crimes. He eventually died in prison.[17]

By comparison with such recruits as Klaus Barbie who had a notorious past, members of the Secret Field Police were seen as relatively benign candidates for American intelligence. The problem with this hasty creation of counterintelligence and spy groups in Europe was that many former Nazi Party members were recruited for service in Allied intelligence organizations:

> From September 1945 Hermann Baun and Gerhard Wesel served in what later was referred to by the code name "Organization X" operating from Oberursel [a suburb in northwestern Frankfurt] for American intelligence. Their intelligence and espionage activity was geared against the Soviet Union. [The American] staff was looking for [men] with appropriate experience. There were isolated outposts called *Generalvertretungen* (General Agencies). Founded in early 1946 in Karlsruhe [Germany], early on "Unit 114" was under a [German] intelligence officer and [former] sergeant of the Secret Field Police (GFP), Alfred Bentzinger (1912–1967). The organization was established quickly and immediately came under the jurisdiction of the camp commander: Colonel Philip, who was removed when Lieutenant-Colonel John Deane (1919–2013) assumed the post as project officer. On April 1, 1946, the group began operations, now under the codename "Operation Rusty" whose official mission was the collection of information about the Soviet armed forces in the occupied regions of Germany and Eastern Europe.[18]

Another example of a former member of the Secret Field Police joining Allied intelligence and later working for the West German government in intelligence matters was Joachim Kaintzik, who had been working for the Gestapo since 1937.[19] Kaintzik joined the American counterintelligence organization beginning in 1948:

> Joachim Kaintzik (1905–1961) the criminal inspector and member of NSDAP member since 1933, was head of the *Gestapo* and the *Reichskriminalpolizei amt* [Reich Criminal Police Department] which was responsible for the persecution of homosexuals. From 1942, he was employed in the Secret Field Police, including service in Lodz [Poland] and from 1943 was *Leitender Feldpolizeidirektor bei der Heeresgruppe Süd* [Senior Field Police Director for Army Group South]. From 1948 to 1954 he was a member of the organization. In Pullach he was in charge of security at the headquarters of the German camp administration. In 1954, unhappy with the organization, he transferred to the Support Group for the Bonn [government] and became Head of the Federal Criminal Department.[20]

Although the majority of the GFP officer corps and its lower ranks walked away from the horrors of the Second World War without any criminal indictments of a death sentence or even a period of incarceration, this was not the case with those in Greece who collaborated with the Nazis during the war:

- Friedrich Schubert (a.k.a. Peter Constantine, a.k.a. Petros Konstantinidis) was executed after a quick trial by a shot in the back of his head in 1947.
- Colonel Georgios Poulos was likewise convicted of treason in 1947 and executed. His final epitaph was spoken when after sentencing he uttered: "What I did, I did for Greece."
- Lieutenant-General Georgios Tsolakoglou was sentenced to death but died of ill treatment shortly before his execution in 1945.
- Major-General Georgios Bakos, the Defense Minister under the Rallis Government was executed in December 1944.
- Georgios Pirrounakis, Supply Minister, was executed in December 1944.
- Ioannis Rallis was sentenced to life in prison, but died of ill treatment on October 26, 1946.

Some senior members of the GFP were killed at the end of the war, like Richard Sithoff who died in a Soviet prison camp in September 1945. Ernst Rassow, initially the senior

GFP official on the Eastern Front who later became a senior member of Wilhelm Krichbaum's GFP staff in Berlin, was captured by the Soviet Army during the final days of the war. He was imprisoned and after being held for several months Rassow was tried and ordered shot on December 24, 1945. However, the overwhelming majority of the Secret Field Police personnel escaped justice. Paul B. Brown put it best when he concluded that:

> The senior GFP officials who found themselves interned in the American zone of occupied Germany after the war conspired to remake the image of their organization in the eyes of their captors. Their apparent reasoning was simple: they hoped to gain an earlier release from internment, and to avoid individual charges of war crimes as well as enhancing their ability to find jobs in a Germany occupied by the victorious Allies. For years after the war, they portrayed themselves as simple police officials conscripted for military service. Their self-image drew heavily upon the idea that political reliability played no role in the selection of GFP personnel.[21]

Although the leadership of the GFP was successful in creating a banal image of their organization shortly at the end of World War II, that picture has now faded. This happened, not because of the passage of time, but as a result of the diligent work of researchers like Jean-Leon Charles, Philippe Dasnoy, Klaus Geßner, Paul B. Brown, and Robert Winter. Because of their efforts, the criminality of the Secret Field Police during World War II has now been firmly established.

Krichbaum in the Postwar Era

After the war, Wilhelm Krichbaum very quickly distanced himself and his organization from the excesses of the Nazi regime. Krichbaum's post-war debriefing was deceptive since he made every effort to mitigate any links with the SS and never mentioned the more nefarious actions of the GFP. The rest of the Secret Field Police officials captured by the Allies did the same. Krichbaum's 1947 monograph, written at the request of the U.S. Army Historical Division, was replete with falsehoods regarding the connection and relationship between the Secret Field Police and the SS.[22] In the report, Krichbaum described the many missions assigned to the GFP, like catching deserters, investigating theft and murder, apprehending Black Market peddlers, and other seemingly mundane jobs that an army intelligence unit would perform.[23] However, he failed to mention the various criminal orders that GFP units followed, like the killing of captured Jews, partisans, and Red Army political commissars. Secret Field Police members who at the end of the war fell into the hands of the western Allies made every attempt to portray the GFP as just another German Army intelligence unit—thus avoiding having to explain the tens of thousands of deaths that, after many decades and much research, was finally attributed to the organization. In fact, it took many decades for the truth about the German Army's participation in wartime atrocities to come out as well.

Even after the war, Krichbaum would be involved in controversy. The West German government had created the *Bundesnachrichtendienst* (BND), or Federal Intelligence Service under the auspices of Reinhard Gehlen. In 1948 Krichbaum was recruited by Gehlen, who had been the former head of German Army intelligence in Russia, into the BND. Having a need for people with an intimate knowledge of the Soviet Union, its people, and Eastern Europe in general, the United States began recruiting many former Germans from the *Abwehr* and even the *SD* and the *Gestapo*. In addition, former members of the GFP were also recruited to work for the either the Americans or the West German government. Wilhelm Krichbaum would eventually become a District Chief for Gehlen's counterintelligence group working for the Americans. U.S. Army intelligence apparently knew as early as 1946 that Wilhelm Krichbaum's description of the activities of the GFP were not completely true. His deception in order to avoid that he and his organization would be prosecuted for war crimes, was allowed to go unchecked because the United States needed former Nazi intelligence officials to fight the growing Cold War. However, the earliest mention of U.S. intelligence questioning Krichbaum's reliability occurred in the early 1950s when he was connected to Otto Verber and Curt Ponger. Both of these men were suspected by the U.S. to be double agents working for the Russians. Verber and Ponger became brothers-in-law and were friends from before the war. They were both Viennese Jews who had emigrated from Austria to the United States in 1938.

Otto Verber and Curt Ponger

During the American investigation, it was discovered that both Verber and Ponger had been card carrying members of the American Communist Party. During World War II they had volunteered for service with the U.S. Army. Their fluency in German and their religious affiliation, which assured they would never be turned by the Nazis if captured, made them extremely useful to Army intelligence. These qualifications also made them ideal officers to help try Nazi war criminals. That is how Ponger and Verber were next assigned as officers working for the International Military Tribunal at Nuremberg. Shortly after the war both Ponger and Verber were sent to the Soviet occupied region of Vienna and established the Central European Literary Agency. According to Paul Brown, both men were working for Soviet intelligence:

> The Ponger-Verber case lasted for a period of five years (1949–1953). During this period, agents of the 430th CIC Detachment, based in Vienna, "wrote approximately 2,000 Top Secret Agent Reports concerning this case." Ponger and Verber were arrested, separately but simultaneously in Vienna on charges of espionage on 14 January 1953. The most significant document in the file is an "MLB Contact Report," dated 10 July 1963, which states that Krichbaum was "also working for the Soviets when he recruited Heinz Felfe" in 1951. The file shows clearly that the CIA and the Gehlen Organization had no knowledge of Krichbaum's association with Ponger and Hoettl prior to Ponger's arrest and extradition to the United States in January 1953. The file also shows that the CIA had no particular interest in Krichbaum's SS past prior to the 1961 arrest of Heinz Felfe, the KGB's mole inside the BND, since no record of a BDC records check prior to November 1961 is included in the file. The release of the CIA file on Krichbaum is unlikely to generate a great deal of interest, despite the rather significant conclusion that Krichbaum was working for the KGB as early as 1950.[24]

Was Krichbaum a Russian Spy?

It wasn't until 1961 therefore, during the course of the unmasking of three Soviet spies who worked for the BND that the West German government discovered that Wilhelm Krichbaum had also been recruited by the KGB.[25] Those accused of espionage in 1961 included Heinz Felfe, Hans Clemens and Erwin Tiebel. That same year Krichbaum, though now deceased since 1957, once again came under suspicion as having worked for the KGB. This was principally due to the fact that two former SD officers (Heinz Felfe and Hans Clemens) were recruited by Krichbaum in 1951 and turned out to be Soviet spies.[26] In total, about forty-six senior staff members of the BND have so far been unmasked as cooperating with foreign nations. A document from 1963 proved that one action which Krichbaum took on behalf of the KGB was to give away the "Gladio" espionage network which had been operating within the Soviet Union. Its members were arrested and executed.

According to the latest findings, it was Hans Clemens (aka, "John" Clemens), who had approached Krichbaum and recruited him for the KGB. Both Clemens and Krichbaum were BND officers who had recruited Heinz Felfe—also a former member of the SS and SD.[27] Felfe was arrested a year later, in 1962. It was a sensational event since Felfe was serving as anti–Soviet counterintelligence chief in the BND. All of these bombshells eventually worked to remove Konrad Adenauer as Chancellor of West Germany. Until his sudden death, Wilhelm Krichbaum was headed towards a higher position within the West German government. Gehlen had actually promoted Krichbaum as head of the district council of Bad Reichenhall. What all of this shows perhaps, is that Krichbaum most likely had a chameleon-like personality. He appears to have had a knack for assimilating himself into existing conditions, making the most of his capabilities in the field of intelligence. He also appears to have preferred working for a totalitarian regime, because he had no problem betraying West German intelligence. Given these intrinsic characteristics, it probably took Hans Clemens little effort to convince Wilhelm Krichbaum to work for the Soviet Union.

Conclusions

The conduct of the Secret Field Police in the Balkans was regulated by a mixture of official German orders and decrees, combined with the local political, social, and military conditions of the region. The attitudes of the German occupation forces towards the non–Jewish Greek population was initially fairly lenient when compared to the German occupation in the former Yugoslavia and especially with regard to what the Germans were doing in the Soviet Union. This position changed progressively for the worse beginning in 1943 for three principal reasons. First the Italian surrender allowed the Germans to acquire the Jewish population that had so far been fairly safe under Italian control, sending them to Nazi death camps. Second, the growing Allied advance and continued victories signaled to Germans that they were going to lose the war. This made the Germans in the Balkans feel that a vice grip was slowly being tightened around them, causing them to react increasingly with terror. Third, by 1943 the partisan movement was a force to be reckoned with which was constantly harassing and damaging the German war effort in Greece. For all of these reasons, the German SS as well as the Wehrmacht began to take more repressive measures against the Greek population as a whole. The very wording of the commands and orders emanating from the headquarters of the *Militärbefehlshaber Griechenland* (Military Commander Greece) indicated the growing desperation on the part of the Germans.[1]

One only needs to look at the murders committed by the Germans in Greece and list them by year, and it becomes quite apparent that most of them occurred during the years 1943–1944. This downward spiral into violence and repressive measures against the general Greek population was followed by the Germans as a whole. During the entire occupation period, the Germans alone executed over 21,000 Greeks.[2] This figure does not even include victims of massacres, but simply counts Greeks executed for activities against the German occupation and hostages shot in retaliation for partisan attacks. The Secret Field Police actively took part in these arrests and shootings. Throughout the occupation, the GFP also operated their own jails which handled thousands of prisoners. For the members of the GFP in Greece, their conduct proved harsher and more severe than their deportment in the West. For example, GFP units operating under Army command did not execute French prisoners even as the western Allies were liberating that country in the summer and fall of 1944. The behavior of the GFP in the so-called "Nordic" countries was even more lenient. With few exceptions, this harsh conduct in Greece did not appear as a general policy until 1943. Before 1943, brutalization of the Greek population was centered on the island of Crete. The chief culprit for this was GFP member Fritz Schubert, and his infamous collaborationist unit. However, in the former Yugoslavia, the GFP as well as the rest of the German forces treated the local population abysmally from the start of the occupation in 1941.

What caused these distinctions to be made by the Germans? We know that a great number of the Wehrmacht forces occupying Serbia were principally composed of Austrians. Many Austrians blamed the Serbians for starting World War I and therefore, for the fall of the Austro-Hungarian Empire. The Greeks were considered by Hitler to be mostly Aryan and had been instrumental, along with the Romans, in helping to create the foundations of Western Civilization. On the other hand, the Serbians were Slavic and considered inferior. The German war of annihilation in the East indicated all too well what the Nazis thought about the value of Slavic life. This racial consideration too might have been a deciding factor in the German decision to initially treat the Greeks less harshly than say, the Serbians. Before the Italian invasion of Greece, Hitler had been courting the right-wing government of Ioannis Metaxas, hoping that it might join the Axis side. Even after the German attack on Greece, launched to bail out Mussolini's faltering invasion of that Balkan nation, Hitler initially attempted to mitigate Greek anger at the German occupation. However, as events showed, this initial olive branch came with the plundering of the Greek nation that caused a great famine from 1941/42.

What of the personnel that made up the Secret Field Police in Greece? The personality description of these GFP men runs almost the entire gamut of human emotions—but with few exceptions they were mostly negative. The vast majority of GFP members in Greece acted as the Nazi dictatorship hoped they would behave. They complied with all orders and decrees and defended the goals of the Nazi regime. Some appear to have enjoyed inflicting pain and agony on the Greek people. They actively pursued, persecuted, tortured and eliminated all enemies of Nazi Germany, even when it meant the torture and death of innocent civilians. The character traits of the GFP personnel who operated in Greece described the hatred, cruelty, and malevolent temperament these officials radiated. These "natural tendencies" were freed when any controls the Germans had towards not brutalizing the general Greek population were removed on account of the dire military situation facing the Germans beginning in 1943. This is borne out by the testimony, not only of those hundreds of Greeks who were imprisoned in GFP jails all across the country, but by the POW interrogation reports of some former Wehrmacht personnel who served with Secret Field Police in Greece.

Members of the GFP acted fully to repress, persecute, and transport as many of Greece's Jewish population to their deaths in Nazi extermination camps. The effectiveness of the Secret Field Police and their actions was proven to be valuable with regard to this Nazi goal, given that most of Greece's pre-war Jewish population was destroyed. Most members of the GFP acted fully to repress, persecute, and eliminate any and all Greeks who resisted the occupation. Those deemed an enemy of the German war effort often included innocent civilians caught up in anti-partisan operations or through the Nazi execution of hostages. The effectiveness of the Secret Field Police and their actions ended in the deaths of thousands of Greek citizens, irrespective of whether they were combatants or non-combatants. The efficacy of the Secret Field Police in repressing the Greek guerrilla movement however was minimal and not well-organized. For example, the agents and spies employed by the GFP tended to be opportunists, more interested in gaining financially and were, for the most part, not politically motivated in their support of the Third Reich. Their actions therefore were minimal and mostly ineffective. Nevertheless, the GFP performed other missions efficiently, like aiding the German military to plunder the country's resources, even at the expense of creating an artificial famine that killed hundreds of thousands.

The actions of Secret Field Police in Greece were initially mostly measured, especially during the 1941–1943 period of trilateral Axis occupation. When the German withdrawal from the Balkans began in 1944, GFP units were tasked with directing the destruction of vital Greek infrastructure as a way of denying their use by the Allies. This destruction caused further pain and suffering on the Greek population. An example of this was the order by the German High Command in Greece for the GFP to take part in the destruction of the militarily vital port facilities on Rhodes. These orders were duplicated throughout the countryside and were meant to (1) deny the Allies anything of value to the war effort, and (2) as a final repressive measure against the Greek people on account of the brave and hard resistance which the nation as a whole put up during the occupation.

When the Italian Fascist regime surrendered, those Italian units who chose to resist disarmament and/or joined the Greek resistance movement were in many instances, massacred upon capture. In particular, the GFP took part in the murder (after surrendering) of approximately 4,000–5,000 Italian soldiers in Cephalonia (from the 33rd Mountain Infantry Division "Acqui"), and another 1,200 Italian troops stationed on the islands of Cos and Leros by members of the Wehrmacht.[3] It appears from the available evidence that the GFP force stationed on Rhodes (GFP-510) did not take direct part in the mass shootings but were involved in an ancillary role. However, as late as the spring and summer of 1944 *Feldpolizeiinspektor* Manshausen from the GFP-510 *"Sekretariat"* on the island of Rhodes was still making reports regarding the aid that local Greeks were giving to runaway Italian soldiers still hiding out in the hills.[4] In addition, Manshausen made reports on German officers, NCOs, and men who were being killed by these runaway Italians, or by local Greek partisans and even British commandos. One such report stated that on March 7, 1944, Sergeant Brunn had most likely been killed by a British commando, given that when the Italians surrendered the British made an effort to send in troops to augment Italian units in the Dodecanese islands who wished to fight the Germans.[5]

Corruption also appears to have been a factor in some of the men involved in the Secret Field Police. The employment of starvation as a tool of repression was also apparent. Quite often GFP officials would withhold food from a particular region or town, as a form of punishment for the local people supporting the Andartes. Most assuredly people died on account of this war crime. Some hotels in Athens and Salonika were used as sexual meeting places by German officers and their Greek acquaintances. Often payment was not made in currency, but rather in foodstuffs. We can consider this a form of psychological subjugation of the Greek nation by the Nazis; the fact that Greek women had to resort to providing sexual favors in exchange for food in order to feed themselves or their children. The psychological cost of the occupation and the depredations that the Greek people underwent has never been fully measured. Frankly, what price can a woman put on her honor? But this kind of emotional torture almost certainly caused untold suffering on the Greek nation.

Where possible as in elsewhere, the GFP would make use of local collaborators and informers. The local population was made responsible by the German occupation authorities for any acts of sabotage or guerrilla resistance. In the USSR, GFP units took an active role by joining in individual and/or mass shootings of ordinary Soviet citizens, Russian Jews, Gypsies, and Communist Party commissars alongside the SS killing units and rear area army formations. This was usually done on the pretext of performing "anti-partisan" or "pacification" operations. GFP units in the Balkans seem to have operated in almost the same manner as in the USSR, although they confined their principal crimes to (1) imprisoning and eventually executing random civilians in retaliation for partisan attacks, (2) the torture and executions of suspected resistance fighters and captured Allied commandos, (3) taking part in several massacres around the countryside; as well as (4) the wanton destruction of Greek property, towns and villages. The hostages who were initially selected for execution were usually Jews and/or communists. When the supply of Jews and communists was not available or ran out, ordinary Greek civilians were selected. There was at least one instance when an individual GFP official executed a suspected partisan leader. This turned out to be GFP official, Ferdinand Friedensbacher, who personally shot pharmacist Joseph Sakkadakis.

The Secret Field Police in Greece and Yugoslavia was responsible for the direct and indirect repression of the local population. Their actions involved the selection and apprehension for forced labor of the civilian population, as well as the random arrest and murder of civilians in retaliation for guerrilla attacks. The GFP also took part in individual and mass arrests, and the imprisoning of hundreds of people in numerous Army, SS, and Gestapo jails. The Secret Field Police even had their own prisons. In the cities of Athens and Salonika they had several. Individual cases where GFP officials took justice into their own hands and executed partisan suspects also took place. Once Hitler issued his infamous "Commando Order" of October 18, 1942, the GFP took this decree as a virtual license to kill, since the order stated that commandos, even those taken in enemy uniform, were to be immediately shot without trial, even if they attempted to surrender.

The principal goal of the Germans in Greece was (1) economic exploitation and (2) safeguarding the "soft underbelly" of Europe from Allied assault. It also included (3) the Nazi goal of extermination all the Jews of Europe. Based on the findings of this study, it appears that the behavior of the GFP in Greece altered as the war progressed. In the initial 1941–1942 period the GFP (and German military as a whole) attempted to achieve the goals of the Nazi regime with a minimum of force, as was seen in Western Europe. This was not the case in Yugoslavia, where cruel treatment occurred from the start of the German occupation. However, as the war intensified and German military reversals increased, the comportment of the Germans in Greece became increasingly harsh and brutal, more akin to the manner in which they acted in the USSR. This was especially true after the Italian surrender in September 1943.

We can attribute this increasingly harsh conduct to a growing awareness, and increasing desperation, on the part of the Germans that their military situation was leading Germany towards inevitable defeat. By 1943 the Germans began to behave like a wounded animal that is cornered and knows it is about to die, and wishes to lash out before it is killed. German occupation policies in Greece, and the rest of the Balkans became increasingly brutal. The GFP, like the rest of the German Armed Forces in this region of Europe, followed this pitiless path to its horrific end. Finally like elsewhere in Europe, the GFP in Greece assisted in the repression, roundup, and arrest of the Jewish population. The GFP performed its role and was a vital part in the eventual expulsion and transfer of most of the Jewish population to extermination camps.

The assistance given by the GFP to completing this heinous goal appears to have increased in size and tempo as the war was drawing to an end. Again, we see a kind of rushed frenzy on the part of the Germans to complete the collection and transport of Greece's Jewish population to the death camps before the Nazi regime collapsed; the logic being "we will shortly be defeated, but we will kill as many of you as we can before that happens." The GFP and Wehrmacht as a whole assisted the SS in attempting to achieve this goal. The GFP also acted as a vital link in cooperation between the SS and German Army. By doing all of this, the Secret Field Police did its part in maintaining the mechanism that kept the gas chambers and crematoriums of the Nazi killing machine running 24/7. Although the Secret Field Police did not come up with the plan to exterminate millions of Europe's Jews, by carrying out the orders of Hitler's regime, the GFP enabled the killing apparatus created by the Third Reich. In Greece, this "commitment" allowed for the eventual elimination of about 80 percent of Greece's Jewish population.

Within the context of the goals mentioned above, it appears that the GFP in Greece operated with the intent of supporting these objectives. The comportment of the GFP in Greece was a mixture of their behavior in the West and in the East. At times, it was polite and correct so long as this attitude did not cost the Germans anything. At other times, it was extremely harsh and brutal. However, there does not appear to have been any attempt by the Germans at the preservation of the basis of wealth and prestige of the Greek people, as was the case in France and other Western countries. With the exemption of operations on Crete, which were harsh as early as 1942, the harsher German conduct appears to have increased with the Italian surrender in 1943. This may have also been a reflection of mounting German desperation at continued military reversals. Finally, this study affirms that the GFP represented a vital link between the Wehrmacht and SS and was therefore an indispensable instrument allowing for cooperation between the German Armed Forces and Hitler's SS, facilitating the Holocaust.

At the end of World War II, SS Chief Heinrich Himmler attempted to evade capture by dressing himself up in the uniform of a *Wehrmacht* corporal. When he was discovered, he bit into a cyanide tablet hidden in his mouth and died instantly—thus avoiding having to answer for his many crimes. It should be noted however, that the disguise that he wore was the uniform of a corporal in the Secret Field Police. It appears then, that even in costume, Himmler wished to portray himself in a position of power.

Appendix I
The Structure of the SS Command in Serbia, 1941–1942
SS und Polizeiführer "Serbien"

- CO—*SS Gruppenführer und Generalleutnant der Polizei* August Meyszner.
- CO—*SS Gruppenführer und Generalleutnant der Polizei* Dr. Hermann Behrends (who assumed command from Meyszner March 15, 1944 and held this post until April 1945).[1]
- Adjutant—*Hauptmann der Schutzpolizei* Anton Kaiser.
- Secretary—Keil
- Transport Officer—*SS Obersturmführer* Frank.
- *SS Wirtschafter "Südost"*—*SS Obersturmbannführer* Otto Bonnes.
- Head Physician—*SS Obersturmbannführer der Reserve* Dr. Ernst-Georg Meyer
  - *Stabskompanie / Höhere SS und Polizeiführer Serbien*
  - *Wehrgeologien Bataillon der Waffen-SS.*
  - *Einsatzgruppe Ring.*
  - *SS und Polizeigericht.*
  - *SS und Polizei Standortführer Belgrad.*
    - CO—*SS Sturmbannführer* Wilhelm Stüwe.
    - Staff—*SS Hauptsturmführer und Hauptmann der Schutzpolizei* Dollmann.
    - Staff—*SS Hauptsturmführer* Kraft.
    - Staff—*SS Hauptsturmführer* Rath.
    - Staff—*SS Hauptsturmführer und Hauptmann der Schutzpolizei* von Ullisperger.
    - Staff—*Hauptmann der Schutzpolizei* Schwarz.
    - Staff—*SS Obersturmführer* Geese.
    - Staff—*SS Obersturmführer* Müller.
    - Staff—*SS Obersturmführer* Schmidt.
    - Staff—*Revier Oberleutnant der Schutzpolizei* Sucherdt.
    - Staff—*SS Untersturmführer* Dr. Michl.
    - Staff—*SS Untersturmführer* von Sarközy.

Appendix II
Structure of the SD in the Occupied Regions of Western Europe
Befehlshaber der Sicherheitsdienst

BdS Niederlande [the Netherlands]
- *SS-Brigadeführer und Generalmajor der Polizei* Hans Nockemann (May 1940–July 1940)
- *SS-Gruppenführer* Wilhelm Harster (15 July 1940–29 August 1943)
- *SS-Gruppenführer* Erich Naumann (September 1943–July 1944)
- *SS-Oberführer* Karl Eberhard Schöngarth (from September 1944)

BdS Frankreich in Paris [France]
- *SS-Standartenführer* Helmut Knochen (Mai 1940–September 1944)
- *SS-Obersturmbannführer* Friedrich Suhr (from November 1944)
    - KdS Angers
    - KdS Bordeaux
    - KdS Châlons-sur-Marne
- *SS-Hauptsturmführer* Modest Graf von Korff (July 1942–May 1943)
- *SS-Sturmbannführer und Regierungsrat* Dr. Karl Lüdcke (24 July 1943– 28 August 1944)
    - KdS Dijon
    - KdS Lyon
    - KdS Limoges
    - KdS Marseille
    - KdS Montpellier
    - KdS Nancy
    - KdS Orléans
    - KdS Paris
    - KdS Poitiers
    - KdS Rennes
    - KdS Rouen
- *SS-Obersturmbannführer* Bruno Müller (May 1944–November 1944)
    - KdS Saint-Quentin
    - KdS Toulouse
    - KdS Vichy

BdS Belgien und Nordfrankreich (Brüssel)–[Belgium & Northern France]
- *SS-Standartenführer* Dr. Constantine Canaris
- *SS-Obersturmbannführer* Hasselbacher

Structure of the SD in the Occupied Regions of Western Europe

- *SS-Obersturmbannführer* Ehlers
- *SS-Standartenführer* Dr Constantin Canaris
  - KdS Wallonien
- *SS-Obersturmbannführer* Eduard Strauch (31 May 1944–October 1944)

BdS Westmark (Metz) [annexed eastern France]
- *SS-Brigadeführer* Anton Dunckern (July 1940–June 1944)
  - KdS Metz
- *SS-Obersturmbannführer* Herbert Zimmermann (1944)

BdS Elsass (Straßburg) [annexed eastern France]
- *SS-Obergruppenführer* Gustav Adolf Scheel (August 1940–January 1941)
- *SS-Oberführer* Hans Fischer (November 1941–December 1943)
- *SS-Standartenführer* Erich Isselhorst (January 1944–10 December 1944)

BdS Norwegen
- *SS-Brigadeführer und Generalmajor der Polizei* Walter Stahlecker (from May 1940 until the fall of 1940)
- *SS-Standartenführer und Oberst der Polizei* Heinrich Fehlis (from the fall of 1940 until the end of the war)
  - KdS Oslo
- *SS-Standartenführer und Oberst der Polizei* Heinrich Fehlis (fall of 1940 to the end of the war)
  - KdS Stavanger
- *SS-Sturmbannführer* Karl-Heinz Stoßberg (April 1940–November 1940)
- *SS-Obersturmbannführer* Heinrich Jennessen (November 1940–September 1941)
- *SS-Obersturmbannführer* Friedrich Wilkens (September 1941–April 1945)
- *SS-Sturmbannführer* Franz Hoth (April 1945–May 1945)
  - KdS Bergen
- *SS-Obersturmbannführer* Gerhard Flesch (April 1940–October 1941)
- *SS-Obersturmbannführer* Hans Wilhelm Blomberg (October 1941–April 1944)
- *SS-Obersturmbannführer* Ernst Weimann (24 June 1944–May 1945)
  - KdS Trondheim
- *SS-Sturmbannführer* Ingo Eichmann (April 1940–September 1940)
- *SS-Sturmbannführer* Hermann Ling (September 1940–October 1941)
- *SS-Obersturmbannführer* Gerhard Flesch (October 1941–May 1945)
  - KdS Tromsö (since 1944 located in Narvik)
- *SS-Obersturmbannführer* Hans Wilhelm Blomberg (May 1940–October 1941)
- *SS-Obersturmbannführer* Heinrich Jennessen (October 1941–September 1942)
- *SS-Sturmbannführer* Kurt Stage (October 1942–27 May 1944)
- *SS-Obersturmbannführer* Oswald Poche (May 1944–April 1945)

Appendix III
Commander of the Order Police "Serbia"
Befehlshaber der Ordnungspolizei "Serbien"

- CO—*Oberstleutnant der Schutzpolizei* (later: *Generalmajor der Ordnungspolizei*) Andreas May.[1]
- Chief of Staff—*Hauptmann der Schutzpolizei* Langsfeld.
- Administration—*Revier Leutnant der Polizei* Hentschel.
- Ia—*Major der Schutzpolizei* Holst.
    - Adjutant—*Oberleutnant der Schutzpolizei* Werft.
    - Assistant—*Revier Oberleutnant der Polizei* Erdmann.
- Ib—*Hauptmann der Schutzpolizei* Lorenz.
- WuG—*Oberleutnant der Schutzpolizei* Bergner.
- NO—*Revier Leutnant der Polizei* Janda.
- K (*Kraftfahr Offizier?*)—*Major der Schutzpolizei* Friedrich Heine.
    - Adjutant—*Revier Leutnant der Polizei* Dreier.
- N (*Nachrichten Offizier?*)—*Major der Schutzpolizei* Kleinbaum.
    - Adjutant—*Revier Leutnant der Polizei* Gerhardt.
- R/F—*Major der Schutzpolizei* Lehmann.
- IIa / IIb—*Hauptmann der Schutzpolizei* Franz.
    - Adjutant—*Revier Leutnant der Polizei* Magelle.
- Ic / IIc—*Major der Schutzpolizei* Kober.
- IId—*Hauptmann der Schutzpolizei* Scholz.
- III—*Oberleutnant der Schutzpolizei* Puls.
- IVa—*Polizei Oberinspekteur* Offermann.
- IVb—*Feldarzt SS Obersturmbannführer der Reserve* Dr. Ernst-Georg Meyer
    - *Polizei Klinik* (Police Clinic):
- *Stabsarzt* (Staff Physician) Dr. Harassti.
- *Stabsarzt* (Staff Physician) Dr. Zellmar.
- Interpreter Section—*Hauptmann der Schutzpolizei* Zoufaly.
- Amt VuR—CO: *Oberregierungsrat* Dr. Hanse.
    - Representative—*Regierungsrat* Dr. Spindelböck
    - Adjutant—Antmann Bothke.
    - I—*Polizei Oberinspekteur* Dohmen.
    - II—*Polizei Rat* Luckmann.
- Attached Formations of the *Befehlshaber der Ordnungspolizei Serbien*:
    - *Hilfspolizei Regiment 2*
    - *Hilfspolizei Bataillon I*
- CO—*Major der Schutzpolizei* Leteit.

- Adjutant—*Oberleutnant der Schutzpolizei* Gerhart.
- First Company CO—?
- Second Company CO—*Hauptmann der Schutzpolizei* Schier.
- Third Company CO—?
- Stabsarzt (IVc)—*Stabsarzt* Dr. Michler.
    - *Hilfspolizei Bataillon II*
    - *Hilfspolizei Bataillon III*
- CO—*Major der Schutzpolizei* Stumpf.
- Stabsarzt (IVc)—*Stabsarzt* Dr. Manimoff.
    - *Polizei Reiter Schwadron*
    - *Sonderkompanie*
    - *Wassrschutzpolizei Flottille Serbien*
- CO—*Hauptmann der Wasserschutzpolizei* Friedrich.

Appendix IV
Uniform and Rank Insignia of the Geheime Feldpolizei

When the GFP was officially established on July 24, 1939, its members were classified as *Wehrmachtsbeamten* or 'military officials.' They wore the field grey uniforms of the Wehrmacht, but GFP officials were identified by a light grey blue (*Graublau*) intermediate underlay piping on the shoulder straps and collar patches (dark green for the *Heer* and wine red for the *Luftwaffe*), together with a white metal cipher (monogram) bearing the initials: "GFP" in white metal Latin characters (gilt for *Luftwaffe*), pinned on the collar tabs. A cuff band, to be worn on the left lower sleeve of the tunic, with the inscription "*Geheime Feldpolizei*" woven in aluminum thread (on a black cloth background) was produced but there is no photographic evidence of it ever being worn.[1] In point of fact, photos of GFP personnel are woefully few and many are blurry or of poor quality. It is obvious that discretion was a watchword that the men who served in the GFP chose to abide by.

Each member of the secret field police had, in addition to his ID disc and Soldbuch, a green pass card showing his photo in civilian and military attire, as well as a police warrant disc. During the First World War the round metal ID disc was made of bronze. On one face was the Imperial German Eagle; while on the other side the center of the disc had the words "Feldpolizei Beamter" imprinted in two rows ("Feldpolizei" in the top row, centered, and "Beamter" in the second row, centered). The word "Feldpolizei" ended with a dash: "Feldpolizei—" Above that title and in a circular arc around the disc were the words "Geheime Feldpolizei." These words were separated by the hole through which a chain link or small rope went through as a way to attach the identity disc to the owner (most likely around the neck). Below the center of the disc with the words "Feldpolizei Beamter," and likewise in an arc around the bottom of the disc were the words "Chef des Generalstabes der Armee."

The identity disc for the *Geheime Feldpolizei* obviously differed during the Second World War (since "Imperial Germany" no longer existed). One side had the words "Geheime Feldpolizei" imprinted in the center in two rows. Above that in a circular arc around the top edge of the disc were the words "Oberkommando des Heeres." Below the "Geheime Feldpolizei" title was a numbered sequence that could be three or four digits in length and you can tell was imprinted onto the disc *after* it arrived from the manufacturer. This number obviously was supposed to correspond to one individual serving in the GFP and was meant to be a security check in case someone got a hold of the disc that didn't belong to it. All that was needed to be done was check the records to see whose name was assigned that number and woe to that person who was holding onto it illegally! On the other side of the World War II GFP disc was the German national eagle—the *Reichsadler,* or German Third Reich eagle—in the style as it appeared on the German jackets, with the elongated wings and talons holding the swastika.

By virtue of his special position and identification, the officials of the GFP were permitted to commandeer military vehicles, pass through any military roadblock, enter military installations;

obtain military supplies, and use any military equipment which was deemed necessary for the accomplishment of their task. They could also use the German and occupied public transportation systems without having to pay. Wilhelm Krichbaum summed up the police powers of the GFP when he wrote:

> All members of the Armed Forces were obliged to identify themselves upon the request of the GFP, and all agencies of the Armed Forces were to cooperate with the GFP if so requested. Investigations within the Armed Forces could only be carried out by the GFP if the disciplinary authority had been duly informed. Members of the GFP worked either in uniform or plain clothes.... It was the principal mission of the GFP to prevent sabotage and espionage, graft, damage to Army property and the undermining of morals. The GFP also acted as a fact-finding organ of the courts-martial, under the authority it came in such cases. In addition, the GFP had to carry out certain measures designed to maintain discipline, in the same manner as the military police services especially charged with this task. Tracing of deserters, tracing in general and counterintelligence tracing in the theater of war was also part of their mission. The GFP had to obey all orders and comply with all requests of the intelligence agencies as far as they concerned intelligence matters.[2]

In World War I the rank of major was the highest grade attainable in the GFP. Initially, for the *Dritte Reich* period from 1933 to 1939, the rank of major remained the highest rank that a GFP official could have. The top man in the GFP at this time was titled *Heerespolizeichef*[3] or "Chief of Army Police." The *Heerespolizeichef* was only responsible to the Armed Forces High Command (*Oberkommando der Wehrmacht*). Below him was the *Oberfeldpolizeidirektor*, and below that post was the position of *Feldpolizeidirektor*. The ranks as established during World War II were as follows:

Table 13—*Geheime Feldpolizei* Rank Equivalents

GFP Rank	German Army Rank	U.S. Army Rank Equivalent
Feldpolizeichef der Wehrmacht	*Generalmajor*	Major General
Heerespolizeichef	*Oberst*	Colonel
Oberfeldpolizeidirektor	*Oberstleutnant*	Lieutenant Colonel
Feldpolizeidirektor	*Major*	Major
Feldpolizeikommissar	*Hauptmann*	Captain
Feldpolizeiinspektor[4]	*Oberleutnant*	1st Lieutenant
Feldpolizeiobersekertar[5]	*Oberleutnant*	1st Lieutenant
Feldpolizeisekretär	*Leutnant*	2nd Lieutenant
Feldpolizeibeamter[6]	*Wachtmeister*	Sergeant (NCO)
Feldpolizeiassistant	*Wachtmeister*	Sergeant (NCO)
Feldpolizeiassistant	*Obergefreiter*	Corporal (NCO)
Feldpolizeiassistant	*Gefreiter*	Private First Class
Hilfspolizeibeamte	*Unteroffizier / Soldat*	NCO or private

Appendix V
Organization of the Secret Field Police

Organization of the Secret Field Police

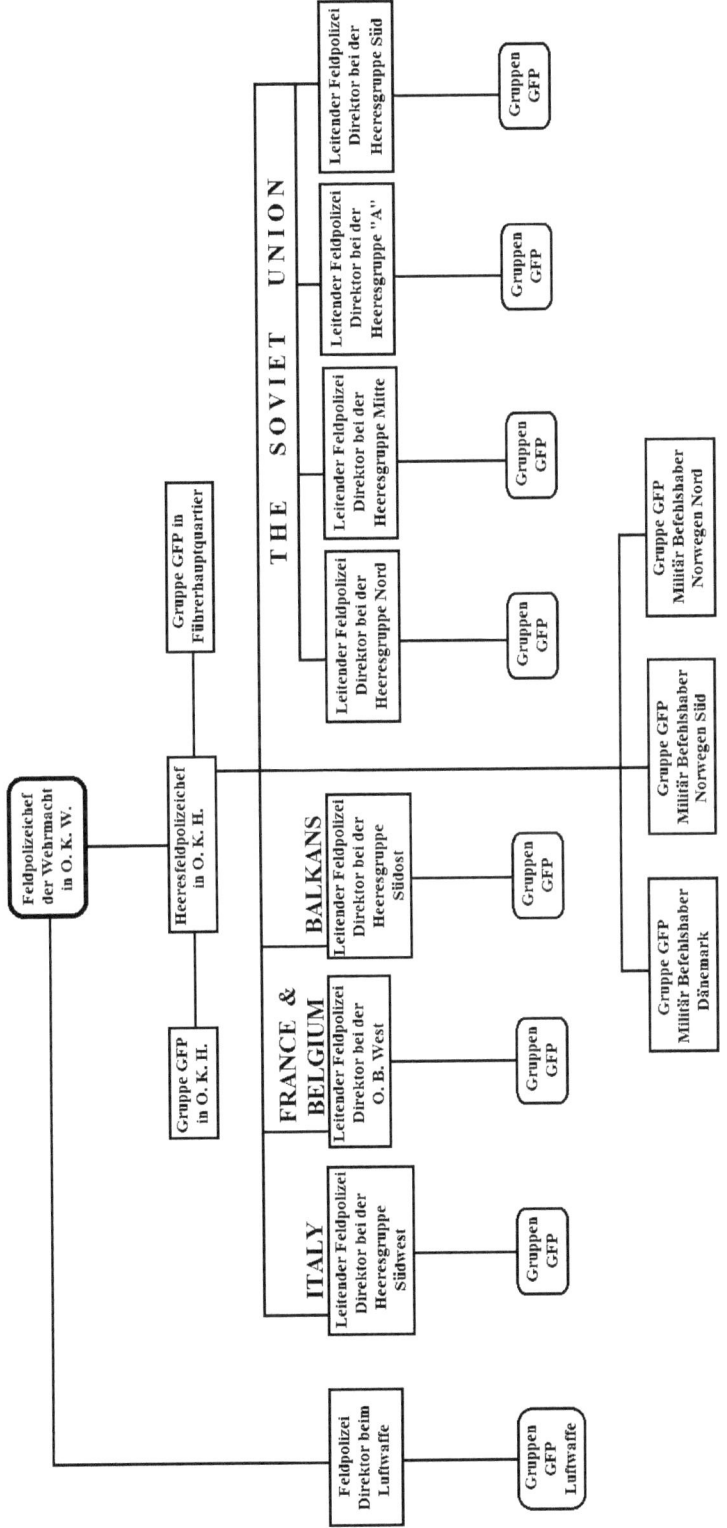

Appendix VI
Order of Battle—Secret Field Police Forces in France, Spring 1941

Table 14—GFP Units Stationed in France & Belgium, January–June 1941

#	GFP Unit	Location	Higher Command
29	1	Brussels–Guarding the Belgian King	*Militärbefehlshaber Belgien-Nord Frankreich*
30	2	Rennes, France	*Militärbefehlshaber in Frankreich*
31	3	Lille, Pas-de-Calais (Northern France)	*Militärbefehlshaber Belgien-Nord Frankreich*
32	7	Dijon, France	*Militärbefehlshaber in Frankreich*
33	8	Ghent (Flemish region of Belgium)	*Militärbefehlshaber Belgien-Nord Frankreich*
34	9	Scheveningen, Netherlands	*Militärbefehlshaber Nederland*
35	11	Paris, France	*Militärbefehlshaber in Frankreich*
36	14	Bordeaux, France under Seventh Army	*Militärbefehlshaber in Frankreich*
37	30	Nancy, France under First Army	*Militärbefehlshaber in Frankreich*
38	131	Dinard, France under 15th Army	*Militärbefehlshaber in Frankreich*
39	171	Copenhagen, Denmark (transferred to Romania in June 1941)	*Militärbefehlshaber Dänemark*
40	312	Caen, France under Seventh Army	*Militärbefehlshaber in Frankreich*
41	501	Tourcoing (near Lille) in France under 16th German Army (in the process of moving to Poland)	*Militärbefehlshaber Belgien-Nord Frankreich*
42	520	Southwest France under 18th Army (in the process of moving to Poland)	*Militärbefehlshaber in Frankreich*
43	530	Brussels, Belgium	*Militärbefehlshaber Belgien-Nord Frankreich*
44	540	Lyon, France under First Army	*Militärbefehlshaber in Frankreich*
45	550	Paris, France	*Militärbefehlshaber in Frankreich*
46	560	Dinard, France under 15th Army	*Militärbefehlshaber in Frankreich*
47	580	Rouen, France under Ninth Army (in the process of moving to Poland)	*Militärbefehlshaber in Frankreich*
48	581	Nancy, France under First Army	*Militärbefehlshaber in Frankreich*
49	590	Nancy, France under First Army	*Militärbefehlshaber in Frankreich*
50	603	Paris, France	*Militärbefehlshaber in Frankreich*
51	610	Paris, France	*Militärbefehlshaber in Frankreich*
52	611	France under First Army until March 1941 when it was transferred to the Balkans	*Militärbefehlshaber in Frankreich*
53	612	France under First Army until February '41 when it was transferred to the Balkans	*Militärbefehlshaber in Frankreich*

Order of Battle—Secret Field Police Forces in France, Spring 1941

#	GFP Unit	Location	Higher Command
54	621	Belgium until March 1941 when it was transferred to 12th Army in the Balkans	*Militärbefehlshaber Belgien-Nord Frankreich*
55	625	Paris/Falaise, France–Composed of LW (*Luftwaffe*) personnel under *Luftflotte 3*	*Militärbefehlshaber in Frankreich*
56	626	Paris, France until transferred in March to Poland & stationed with Panzer Group 1	*Militärbefehlshaber in Frankreich*
57	627	Troyes, France under First Army	*Militärbefehlshaber in Frankreich*
58	629	Oslo, Norway	*Militärbefehlshaber Norwegen*
59	632	La Rochelle, France	*Militärbefehlshaber in Frankreich*
60	633	Orleans, France	*Militärbefehlshaber in Frankreich*
61	637	Brussels, Lille, Noailles, Belgium. Employment under *Luftflotte 2*	*Militärbefehlshaber Belgien-Nord Frankreich*
62	639	Nancy, France under First Army	*Militärbefehlshaber in Frankreich*
63	644	Bordeaux, France under Seventh Army	*Militärbefehlshaber in Frankreich*
64	647	Bordeaux, France under Seventh Army until transferred in April to Romania	*Militärbefehlshaber in Frankreich*
65	648	Lüttich (Liege) & Namur (in Walloon areas of Belgium)	*Militärbefehlshaber Belgien-Nord Frankreich*
66	649	Paris, France	*Militärbefehlshaber in Frankreich*
67	701	Formed April 26, 1941. Sent to Rouen, France	*Militärbefehlshaber in Frankreich*
68	712	Namur	*Militärbefehlshaber Belgien-Nord Frankreich*
69	716	Arras	*Militärbefehlshaber in Frankreich*
70	731	Maisons-Lafitte, France	*Militärbefehlshaber in Frankreich*
71	732	Created June 21, 1941 and stationed in Angers, France in July 1941	*Militärbefehlshaber in Frankreich*
72	733	Created June 21, 1941 and stationed in Paris, France in July 1941 *Feldpolizeikommissar* Jetzick	*Militärbefehlshaber in Frankreich*
73	734	Created June 21, 1941 and stationed in Paris, France in July 1941	*Militärbefehlshaber in Frankreich*
74	735	Created June 21, 1941 and stationed in Paris, France in July. Transferred to 20th Mountain Army in 1941	*Militärbefehlshaber in Frankreich*
75	736	Created June 21, 1941 and stationed in Paris, France in July 1941	*Militärbefehlshaber in Frankreich*
76	737	Created June 21, 1941 and stationed in Paris, France in July 1941	*Militärbefehlshaber in Frankreich*
77	738	Created June 21, 1941 and stationed in Brussels, Belgium in July 1941	*Militärbefehlshaber Belgien-Nord Frankreich*
78	739	Created June 21, 1941 and stationed in Namur, Belgium in July 1941	*Militärbefehlshaber Belgien-Nord Frankreich*
79	740	Created June 21, 1941 and stationed in Brussels, Belgium in July 1941	*Militärbefehlshaber Belgien-Nord Frankreich*

Chapter Notes

Preface

1. *Geheime Feldpolizei* is German for "Secret Field Police"—hereafter referred to as the "GFP."
2. In 1940, Greece had 7,335,000 people living within the borders of her country. By 1944, the population had plummeted to 6,805,000 people.
3. Klaus Geßner. *Geheime Feldpolizei. Zur Funktion und Organisation des geheimpolizeilichen Exekutivorgans der faschistischen Wehrmacht* (Berlin: Militärverlag der Deutschen Demokratischen Republik, 1986); and a revised and updated edition: *Geheime Feldpolizei: Die Gestapo der Wehrmacht* (Berlin: Miliärverlag, 2010).
4. Robert Winter, *Die Geheime Feldpolizei* (Wolfenbüttel: Melchior Verlag, 2013).
5. Paul B. Brown, "The Senior Leadership Cadre of the Geheime Feldpolizei 1939–1945" in *Holocaust and Genocide Studies*, Vol.17, No.2 (Fall 2003): 278–304.
6. See, for example Mark Mazower, *Inside Hitler's Greece: The Experience of Occupation, 1941–44* (New Haven: Yale University Press, 1993).
7. Reinhard Gehlen had been the German Army's chief of intelligence on the Russian Front. As a result, he and his organization *Fremde Heere Ost (FHO)*, was the German Army's military intelligence unit on the Eastern Front and as such was extremely valued by the Allies after the war because of the extensive knowledge of the USSR and other peoples now living under Soviet control during the Cold War.
8. Robert Winter. *Täter im Geheimen: Wilhelm Krichbaum zwischen NS-Feldpolizei und Organisation Gehlen* (Leipzig: Militzke Verlag GmbH, 2010).
9. Jean-Léon Charles, and Philippe Dasnoy. *Les Dossiers Secrets de la Police Allemande en Belgique*—2 Vols. (Brussels: Editions Arts & Voyages, 1972).
10. Raul Hilberg. *The Destruction of the European Jews*, 3 vols. (New Haven: Yale University Press, 2003), 3rd Edition.
11. *Vernichtungskrieg* ("war of annihilation").
12. Hannes Heer, and Klaus Naumann, *Vernichtungskrieg: Verbrechen der Wehrmacht 1941–1944* (Hamburg: Hamburger Edition, 1995), as well as their amended and abridged English language version: *War of Extermination: the German Military in World War II–1944* (New York: Berghan Books, 2000).
13. Christian Hartmann, Johannes Hürter and Ulrike Jureit. *Verbrechen der Wehrmacht: Bilanz einer Debatte* (Munich: Verlag C.H. Beck, 2005).
14. Klaus-Michael Mallmann, Volker Rieß, and Wolfram Pyta. *Deutscher Osten 1939–1945: Der Weltanschauungskrieg in Photos und Texten* (Darmstadt: Wissenschaftliche Buchgesellschaft, 2003).
15. Ulrich Herbert, editor. *National Socialist Extermination Policies: Contemporary German Perspectives and Controversies* (New York: Berghan Books, 2000).
16. Jürgen Förster, "The German Army and the Ideological War against the Soviet Union" in *The Policies of Genocide: Jews and Soviet Prisoners of War in Nazi Germany*, Gerhard Hirschfeld, editor (London: Allen and Unwin, 1986).
17. Omer Bartov, *The Eastern Front, 1941–45: German Troops and the Barbarization of Warfare* (Oxford: Oxford University Press, 1985); also: *Hitler's Army: Soldiers, Nazis, and War in the Third Reich* (Oxford: Oxford University Press, 1992); and *Mirrors of Destruction: War, Genocide, and Modern Identity* (Oxford: Oxford University Press, 2000); as well as his most recent work on the topic: *Germany's War and the Holocaust: Disputed Histories* (Cornell: Cornell University Press, 2003).
18. Thomas J. Laub, *After the Fall: German Policy in Occupied France, 1940–1944* (Oxford: Oxford University Press, 2010).
19. The *Kommissar Befehl* (Commissar Order) was a decree that after interrogation, all Red Army political commissars were to be eliminated.
20. For a complete list of all primary source documents and sources please refer to the bibliography.
21. The *Bundesarchiv-Militärarchiv* in Berlin is the former U.S. run "Berlin Document Center," which was turned over to the German government in 1994.
22. In March and September 1947.
23. *CROWCASS*, Allied Control Authority, APO 742, U.S. Army, Part 1 & 2—March, 1947; Supplementary Wanted List, September 1947. Republished together by The Naval & Military Press Ltd, Uckfield, 2005.
24. Isabel V. Hull, *Absolute Destruction: Military Culture and the Practices of War in Imperial Germany* (Ithaca: Cornell University Press, 2005).
25. Including the very excellent and classic study by Mark Mazower: *Inside Hitler's Greece*.
26. Mark Mazower, *Inside Hitler's Greece: The Experience of Occupation, 1941–44* (New Haven: Yale University Press, 1993), 365.

Introduction

1. A fourth convention was established after the Second World War, in 1949.
2. Robert M. Citino, *The German Way of War: From*

the *Thirty Years' War to the Third Reich*. (Lawrence: University Press of Kansas, 2005), 5–6.

3. Isabel V. Hull, *Absolute Destruction: Military Culture and the Practices of War in Imperial Germany* (Ithaca: Cornell University Press, 2005), 325.

4. Wilhelm Krichbaum, *The Secret Field Police*. MS # C-029. Edited by George Vanderstadt. Translated by M. Franke. U.S. Army Historical Division, 18 May 1947, 6.

5. Jeffrey Wawro, *The Austro-Prussian War: Austria's War with Prussia and Italy in 1866* (New York: Cambridge University Press, 1996), 17.

6. Philip W. Blood, *Hitler's Bandit Hunters: The SS and the Nazi Occupation of Europe* (Washington, D.C.: Potomac Books, 2006), 13.

7. Gordon Williamson, *German Military Police Units 1939–45* (London: Reed International Books, 1997), 6.

8. Michael Howard, *The Franco-Prussian War: The German Invasion of France 1870–1871* (London: Rupert Hart-Davis Ltd., 1961), 249–256, and 374–381.

9. Mark R. Stoneman, "The Bavarian Army and French Civilians in the War of 1870–71" (PhD diss., Universität Augsburg, 1994).

10. Krichbaum, *The Secret Field Police*, 6–7.

11. René Albrecht-Carrié, *A Diplomatic History of Europe Since the Congress of Vienna* (New York: Harper & Row, Publishers, 1958), 165.

12. "Alsace-Lorraine Ministry Quits: Resignations Which Caused No Surprise, Echo of Zabern Affair," in *The Toronto World* (January 29, 1914).

13. The town was known as "Zavern" in German.

14. Henri Domelier, *Behind the Scenes at German Headquarters* (London: Hurst & Blackett, 1919), 144.

15. The Germans never forgot about Jean-Jacques Waltz. In fact, when the *Dritte Reich* defeated the French army in mid-June 1940 a serious search was made by the Nazis to hunt down Hansi and arrest him. He fled to unoccupied France (Vichy France) in July 1940, but was found by German agents and severely beaten. He survived the attack and eventually fled to Switzerland, where he died from his sustained injuries in 1951.

16. Wolfgang Förster, *Kämpfer an vergessenen Fronten: Feldzugsbriefe, Kriegstagebücher und Berichte. Kolonialkrieg, Seekrieg, Luftkrieg Spionage.* (Berlin: deutsche Buchvertriebsstelle, Abteilung für Veröffentlichungen aus amtlichen Archiven, 1931), 545.

17. Förster, *Kämpfer an vergessenen Fronten*, 546.

18. Krichbaum, *The Secret Field Police*, 7.

19. Domelier, *Behind the Scenes at German Headquarters*, 148.

20. The military term "Ic" was in the tactical detachment of a *Division* HQ whose official title was: *3. Generalstabsoffizier* (3rd General Staff Officer). The "Ic," otherwise known as the Chief Intelligence Officer, was responsible for all matters that dealt with intelligence and charged with gathering and presenting as much data on the enemy. All intelligence information was then used by the other members of the *Division* staff to plan and execute combat and movement operations. This made the position of "Ic" very important to the operations of the unit as a whole. The "Ic" also was in charge of the discipline and spiritual guidance of the men of a *Division*.

21. Manfred Messerschmidt, et al, *The Waldheim Report* (University of Copenhagen: Museum Tusculanum Press, 1993), 86–90.

22. Domelier, *Behind the Scenes at German Headquarters*, 142.

23. Klaus Geßner, *Geheime Feldpolizei—Zur Funktion und Organisation des geheimpolizeichen Executivorgans der faschistischen Wehrmacht* (Berlin: Militärverlag der DDR, 1986), i–vii.

24. Jürgen Schmidt, "Political Police and German Occupational Forces in Romania, Fall 1918," in *The Journal of Intelligence History* (Vol.1, No.2, Winter 2001): 146.

25. Andrea Schmidt-Rösler, "Autonomie und Separatismusbestrebungen in Oberschlesien 1918–1922," in *Zeitschrift für Ostmitteleuropa-Forschung* (Vol.48, No.2, 1999): 1–49.

26. T. Hunt Tooley. *National Identity and Weimar Germany: Upper Silesia and the eastern border* (Lincoln: University of Nebraska Press, 1997), 140.

27. Richard C. Lukas. *Forgotten Holocaust: The Poles Under German Occupation, 1939–1944* (Lexington: University Press of Kentucky, 1986), 7.

28. Krichbaum, *The Secret Field Police*, op cit, 9.

29. The *Reichswehr* was the army of the Weimar Republic from 1920–1935.

30. The heads of the *Abwehr* were as follows: *Oberst* Friedrich Gempp (1920–1927); *Major* Günther Schwantes (1927–1929); *Oberstleutnant* Ferdinand von Bredow (1929–1932); *Konteradmiral* Konrad Patzig (1932–1935); *Admiral* Wilhelm Canaris (1935–1944); and *SS-Brigadeführer* Walter Schellenberg (1944–1945).

31. On February 18, 1944 Canaris was relieved of his command at Heinrich Himmler's insistence, and *SS-Brigadeführer* Walter Schellenberg replaced him. Canaris had long opposed the Third Reich, and had worked against Nazi interests. By the beginning of 1944 suspicion of his pro-Allied activities had grown. On the same day that Schellenberg was tasked with leading the *Abwehr*, Hitler signed a decree that abolished it. Henceforth the *RSHA* (*Reichssicherheitshauptamt*—the Reich Main Security Office) would be in charge of intelligence for the German armed forces. The Secret Field Police remained under the direct control of the *Oberkommando der Wehrmacht* (OKW—the Armed Forces High Command). After the attempt on Adolf Hitler's life on July 20, 1944, the Army fell in disgrace since the principal ring leaders of the plot had been *Wehrmacht* officers. Admiral Canaris was soon implicated in the plot, and was arrested on July 23, 1944.

32. The abbreviation "z.b.V." stood for *"zur besondere Verwendung"* ("For Special Employment").

33. Klaus Geßner, *Geheime Feldpolizei: Die Gestapo der Wehrmacht.* (Berlin: Militärverlag, 2010), 25.

34. RH 20-4/640, 1124–1127: Kriegstagebuch, Okt. 1939—Sept. 1940 RH 20-4/1130: Einsatzplan Mai 1941—März 1942 RH 23/129–130; RH 20-4/1132–1134: Tätigkeitsbericht, Feb. 1942—Juli 1943.

35. RH 20-8/297: Tätigkeitsbericht, Aug.–Sept. 1939.

36. Krichbaum, *The Secret Field Police*, op cit, 13.

37. Rainer Longhardt-Söntgen, *Partisanen, Spione und Banditen: Abwehrtätigkeit in Oberitalien 1943–1945* (Neckargemünd: Kurt Vowinckel Verlag, 1961), 9.

38. *Kommissariat der GFP für Deutsche Afrika-Korps*—translation: Commissariat of the Secret Field Police for the German Africa Corps.

39. Tessin, Georg. *Verbände und Truppen der deutschen Wehrmacht und Waffen-SS 1939–1945* (Osnabrück: Biblio Verlag GmbH, 1973–2002), twenty-four volumes, Volume 12, 244.

40. Where "z.b.V." is an abbreviation of *zur Besondere verwendung* (for Special Employment).

41. Robert Winter. *Die Geheime Feldpolizei* (Wolfenbüttal: Melchior Verlag, 2013), 130.

42. Richard J. Evans. *The Third Reich in Power* (New York: The Penguin Press, 2005), 16.

43. Jeffrey Herf. *Reactionary Modernism* (New York: Cambridge University Press, 1984), 20.

Chapter 1

1. Mark Mazower, *Dark Continent: Europe's Twentieth Century* (New York: Vintage Books, 1998), 17.
2. For a discussion of the social transformations that industrialization prompted in Europe, see for example, Patrick O'Brien, "The Foundations of European Industrialization: From the Perspective of the World," in *Journal of Historical Sociology*, 4.3 (1991): 288–317.
3. The European nations with overseas colonies at this time included the United Kingdom, France, Imperial Germany, Italy, Portugal, Spain, The Netherlands, Denmark, Imperial Russia, Belgium, and even the Austro-Hungarian Empire, if you consider Tianjin and Bosnia and Herzegovina (which they annexed in 1909). For a list of all overseas possessions and colonies by European powers before 1914, see: Daniel R. Headrick. *The Tools of Empire: Technology and European Imperialism in the Nineteenth Century* (Oxford: Oxford University Press, 1981).
4. See Dean Konstantaras, "Culture, structure and reciprocity: histoire croisée and its uses for the conceptualization of the rise and spread of national movements in Europe and the Atlantic World during the Age of Revolutions," in *European Review of History*, Vol. 20 Issue 3 (June 2013): 383–405.
5. The Byzantine Empire was the eastern half—the remnant that remained of the old Roman Empire when the city of Rome officially fell in 476 A.D. and its western possessions were seized by numerous Germanic Barbarian tribes. By the sixth century A.D. the eastern half of the Roman Empire was increasingly being influenced by all things Greek. Indeed, even the language of the Romans—Latin—which was still spoken in the court of the emperor in Constantinople in the 5th Century A.D. had been replaced by Greek in the 6th Century. Increasingly, the remains of the eastern half of the Roman Empire became more and more Hellenized. Even the Christian religion became divided and finally, in 1054 the aptly named "Great Schism" finalized the separation of the Roman Catholic Church (based in Rome) and the Eastern Orthodox Christian faith (based in Constantinople).
6. David Brewer, *The Flame of Freedom: The Greek War of Independence, 1821–1833* (London: John Murray, 2001), 215.
7. John A. Petropulos. *Politics and Statecraft in the Kingdom of Greece* (Princeton: Princeton University Press, 1968), 523.
8. J. W. Duffield article in *The New York Times*, October 30, 1921, Sunday Edition. http://query.nytimes.com/gst/abstract.html?res=9505E1DD103EEE3ABC4850DFB667838A639EDE, accessed January 30, 2015.
9. Mark Mazower. *Inside Hitler's Greece: The Experience of Occupation 1941–1944* (New Haven: Yale University Press, 1993), 12–13.
10. Ibid., 12.
11. Richard C. Hall, "Balkan Wars," in *History Today*, Vol. 62, Issue 11 (November 2012): 36–42.
12. When Greece had won independence in 1832, the French, Russians, and the English had imposed the Bavarian born Prince Otto von Wittelsbach as monarch of the Kingdom of Greece. However, in 1862 after he continued to rule Greece as an authoritarian ruler (ignoring Parliament), he was overthrown. His place was taken over by Prince William of Denmark. In order to make this other foreign-imposed king more palatable to the Greek people, the United Kingdom offered the Ionian Islands as a "coronation gift" (with Corfu being the largest of these islands). For a more detailed history of King George I see: *King of Greece George I* [New York: Columbia University Press, Columbia Electronic Encyclopedia], 6th Edition. Q1 2014, 1–11.
13. http://goldcoin.org/gold-coins/the-latin-monetary-union-1865/691/, accessed on January 30, 2015.
14. Kris James Mitchener, and Marc D. Weidenmier. "Supersanctions and Sovereign Debt Repayment"—National Bureau of Economic Research—Working Paper Series, 1050 Massachusetts Avenue, Cambridge, MA 02138—Working Paper 11472 (2005): 33; http://www.nber.org/papers/w11472, accessed January 31, 2015.
15. Catherine Bregianni, "The Gold Exchange Standard, the Great Depression and Greece; Lessons from the Interwar Greek Default"—*Modern Greek History Research Center of the Academy of Athens* (2002), 4–5. http://www.academyofathens.gr/ecportal.asp?id=71&nt=109&lang=2, accessed on January 31, 2015.
16. Fischer, *Balkan Strongmen*, op cit., 169.
17. Panagiotis Dimitrakis. *Greece and the English: British Diplomacy and the Kings of Greece* (London: Tauris Academic Studies, 2009), 8.
18. George Kaloudis, "Ethnic Cleansing in Asia Minor and the Treaty of Lausanne" in *International Journal on World Peace*, Vol. XXXI, No.1 (March 2014): 60.
19. Bernd J. Fischer, ed. *Balkan Strongmen: Dictators and Authoritarian Rulers of Southeast Europe* (West Lafayette: Purdue University Press, 2007), 166–167.
20. Keith Legg, and John Roberts, *Modern Greece: A Civilization on the Periphery* (Boulder, Colorado: Westview Press, 1997), 35.
21. Fischer, *Balkan Strongmen*, op cit., 169.
22. Joshua Teitelbaum, "Taking Back the Caliphate: Sharif Husayn ibn Ali, Mustafa Kemal and the Ottoman Caliphate" in *Welt des Islams*, Vol. 40 Issue 3 (2000): 414–424.
23. Fischer, *Balkan Strongmen*, 170.
24. http://www.theverge.com/2015/2/2/7963911/greek-austerity-increased-suicides-financial-crisis-bmj-study, accessed on 03/24/2017.
25. Peter Davies, and Derek Lynch. *The Routledge companion to fascism and the far right* (New York: Routledge, 2002), 276.
26. John Van der Kiste. *Kings of the Hellenes* (Gloucestershire: Alan Sutton Publishing, 1994), 144.
27. Richard Clogg. *A Concise History of Greece* (Cambridge: Cambridge University Press, 1992), 4.
28. C.M. Woodhouse. *Modern Greece: A Short History* (London: Faber & Faber Publishing, 2000), 224.
29. Fischer, *Balkan Strongmen*, op cit., 175.
30. Mazower, *Inside Hitler's Greece*, op cit., 12.
31. Bregianni, "The Gold Exchange Standard," 2–3.
32. Mazower, *Inside Hitler's Greece*, op cit., 13.
33. Clogg, *A Concise History of Greece*, op cit., 114.
34. Fischer, *Balkan Strongmen*, op cit., 179.
35. Clogg, *A Concise History of Greece*, op cit., 116.
36. Marina Petrakis. *The Metaxas Myth: Dictatorship and Propaganda in Greece* (London: I. B. Tauris, 2005), 32.
37. Robin W. Winks, and R. J. Q. Adams. *Europe, 1890–1945: Crisis and Conflict* (Oxford: Oxford University Press, 2003), 160.
38. Greg Anderson, "The Personality of the Greek

State" in *The Journal of Hellenic Studies*, Vol. CXXIX (November 2009): 1–22.
    39. K. E. Fleming. *Greece: A Jewish History* (Princeton: Princeton University Press, 2008), 1.
    40. John Edwards. *The Spain of the Catholic Monarchs 1474–1520* (Oxford: Blackwell Publishers, 2000), 1–37.
    41. Avigdor Levy (ed.), *Jews, Turks, Ottomans: A Shared History, Fifteenth through the Twentieth Century* (New York: Syracuse University Press, 2002), 194–195.
    42. Michael Matsas. *The Illusion of Safety: The Story of the Greek Jews During the Second World War* (New York: Pella Publishing, 1997), 83.

Chapter 2

    1. Ian Kershaw, *Fateful Choices: Ten Decisions That Changed the World, 1940–1941* (New York: Penguin, 2007), 177.
    2. Ian Kershaw, *Fateful Choices*, op cit, 62.
    3. Patrick J. Buchanan, *Churchill, Hitler, and The Unnecessary War: How Britain Lost Its Empire and the West Lost the World* (New York: Crown Press, 2008), 293.
    4. David.Faber. *Munich 1938: Appeasement and World War Two* (New York: Simon & Schuster, 2010), 346.
    5. Henri Nogueres. *Munich: "Peace for our Time"* (London: George Weidenfeld and Nicholson, Ltd., 1965), 309.
    6. Franklin D. Roosevelt, "No Peace With Hitler: Eight Common Principles for a Better World," in *Vital Speeches of the Day*. Vol. 7 Issue 22 (September 1, 1941): 678–679.
    7. Winston S. Churchill, *Never Give In! The Best of Winston Churchill's Speeches* (New York: Hyperion, 2003), 218.
    8. Ian Kershaw, *Fateful Choices*, op cit, 54.
    9. David Stahel, *Operation Barbarossa and Germany's Defeat in the East* (New York: Cambridge University Press, 2011), 35.
    10. Eddy Bauer, *The History of World War II* (London: Galley Press, 1984), 95.
    11. John Keegan, *The Second World War* (Toronto: Key Porter Books, 1989), 327.
    12. Leni Riefenstahl, *Leni Riefenstahl: A Memoir* (New York: Picador, 1987), 295–296.
    13. Gani Manelli, "Partisan Politics in WWII Albania: The Struggle for Power, 1939–1944" in *East European Quarterly*, XL, No.3 (2006): 333–348.
    14. Besnik Pula, "Becoming citizens of empire: Albanian nationalism and fascist empire, 1939–1943" in *Theory & Society*, Vol. XXXVII, Issue 6, 567–596 (December 2008): 579.
    15. John Gooch, *Mussolini and His Generals: The Armed Forces and Fascist Foreign Policy, 1922–1940* (Cambridge: Cambridge University Press), 332.
    16. Mario Cervi, *The Hollow Legions: Mussolini's blunder in Greece, 1940–1941* (New York: Doubleday, 1971), 137–39.
    17. Richard J. Evans, *The Third Reich at War* (London: Penguin Books Ltd., 2008), 147.
    18. Hugh Gibson and Sumner Welles, eds. *Ciano Diaries 1939–1943, Complete, Unabridged Diaries of Count Galeazzo. Italian Minister for Foreign Affairs 1936–1943* (New York: Doubleday & Co., 1946), 247.
    19. Doris L. Bergen, *War & Genocide: A Concise History of the Holocaust* (New York: Rowman & Littlefield, 2009), 36.
    20. When the nation of Czechoslovakia was finally occupied in March 1939, Slovakia became an independent Fascist state under Father Tiso (a defrocked Catholic priest). The Czech territories became the German "protectorates" of *Böhmen* (Bohemia) and *Mähren* (Moravia).
    21. David G. Williamson, *The Age of the Dictators* (New York: Routledge Publishing, 2007), 435.
    22. This force included 7,702 New Zealand, 6,540 Australians, and 17,004 British troops (of which 1,941 were Royal Marines held in reserve).
    23. David E. Murphy, *What Stalin Knew: The Enigma of Barbarossa* (New Haven: Yale University Press, 2005), 262.
    24. Robert Whymant, *Stalin's Spy: Richard Sorge and the Tokyo Espionage Ring* (London: I. B. Tauris, 2007), 157.
    25. Marina Petrakis, *The Metaxas Myth: Dictatorship and Propaganda in Greece* (London: I. B. Tauris, 2011), 234.
    26. At this time, right-wing states existed in Spain, Slovakia, Hungary, Romania, and Bulgaria.
    27. Besnik Pula, "Becoming citizens of empire," 573.
    28. Clogg, *A Concise History of Greece*, op cit., 116.
    29. Walter Görlitz, and David Irving, eds. *In the Service of the Reich* (New York: Stein & Day, 1979), 165.
    30. http://www.jewishvirtuallibrary.org/jsource/Holocaust/hitler050441.html, accessed on February 4, 2015.
    31. Murat Önsoy, *The World War Two Allied Economic Warfare: The Case of Turkish Chrome Sales* (Saarbrücken: VDM Verlag, 2009), 147.
    32. Mazower, *Inside Hitler's Greece*, 44–48.
    33. Violetta Hionidu. *Famine and Death in Occupied Greece, 1941–1944* (New York, Cambridge University Press, 2012), 237.

Chapter 3

    1. William L. Shirer, *The Rise and fall of the Third Reich: A History of Nazi Germany* (New York: Simon & Schuster, 1960), 937.
    2. Jeffrey Herf, *Reactionary Modernism: Technology, Culture, and Politics in the Third Reich* (New York: Cambridge University Press, 1984), 20.
    3. Paul B. Brown, "The Senior Leadership Cadre of the Geheime Feldpolizei 1939–1945" in: *Holocaust and Genocide Studies*, Vol. 17, No. 2 (2003): 278–304.
    4. Wilhelm Krichbaum. *The Secret Field Police*. MS # C-029. Edited by George Vanderstadt. Translated by M. Franke. U.S. Army Historical Division, 18 May 1947, 23.
    5. Historians believe that the origin of Europe's Gypsies lies in the northwest region of the Indian subcontinent. There lived an Indian tribe known for their squabbling, banditry, and fierce independence. They proved to be particularly troublesome to the local Gupta rulers, who wished to get rid of them. Sometime around 500 A.D. the tribe was ordered to leave their ancestral home and head west as "ambassadors." The truth is that they were expelled by force by the Gupta rulers, who considered them too difficult and bothersome to handle. Another story has them leaving on account of the invasion of the Indian subcontinent by the Huns. In any event, they wandered westward through Afghanistan, Iran, Mesopotamia, and other regions of the Near East. By the time of the Middle Ages they had reached the Balkans. In order to be more readily accepted by the people whom they encountered there, they claimed that

they were Christian pilgrims from Egypt—thus the term "Gypsies" (Egyptians). When they mixed with the population of the Balkans, they became the Romani people of today, with their particular customs and ways. The Romani have been the subject of persecution and hatred for hundreds of years. Even as late as the 1970s, numerous German municipalities had laws on their books which made discrimination against *Zigeuner* (Gypsies) legal.

6. Raphael Lemkin, *Axis Rule in Occupied Europe: Laws of Occupation, Analysis of Government. Proposals for Redress* (Washington, D.C.: Carnegie Endowment for International Peace, 1944), 8–9.

7. *Ibid.*, 9.

8. http://lefthumanism.blogspot.com/2011/08/roth-karl-heinz-die-zerstorung-der.html, accessed on January 27, 2015.

9. *Ibid.*

10. http://www.japantimes.co.jp/news/2015/02/09/world/politics-diplomacy-world/greece-to-demand-that-germany-pay-reparations-for-wwii, accessed on June 30, 2016.

11. Office of Strategic Services Research and Analysis Branch, R & A N, 2500.15, "German Military Government Over Europe: Economic Controls in Occupied Europe," Washington. D.C., 28 August, 1945, 160pp.

12. Frank J. Coppa. *The Life & Pontificate of Pope Pius XII: Between History & Controversy* (Washington, D.C.: The Catholic University of America Press, 2013), 148.

13. When the Germans refused to employ their paratroopers for the planned invasion of Malta (code-named "Operation Hercules"), the Italians scrapped the idea altogether.

14. http://www.yadvashem.org/odot_pdf/Microsoft%20Word%20-%204803.pdf, accessed on March 30, 2017.

15. The Bulgarians eventually employed and entire corps: the Bulgarian I Corps, with the 22nd, 24th, 25th, and 27th Infantry Division.

16. Franz Kurowski, *The Brandenburgers: Global Mission* (Winnipeg: J.J. Fedorowicz Publishing, 1997), 227.

17. NARA Microfilm T-501, Roll 260, Frame 000625.

18. BA/Frieberg, RH 26-1007/25, *Lagebericht—Kommandant Ost-Aegaeis*, 11 August 1944, *Unerlaubte Entfernungen und Fahnenfluchtsfälle*, pages 8 and 12.

Chapter 4

1. The table was devised using various sources. See: *The Secret Field Police in the West*, C.S.D.I.C., 24 May 1945, The National Archives, Kew, Richmond, Surrey, TW9 4DU, United Kingdom; Records of the Army Staff—Box No.5, NND 881019, File No. XE019650— *Geheime Feldpolizei* (GFP) [Secret Field Police], Vol. I & Vol. II—U.S. Army Historical Division, 18 May 1947; as well as: Robert Winter, *Die Geheime Feldpolizei: Die Abwehrpolizei des Feldheeres* (Wolfenbüttel: Melchoir Verlag, 2013), 69–70.

2. One other source gives the rank and title of Alois Uch as "*SS-Obersturmführer und Kriminal Kommissar*"—see *The Waldheim Report*, 86–87. In addition, Uch is listed as "the group commander of GFP-621 and GFP-510," 86. The confusion appears to stem from the fact that Alois Uch was transferred from GFP-510 to GFP-621 in March 1944.

3. Winter, *Die Geheime Feldpolizei*, op cit, 69.

4. Wilhelm Krichbaum and Franz Groscheck. *Geheime Feldpolizei* (Secret Field Police), Vol.I XE 019650 Par 43, SR 380-320-10. General Staff, U.S. Army G2 Central Records Facility, Fort Holabird, Baltimore, MD, 1948, Appendix III, 20.

5. Corporal Hermann Westhauser was born on March 4, 1912. He was attached to GFP-621 in November 1943, and served on the island of Chios. He was later transferred to *Abwehrtrupp 383*. After the war he received a PhD.

6. This unit served in southern Greece from 1942–44. In 1944, it was transferred to Sofia, Bulgaria and attached to the German liaison staff. In the late summer of 1944, when the Russian front reached the Balkans, the unit was shifted to Croatia where it ended the war.

7. Georg Tessin, *Verbände un Truppen der deutschen Wehrmacht und Waffen-SS, 1939-1945* (Osnabrück: Biblio Verlag GmbH, 1973–2015) 18 volumes, Vol. 11, 34.

8. Hans Rudolf Kurz, et al, *The Waldheim Report: Submitted February 8, 1988 to Federal Chancellor Dr. Franz Vranitzky* (Copenhagen: Museum Tuscalanum Press, 1993), 90.

9. Kurz, *The Waldheim Report*, op cit, 89–90.

10. Tessin, *Verbände un Truppen*, op cit, Vol. 11, 298.

11. Feldpostbrief vom 5.7.41, mit Inhalt, FpNr: 10448, Einheit: Gruppe Geheime Feldpolizei 611, Stempel der eigenen Dienststelle gut erhalten, Inhalt: 3 Seiten A4 beidseitig beschrieben, griechenland, 1941. http://www.feldpost-angebote.de/Polizei.htm, accessed April 26, 2016.

12. Wilhelm Krichbaum, and Franz Groscheck. *Geheime Feldpolizei* (Secret Field Police), Vol.I XE 019650 Par 43, SR 380-320-10. General Staff, U.S. Army G2 Central Records Facility, Fort Holabird, Baltimore, MD, 1948, 225.

13. Winifried R. Garscha, "Ordinary Austrians: Common War Criminals during World War II" in *Austrian Lives: Contemporary Austrian Studies* (Innsbruck: Innsbruck University, 2012), 313.

14. BA/MA, RH 48 Dienststellen und Einheiten der Ordnungstruppen, der Geheimen Feldpolizei, der Betreuungs und Streifendienste des Heeres. RW 40/170: Fester Platz Kreta, Sept. 1944 RW 40/172: Tätigkeitsbericht, Juli—Aug. 1944.

15. BA/MA RH-24-22/21, folio 88–89.

16. BA—RW 40/170: Fester Platz Kreta, Sept. 1944 RW 40/172: Tätigkeitsbericht, Juli—Aug. 1944.

17. Kurz, *The Waldheim Report*, op cit, 59.

18. Kurz, *The Waldheim Report*, op cit, 70.

19. Antonio Muñoz, *Hitler's Green Army: The German Order Police and their European Auxiliaries, 1933-1945* (New York: Europa Books, 2005), 335.

20. Tessin, *Verbände un Truppen*, op cit, Vol.11, 327.

21. Up until the Italian surrender on September 8, 1943, Italian Jews were protected by their government from Nazi persecution. It was only after the Italian surrender that the roundup of Italian Jews for transport to extermination camps began.

22. Mark Mazower. *Inside Hitler's Greece: The Experience of Occupation, 1941-1944* (New Haven: Yale University Press, 1993), 246–247.

23. http://medienfresser.blogspot.com/2014/12/chios-vor-70-jahren-endete-die-deutsche.html, accessed on July 8, 1916.

24. Bowman, Steven. *The Agony of Greek Jews, 1940-1945* (Stanford: Stanford University Press), 2009, 72–73.

25. Mazower, op cit., 244.

26. BA/MA RH24-22/23, folio 50–51. *Geheime Feldpolizei Gruppe 621 Kommando der XXII. Geb. AK, 27 Marz 1944*.

27. Hans Safrian, *Eichmann's Men* (New York: Cambridge University Press, 2010), 184.
28. Kurz, *The Waldheim Report*, op cit, 80.
29. Ibid.
30. Kurz, *The Waldheim Report*, op cit, 58.
31. According to Tessin, *Sturm Division Rhodes* (Assault Division "Rhodes") was created from elements from parts of the German 22nd Air Landing Division and Fortress Division "Crete."
32. Kurz, *The Waldheim Report*, op cit, 86.
33. Tessin, *Verbände un Truppen*, op cit, Vol. 12, 19.
34. Rigas Rigopoulos. *Secret War: Greece—Middle East, 1940–1945. The Events Surrounding the Story of Service 5-16-5* (Paducah: Turner Publishing Company), 2003, page 87.
35. Bundesarchiv-Militärarchiv, RH 19 VII/31, folio 2.
36. Martin Seckendorf, "Ein Einmaliger Raubzug—Die Wehrmacht in Griechenland 1941 Bis 1944," in *Europa unterm Hakenkreuz, Band 8, Die Okkupationspolitik des deutschen Faschismus in Jugoslawien, Griechenland, Albanien, Italien und Ungarn 1941–1945*" (Heidelberg: Decker/Müller Verlag GmbH, 2000), 118.
37. NARA Microfilm T-501, Roll 259, Frame 000545.
38. The unit's Field Post Number at this time was 47 661.
39. NARA Microfilm T-501, Roll 259, Frame 000545-46.
40. Winter, *Die Geheime Feldpolizei*, op cit., 117.
41. Ibid.
42. Paul B. Brown, "The Senior Leadership Cadre of the Geheime Feldpolizei, 1939–1945," in *Holocaust and Genocide Studies*, Oxford: Oxford University Press, Vol. 17, No.2 (2003): 278–304.
43. CSDIC Reports: Otto Begus, U.S. NARA Microfilm, RG 226.
44. BA/MA, R19/2050 Folio 1.
45. *SS Dienstalterliste der Schutzstaffel der NSDAP (SS-Obersturmbannführer und SS-Sturmbannführer) Stand vom 1. Oktober 1944* (Berlin: Herausgegeben vom SS Personalhauptamt, 1944), 83.
46. Garscha, "Ordinary Austrians: Common War Criminals during World War II," op cit, 313.
47. BA Berlin-Lichterfelde, SS Personalnachweis Heinrich Deubel.
48. https://en.wikipedia.org/wiki/Heinrich_Deubel, accessed on July 7, 2015.
49. French MacLean, *The Camp Men: The SS Officers Who Ran the Nazi Concentration Camp System* (Atglen: Schiffer Military History, 1999), 62.
50. BA Berlin-Lichterfelde, *SS Führerpersonalakten der Heinrich Deubel*.
51. *SS Dienstalterliste der Schutzstaffel der NSDAP (SS-Oberst-Gruppenführer—SS-Standartenführer) Stand vom 9. November 1944* (Berlin: Herausgegeben vom SS Personalhauptamt, 1944), 24.
52. Thomas Kempter, "Gott Feiern In Dachau: Die Feier Der Eucharistie Im KZ Dachau" (Master's Thesis, Albert-Ludwigs University, 2005), 12.
53. https://de.wikipedia.org/wiki/Heinrich_Deubel, accessed on July 7, 2015.
54. BA Berlin-Lichterfelde, *SS Führerpersonalakten der Heinrich Deubel*.
55. BA Berlin-Lichterfelde, *SS Führerpersonalakten der Leo Eder*.
56. The various terms here need to be explained, given that only an expert in the Third Reich would most likely understand these abbreviations. *NS Frauenwerk* (NSF)—National Socialist Association for Women; *Nationale Sozialistische Volkswohlfahrt* (NSV)—Nazi People's Welfare Organization; *Reichsbund der Deutschen Beamten* (RDB)—Reich Federation of German Civil Servants; *Reichsluftschutzbund* (RLB)—the National Air Raid Protection League. *Frauen Warte* (FW)—Nazi Party's biweekly illustrated magazine for women; *Völkischer Beobachter* (VB)—the newspaper of the National Socialist German Workers' Party.
57. Robert Winter, *Tater im Geheimen: Wilhelm Krichbaum zwischen NS-Feldpolizei und Organisation Gehlen* (Leipzig: Militzke Verlag GmbH, 2010), 126.
58. BA Berlin-Lichterfelde, *SS Führerpersonalakten der Karl Eschweiler*.
59. Winter, *Tater im Geheimen*, op cit., 51.
60. Winter, *Die Geheime Feldpolizei*, op cit., 126.
61. Paul B. Brown, "The Senior Leadership Cadre of the Geheime Feldpolizei, 1939–1945," in *Holocaust and Genocide Studies*, Oxford: Oxford University Press, Vol. 17, No.2 (2003): 278–304.
62. Günther Bischof, Fritz Plasser, Eva Maltschnig, eds. *Austrian Lives: Contemporary Austrian Studies Vol. 21* (New Orleans: University of New Orleans Press, 2012), 311–312.
63. BA Berlin-Lichterfelde, *SS Führerpersonalakten der Paul Härtel*.
64. Krichbaum, *Geheime Feldpolizei*, op cit., 90.
65. BA Berlin-Lichterfelde, *SS Führerpersonalakten der Roman Loos*.
66. NARA Microfilm T-1019, Roll 38, Frame 000144.
67. Gordon Williamson. *German Military Police Units, 1939–1945* (London: Osprey, 1997), 15.
68. C.S.D.I.C. (UK) Special Interrogation Report 818: 20 August 1944 Geheime Feldpolizei in Greece 1942, 3.
69. Mark Mazower, *Inside Hitler's Greece: The Experience of Occupation 1941–1944* (New Haven: Yale University Press, 1993), 225.
70. C.S.D.I.C. (UK) Special Interrogation Report 818: 20 August 1944 Geheime Feldpolizei in Greece 1942, 2.
71. *Befehlsblatt des Chefs der Sicherheitspolizei und der SD, Nr. 14/44 Berlin, 1. April 1944*. (Berlin: Herausgegeben vom Reichssicherheitshauptamt, Gedruckt in der Reichsdruckerei, 1944), 68.
72. Kurz, *The Waldheim Report*, op cit, 87.
73. Hereafter referred to as *GFP Südost*.
74. The report did not list his first name.
75. Tessin, *Verbände und Truppen*, Vol. 13, op cit., 189.
76. C.S.D.I.C. (UK) Special Interrogation Report 818, op cit, 1.
77. Ibid., 5.
78. *Wehrmachtsangehörige*—literally "member of the armed forces."
79. Winter, *Die Geheime Feldpolizei*, op cit., 68.
80. C.S.D.I.C. (UK) Special Interrogation Report 818, op cit, 3.
81. C.S.D.I.C. (UK) Special Interrogation Report 818, op cit, 1.
82. Garscha, "Ordinary Austrians," op cit., 313.
83. Ibid.
84. C.S.D.I.C. (UK) Special Interrogation Report 818, op cit, 3.
85. C.S.D.I.C. (UK) Special Interrogation Report 818, op cit, 3.
86. http://de.wikipedia.org/wiki/Alfons_Hochhauser, accessed on April 10. 2015.
87. http://www.alfons-hochhauser.de/bei-der-wehrmacht.html, accessed on March 25, Accessed on 2015.
88. Mark Mazower, *Inside Hitler's Greece*, op cit, 225.
89. Thomas J. Laub, *After the Fall: German Policy in*

Occupied France, 1940–1944 (New York: Oxford University Press, 2010), 183.

90. Paul B. Brown, "The Senior Leadership Cadre of the Geheime Feldpolizei, 1939–1945," in *Holocaust and Genocide Studies* (Volume 17, Number 2): 302–304.

91. Douglas Porch, *The French Secret Services: A History of French Intelligence from the Dreyfus Affair to the Gulf War* (New York: Farrar, Straus and Giroux, 1995), 232.

92. The *Höherer SS und Polizeiführer* were German SS headquarters created to control SS and SD forces in the occupied regions.

93. C.S.D.I.C. (UK) Special Interrogation Report 818, op cit, 2.

94. Michael Wildt, *An Uncompromising Generation: The Nazi Leadership of the Reich Security Main Office* (Madison: University of Wisconsin Press, 2003), 104–106.

Chapter 5

1. Mark Mazower, "Military Violence and the National Socialist Consensus. The Wehrmacht in Greece, 1941–44" in *War of Extermination: the German Military in World War II 1941–1944*, ed. Hannes Heer & Klaus Naumann (New York: Berghahn Books, 2000), 167.

2. C.S.D.I.C. (UK) Special Interrogation Report 818, op cit, 3.

3. *Ibid.*

4. http://articles.philly.com/1995-04-29/news/25687513_1_deserters-adolf-hitler-mein-kampf, accessed on July 1, 2016.

5. C.S.D.I.C. (UK) Special Interrogation Report 818, op cit, 6.

6. *Ibid.*, 2.

7. C.S.D.I.C. (UK) Special Interrogation Report 818, op cit., 3.

8. Christer Jörgensen, *Hitler's Espionage Machine: The True Story Behind One of the World's Most Ruthless Spy Networks* (Guilford: The Lyons Press, 2004), 166.

9. Mazower, *Inside Hitler's Greece*, op cit., 261.

10. Procedures for the Capture & Treatment during Partisan Battles through Immediate Punishment and Evacuation.

11. BA-MA, RH-40, 10.

12. BA-MA, RH-40, 11.

13. *Ibid.*

14. Mazower, *Inside Hitler's Greece*, op cit., 206.

15. http://www.nachkriegsjustiz.at/prozesse/geschworeneng/friedensbacher.php, accessed on July 16, 2016.

16. Mazower, *Inside Hitler's Greece*, op cit., 212.

17. BA-MA RH-19 VII/2, 2.

18. http://mittenwald.blogsport.eu/2010/03/30/aufzur-befreiungsfeier-nach-mittenwald/, accessed on 8 August 2015.

19. Hermann Frank Mayer, *Blutiges Edelweiß, Die 1. Gebirgs-Division im Zweiten Weltkrieg* (Berlin: Christoph-Links Verlag, 2008), 178–179.

20. Mayer, *Blutiges Edelweiß*, op cit., 178.

21. *Weitere Verbrechen, die den Gebirgsjägern eindeutig zuzuordnen sind*—Ulrich Sander, Landessprecher der VVN-BdA, Postfach 321, 44388 Dortmund, Büro: Gathe 55 (VVN-BdA) 42107 Wuppertal.

22. BA–Berlin-Lichterfelde, Personalakte von Leo Eder.

23. BA–Berlin-Lichterfelde, Personalakte von Georg Koch.

24. http://www.merkur.de/lokales/regionen/pfingsttreffen-unter-polizeischutz-330276.html

25. Meyer, *Blutiges Edelweiß*, op cit., 476.

26. BA/MA RH 22/465. *Tätigkeitbericht des 1 Gebirgsdivision, 1.—15 September 1943*.

27. Martin Zöller, and Kazimirz Leszczyński, *Das Urteil im Geiselmordprozess, gefällt vom Militärgerichtshof V der Vereinigten Staaten von America* (Berlin: VEB Verlag der Wissenschaften, 1965), 172.

28. The term "*landser*" is the German military term for "foot soldier" or "G.I."

29. Robert H. Jackson, *Tyranny on Trial: The Evidence at Nuremberg* (Dallas: Southern Methodist University Press, 1954), 199.

30. The hostage trial, trial of Wilhelm Speidel, Wilhelm List and others: Notes held at University of the West of England original source: United Nations War Crimes Commission. Law Reports of Trials of War Criminals. Volume VIII, 1949. Records of the Speidel Case are closely related to other microfilmed records in Record Group 238; prosecution submitted to the International Military Tribunal, T988; Series T301 (Nuremberg Armed Forces High Command) Series, T1119; NG (Nuremberg Government) Series, T1139; M89S.

31. BA—Berlin-Lichterfelde, Personalakte von Gottfried Torkler.

32. BA-MA RH-26 / 117/16.

33. "Greeks Lose Nazi Massacre Claim," http://news.bbc.co.uk/2/hi/europe/3023144.stmaccessed January 26, 2015.

34. David T. Zabecki, ed. *Germany at War: Four Hundred Years of Military History*, Vol. I (Santa Barbara: ABC-CLIO, LLC, 2014), 327.

35. Mazower, *Inside Hitler's Greece*, op cit., 212; and http://gskk.eu/?page_id=794, accessed January 26, 2015.

36. Mazower, *Ibid.*, 214–215.

37. www.fontanafilm.ch/DOKFILME/argyris/pdf/DI-10062005.pdf, accessed on January 26, 2015.

38. Rab Bennett, *Under the Shadow of the Swastika: The Moral Dilemmas of Resistance and Collaboration in Hitler's Europe* (New York: NYU Press, 1999), 103.

39. *Ibid.*

40. In March 1970, he was acquitted of the murder of the Greek pharmacist, Joseph Sakkadakis.

41. Innsbruck Court Case: GG Innsbruck 10 Nr. 415170–23 10 H 7170, 43.

42. http://www.nachkriegsjustiz.at/prozesse/geschworeneng/35prozesse56_04.php, accessed on 21 July 2015.

43. http://www.u-berg.at/texte/nachkriegsjustiz.htm, accessed on 23 July 2015.

44. The garrison commander of Crete, General Friedrich-Wilhelm Müller, was nicknamed the "Butcher of Crete."

45. He was born in Dortmund, Germany which lies south of Münster, and east of Düsseldorf, not far from the frontier with The Netherlands which lay about 137 kilometers.

46. War brings out the worst in human beings. Many people who owed money to their neighbor or who had an ax to grind found the German occupation as a perfect opportunity to exact revenge or to renege on a loan. Envy or dislike was sometimes reason enough for a fellow Greek to denounce a neighbor, whether the accusation was true or not.

47. G. C. Kiriakopoulos, *The Nazi Occupation of Crete, 1941–1945* (Westport: Praeger, 1995), 222.

48. https://en.wikipedia.org/wiki/Friedrich_Schubert, accessed on 23 July 2015.

49. Rudolph J. Rummel, *Death by Government* (New Brunswick: Transaction Publishers, 1994), 233.
50. The American sponsored "Dawes Plan" would eventually stabilize the German economy by a massive influx of loans from American banks, but the German economy did not begin to regain its footing until beginning 1925/26.
51. Anthony Beevor, *Crete: The Battle and the Resistance* (New York: Penguin Books, 2014), 287–288.
52. Suspected War Criminals to be Apprehended on Sight—*Central Registry of War Criminals and Security Suspects* (CROCASS Allied Control Authority, Part 1 & 2, U.S. Army, APO 742, 1947), 121.
53. Schubert's unit was perhaps one hundred men, but an additional 50–100 local and mainland Greeks served as spies whose job it was to travel through the villages and towns and, on the pretext of getting a drink, would linger in the local bars and try to listen in on what the locals were discussing.
54. Antonio Muñoz, *Hitler's Green Army: The German Order Police and their European Auxiliaries, Volume 2* (New York: Europa Books, 2006), 338.
55. All of these villages were located west and southwest of Heraklion on the island of Crete.
56. Alan Ogden, *Sons of Odysseus, SOE Heroes in Greece* (London: Bene Factum Publishing Ltd, 2012), 319.
57. Ulrich Kadelbach. *Schatten ohne Mann: Die deutsche Besetzung Kretas 1941–1945* (Mähringen: Balistier Verlag, 2002), 54.
58. Hans Dieter Berthel, *Die Feldgendarmerie im Zweiten Weltkrieg und ihre Teilnahme an völkerrechtswidrigen Aktionen 1939–1945* (Norderstedt: Herstellung und Verlag, 2006), 53.
59. BA/Frieberg, RH 26–1007/25—*Geheime Feldpolizei Gruppe 510*, page 153.
60. *CAB/129/28*, British National Archives—USPGO (U.K.) translation of the order.
61. Wes Davis, *The Ariadne Objective: Patrick Leigh Fermor and the Underground War to Rescue Crete from the Nazis* (New York: Crown, 2013), 230.
62. Hans Rudolf Kurz, ed., *The Waldheim Report*, 91.
63. Vasiliki Fouka and Hans-Joachim Voth, "Reprisals Remembered: German-Greek Conflict and Car Sales during the Euro Crisis" (September 2014): 8, http://www.econ.upf.edu/gpefm/jm/pdf/paper/Reprisals.pdf, accessed on April 19, 2015.
64. Vasiliki Fouka, and Hans-Joachim Voth, "Reprisals Remembered: German-Greek Conflict and Car Sales during the Euro Crisis" (September 2014): 8, http://www.econ.upf.edu/gpefm/jm/pdf/paper/Reprisals.pdf, accessed on April 19, 2015.
65. Map adapted from data presented in the following paper by: Vasiliki Fouka and Hans-Joachim Voth, "Reprisals Remembered: German-Greek Conflict and Car Sales During the Euro Crisis" UBS International Center of Economics in Society; Center for Economic Policy Research, CEPR (Zurich: University of Zurich, 2013).
66. http://www.dw.com/en/greece-puts-a-price-tag-on-ww2-reparations-279-billion-euros/a-18364143, accessed on July 17, 2015.
67. RH 19 XI/37, BA-MA, *Bericht des GFP-Angehörigen Georg Koch*, 37.
68. http://www.lexikon-der-wehrmacht.de/Gliederungen/PionierBat/PiBat659-R.htm, accessed 23 July 2016.

Chapter 6

1. *ha Shoah*: The Holocaust.
2. Wilhelm Krichbaum, *Geheime Feldpolizei* (Secret Field Police), Vol.I XE 019650 Par 43, SR 380-320-10. General Staff, U.S. Army G2 Central Records Facility, Fort Holabird, Baltimore 19, Maryland, 1948.
3. https://www.jewishvirtuallibrary.org/jsource/Holocaust/sephardimsalonica.html, accessed January 11, 2015.
4. According to professor Raoul Hilberg, 43,850 in the city itself, while 1,132 lived in towns near Salonika and another 1,002 in the East-Aegean (facing the Turkish border)
5. http://www.yadvashem.org/yv/en/education/learning_environments/salonika/salonika.asp#!pretty Photo, accessed on 24 July 2016.
6. Hilberg, *The Destruction of the European Jews, Volume II*, 738.
7. Walter Laqueur, ed., *The Holocaust Encyclopedia* (New Haven: Yale University Press, 2001), p 268.
8. Rosenberg was a Baltic German—having been born in Reval (modern-day Tallinn, in Estonia) during the reign of Tsar Nicholas II.
9. Winter, *Die Geheime Feldpolizei*, op cit., 71.
10. Nuremberg Trial, document NOKW 1382, Directive of the Quartermaster of the *Kommandant rückwärtiges Armeegebiet 560* (Army Groups A, Twelfth Army, 560th Army Rear Area Security Command), May 21, 1941.
11. http://www.yadvashem.org/yv/en/education/learning_environments/salonika/salonika.asp#!pretty Photo, accessed on 24 July 2016.
12. "Famine, Starvation, and Disease in Europe." in *Social Service Review* (Chicago: The University of Chicago Press, Vol. 16, No. 3, 1942): 544–47.
13. Mark Mazower, *Salonica, City of Ghosts: Christians, Muslims and Jews 1430–1950* (New York: Vintage Press—a division of Random House, 2007), 395.
14. Robert Gildea, and Anette Warring, and Olivier Wieviorka, eds., *Surviving Hitler and Mussolini: Daily Life in Occupied Europe* (New York: Bloomsbury Academic, 2006), 23.
15. NARA T-501, Roll 259, Frames 000107–115.
16. *Ibid.*, Frame 000471.
17. Mazower, *Salonica, City of Ghosts*, op cit., 395.
18. *Ibid.*, 396.
19. Safrian, *Eichmann's Men*, op cit., 185.
20. Testimony of *SS Hauptsturmführer* Dieter Wisliceny, *Trial of the Major War Criminals Before the International Military Tribunal, 14 November 1945–1 October 1946* (Nuremberg: International Military Tribunal, Vol. IV, 1946), 365.
21. Mazower, *Inside Hitler's Greece*, op cit., 244.
22. Yad Vashem: Tel-Aviv University. German Foreign Office documents on the Holocaust in Greece (1937–1944)—The Goldstein-Goren Diaspora Research Center, 2007. Document title: *Abteilung für Verwaltung MV 2165/43 [Geheime] Dr. Merten / 26.4.43—Die Überfahrt von Juden italienischer Staatsangehörigkeit über die Grenze nach Süden Griechenlands ins Italienische besetzten Gebiet*.
23. Raul Hilberg, *The Destruction of the European Jews* (New Haven: Yale University Press, Vol. II, 2003), 749.
24. http://www.gedenkdienst.at/index.php?id=832, accessed on july 26, 2015.
25. Andreas Schulz and Dieter Zinke, *Die Generale*

der Waffen-SS und der Polizei, Band 4 (Bissendorf: Biblio Verlag GmbH, 2009), 562.

26. Schulz, *Die Generale der Waffen-SS und der Polizei*, op cit., 562.

27. Rallis had assumed the post on April 7, 1943. He held this position until October 12, 1944 when the Greek collaborationist government withdrew, following the German withdrawal. Prior to Rallis the leader of the Greek collaborationist government was Konstantinos Logothetopoulos.

28. http://blog.acton.org/archives/77044-the-greek-orthodox-bishop-who-stood-up-to-the-nazis.html, accessed on 27 July 2016.

29. Mazower, *Inside Hitler's Greece*, op cit., 224.

30. Telex—General Löhr to the *Befehlshaber Südost*, dated October 1, 1944—RH 19 VII/37, Part 1, Annex 12.

31. BA/MA Berlin, Personalakte von Roman Loos.

32. Hermann Franz, *Gebirgsjäger der Polizei: Polizei-Gebirgsjäger-Regiment 18 und Polizei-Gebirgs-Artillerieabteilung 1942* (Verlag Hans Henning: Bad Nauheim 1963), 90.

33. Mazower, *Inside Hitler's Greece*, op cit., 344–345.

34. NARA Microfilm T-501, Roll 259, frames 000551.

35. "Higher SS & Police Leader in Greece by the [Army] Military Commander in Greece"

36. "SS Brigadier General and Major General of the Police" Jürgen Stroop.

37. Schimana was promoted to on April 20, 1944. His rank was now as follows: "SS Major General and Lieutenant-General of the Police."

38. "Higher-SS & Police Leader for Greece."

39. "Commander of the Security Police and the Security Service in Greece."

40. The term *"Kriminalrat"* was equivalent to the rank of "major" in the State Secret Police—the *Geheimstaatspolizei*, whose acronym was *"Gestapo."*

41. "SS Colonel and Ministerial Counselor."

42. "Commander of the Order Police in Greece."

43. Friedrich Hermann Franz was promoted to SS-*Oberführer* on December 21, 1943.

44. "Commander of the Order Police in Athens." Note that the title *"Befehlshaber"* was a higher administrative headquarters command than that of *"Kommandeur."* Above the *"Befehlshaber"* was the headquarters of the *"Oberfehlshaber"* ("Supreme Commander").

45. Nagel was the former commander of the 322nd German Police Battalion.

46. Hans Safrian, *Eichmann's Men* (New York: Cambridge University Press), 272, n6.

47. Norbert Frei. *Vergangenheitspolotik* (Einbeck: AHA-BUCH GmbH, 1996), 222–223.

48. *Trial of the Major War Criminals*, Case No.7, Closing Statements (Nuremberg: Germany, 1948), 2c.

49. *Ibid.*, 1c.

50. Walter Laqueur, Editor. *The Holocaust Encyclopedia* (New Haven: Yale University Press, 2001), 269.

51. Antonio Muñoz, *Heracles and the Swastika: Greek Volunteers in the German Army, SS and Police 1943-1944* (New York: Europa Books, 2002), 8.

52. Laqueur, *The Holocaust Encyclopedia*, 269.

53. Hermann Frank Mayer, *Blutiges Edelweiß: die 1. Gebirgsdivision im Zweiten Weltkrieg* (Berlin: Christoph Links Verlag GmbH, 2008), 586.

54. Muñoz, *Greek Volunteers in the German Army, SS and Police*, op cit, 42.

55. Raymond P. Scheindlin, *A Short History of the Jewish People* (New York: Oxford University Press, 1998), 139.

56. Hilberg, *The Destruction of the European Jews*, Vol. II, 754.

57. http://www.ushmm.org/information/exhibitions/online-features/special-focus/holocaust-in-greece/corfu, accessed on January 19, 2015.

58. Hilberg, *The Destruction of the European Jews*, op cit., 752.

59. NARA T-78, Roll 405, and Tessin, *Verbände und Truppen der deutschen Wehrmacht*, Vol.14, op cit., 207.

60. Samuel W. Mitcham, *Hitler's Legions: The German Army Order of Battle, World War II* (New York: Dorset Press, 1985), 274.

61. Franz Kurowski, *The Brandenburger Commandos: Germany's Elite Warrior Spies in WWII* (Mechanicsburg: Stackpole Books, 2005), 325.

62. Kurt Mehner. *Die Geheimentagesberichte der Deutschen Wehrmachtführung Im Zweiten Weltkrieg 1939-1945* (Osnabrück: Biblio Verlag GmbH, zwölf Bände, 1985–1994), 24 u. 768.

63. BA-MA, RH-24, 23–24.

64. Unfortunately, records about the number of deported Jews from Ioannina vary somewhat.

65. Steven Bowman, *The Agony of Greek Jews, 1940-1945* (Stanford: Stanford University Press, 2006), 71–72.

66. During this same period, GFP-611 was stationed in Crete.

67. BA/MA RH-24-22/21, folio 88–89.

68. BA-MA RH 24-22/23, Jäger—Gen.Kdo.22 AK, 14 May 1944, Ic—Aussenstelle Korfu—Korpsgruppe Joannina / Ic, 25 April 1944.

69. NARA T-311, Roll 177, Frame 000047, *Kriegstagebuch der Heeresgruppe E*, Eintragung 12 Mai 1944, Abtransport von Juden.

70. BA—RW 40/170: Fester Platz Kreta, Sept. 1944 RW 40/172: Tätigkeitsbericht, Juli—Aug. 1944.

71. BA—RW 40/170: Fester Platz Kreta, Sept. 1944 RW 40/172: Tätigkeitsbericht, Juli—Aug. 1944.

72. http://db.yadvashem.org/deportation/transportDetails.html?language=en&itemId=5093698, accessed on January 19, 2015

73. NARA Microfilm T-501, Roll 260, Frame 000536.

74. Hans Rudolf, Kurz, et al. *The Waldheim Report* (Copenhagen: Museum Tusculanum Press—University of Copenhagen, 1993), 86.

75. Gavin Mortimer, *The SBS in World War II: An Illustrated History* (London: Osprey Publishing, 2013), 155.

76. OKH: *Oberkommando des Heeres* (High Command of the Army).

77. NARA Microfilm T-501, Roll 260, Frames 000556–557.

78. NARA Microfilm T-501, Roll 260, Frame 000548.

79. NARA Microfilm T-501, Roll 260, Frame 000618.

80. *Ibid.*, Frame 000618–000619.

81. NARA Microfilm T-501, Roll 260, Frame 000620.

82. Hilberg, *The Destruction of the European Jews*, Vol. II, 754.

83. NARA Microfilm T-501, Roll 260, Frame 000510.

84. Because Eichmann was dissatisfied with Wisliceny's poor showing.

85. Hilberg, *The Destruction of the European Jews*, Vol. II, 753, and Mazower, *Inside Hitler's Greece*, 260.

86. Munoz, *Hitler's Green Army*, Vol. II, 325.

87. Mazower, *Inside Hitler's Greece*, 256.

88. Mazower, *Inside Hitler's Greece*, op cit., 229.

89. http://www.haidari.gr/Default.aspx?tabid=649&language=en-U.S., accessed on January 12, 2015.

90. NARA Microfilm T-501, Roll 259, Frame 000543.

91. Kurz, *The Waldheim Report*, op cit., 90n.

92. *Geheime Feldpolizei* (GFP) Vol. I XE 019650, Par 43, SR 380-320-10, General Staff, U.S. Army, G2 Central Records Facility, Baltimore, MD.

Chapter 7

1. *Geheime Feldpolizei*, G-2 Department of the Army, op cit., 191.
2. *Geheime Feldpolizei*, General Staff, U.S. Army, G2 Central Records Facility, op cit.
3. NARA Microfilm T-501, Roll 259, Frame 000568.
4. Anna Maria Grünfelder, *Arbeitzeinsatz Für Die Neuordnung Europas: Zivil und Zwangsarteiterlnnen aus Jugoslawien in der "Ostmark" 1938/41–1945* (Vienna: Böhlau Verlag, 2010), 74.
5. Tessin, *Verbände un Truppen*, op cit, Vol.4, 289.
6. Wolfgang Curilla, *Die deutsche Ordnungspolizei und der Holocaust im Baltikum imd im Weißrußland 1941–1944* (Paderborn: Verlag Ferdinand Schöningh GmbH, 2006), 706.
7. Antonio Muñoz, and Oleg Romanko, *Hitler's White Russians: Collaboration, Extermination and Anti-Partisan Warfare in Byelorussia, 1941–1944* (New York: Europa Books Inc., 2002), 160.
8. BA-MA, RH 21-2/639: Gruppe Geheime Feldpolizei 639 beim Pz. AOK2, "Tätigkeitsbericht für Monat April 1942" vom 25.4.1942.
9. www.znaci.net, accessed on January 25, 2015.
10. Winter, *Die Geheime Feldpolizei*. op cit., 95.
11. Hilberg, *The Destruction of the European Jews*, Vol. II, 761.
12. Gerald Reitlinger, *The Final Solution: The Attempt to Exterminate the Jews of Europe 1939–1945* (South Brunswick: Thomas Yoseloff, 1968), 385.
13. Edmund Paris, *Genocide in Satellite Croatia, 1941–1945* (Chicago: The American Institute for Balkan Affairs, 1961), 129.
14. Safrian, *Die Eichmann Männer*, op cit., 200.
15. The *Wehrmannschaft* were the Slovenian ethnic-German community who had been organized into a defense militia.
16. Antonio Muñoz, *Slovenian Axis Forces in World War II, 1941–1945* (New York: Europa Books, 1998), 67.
17. http://www.sinagogamaribor.si/en/heritage/holocaust-in-slovenia/, accessed on August 17, 2015.
18. This rear area command in Serbia was organized as follows:
- *Feldkommandantur 599* (*Generalmajor* Adalbert Lontschar)—Belgrade
  - *Ortskommandantur 378*—(Pozarevac)
- *Feldkommandantur 610*—Vrnjaeka Banja
  - *Ortskommandantur 823*—(Velicki Beckerek, then Petrovograd)
  - *Ortskommandantur 832*—(Kragujevac)
  - *Ortskommandantur 833*—(Krusevac)
  - *Ortskommandantur 834*—(Cuprija)
  - *Ortskommandantur 838*—(Kosovska Mitrovica)
  - *Ortskommandantur 847*—(Uzice)
- *Feldkommandantur 809*—Nish
  - *Ortskommandantur 857*—(Zajecar)
  - *Ortskommandantur 867*—(Leskovac)
- *Feldkommandantur 816*—Uzice, then Sabac (Schabatz)
  - *Ortskommandantur 861*—(Valjevo)
19. NARA Microfilm T-501, Roll 259, Frame 000573.
20. *Ibid.*, Frame 000568.
21. Walter Manoschek, "Serbien: Partisanenkrieg und Völkermord," in *Anpassung—Kollaboration—Widerstand: Kollektive Reaktionen auf die Okkupation* (Metropol Verlag: Berlin, 1996), 136.
22. Jozo Tomasevich. *"War and Revolution in Yugoslavia, 1941–1945"* (Stanford University Press: Stanford, 2001), 77.
23. For a structure of the SS command in Serbia see the Appendices.
24. NARA Microfilm T-501, Roll 259, Frame 000570.
25. For a complete listing of the BdO command, please refer to the Appendices.
26. Hilberg, *The Destruction of the European Jews*, Vol. II, 727.
27. Manoschek, "Serbien: Partisanenkrieg und Völkermord," op cit., 138.
28. Georg Tessin, and Walter Kannapin, *Waffen-SS und Ordnungspolizei im Kriegseinsatz 1939–1945: Ein Überblick anhand der Feldpostübersicht* (Biblio Verlag GmbH, 2002), 631 & 637.
29. Mark Yerger, *Allgemeine-SS* (Atglen: Schiffer Publishing, 1997), 59.
30. Gerald Reitlinger, *The Final Solution: The Attempt to Exterminate the Jews of Europe 1939–1945*. (South Brunswick: Thomas Yoseloff, 1968), 390.
31. NARA Microfilm T-501, Roll 259, Frame 000572.
32. The principle Gestapo officers in Serbia were:
- CO—*SS Oberführer und Oberst der Polizei* Dr. Emanuel Schäfer.
- Adjutant—*SS Obersturmbannführer* Ludwig Teichmann.
- Staff Physician—*SS Sturmbannführer* Dr. Rudolf Jung.
- *SS Sturmbannführer* Franz Marmon.
- *SS Sturmbannführer* Dr. Erwin Weinmann.
- *SS Sturmbannführer* Kopenhöfer.
- *SS Sturmbannführer* Hans Rexeisen.
- *SS Hauptsturmführer* Heintschel.
- *SS Hauptsturmführer* Heller.
- *SS Hauptsturmführer* Möller.
- *SS Obersturmführer* Müller.
- *SS-Sturmbannführer* Bruno Sattler.
33. Reitlinger, *The Final Solution*, op cit., 390.
34. Hilberg, *The Destruction of the European Jews*, vol. II, op cit., 725.
35. Turner was the "Military Administrator in Serbia," while *Luftwaffe* General Heinrich Danckelmann was "Military Commander in Serbia."
36. Siegfried Grundmann, *Die V-Leute des Gestapo-Kommissars Sattler* (Berlin: Hentrich und Hentrich Verlag, 2010), 283.
37. Walter Manoschek, *"Serbien ist Judenfrei": Militärische Besatzungspolitik und Judenvernichtung in Serbien 1941/42* (Munich: Oldenbourg Verlag GmbH, 1993), 64.
38. During this time period this unit's commander was *Hauptmann der Feldgendarmerie* Geisler.
39. This was the single *Sekretariat* which remained behind in Serbia when the bulk of GFP-9 was sent to northern France in January 1942.
40. Walter Manoschek, "The Extermination of the Jews of Serbia" in *National Socialist Extermination Policies: Contemporary Perspectives and Controversies*, ed. Ulrich Herbert (New York: Berghahn Books, 2000), 167.
41. Christopher R. Browning, "The Wehrmacht in Serbia Revisited" in *Crimes of War: Guilt and Denial in the Twentieth Century*, ed. Omer Bartov, Atina Grossmann, and Mary Nolan (New York: The New Press, 2002), 36–37.
42. Martin Seckendorf, "Ein Einmaliger Raubzug—

Die Wehrmacht in Griechenland 1941 Bis 1944," in *Europa unterm Hakenkreuz, Band 8, Die Okkupationspolitik des deutschen Faschismus in Jugoslawien, Griechenland, Albanien, Italien und Ungarn 1941–1945* (Heidelberg: Decker/Müller Verlag GmbH, 2000), 118.

43. Hilberg, *The Destruction of the European Jews*, Vol. II, 724.

44. The Reich Main Security Office.

45. Mihai Serban, "Special Intelligence Service in the Black Sea Region (1940–1948)," in *Challenges and Opportunities For a Multilateral Cooperation*, Antonello F. Biagini, Constantin Hlihor, and Andrea Carteny, eds. (Bagheria: Giovanni Mineo Editore, 2012), 185.

46. Antonio Muñoz, "The German Anti-Partisan War in the Ukraine" in *World at War*, Decision Games, Inc. (June-July 2015), 35.

47. *Einsatzgruppe D* was an SS killing formation specifically created to murder Jews, Gypsies, and Red Army commissars behind the lines. In total, there were four SS killing units named "A," "B," "C," and "D."

48. Radu Ioanid, *the Holocaust in Romania: The Destruction of Jews and Gypsies under the Antonescu Regime, 1940–1944* (Chicago: Ivan R. Dee, 2008), 69.

49. Radu Ioanid, "The Holocaust in Romania: The Iasi Pogrom of June 1941" in *Contemporary European History*, Cambridge University Press (Vol. 2, No. 2, July 1993), 123.

50. Ioanid, *the Holocaust in Romania: The Destruction of Jews and Gypsies under the Antonescu Regime*, 65.

51. Given that Simeon II was a child at the time, the actual policy was enforced by Simeon's uncle, Prince Kiril who acted as Regent, as well as General Nikola Mihov and Prime Minister Bogdan Filov.

52. Turner was the "Military Administrator in Serbia," while *Luftwaffe* General Heinrich Danckelmann was "Military Commander in Serbia."

Chapter 8

1. Thomas J. Laub, *After the Fall: German Policy in Occupied France, 1940–1944* (New York: Oxford University Press, 2010), 209.

2. The border provinces situated between France & Germany, known as Alsace and Lorraine had belonged to France since 1648. They had been given to France in that year in exchange for French support of Protestant forces against the Catholic armies of the Holy Roman Emperor during the Thirty Years' War (1618–1648). After the Franco-Prussian War (1870–1871), and the establishment of the German nation under Prussian tutelage, these two regions were made a part of Germany. The French never forgave the Prussians and never forgot the humiliation. At the end of the First World War, these two regions were returned to France.

3. *Geheime Feldpolizei* (GFP) [Secret Field Police] Vol. I XE 019650 Par.43, SR 380–320–10 (General Staff, U.S. Army G2 Central Records Facility, Fort Holabird, Baltimore, MD): 190.

4. In the West, the greatest need for SD personnel came from France, which contained the largest amount of territory and heaviest partisan activity of any western occupied nation. Each occupied nation or region had a "Befehlshaber der Sicherheitspolizei" (Supreme Commander of the Security Police), abbreviated to "BdS." In turn, each "BdS" had several "Kommandeur der Sicherheitspolizei" (Commander of the Security Police) posts, abbreviated to "KdS." To see the structure of the SD organization in the occupied regions of Western Europe please refer to the Appendices.

5. "Senior Field Superintendent for the Military Commander Northern France."

6. FBI Case Report: *Regierungs und Kriminaldirektor* Philipp Greiner—Reference No. NW 38568, FIR No.98 (IRR Image File D011513) obtained through the Freedom of Information Act, September 14, 2012. Redacted, 6.

7. The position of *Regierungs und Kriminalrat* in the SD was equivalent to the rank of major in the Army or *Sturmbannführer* in the SS.

8. C.S.D.I.C. U.K. S.I.R. / 1676 / 24 May 1945 "Notes on the GFP and other security services in the West, 1939–1942," 1.

9. *Ibid.*, appendix III

10. From June 1941 until January 1942 Ernst Rassow was *Leiter der Geheime Feldpolizei Ost* ("Leader of the Secret Field Police in the East").

11. Dr. Hermann Herold eventually became commander of the Sipo/SD in Poitiers.

12. The position of the Paris GFP command was to be left under the command of *Feldpolizeidirektor* Vogel.

13. Laub, *After the Fall*, op cit., 16.

14. *Geheime Feldpolizei* (GFP) [Secret Field Police]— Volume I XE 019650, Par. 43, SR 380–320–10—General Staff, U.S. Army, G2 Central Records Facility, Fort Holabird, Baltimore, MD, pg. 225.

15. Geßner, *Geheime Feldpolizei*, op cit., 72.

16. This unit was made up of *Luftwaffe* (Air Force) personnel and attached to *Luftflotte Kommando 3* which was the headquarters for the German Air Force in the West.

17. This unit remained in Paris, France until March 1941 when it was transferred East in anticipation of employing it in the Russian campaign.

18. NARA Microfilm T-501, Roll 266, Frame 1272.

19. Paul B. Brown, "The Senior Leadership Cadre of the Geheime Feldpolizei 1939–1945," in: *Holocaust and Genocide Studies*, Volume 17, Nr. 2 (2003): 281.

20. A section from the GFP units stationed in this region, were supposed to keep an eye and "protect" the Belgian king.

21. NARA Microfilm T-78, Roll 520, Frame 000039.

22. GFP-639 was created on September 10, 1940 in *Wehrkreis V*. Although it was stationed in Nancy in the fall of 1940 and spring of 1941, it was eventually posted to serve under *Panzer Gruppe 2*, in the region of central Russia during the German invasion of Russia. In 1943 when 2nd Panzer Army was transferred to Yugoslavia, it served in Montenegro in 1943 and was eventually posted to Bosnia in 1944. By 1945 it was operating on Croatian territory.

23. GFP-312 was operating in Caen, Saint-Lo, Rouen, Maisons-Lafitte, Saint-Helier and Le Havre.

24. GFP-540 was stationed in Laon, between Reims and St. Quentin. It was led by *Feldpolizeikommissar* Dr. Orehs.

25. GFP-610 was eventually posted to the region of Paris and employed there. It was initially led by *Feldpolizeidirektor* Hargard, but later *Feldpolizeikommissar* Kallenborn assumed command.

26. Geßner, *Geheime Feldpolizei*, op cit., 73.

27. Krichbaum, *The Secret Field Police*, op cit., 53–55.

28. Giles Macdonogh, *The Last Kaiser: The Life of Wilhelm II* (New York: St. Martin's Press, 2000), 458.

29. A good number of the more able-bodied GFP personnel were sent to the Russian front.

30. Geßner, *Geheime Feldpolizei: Zur Funktion Und Organization*, 68.
31. Peter Lieb, *Konventioneller Krieg oder NS-Weltanschaungskrieg? Kriegfürung und Partisanenbekämpfung in Frankreich 1943/44* (Munich: R. Oldenbourg Verlag, 2007), 65.
32. Laub, *After the Fall,* op cit., 182.
33. See Geßner, *Geheime Feldpolizei,* op cit., 68; and Peter Lieb. *Konventioneller Krieg oder NS-Weltanschaungskrieg? Kriegfürung und Partisanenbekämpfung in Frankreich 1943/44* (Munich: R. Oldenbourg Verlag, 2007), 65.
34. Laub, *After the Fall,* op cit., 80.
35. Harry Levy. *The Dark Side of the Sky* (London: The London Press, 2007), 210.
36. Born in Dresden on February 15, 1903.
37. Born in Breskow on November 27, 1906.
38. Born in Israeldorf on June 4, 1900.
39. Jean-Leon Charles and Philippe Dasnoy, *Des dossiers secrets de la police allemande en Belgique. La Geheime Feldpolizei en Belgique et dans le Nord de la France* (Brüssel: Arts et Voyages / Lucien De Meyer, 1972), 127.
40. Robert Winter,. *Täter in Geheimen: Wilhelm Krichbaum zwischen NS-Feldpolizei und Organisation Gehlen.* (Leipzig: Militzke Verlag, 2010), 59.
41. Robert Winter, *Täter in Geheimen,* op cit., 59.
42. http://www.glennshafer.com/assets/downloads/borel_revised_14_feb_2011.pdf accessed July 1, 2012. The following article was written by Laurent Mazliak1 and Glenn Shafer and dated "February 14, 2011": *What does the arrest and release of Emile Borel and his colleagues in 1941 tell us about the German occupation of France?*
43. Krichbaum, *The Secret Field Police,* op cit., 54–56.
44. The *Maquisards* were the *FFI,* the French Forces of the Interior—the guerrilla forces fighting the German occupation.
45. Manfred Messerschmidt, *Die Wehrmachtjustiz 1933–1945.* (Paderborn: Ferdinand Schöningh Verlag, 2005), 247.
46. Henry Leide. *NS-Verbrecher und Staatssicherheit: Die geheime Vergangenheitspolitik der DDR* (Göttingen: Vandenhoeck & Ruprecht GmbH & Co., 2007), 378.
47. Lieb, *Konventioneller Krieg oder NS-Weltanschaungskrieg,* 65.
48. Tessin, *Verbände und Truppen,* Vol. 1, 128.
49. Telford Taylor, *The March of Conquest: The German Victories in Western Europe, 1940* (New York: Simon & Schuster, 1958), 184.
50. Geßner, *Geheime Feldpolizei,* op cit., 61.
51. Please see his image on the photo-page of his *Soldbuch* on the next page.
52. Dasnoy, *Les Dossiers Secrets,* op cit., 129.
53. Tessin, *Verbände und Truppen,* Vol. 3, op cit., 74.
54. Geßner, *Geheime Feldpolizei,* op cit., 74.
55. Samuel W. Mitcham. *German Order of Battle, Volume One: 1st–290th Infantry Divisions in WWII.* (Mechanicsburg: Stackpole Books, 2007), 313.
56. Tessin, *Verbände und Truppen,* Vol. 3, op cit., 74.
57. http://www.bills-bunker.privat.t-online.de/122422.html, accessed October 15, 2010.
58. *Abwehrtrupp 364* was a unit making up part of regular German Army intelligenece (the so-called "Abwehr"). Each German army, and corps command was assigned one of these groups under the direct control of the "Ic" (intelligence officer). After the 20 of July 1944 attempted bomb plot against Adolf Hitler, the German Army fell into disgrace with Hitler and the Nazis. Admiral Canaris, who was head of the *Abwehr* was arrested and the entire German Army intelligence branch was absorbed into the SD department of the RSHA.
59. Jean-Leon Charles, and Philippe Dasnoy. *Les dossiers secrets de la pólice allemande en Belgique, 1942–1944* (Brussels: Editions Arts & Voyages Lucien de Meyer, Editeur, 1972), 126.
60. NARS Microfilm T501, Roll 108.
61. The flyer included pro-Allied news and propaganda and was titled "The Red Flag." Apparently it was produced on a regular basis.
62. Samuel W. Mitcham, *German Order of Battle, Volume One: 1st–290th Infantry Divisions in WWII* (Mechanicsburg: Stackpole Books, 2007), 239.
63. Charles & Dasnoy, *Les dossiers secrets,* op cit., 126.
64. Alexander V. Prusin, "A Community of Violence: The Sipo/SD and its Role in the Nazi Terror System in Generalbezirk Kiev," *Holocaust and Genocide Studies,* Vol. XXI, no.1 (2007): 7.
65. NARA Microfilm T-501, Roll 108, Frame 000236.
66. François Marcot, *Dictionnaire historique de la Résistance* (Paris: Éditions Robert Laffont, 2006) 607–608.
67. The position of *Militär Befehlshaber in Frankreich* from October 25, 1940 to February 13, 1942 was *General der Infanterie* Otto von Stülpnagel.
68. Ahlrich Meyer, "Kleitische Prosa oder Polizeibericht? Anmerkungen zu Ernst Jüngers Denkschrift 'Zur Geiselfrage,'" in *Vierteljahrshefte Für Zeitgeschichte* (April 2004): 282.
69. http://www.geocities.com/orion47.geo/WEHRMACHT/HEER/General/GIENANTH_CURT.html, accessed on October 17, 2010.
70. Andris Kursietis, *The Wehrmacht at War 1939–1945.* (Soesterberg: Aspekt, 1999), 46.
71. Antonio Muñoz, *Hitler's Green Army: the German Order Police in World War Two, 1939–1945* (New York: Europa Books, Inc., 2006), 133.
72. Albert-Marie Pfund, *Wenn Ich Nicht Wiederkomme* (Halle: Projekte-Verlag Cornelius, 2010), 299.
73. Geßner, *Geheime Feldpolizei,* op cit, 73.
74. Tessin, op cit, Vol.7, op cit., 6.
75. Tessin, *Verbände und Truppen,* Vol. 7, op cit., 128.
76. Personnel file of Philipp Greiner DO11513, declassified through a Freedom of Information Act request: NWCDA 9/14/2012 7:57:01 AM.
77. Personnel file of Philipp Greiner DO11513, interrogator's spelling.
78. Personnel file of Philipp Greiner DO11513.
79. The rank of *Kriminal Rat* could be equivalent either to a German army captain (*Hauptmann*) or major (*Major*). If the officer with the rank of *Kriminal Rat* had less than three years in that rank, he would be the lower rank (*Hauptmann*).
80. Personnel file of Philipp Greiner DO11513, declassified through a Freedom of Information Act request: NWCDA 9/14/2012 7:57:01 AM.
81. Ibid.
82. Personnel file of Philipp Greiner DO11513, declassified through a Freedom of Information Act request: NWCDA 9/14/2012 7:57:01 AM.
83. Tessin, op cit, Vol. 11, page 335.
84. Jacques Benoist-Méchin, *Sixty Days That Shook the West: The Fall of France, 1940* (New York: G.P. Putnam's Sons, 1963), 469.
85. Personnel file of Philipp Greiner DO11513, op cit.
86. *Abwehr III* (Department Three) of the German Armed Forces High Command dealt with intelligence and counter-intelligence matters of the *Wehrmacht.*
87. http://ablhistoryforum.be/viewtopic.php?f=51&t=128, accessed on June 20th 2012.

88. Charles and Dasnoy, *Les Dossiers Secrets*, op cit., 127, 137.
89. Tessin, *Verbände und Truppen*, Vol. 12, op cit., 174.
90. Tessin, op cit, Vol. 12, op cit., 225.
91. BA/MA, RH 20–20/306/210.
92. http://www.arkisto.fi/uploads/Palvelut/Julkaisut/SOTAVANGIT%20JA%20INTERNOIDUT_WEB.pdf, accessed on April 26, 2015.
93. Van Riet, F. A. M. *Handhaven onder de nieuwe orde: de politieke geschiedenis van de Rotterdamse politie tijdens de Tweede Wereldoorlog* (Amsterdam: University of Amsterdam, PhD Thesis in partial fulfillment for Doctor of Philosophy degree) 2008, pages 288–289.
94. *Geheime Feldpolizei* (Secret Field Police) Vol.I XE 019650, General Staff, U.S. Army G2 Central Records Facility, Fort Holabird, Baltimore 19, Maryland, n.d., 270–271.

Chapter 9

1. The original invasion date was had been set as May 15, 1941. However, the need to occupy Greece and Yugoslavia delayed the German invasion by about five weeks. The Russians themselves have always admitted that this delay where the Germans lost five good weeks of summer campaigning weather may have ultimately saved the USSR from destruction and total annihilation in 1941.
2. NARA Microfilm T-315, Roll 2214, Frame 1163.
3. *Ibid.*, 1164.
4. Jeff Rutherford, *Combat and Genocide on the Eastern Front: The German Infantry's War, 1941–1944* (Cambridge: Cambridge University Press, 2014), 184.
5. Alexander Hill, *The War Behind the Eastern Front: The Soviet Partisan Movement in North-West Russia, 1941–44* (New York: Frank Cass, 2005), 97.
6. Christopher Browning, *The Origins of the Final Solution: The Evolution of Nazi Jewish Policy, September 1939—March 1942* (Lincoln: University of Nebraska Press, 2004), 259.
7. BA-MA WF 03/15831, Feldpolizeidirektor beim Befehlshaber Heeresgebiet 103.
8. BA-MA RH 22/31, Meldung Direktor GFP, Mai 1942.
9. BA-MA RH 22/173, Meldung Direktor GFP, Juli 1942.
10. BA-MA RH 22/60, Bericht GFP für Heeresgebiet B, August 1942.
11. BA-MA RH 22/86, 27.
12. Christian Gerlach, "Men of 20 July and the War in the Soviet Union," in *War of Extermination: The German Military in World War Two 1941–1944*, Hannes Heer, and Klaus Naumann, eds. (New York: Berghahn Books, 200), 134.
13. Nor is this even a complete picture. For example, GFP-723 kept incomplete reports. The unit claimed in their reports that between July 1941 and the end of 1942 it had shot a total of 1,486 (including about 133 Jews).
14. BA-MA WF 01/2151, Bl. 816.
15. Alexander Hill, *The War Behind the Eastern Front: The Soviet Partisan Movement in North-West Russia, 1941–44* (New York: Frank Cass, 2005), 42.
16. Christopher Browning, *The Origins of the Final Solution: The Evolution of Nazi Jewish Policy, September 1939—March 1942* (Lincoln: University of Nebraska Press, 2004), 216.
17. GFP-716 would be employed under the German 286th Security Division in the central sector of the Russian front until March 1944 when the unit was withdrawn and sent to the West to be in charge of security for the V-1 and V-2 weapons under the German LXV Army Corps in Belgium and the Netherlands.
18. Initially GFP-1 was attached to Army Group "North" but later transferred to southern Russia.
19. In July 1942 GFP-1 was located in Konotop, in northeastern Ukraine (in the region of Army Group "South").
20. Hartmann, Christian, with Johannes Hürter, Peter Lieb, and Dieter Pohl, *Der deutsche Krieg in Osten 1941–1944: Faceten einer Grenzüberschreitung* (Oldenbourg: Wissenschaftsverlag, 2009), 177.
21. BA/MA, RH22/199 *Befehlshaber rückwärtiger Heeresgebiete* Tätigkeitsberichte der Geheimen Feldpolizeigruppen 1, 708, 719, 725, 730, 739, 721.—Stärkemeldungen Laufzeit: Jan.–Aug. 1942.
22. BA/MA, RH22/200 *Befehlshaber rückwärtiger Heeresgebiete* Tätigkeitsberichte der Geheimen Feldpolizeigruppen 1, 708, 719, 725, 730, 739, 721.—Stärkemeldungen Laufzeit: Sept.–Dez. 1942.
23. GFP-729 was transferred to the 286th Security Division on November 6th 1941.
24. The only person higher in the Secret Field Police than Cuno Schmidt was his boss, Wilhelm Krichbaum as head of the entire GFP organization.
25. Winter, *Die Geheime Feldpolizei*, op cit, 44.
26. There's a dispute as to whether Kaintzig left this post in January or in May 1942.
27. Winter, *Täter in Geheimen*, op cit., 125.
28. T. O. Anderson, "Germans, Ukrainians and Jews: Ethnic Politics in Heeresgebiet Süd, June–December 1941," in *War in History*, Vol. 7, No. 3, 2000).
29. Paul B. Brown, "The Senior Leadership Cadre of the Geheime Feldpolizei, 1939–1945," in *Holocaust and Genocide Studies* (Vol. 17, No. 2, 2003): 284.
30. Alexander Prusin, "Fascist Criminals to the Gallows! The Holocaust and Soviet War Crimes Trials," in *Holocaust and Genocide Studies* (Vol. 17, No. 1, spring 2003):1–31.
31. Alexander Hill, *The War Behind the Eastern Front: The Soviet Partisan Movement in North-West Russia 1941–44* (London: Frank Cass & Co., 2005), 36 & n37.
32. Hill, *The War Behind the Eastern Front*, op cit., 25.
33. The National Archives, Kew, Richmond, Surrey,—C.S.D.I.C. (U.K.) S.I.R. 1675–24 May 1945. "Notes on the GFP and Other Security Services in the Area of Army Group North (Later Kurland)," 1.
34. GFP-727 was a late-comer to the Russian front. It had been created from *Luftwaffe* (Air Force) personnel during the winter of 1943/1944 in Posen (Poznan) in *Wehrkreis XXI* (21st Military District). This area was a part of Poland that in October 1939 had been absorbed as part of *Reich* national territory.
35. The *Aussenkommando Sondernat "R"* was created to interrogate all German POWs who had returned from Russian captivity bearing sealed letters from the Russian-sponsored National Committee "Freies Deutschland," which was led by captured German general Seydlitz.
36. The National Archives, Kew, Richmond, Surrey,—C.S.D.I.C. (U.K.) S.I.R. 1675–24 May 1945. "Notes on the GFP and Other Security Services in the Area of Army Group North (Later Kurland)," 2.
37. Johannes Hürter, "Die Wehrmacht vor Leningrad: Krieg und Besatzungspolitik der 18. Armee im

Herbst und Winter 1941/42" in Institut für Zeitgeschichte: Oldenbourg (Jahrgang 49, 2001): 387. See also the following web site: http://www.ifz-muenchen.de/heftarchiv/2001_3_1_huerter.pdf. Accessed on March 22, 2015.

38. GFP-709 began its operations in Russia under the 286th Security Division (Bialystok/Osrha), and was later shifted to the 339th Static Division (Vitebsk/Bobruisk).

39. In July 1942, the 403rd Security Division was transferred to the region of Army Group South.

40. The 339th Static Division as well as GFP-709 were involved in the murder of approximately 7–8,000 Jews in Mogilev beginning in October 1941. While the 339th Static Division cordoned off the Jewish ghetto in Mogiolev, GFP-709 provided security at the murder site while the SS and SD provided the killing units. For a full detail of this massacre see: Dieter Pohl, *Die Herrschaft der Wehrmacht: Deutsche Militärbesatzung und einheimische Bevölkerung in der Sowjetunion 1941–1944* (München: R. Oldenbourg Verlag, 2008), 269–270.

41. In 1944, the 339th Static Division was reorganized as a "1944" infantry division and employed at the front.

42. This armored group was transferred to the region of Army Group South in the spring of 1942.

43. Antonio J. Munoz, *Hitler's White Russians: Collaboration, Extermoination, and Anti-Partisan Warfare in Byelorussia, 1941–1944* (New York: Europa Books, 2003), 159.

44. Rolf-Dieter Müller, and Hans Erik Volkmann, *Die Wehrmacht: Mythos und Realität* (Oldenbourg: Wissenschaftsverlag, 1999), 1084.

45. Horst Boog, et al. *Germany and the Second World War, Volume IV The Attack on the Soviet Union* (Oxford: Clarenden Press, 1998), 1220.

46. Nicolo Machiavelli, *The Prince* (Mineola: Dover, 1992), 43.

47. During the Russo-German War, Shcherbakov served as the head of the political directorate of the Red Army in Moscow with the rank of colonel-general. At the same time Shcherbakov was director of the Soviet Information Bureau.

48. Pohl, *Die Herrschaft der Wehrmacht*, op cit, 269.

49. Hoppe, Bert and Hildrun Glass. *Die Verfolgung und Ermordung der europaische Juden durch das nationalsoz. Deutschland 1933–1945: Deutsches Reich und Protektorat September 1939—September 1941* (Munich: Oldenbourg Wissenschaftsverlag, 2012), page 43.

50. Martin Gilbert, *Atlas of the Holocaust* (London: Lester Publishing, 1993), 75.

51. Later the division was reinforced by the assignment of the 824th Divisional Signals Battalion (January 21, 1941), 91st Police Battalion (later becoming the 1st Battalion of the 8th Police Regiment), 221st Cavalry Squadron, and the 1st & 2nd Eastern Cavalry Squadron (Winter 1942/1943). On October 15, 1942, the Staff headquarters of the 45th Regional Defense Regiment was incorporated into the division along with the 302nd, 352nd, and 230th Battalions of the 45th Regiment. The divisional infantry was then formed into the 350th Grenadier Regiment and the 45th Security Regiment. In 1942, the 350th Grenadier Regiment was dispatched to the 2nd Panzer Army, and in 1944 it was dispatched to the 3rd Panzer Army. At that time, it was sent back to the 221st Security Division. The division had several different regiments assigned during that period; like the 27th Security Regiment (containing the 325th, 706th & 862nd Battalions), as well as the 44th Security Regiment (573rd & 701st Battalions) in August 1942.

52. Wendy Lower, and Ray Brandon, *The Shoah in Ukraine* (Bloomington: Indiana University Press, 2008), 26.

53. Muñoz and Romanko, *Hitler's White Russians*, op cit, 438.

54. Alexander Dallin, *German Rule in Russia 1941–1945: A Study of Occupation Policies* (London: MacMillan, 1957), 205.

55. According to NARA T-315, Roll 2215, Frame 554 states that this GFP group also served in the 454th Security Division. It also listed its home station as Liebenau. On 26 July 1941, the unit was located in Berdichev.

56. *GFP-708* was attached to the 1st Panzer Army in November–December 1941.

57. According to NARA T-315, Roll 2215, Frame 553, this unit served initially with the 454th Security Division.

58. According to NARA T-315, Roll 2215, Frame 893, *GFP-721* and *GFP-730* were located in Zhitomir in July 1941.

59. *GFP-721* was attached to 1st Panzer Army in November–December 1941. On 26 July 1941 the unit was located in Zhitomir. However, according to NARA T-315, Roll 2216, Frame 47, *GFP-721* was located in Korosten on 1 September 1941 and directly under the control of the 454th Security Division.

60. On July 26, 1941 GFP-730 was located in Zhitomir.

61. James F. Dunnigan, David Isby, E. C. McCarthy, Stephen Patrick, and Trevor N. Dupuy, eds., *War in the East: The Russo-German Conflict, 1941–45* (New York: Simulations Publications Inc., 1977), 82.

62. Percy Schramm, ed., *Kriegstagebuch Des Oberkommandos Der Wehrmacht 1939–1945*, 8 Volumes (Herrsching: Manfred Pawlak, 1982), Vol. 2, Part II, 1135.

63. Tessin, *Verbände und Truppen*, Vol. 8, 63.

64. Kurt Arlt had begun his career in the Secret Field Police as leader of GFP-14.

65. Not to be confused with Cuno Schmidt.

66. Winter, *Die Geheime Feldpolizei*, op cit., 60.

67. BA-MA, RH 22/199 u. RH 22/200.

68. BA-MA, RH 22/199 u. RH 22/200.

69. Westermann, "Himmler's Uniformed Police on the Eastern Front," 309–329.

70. Browning, *The Origins of the Final Solution*, 185.

71. Walter Manoschek, *Die Wehrmacht Im Rassenkrieg: Der Vernichtungskrieg Hinter der Front* (Vienna: Picus Verlag, 1996), 121.

72. Hilberg, *The Destruction of the European Jews*, Volume 3, op cit., 1022–23.

73. Omer Bartov, *The Eastern Front, 1941–45: German Troops and the Barbarization of Warfare* (Oxford: Oxford University Press, 1985), 155–56.

74. Geßner, *Geheim Feldpolizei*, op cit, 51.

75. Antonio Muñoz, *Hitler's Green Army: The German Order Police and their European Auxiliaries, 1933–1945, Volume 2.* (New York: Europa Books, Inc., 2006), 22.

76. Michael Wildt. *An Uncompromising Generation: The Nazi Leadership of the Reich Security Main Office.* (Madison: The University of Wisconsin Press, 2009), 220.

77. Geßner, *Geheim Feldpolizei*, op cit, 51.

78. *Ibid.*, 52.

79. Winter, *Geheim Feldpolizei*, op cit, 122.

80. http://www.wehrmacht-awards.com/forums/showthread.php?t=249494—accessed on July 3, 2012.

81. Winter, *Die Geheime Feldpolizei*, op cit., 123.

82. http://forum.axishistory.com/viewtopic.php?f=38&t=81897, accessed June 5th 2012; And NARS Microfilm T-312, Roll 1353/ 1272–1410.

83. *Amtliches Material zum Massenmord von KATYN* found on the following web site: http://katyn.ru/index.php?go=Pages&file=print&id=831, accessed on July 1, 2012.
84. http://www1.jur.uva.nl/junsv/brd/Dienstdeufr.htm, Justiz und NS-Verbrechen, accessed October 16, 2010.
85. Veröffentlicht in Justiz und NS-Verbrechen Band XXXIX.
86. http://www1.jur.uva.nl/junsv/ddr/ddrdienststfr.htm, accessed 16 October 2010.
87. Court decisions: LG/BG Berlin 780814 Az.: 101aBs42/78 211–54/78 and court case GDR 781016 Az.: 1OSB68/78.
88. http://www1.jur.uva.nl/junsv/ddr/ddrdienststfr.htm, accessed 16 October 2010.
89. NARA Microfilm T-312, Roll 1347, Frames 000342–000343.
90. NOTE: At this time, GFP-570 comprised about 75 men, although the standard average size of a GFP unit was closer to 100 men (roughly three platoons making up an under-strength company). The list above includes only significant staff. The rest of the personnel were rank and file enlisted men.
91. A V-Mann (V-Manner) was a local individual, hired by the Germans to act as a liaison personnel. After a thorough screening, these individuals (they could be both men and women) were trusted to work as a permanent informant for the secret field police.
92. NARA Microfilm T-312, Roll 1347, Frame 000343.
93. *Ibid.*, Frame 000047.
94. NARA Microfilm T-312, Roll 1351, Frame 000042.
95. *Ibid.*, Frame 000043.
96. *Ibid.*, Frame 000059.
97. Tadeusz Piotrowski. *Poland's Holocaust: Ethnic Strife, Collaboration with Occupying Forces and Genocide in the Second Republic, 1918–1947* (Jefferson, NC: McFarland, 1998), 164.
98. NARA Microfilm T-312, Roll 1351, Frame 000043.
99. NARA Microfilm T-312, Roll 1351, Frame 000037.
100. Leonid Grenkevich. *The Soviet Partisan Movement 1941–1944* (London: Frank Cass & Co. Ltd., 1999), 94.
101. NARA Microfilm T-312, Roll 1351, frame 000037.
102. Kenneth Slepyan. *Stalin's Guerrillas: Soviet Partisans in World War II* (Lawrence: University Press of Kansas, 2006), 12.
103. NARA Microfilm T-312, Roll 1351, frame 000028.
104. Matthew Cooper. *The Nazi War Against Soviet Partisans 1941–1944* (New York: Stein & Day, 1979), 82.
105. NARA Microfilm T-312, Roll 1351, Frame 000040.
106. *Ibid.*, Frame 000041.
107. *Ibid.*, Frame 000031.
108. At this time, the 263rd Infantry Division was part of the 43rd Army Corps of 4th German Army and was operating in the region of Spas-Demensk.
109. NARA Microfilm T-312, Roll 1351, Frame 000031.
110. NARA Microfilm T-312, Roll 1351, Frame 000034.
111. Komsomol was the abbreviation for "*Kommunisticheskii Soyuz Molodyozhi*" (Communist Union of Youth).
112. NARA Microfilm T-312, Roll 1351, Frame 000035.
113. *Ibid.*, Frame 000023.
114. NARA Microfilm T-312, Roll 1351, Frame 000024.
115. *Ibid.*, Frame 000024–25.
116. *Ibid.*, Frame 000025.
117. *Ibid.*, Frame 000003.
118. Werner Haupt. *Army Group Center: The Wehrmacht in Russia 1941–1945* (Atglen: Schiffer Publishing, 1997), 143.
119. NARA Microfilm T-312, Roll 1351, Frame 000003.
120. *Ibid.*, Frame 000003.
121. *Ibid.*, Frame 000004.
122. *Ibid.*, Frame 000004.
123. NARA Microfilm T-312, Roll 1351, Frame 000011.
124. *Ibid.*, Frame 000008.
125. *Ibid.*, Frame 000009.
126. *Ibid.*, Frame 000058.
127. *Ibid.*, Frame 000058.
128. NARA Microfilm T-312, Roll 1351, Frame 000012.
129. Tessin, *Verbände und Truppen*, volume 7, op cit., 208.
130. The 2nd Company of the 359th Infantry Regiment would have been a part of the 1st Battalion.
131. Samuel W. Mitcham, *German Order of Battle, Volume One: 1st–290th Infantry Divisions in WWII* (Mechanicsburg: Stackpole Books, 2007), 234.
132. NARA Microfilm: RG 242—T-312 Rolls 1353/1272–1410; and Roll 1355.
133. NARA Microfilm T-312, Roll 1351, Frame 000056.
134. Robert Winter, *Täter in Geheimen: Wilhelm Krichbaum zwischen NS-Feldpolizei und Organisation Gehlen* (Leipzig: Militzke Verlag GmbH, 2010), 122.
135. Hans Friedrich von Ehrenkrook, *Genealogisches Handbuch des Adels, Adelslexikon*, Volume XIV (Glücksburg: C. A. Starke Verlag, 2003), 131.
136. The Field Post number for *Abwehrkommando 150* was "10505"—(1.8.1943–23.3.1944) *Abwehr-Kommando 150 (Wirtschaft)*; then: (24.3.1944–6.11.1944) *Frontaufklärungs-Kommando (Abwehr) 150 (Wirtschaft)*.
137. Dieter Pohl, *Die Herrschaft der Wehrmacht. Deutsche Militärbesatzung und einheimische Bevölkerung in der Sowjetunion* (München: R. Oldenbourg Verlag, 2008), 329.
138. Pohl, *Die Herrschaft der Wehrmacht*, op cit., 329.
139. United States Holocaust Memorial Museum Archives, RG-14.068, Acc. 2004.300.
140. http://www1.jur.uva.nl/junsv/ddr/ddrdienststfr.htm, accessed August 2, 2015.
141. Robert Kirchubel, *Hitler's Panzer Armies on the Eastern Front*. (London: Pen & Sword, 2009), 19.
142. Brigadier Aubrey Dixon, and Otto Heilbrunn, *Communist Guerrilla Warfare* (New York: Frederick A. Praeger, 1954), 50–51.
143. *Ibid.*, 52.
144. Dixon and Heilbrunn, *Communist Guerrilla Warfare*, op cit., 52.
145. Peter Schmitz, and Klaus-Jürgen Thies, *Die Truppenkennzeichen der Verbände und Einheiten der deutschen Wehrmacht und Waffen-SS und ihre Einsätze im Zweiten Weltkrieg 1939–1945*, Vol. 1 (Osnabrück: Biblio Verlag GmbH, 1987), 4.
146. Tessin, *Verbände und Truppen*, Vol. 11, op cit., 337.
147. In September 1943 2nd Panzer Army was transferred to Yugoslavia.
148. Wolfgang Curilla, *Die deutsche Ordnungspolizei und der Holocaust im Baltikum imd in Weißrußland 1941–1944* (Paderborn: Verlag Ferdinand Schöningh GmbH, 2006), 706.
149. Muñoz and Romanko, *Hitler's White Russians*, op cit, 159.
150. *Ibid.*, 160.
151. Winter, *Geheime Feldpolizei*, op cit, 95.
152. BA-MA, RH 21-2/639: Gruppe Geheime Feldpolizei 639 beim Pz. AOK2, "Tätigkeitsbericht für Monat April 1942" vom 25.4.1942.

153. Willi Dreßen. "The Role of the Wehrmacht and Police in the Annihilation of the Jews; the Prosecution and Postwar Careers of Perpetrators in the Police Forces of the Federal Republic of Germany" in *Yad Vashem Studies XXIII* (Jerusalem, 1993): 312.

154. "Generalkommando LIV.A.K., Abt.Ic/A.O. vom 2.8.41, An den Führer des Sonderkommandos Xia Herrn SS-Sturmbannführer Zapp.," MAP, microfilm 56748, fr. 954; "Geheime Feldpolizei 647, Koat II beim LIV.A.K., Tgb. -Nr. 77/41 vom 2.8.1941, An den Stab der Geheimen Feldpolizei 647 beim A.O.K. 11.," *Ibid.*, fr. 945. During thesubsequent period, neither reported about any difficulties at the Dniestercrossing points. For the Sk 11a, see Nuremberg Doc. NO-2067, "Der Beauftragte des Chefs der Sicherheitspolizei und des SD beim Befehlshaberdes rückwartigen Heeresgebiet Süd, Sonderkommando 11a, Tgb. 83/41 vom4.8.1941, Betrifft: Bericht über die Tätigkeit des Sonderkommandos in der Zeit vom 17. Juli bis 3. August und die Einsatzplanung für die erste Augusthalfte 1941." On the concentration of Jews in labor camps in Bessarabia, see "Die Gesandschaft in Bukarest an das Auswartige Amt," August 6, 1941, reproduced in ADAP, Series D, vol. XIII/1, 238–39.

155. BA-MA, WF-03/10414, Bl. 544, War Diary of the "Ia" of the German 11th Army, entry date of January 6, 1942.

156. Wolfgang Curilla. *Die deutsche Ordnungspolizei und der Holocaust im Baltikum und in Weißrußland 1941–1944* (Paderborn: Ferdinand Schöning Verlag, 2006), 424.

157. Curilla, *Die deutsche Ordnunspolizei und der Holocaust*, op cit., 424.

158. Muñoz and Romanko, *Hitler's White Russians*, op cit., 160.

159. Rolf-Dieter Müller, and Hans Erik Volkmann. *Die Wehrmacht: Mythos und Realität.* (Oldenbourg: Wissenschaftsverlag, 1999), 1084.

160. http://www.forum-der-wehrmacht.de/index.php/Thread/8929/ accessed on March 25, 2015.

161. Tessin, *Verbände und Truppen*, Vol. 12, op cit., 187.

162. Tessin, *Verbände und Truppen*, Vol. 8, op cit., 3.

163. *The German Army High Command Trial: The United States vs. Wilhelm von Leeb et al.* U.S. Military Tribunal, Judgment of 27 October 1948, Nuremberg Tribunal, ETO, 612.

164. Bruns, Friedrich. *Die Brücke von Neuenburg: Eine Dokumentation über den Endkampf der 19 Armee in Elsaß 1945* (Celle: Self Published, 1990), 13.

165. Winter, *Geheime Feldpolizei*, op cit, 95.

166. http://www1.jur.uva.nl/junsv/ddr/ddrdienststfr.htm, accessed on August 2, 2015.

167. Wolfgang Curilla. *Die deutsche Ordnungspolizei und der Holocaust im Baltikum und Weißrußland 1941–1944.* (Paderborn: Ferdinand Schöningh, 2006), 897.

168. *Ibid.*

169. Pohl, *Der Herrschaft der Wehrmacht*, op cit, 163.

170. Tessin, op cit, Vol. 12, op cit., 201.

171. NARA microfilm T-315, Roll 2216, Frame 401.

172. According to Tessin, the remnants of the 703rd Guard Battalion were used to create the 703rd Security Battalion on May 28, 1942.

173. The 24th Infantry Division was assigned to the Kiev region, but its component units were used in various anti-partisan operations in October and November 1941.

174. The acronym, *z.b.V.* stood for *zur besondere verwendung* ("for special employment").

175. NARA microfilm T-315, Roll 2216, Frame 00401.

176. Antonio Muñoz, *Army Group South: Rear Area Security and the Holocaust, 1941–1943* (New York: Academic Publishing Group, 2009), 126.

177. According to Tessin, *Landesschützen Regiment 57* was renamed as *Sicherungsregiment 57* (57th Security Regiment) on June 10, 1942.

178. NARA microfilm T-315, Roll 2216, Frame 506.

179. *Ibid.*, Frame 443.

180. *Ibid.*, Frame 508.

181. Brown, "The Senior Leadership Cadre of the Geheime Feldpolizei, 1939–1945," op cit., 280.

182. Tessin, *Verbände und Truppen*, Vol. 13, op cit., 205.

Chapter 10

1. Raul Hilberg, *The Destruction of the European Jews* (New Haven: Yale University Press, 2003), Volume I, 308.

2. Hilberg, *The Destruction of the European Jews*, op cit., Vol. III, 1096.

3. Trial of the Major War Criminals—The International Military Tribunal at Nuremberg, Volume XXII—Proceedings of 27 August 1946–1 October 1946, 508.

4. Edward Crankshaw. *Gestapo: Instrument of Tyranny* (London: Greenhill Books, 1990), 215.

5. Trial of the Major War Criminals—The International Military Tribunal at Nuremberg, Volume XXII—Proceedings of 27 August 1946–1 October 1946, 32.

6. The High Command Trial: *The United States of America vs. Wilhelm von Leeb et al.* U.S. Military Tribunal Nuremberg: Judgment of 27 October 1948, 72–73.

7. Hans Rudolf Kurz, et al., *The Waldheim Report* (Copenhagen: Mueseum Tusculanum, University of Copenhagen, 1993), 81–90.

8. Paul B. Brown, "The Senior Leadership Cadre of the Geheime Feldpolizei, 1939–1945," in *Holocaust and Genocide Studies* (Vol. 17, Nr. 2, fall 2003): 281–303.

9. SHAEF EDF/G/10 Subject: "The German Police" dated: April 1945, 63.

10. Wilhelm Krichbaum, falsified a report on the history and activities of the GFP during World War Two. This 1947 monograph was ordered written by Krichbaum for the U.S. Army Historical Division.

11. T. O. Anderson, "Germans, Ukrainians and Jews: Ethnic Politics in Heeresgebiet Süd, June-December 1941," in *War in History* (Vol. 7, Nr. 3, 2000): 325–351.

12. Brown, "The Senior Leadership Cadre of the Geheime Feldpolizei, 1939–1945," 284.

13. Winter, *Täter im Geheimen*, op cit., 15.

14. Winter, *Täter im Geheimen*, op cit., 49.

15. Geßner, *Geheime Feldpolizei*, op cit., 44.

16. *Geheime Feldpolizei*—EI (GFP) [Secret Field Police] G-2 Department of the Army, Volume II, XE 019650, 193.

17. Alexander Cockburn, and Jeffrey St. Clair. *Whiteout: The CIA, Drugs, and the Press* (New York: Verso Press, 1998), 167–170.

18. Bodo Hechelhammer, and Susanne Meinl. *Geheimobjekt Pullach: Von der NS-Mustersiedlung zur Zentrale des BND* (Berlin: Christoph Links Verlag, 2014), 142–143.

19. Winter, *Die Geheime Feldpolizei*, op cit., 111.

20. Hechelhammer, Geheimobjekt *Pullach*, 162.

21. Brown, "The Senior Leadership Cadre of the Geheime Feldpolizei, 1939–1945," op cit., 294.

22. Brown, "The Senior Leadership Cadre of the Geheime Feldpolizei, 1939–1945," op cit., 281.
23. Jean-Pierre Chantrain, and Gabriel Laforge "Fonctionnaires, Specialistes Et Auxiliariares De La Wehrmacht: 8—Les fonctionnaires de la Geheime Feldpolizei" (Première partie), in *Armes Militaria* (Number 268, November 2007), 26.
24. http://www.archives.gov/iwg/declassified-records/rg-263-cia-records/rg-263-krichbaum.html—accessed July 26, 2014.
25. Winter, *Täter im Geheimen*, op cit., 114.
26. David A. Messenger, and Katrin Paehler, eds., *A Nazi Past: Recasting German Identity in Postwar Europe* (Lexington: University Press of Kentucky, 2015), 277.
27. Ron Edwards, *Spione: Story Now in Cold War Berlin* (Adept Press: Chicago, 2007), 111.

Conclusions

1. Hagen Fleischer, "Die deutsche Militärverwaltung in Griechenland" in *Die Bürokratie der Okkupation: Strukturen der Herrschaft und Verwaltung im besetzten Europa*, edited by Wolfgang Benz, Johannes Houwink ten Cate, and Gerhard Otto (Berlin: Metropol Verlag, 1998), 66.
2. Guido Knopp, *Die Wehrmacht—Eine Bilanz* (Munich: Wilhelm Goldmann Verlag, 2009), 193.
3. *German Anti-Guerrilla Operations in the Balkans, 1941–1944*. DA Pamphlet 20-243, August 1954, Center of Military History, U.S. Army, Washington, D.C., page 46.
4. NARA Microfilm T-501, Roll 260, Frames 000611–616.
5. *Ibid.*, Frame 000617.

Appendix I

1. NARA Microfilm T-501, Roll 259, Frame 000570.

Appendix III

1. NARA Microfilm T-501, Roll 259, Frame 000567.

Appendix IV

1. Gordon Williamson, *German Military Police Units 1939–45* (London: Reed International Books, 1997), 14.
2. Krichbaum, *The Secret Field Police*, op cit., 23.
3. The higher rank of *Feldpolizeichef der Wehrmacht* was only established after 1939.
4. "Elevated Career."
5. "Medium Career." This rank was done away with after 1939.
6. This rank was for the World War One period only.

Bibliography

Primary Sources

National Archives, College Park, Maryland

NARA Microfilm RG 242, T-78, Roll 520; T175, Roll 233; T-312, Rolls 1347, 1348, 1351, 1353, and 1367; T-315, Rolls 1355, 2213, 2214, 2215, and 2216; T-501, Rolls 108, 259, 260, 266, and 349; T-1019, Roll 38.

Bundesarchiv / Militärarchiv

BA-MA RH-19 VII/2, Bl. 2.
BA-MA RH 19 XI/37, *Bericht des GFP-Angehörigen Georg Koch*, 37.
BA-MA RH 22/31, Meldung Direktor GFP, Mai 1942.
BA-MA RH 22/60, Bericht GFP für Heeresgebiet B, August 1942.
BA-MA RH 22/86, 27.
BA-MA RH 22/173, Meldung Direktor GFP, Juli 1942.
BA-MA RH 22/199 *Befehlshaber rückwärtiger Heeresgebiete Tätigkeitsberichte der Geheimen Feldpolizeigruppen* 1, 708, 719, 725, 730, 739, 721.—Stärkemeldungen Laufzeit: Jan.–Aug. 1942.
BA-MA RH 22/200 *Befehlshaber rückwärtiger Heeresgebiete* Tätigkeitsberichte der Geheimen Feldpolizeigruppen 1, 708, 719, 725, 730, 739, 721.—Stärkemeldungen Laufzeit: Sept.–Dez. 1942.
BA/MA RH-24–22/21, folio 88–89.
BA-MA RH 24–22/23, Jäger—Gen.Kdo.22 AK, 14 May 1944, Ic—Aussenstelle Korfu—*Korpsgruppe Joannina* / Ic, 25 April 1944.
BA-MA RH-24, 23–24.
BA-MA RH-26 / 117/16.
BA-MA RH-40, 10.
BA-MA RH-40, 11.
BA-MA RH 48 *Dienststellen und Einheiten der Ordnungstruppen, der Geheimen Feldpolizei, der Betreuungs und Streifendienste des Heeres. RW 40/170: Fester Platz Kreta, Sept. 1944 RW 40/172: Tätigkeits*
BA-MA WF 01/2151, Bl. 816.
BA-MA WF 03/15831, Feldpolizeidirektor beim Befehlshaber Heeresgebiet 103.
bericht, Juli–Aug. 1944; Bundesarchiv.

The National Archives, Kew, Richmond, Surrey, UK

The National Archives, Kew, Richmond, Surrey, United Kingdom also holds these useful British intelligence reports: C.S.D.I.C. (U.K.) S.I.R. (Special Interrogation Report) 730 (8 Aug 1944) "Geheime Feldpolizei Gruppe 644," 4 pages; C.S.D.I.C. (U.K.) S.I.R. (Special Interrogation Report) 818 (20 Aug 1944) "Geheime Feldpolizei in Greece 1942," 5 pages; C.S.D.I.C. (U.K.) S.I.R. (Special Interrogation Report) 1675 (24 May 1945) "Notes on the GFP and Other Security Services in the Area of Army Group Nord (Later Kurland)—1942–1 Jan 45," 33 pages; C.S.D.I.C. (U.K.) S.I.R. (Special Interrogation Report) 1676 (24 May 1945) "Notes on the GFP and Other Security Services in the West—1939–42," 29 pages.
CAB/129/28, British National Archives—USPGO (U.K.) *Kommandobefehl, den 18 Okt. 1942.*

German Armed Forces War Diary

Schramm, Percy. *Kriegstagebuch Des Oberkommandos Der Wehrmacht 1939–1945, 8 Vols.* Herrsching: Manfred Pawlak, 1982.

Supreme Headquarters Allied Expeditionary Force, Office of Assistant Chief of Staff G-2, Counter-intelligence Sub-Division Evaluation, and Dissemination Section.

Box No.4—No. XE003923 German Police System in Occupied Czechoslovakia, Box No.5—NND 881019, File No. XE019650 *Geheime Feldpolizei* (GFP) (Secret Field Police) Volume I & Volume II.
E.D.S. Report No.15—*Geheime Feldpolizei* [GFP—Secret Field Police] 8 January 1945, Supreme Headquarters Allied Expeditionary Force, Office of Assistant Chief of Staff G-2, Counter-intelligence Sub-Division Evaluation and Dissemination Section.
Geheime Feldpolizei (GFP) [Secret Field Police] Vol. I XE 019650 Par 43, SR 380–320-10. General Staff,

U.S. Army G2 Central Records Facility, Fort Holabird, Baltimore 19, Maryland.
Geheime Feldpolizei—EI (GFP) [Secret Field Police] G-2 Department of the Army, Volume II, XE 019650.
Office of Strategic Services Research and Analysis Branch, R & A N, 2500.15, "German Military Government Over Europe: Economic Controls in Occupied Europe," Washington, D.C., 28 August, 1945.

Records of the Army Staff (Record Group 319)—CIC Collection—Declassified Files

From the *Records of the Army Staff* (Record Group 319)—CIC Collection—Declassified Files: Box No.4—No. XE003923 German Police System in Occupied Czechoslovakia, Box No.5—NND 881019 File No. XE019650 *Geheime Feldpolizei* (GFP) (Secret Field Police) Vol. I & Vol. II. From Military Intelligence Service Center/U.S. Forces European Theater CI—Final Interrogation Report No. 98 (14 Mar 1946) "Reg.-u.Krim.Dir. Philipp GREINER, Leitender FP Direktor, Mil.Befh. Frankreich," 6 pages. From the Seventh Army Interrogation Center, Final Interrogation Report No. 20 (8 Aug 1945) "Secret Military Police Unit 712," 4 pages. From the Nuremberg Trial, document NOKW 1382, Directive of the Quartermaster of the *Kommandant rückwärtiges Armeegebiet 560* (Army Groups A, Twelfth Army, 560th Army Rear Area Security Command), May 21, 1941.

Legal Court Cases

Innsbruck Court Case: GG Innsbruck 10 Nr. 415170–23 10 H 7170: 1–43.

Other Primary Sources

"Central Registry of War Criminals and Security Suspects" (CROCASS Allied Control Authority, Part 1 & 2, U.S. Army, APO 742, 1947).
"Generalkommando LIV.A.K., Abt.Ic/A.O. vom 2.8.41, An den Führer des Sonderkommandos XIa Herrn SS-Sturmbannführer Zapp.," MAP, microfilm 56748, fr. 954; "Geheime Feldpolizei 647, Koat II beim LIV.A.K., Tgb.—Nr. 77/41 vom 2.8.1941, An den Stab der Geheimen Feldpolizei 647 beim A.O.K. 11.," Ibid., fr. 945. During thesubsequent period, neither reported about any difficulties at the Dniestercrossing points. For the Sk 11a, see Nuremberg Doc. NO-2067, "Der Beauftragte des Chefs der Sicherheitspolizei und des SD beim Befehlshaber des rückwartigen Heeresgebiet Süd, Sonderkommando 11a, Tgb. 83/41 vom4.8.1941, Betrifft: Bericht über die Tätigkeit des Sonderkommandos in der Zeit vom 17. Juli bis 3. August und die Einsatzplanung für die erste Augusthalfte 1941." On the concentration of Jews in labor camps in Bessarabia, see "Die Gesandschaft in Bukarest an das Auswartige Amt," August 6, 1941, reproduced in ADAP, Series D, vol. XIII/1, 238–39.
Meyer, Brünn. *Dienstalterliste der Waffen-SS: SS-Obergruppenführer bis SS Hauptsturmführer; Stand vom 1 Juli 1944*. Biblio Verlag: Osnabrück, 1987.
Roosevelt, Franklin D. "No Peace with Hitler: Eight Common Principles for a Better World," in *Vital Speeches of the Day*. Vol. 7 Issue 22 (September 1, 1941).
Telex—General Löhr to the *Befehlshaber Südost*, dated October 1, 1944—RH 19 VII/37, Part 1, Annex 12.
Yad Vashem: Tel-Aviv University. German Foreign Office documents on the Holocaust in Greece (1937–1944)—The Goldstein-Goren Diaspora Research Center, 2007. Document title: *Abteilung für Verwaltung MV 2165/43 [Geheime] Dr. Merten / 26.4.43—Die Überfahrt von Juden italienischer Staatsangehörigkeit über die Grenze nach Süden Griechenlands ins Italienische besetzten Gebiet.*

Documents

Nuremberg Trial, document NOKW 1382, Directive of the Quartermaster of the *Kommandant rückwärtiges Armeegebiet 560* (Army Groups A, Twelfth Army, 560th Army Rear Area Security Command), May 21, 1941.

Pamphlets Published by the Third Reich

Befehlsblatt des Chefs der Sicherheitspolizei und der SD, Nr. 14/44 Berlin, 1. April 1944. Herausgegeben vom Reichssicherheitshauptamt, Berlin: Gedruckt in der Reichsdruckerei, 1944.
Dienstalterliste der Schutzstafel der NSDAP (SS Obergruppenführer bis SS Standartenführer) Stand vom 30. Januar 1942. Herausgegeben vom Personalhauptamt. Berlin: Gedruckt in der Reichsdruckerei, 1942.
Dienstalterliste der Schutzstafel der NSDAP (SS Obergruppenführer bis SS Standartenführer) Stand vom 1. Oktober 1944. Herausgegeben vom Personalhauptamt. Berlin: Gedruckt in der Reichsdruckerei, 1944.
Dienstalterliste der Schutzstafel der NSDAP (SS Obersturmbannführer und SS Sturmbannführer) Stand vom 1. Oktober 1944. Herausgegeben vom Personalhauptamt. Berlin: Gedruckt in der Reichsdruckerei, 1944.

The International Military Tribunal and Trial of Major War Criminals

Trial of the Major War Criminals before the International Military Tribunal, 42 Volumes. Nuremberg: Secretary of the Tribunal, 1947–49; as well as *The German Army High Command Trial, The United States vs. Wilhelm von Leeb et al.* U.S. Military Tribunal, Judgment of 27 October 1948, Nuremberg Tribunal, ETO, and *Proceedings of the Interna-*

tional Military Tribunal Sitting at Nuremberg, Germany, Volume 22 (London: HMSO), 1950.
United Nations War Crimes Commission. Law Reports of Trials of War Criminals. Volume VIII, 1949. Records of the Spiedel Case are closely related to other microfilmed records in Record Group 238; prosecution submitted to the International Military Tribunal, T988; Series T301 (Nuremberg Armed Forces High Command) Series, T1119; NG (Nuremberg Government) Series, T1139; M89S.

The High Command Trial

The United States of America vs. Wilhelm von Leeb et al. U.S. Military Tribunal Nuremberg: Judgment of 27 October 1948.

Secondary Sources

Journal Articles

Anderson, Greg. "The Personality of the Greek State" in *The Journal of Hellenic Studies*, Vol. CXXIX (November 2009): 1–22.

Anderson, T. O. "Germans, Ukrainians, and Jews: Ethnic Politics in Heeresgebiet Süd, June-December 1941," in *War in History* (Volume 7, Number 3, 2000): 325–351.

Brown, Paul B. "The Senior Leadership Cadre of the Geheime Feldpolizei, 1939–1945," in *Holocaust and Genocide Studies* (Volume 17, Number 2, fall 2003): 278–304.

Chantrain, Jean-Pierre, and Gabriel Laforge "Fonctionnaires, Specialistes Et Auxiliariares De La Wehrmacht: 8—Les fonctionnaires de la Geheime Feldpolizei"—Première partie, in *Armes Militaria* (Number 268, November 2007): 31–45.

Garscha, Winifried R. "Ordinary Austrians: Common War Criminals during World War II" in *Austrian Lives: Contemporary Austrian Studies* (Volume 21, 2012): 312–318.

Ioanid, Radu. "The Holocaust in Romania: The Iasi Pogrom of June 1941" in *Contemporary European History* (Vol. 2, No. 2, July 1993): 119–148.

Manelli, Gani. "Partisan Politics in WWII Albania: The Struggle for Power, 1939–1944" in *East European Quarterly*, XL, No.3 (2006): 333–348.

Meyer, Ahlrich. "Kleitische Prosa oder Polizeibericht? Anmerkungen zu Ernst Jüngers Denkschrift 'Zur Geiselfrage,'" in *Vierteljahrshefte für Zeitgeschichte* (April 2004): 281–287.

Muñoz, Antonio "The German Anti-Partisan War in the Ukraine" in *World at War* (June-July 2015): 32–38.

Prusin, Alexander. "Fascist Criminals to the Gallows! The Holocaust and Soviet War Crimes Trials," in *Holocaust and Genocide Studies* (Volume 17, Number 1, spring 2003): 1–31.

Prusin, Alexander V. "A Community of Violence: The Sipo/SD and its Role in the Nazi Terror System in Generalbezirk Kiev," in *Holocaust and Genocide Studies*, Vol. XXI, No.1 (spring 2007): 1–30.

Pula, Besnik. "Becoming citizens of empire: Albanian nationalism and fascist empire, 1939–1943" in *Theory & Society* (Vol. XXXVII, Issue 6, December 2008): 567–596.

Dissertations

Kempter, Thomas. "Gott Feiern in Dachau: Die Feier der Eucharistie im KZ Dachau" (Master's thesis, Albert-Ludwigs University, 2005).

Stoneman, Mark R. "The Bavarian Army and French Civilians in the War of 1870–71" (PhD Thesis, Augsburg University, 1994).

Pamphlets

The Case Against General Heusinger. Documents Illustrating the Charges of the USSR Against Former Lieutenant-General Adolf Heusinger, Former Operations Chief of the Wehrmacht High Command. Soviet Government. New York: Translation World Publishers, 1961.

German Anti-Guerrilla Operations in the Balkans, 1941–1944. DA Pamphlet 20-243, August 1954, Center of Military History, U.S. Army, Washington, D.C.

Krichbaum, Wilhelm. *The Secret Field Police.* MS # C-029. Edited by George Vanderstadt. Translated by M. Franke. U.S. Army Historical Division, 18 May 1947.

Books

Aharon Weiss, ed. *Yad Vashem Studies XXI.* Jerusalem: The Holocaust Martyr's And Heroes' Remembrance Authority, 1991.

Albrecht-Carrié, René. *A Diplomatic History of Europe Since the Congress of Vienna.* New York: Harper & Row, Publishers, 1958.

Andrew, Christopher. *Defend the Realm: The Authorized History of MI5.* New York: Knopf Doubleday, 2009.

Angrick, Andrej. *Besatzungspolitik und Massenmord: Die Einsatzgruppe D in der Sowjetunion 1941–1943.* Hamburg: Hamburger Edition, 2003.

Arad, Yitzhak. "The Holocaust of Soviet Jewry in the Occupied Territories of the Soviet Union."

Armstrong, John A. *Soviet Partisans in World War II.* Madison: The University of Wisconsin Press, 1964.

Armstrong, John A. *Ukrainian Nationalism.* Englewood: Ukrainian Academic Press, 1990.

Banach, Jens. *Heydrichs Elite: Das Führerkorps der Sicherheitspolizei und des SD 1936–1945.* Paderborn: Ferdinand Schöningh, 1998.

Bartov, Omer. *The Eastern Front, 1941–45: German Troops and the Barbarization of Warfare.* Oxford: Oxford University Press, 1985.

Bartov, Omer. *Germany's War and the Holocaust:*

Disputed Histories. Cornell: Cornell University Press, 2003.

Bartov, Omer. *Hitler's Army: Soldiers, Nazis, and War in the Third Reich*. Oxford: Oxford University Press, 1992.

Bartov, Omer. *Mirrors of Destruction: War, Genocide, and Modern Identity*. Oxford: Oxford University Press, 2000.

Bauer, Eddy. *The History of World War II*. London: Galley Press, 1984.

Beevor, Anthony. *Crete: The Battle and the Resistance*. New York: Penguin Books, 2014.

Bennett, Rab. *Under the Shadow of the Swastika: The Moral Dilemmas of Resistance and Collaboration in Hitler's Europe*. New York: New York University Press, 1999.

Bergen, Doris L. *War & Genocide: A Concise History of the Holocaust*. New York: Rowman & Littlefield 2009.

Berthel, Hans Dieter. *Die Feldgendarmerie im Zweiten Weltkrieg und ihre Teilnahme an völkerrechtswidrigen Aktionen 1939–1945*. Norderstedt: Herstellung und Verlag, 2006.

Birn, Ruth Bettina. *Die Sicherheitspolizei in Estland, 1941–1944: Eine Studie zur Kollaboration im Osten*. Paderborn: Ferdinand Schöningh, 2006.

Bischof, Günther, Fritz Plasser, and Eva Maltschnig, eds. *Austrian Lives: Contemporary Austrian Studies Vol. 21*. New Orleans: University of New Orleans Press, 2012.

Blood, Philip W. *Hitler's Bandit Hunters: The SS and the Nazi Occupation of Europe*. Washington, D.C.: Potomac Books, 2006.

Bonn, Keith E., ed. *Slaughterhouse: The Handbook of the Eastern Front*. Bedford: The Aberjona Press, 2005.

Boog, Horst, et al. Germany and the Second World War, Volume IV The Attack on the Soviet Union. Oxford: Clarenden Press, 1998.

Boshyk, Yury, Editor. *Ukraine during World War II: History and its Aftermath*. Edmonton: Canadian Institute of Ukrainian Studies, 1986.

Bowman, Steven. *The Agony of Greek Jews, 1940–1945*. Stanford: Stanford University Press, 2006.

Browning, Christopher. *Ordinary Men: Reserve Police Battalion 101 and the Final Solution in Poland*. New York: HarperCollins Publishers, Inc., 1992.

Browning, Christopher. *The Origins of the Final Solution: The Evolution of Nazi Jewish Policy, September 1939–March 1942*. Lincoln: University of Nebraska Press, 2004.

Bruns, Friedrich. *Die Brücke von Neuenburg: Eine Dokumentation über den Endkampf der 19 Armee in Elsaß 1945*. Celle: Self Published, 1990.

Buchanan, Patrick J. *Churchill, Hitler, and The Unnecessary War: How Britain Lost Its Empire and the West Lost the World*. New York: Crown Press, 2008.

Campbell, Stephen. *Police Battalions of the Third Reich*. Atglen: Schiffer Publishers, 2007.

Carell, Paul. *Hitler Moves East 1941–1943*. London: George G. Harrap & Co. Ltd., 1964.

Carell, Paul. *Scorched Earth: The Russo-German War 1943–1944*. Boston: Little, Brown & Co., 1970.

Cervi, Mario. *The Hollow Legions: Mussolini's blunder in Greece, 1940–1941*. New York: Doubleday, 1971.

Charles, Jean-Léon, and Philippe Dasnoy. *Les Dossiers Secrets de la Police Allemande en Belgique*. 2 Vols. Brüssel: Arts et Voyages, 1972.

Churchill, Winston S. *Never Give In! The Best of Winston Churchill's Speeches*. New York: Hyperion, 2003.

Citino, Robert M. *The German Way of War: From the Thirty Years' War to the Third Reich*. Lawrence: University Press of Kansas, 2005.

Clogg, Richard. *A Concise History of Greece*. Cambridge: Cambridge University Press, 1992.

Cockburn, Alexander, and Jeffrey St. Clair. *Whiteout: The CIA, Drugs, and the Press*. New York: Verso Press, 1998.

Cooper, Matthew. *The Nazi War Against Soviet Partisans, 1941–1944*. New York: Stein & Day, 1979.

Coppa, Frank J. *The Life & Pontificate of Pope Pius XII: Between History & Controversy*. Washington, D.C.: The Catholic University of America Press, 2013.

Crankshaw, Edward. *Gestapo: Instrument of Tyranny*. London: Greenhill Books, 1990.

Cüppers, Martin. *Wegbereiter der Shoah: Die Waffen-SS, der Kommandostab Reichsführer-SS und die Judenvernichtung 1939–1945*. Darmstadt: Wissenschaftliche Buchgesellschaft, 2005.

Curilla, Wolfgang. *Die deutsche Ordnungspolizei und der Holocaust im Baltikum imd im Weißrußland 1941–1944*. Paderborn: Verlag Ferdinand Schöningh GmbH, 2006.

Dallin, Alexander. *German Rule in Russia 1941–1945— A study of Occupation Policies*. London: Macmillan & Co Ltd, 1957.

Davies, Peter, and Derek Lynch. *The Routledge Companion to Fascism and the Far Right*. New York: Routledge, 2002.

Davis, Wes. *The Ariadne Objective: Patrick Leigh Fermor and the Underground War to Rescue Crete from the Nazis*. New York: Crown Publishers, 2013.

Dean, Martin. *Collaboration in the Holocaust: Crimes of the Local Police in Belorussia and Ukraine, 1941–1944*. New York: St. Martin's Press, 2000.

Dixon, Brigadier C. Aubrey, and Otto Heilbrunn. *Communist Guerrilla Warfare*. New York: Frederick A. Praeger, 1954.

Domelier, Henri. *Behind the Scenes at German Headquarters*. London: Hurst & Blackett, Ltd., 1919.

Dreßen, Willi. "The Role of the Wehrmacht and the Police in the Annihilation of the Jews; the Prosecution of Postwar Careers of Perpetrators in the Police Force of the Federal Republic of Germany." *Yad Vashem Studies XXIII*, 1993: 295–319.

Dunnigan, James F., David C. Isby, E. C. McCarthy, Stephen Patrick, and Trevor N. Dupuy, Eds., *War in the East: The Russo-German Conflict, 1941–45*. New York: Simulations Publications Inc., 1977.

Edwards, John. *The Spain of the Catholic Monarchs 1474–1520*. Oxford: Blackwell Publishers Inc, 2000.
Edwards, Ron. *Spione: Story Now in Cold War Berlin*. Adept Press: Chicago, 2007.
Ehrenburg, Ilya, and Vasily Grossman. *The Black Book*. New York: Holocaust Library, 1981.
Ehrenkrook, Hans Friedrich von. *Genealogisches Handbuch des Adels, Adelslexikon*, Volume XIV, Glücksburg: C. A. Starke Verlag, 2003.
Evans, Richard J. *The Third Reich at War*. London: Penguin Books Ltd., 2008.
Evans, Richard J. *The Third Reich in Power*. New York: The Penguin Press, 2005.
Ezergailis, Andrew. *The Holocaust in Latvia 1941–1944*. Washington, D.C.: The United States Holocaust Memorial Museum, 1996.
Faber, David. *Munich 1938: Appeasement and World War Two*. New York: Simon & Schuster, 2010.
Federov, Alexander. *Partisans d'Ukraine—2. operations contre la Wehrmacht*. Paris: Editions J'ai Lu, 1951.
Fleming, K. E. *Greece: A Jewish History*. Princeton: Princeton University Press, 2008.
Fontaine, Thomas. "Chronology of Repression and Persecution in Occupied France, 1940–44" in *The Online Encyclopedia of Mass Violence* (19 November 2007): 1–8.
Förster, Jürgen. "The German Army and the Ideological War against the Soviet Union" in *The Policies of Genocide: Jews and Soviet Prisoners of War in Nazi Germany*, 15–29. Gerhard Hirschfeld, editor (London: Allen and Unwin, 1986).
Förster, Wolfgang. *Kämpfer an vergessenen Fronten: Feldzugsbriefe, Kriegstagebücher und Berichte. Kolonialkrieg, Seekrieg, Luftkrieg Spionage*. Berlin: deutsche Buchvertriebsstelle, Abteilung für Veröffentlichungen aus amtlichen Archiven, 1931.
Franz, Hermann. *Gebirgsjäger der Polizei: Polizei-Gebirgsjäger-Regiment 18 und Polizei-Gebirgs-Artillerieabteilung 1942*. Verlag Hans Henning: Bad Nauheim, 1963.
Frei, Norbert. *Vergangenheitspolotik*. Einbeck: AHA-BUCH GmbH, 1996.
Geßner, Klaus. *Geheime Feldpolizei*. Berlin: Militarverlag der Deutschen Demokratische Republik, 1986.
Geßner, Klaus. *Geheime Feldpolizei: Die Gestapo der Wehrmacht*. Berlin: Militärverlag, 2010.
Geldmacher, Thomas. *Wir als Wiener waren ja bei der Bevölkerung beliebt: Östtereichische Schutzpolizisten und die Judenvernichtung in Ostgalizien 1941–1944*. Vienna: Mandelbaum Verlag, 2002.
Gerlach, Christian. "Men of 20 July and the War in the Soviet Union," in *War of Extermination: The German Military in World War Two 1941–1944*, Hannes Heer & Klaus Naumann, eds. (New York: Berghahn Books, 200): 127–145.
Geyer, Michael, Charles S Maier and Andrew Gould, Eds. "Traditional Elites and National Socialist Leadership," 77–133. in *The Rise of the Nazi Regime: Historical Reassessments*. Boulder: Westview Press, 1986.
Gibson, Hugh, and Sumner Welles, eds. *Ciano Diaries 1939–1943, Complete, Unabridged Diaries of Count Galeazzo. Italian Minister for Foreign Affairs 1936–1943*. New York: Doubleday & Co., 1946.
Gilbert, Martin. *Atlas of the Holocaust*. London: Lester Publishing Ltd., 1993.
Gildea, Robert, Anette Warring and Olivier Wieviorka, eds. *Surviving Hitler and Mussolini: Daily Life in Occupied Europe*. New York: Bloomsbury Academic, 2006.
Goldhagen, Daniel Jonah. *Hitler's Willing Executioners: Ordinary Germans and the Holocaust*. New York: Alfred A. Knopf, 1996.
Gooch, John. *Mussolini and His Generals: The Armed Forces and Fascist Foreign Policy, 1922–1940*. Cambridge: Cambridge University Press.
Görlitz, Walter, and David Irving, Eds. *In the Service of the Reich*. New York: Stein & Day, 1979.
Grenkevich, Leonid. *The Soviet Partisan Movement 1941–1944*. London: Frank Cass Ltd, 1999.
Grundmann, Siegfried. *Die V-Leute des Gestapo-Kommissars Sattler*. Berlin: Hentrich und Hentrich Verlag, 2010.
Grünfelder, Anna Maria. *Arbeitseinsatz für die Neuordnung Europas: Zivil und Zwangsarbeiterlnnen aus Jugoslawien in der "Ostmark" 1938/41–1945*. Vienna: Böhlau Verlag, 2010.
Hanusiak, Michael. *Lest We Forget*. New York: Privately Printed, 1973.
Hartmann, Christian, Johannes Hürter, and Ulrike Jureit. *Verbrechen der Wehrmacht: Bilanz einer Debatte*. Munich: Verlag C.H. Beck, 2005.
Hartmann, Christian, with Johannes Hürter, Peter Lieb and Dieter Pohl. *Der deutsche Krieg in Osten 1941–1944: Faceten einer Grenzüberschreitung*. Oldenbourg: Wissenschaftsverlag, 2009.
Haupt, Werner. *Army Group South: The Wehrmacht in Russia 1941–1945*. Atglen: Schiffer Military History, 1998.
Haupt, Werner. *Army Group Center: The Wehrmacht in Russia 1941–1945*. Atglen: Schiffer Publishing, 1997.
Hechelhammer, Bodo, and Susanne Meinl. *Geheimobjekt Pullach: Von der NS-Mustersiedlung zur Zentrale des BND*. Berlin: Christoph Links Verlag, 2014.
Heer, Hannes, and Klaus Naumann, eds. *The German Army and Genocide: Crimes Against War Prisoners, Jews, and Other Civilians in the East, 1939–1944*. New York: The New Press, 1999.
Heer, Hannes, and Klaus Naumann, eds. *Verbrechen der Wehrmacht: Dimensionen des Vernichtungskrieges 1941–1944*. Hamburg: Hamburger Institut für Sozialforschung, 2002.
Heer, Hannes and Klaus Naumann. *Vernichtungskrieg: Verbrechen der Wehrmacht 1941–1944*. Hamburg: Hamburger Edition, 1995.
Heer, Hannes and Klaus Naumann. *War of Extermination: the German Military in World War II–1944*. New York: Berghan Books, 2000.
Herbert, Ulrich, editor. *National Socialist Extermination Policies: Contemporary German Perspectives and Controversies* (New York: Berghan Books, 2000).

Herf, Jeffrey. *Reactionary Modernism: Technology, Culture, and Politics in the Third Reich.* New York: Cambridge University Press, 1984.

Hilberg, Raoul. *Perpetrators, Victims, Bystanders: The Jewish Catastrophe 1933-1945.* New York: HarperCollins Publishers, 1992.

Hilberg, Raul. *The Destruction of the European Jews,* 3 vols. New Haven: Yale University Press, 2003, 3rd Edition.

Hill, Alexander. *The War Behind the Eastern Front: The Soviet Partisan Movement in North-West Russia, 1941-44.* New York: Frank Cass, 2005.

Hionidu, Violetta. *Famine and Death in Occupied Greece, 1941-1944.* New York, Cambridge University Press, 2012.

Hoffmann, Joachim. *Die Ostlegionen 1941-1943.* Friedberg: Verlag Rombach GmbH, 1986.

Höhne, Heinz. *Der Orden unter dem Totenkopf. Die Geschichte der SS.* Frankfurt am Main: Fischer-Bücherei, 1969.

Howard, Michael. *The Franco-Prussian War: The German Invasion of France 1870-1871.* London: Rupert Hart-Davis Ltd., 1961.

Hull, Isabel V. *Absolute Destruction: Military Culture and the Practices of War in Imperial Germany.* Ithaca: Cornell University Press, 2005.

Ioanid, Radu. *The Holocaust in Romania: The Destruction of Jews and Gypsies under the Antonescu Regime, 1940-1944.* Chicago: Ivan R. Dee, 2008.

Jackson, Robert H. *Tyranny on Trial: The Evidence at Nuremberg.* Dallas: Southern Methodist University Press, 1954.

Jörgensen, Christer. *Hitler's Espionage Machine: The True Story Behind One of the World's Most Ruthless Spy Networks.* Guilford: The Lyons Press, 2004.

Jurado, Carlos Caballero. *Rompiendo Las Cadenas: La Division Ucraniana De Las Waffen SS.* Alicante: Garcia Hispan Editor, 1992.

Kadelbach, Ulrich. *Schatten ohne Mann: Die deutsche Besetzung Kretas 1941-1945.* Mähringen: Balistier Verlag, 2002

Kampe, Norbert, Wolfgang Scheffler and Gerhard Schoenberger, eds., *Die Einsatzgruppen in der besetzten Sowjetunion 1941/42. Die Tätigkeits und Lageberichte des Chefs der Sicherheitspolizei und des SD.* Berlin: Edition Hentrich, 1997.

Keegan, John. *The Second World War.* Toronto: Key Porter Books, 1989.

Kershaw, Ian. *Fateful Choices: Ten Decisions That Changed the World, 1940-1941.* New York: The Penguin Press, 2007.

Kirchubel, Robert. *Hitler's Panzer Armies on the Eastern Front.* London: Pen & Sword, 2009.

Kirchubel, Robert. *Operation Barbarossa 1941: Army Group South.* Westport: Praeger Illustrated Military History Series, 2004.

Kiriakopoulos, G. C. *The Nazi Occupation of Crete, 1941-1945.* Westport: Praeger Publishers, 1995.

Klietmann, Dr. K. G. *Die Waffen-SS: eine Dokumentation.* Osnabrück: Verlag "Der Freiwillige" GmbH, 1965.

Knopp, Guido. *Die Wehrmacht—Eine Bilanz.* Munich: Wilhelm Goldmann Verlag, 2009.

Kohl, Paul. *Der Krieg der deutschen Wehrmacht und der Polizei 1941-1944.* Frankfurt am Main: Fischer Taschenbuch Verlag, 1995.

Kurowski, Franz. *The Brandenburgers: Global Mission.* Winnipeg: J.J. Fedorowicz Publishing, 1997.

Kurowski, Franz. *The Brandenburger Commandos: Germany's Elite Warrior Spies in WWII.* Mechanicsburg: Stackpole Books, 2005.

Kursietis, Andris. *The Wehrmacht at War 1939-1945.* Soesterberg: Aspekt, 1999.

Laqueur, Walter. *The Holocaust Encyclopedia.* New Haven: Yale University Press, 2001.

Laub, Thomas J. *After the Fall: German Policy in Occupied France, 1940-1944.* New York: Oxford University Press, 2010.

Leide, Henry. *NS-Verbrecher und Staatssicherheit: Die geheime Vergangenheitspolitik der DDR.* Göttingen: Vandenhoeck & Ruprecht GmbH & Co., 2007.

Lemkin, Raphael. *Axis Rule in Occupied Europe: Laws of Occupation, Analysis of Government. Proposals for Redress.* Washington, D.C.: Carnegie Endowment for International Peace, 1944.

Leumi, Vaad, ed. *The Black Book: The Nazi Crime Against the Jewish People.* New York: The Jewish Black Book Committee, 1946.

Levy, Avigdor, ed. *Jews, Turks, Ottomans: A Shared History, Fifteenth through the Twentieth Century.* New York: Syracuse University Press, 2002.

Levy, Harry. *The Dark Side of the Sky.* London: The London Press, 2007.

Lieb, Peter. *Konventioneller Krieg oder NS-Weltanschauungskrieg? Kriegführung und Partisanenbekämpfung in Frankreich 1943/44.* Munich: R. Oldenbourg Verlag, 2007.

Littlejohn, David. *Foreign Legions of the Third Reich, Volume IV—Poland, the Ukraine, Bulgaria, Rumania, Free India, Estonia, Latvia, Lithuania, Finland and Russia.* San Jose: R. James Bender Publishing, 1987.

Littman, Sol. *Pure Soldiers or Sinister Legion: The Ukrainian 14th Waffen-SS Division.* Montreal: Black Rose Books, 2003.

Longhardt-Söntgen, Rainer. *Partisanen, Spione und Banditen: Abwehrtätigkeit in Oberitalien 1943-1945.* Neckargemünd: Kurt Vowinckel Verlag, 1961.

Lower, Wendy. *Nazi Empire-Building and the Holocaust in Ukraine.* Chapel Hill: The University of North Carolina Press, 2005.

Lower, Wendy and Ray Brandon, eds. *The Shoah in Ukraine: History, Testimony, Memorialization.* Bloomington: Indiana University Press, 2008.

Lukas, Richard C. *Forgotten Holocaust: The Poles Under German Occupation, 1939-1944.* Lexington: University Press of Kentucky, 1986.

Machiavelli, Nicolo. *The Prince.* Mineola: Dover Publications, 1992.

Maclean, French L. *The Field Men: The SS Officers Who Led the Einsatzkommandos—the Nazi Mobile*

Killing Units. Atglen: Schiffer Military History, 1999.

Mallmann, Klaus-Michael, Volker Rieβ, and Wolfram Pyta. *Deutscher Osten 1939-1945: Der Weltanschauungskrieg in Photos und Texten*. Darmstadt: Wissenschaftliche Buchgesellschaft, 2003.

Manoschek, Walter. *Die Wehrmacht im Rassenkrieg: Der Vernichtungskrieg Hinter der Front*. Vienna: Picus Verlag, 1996.

Manoschek, Walter. "Serbien: Partisanenkrieg und Völkermord," in *Anpassung—Kollaboration—Widerstand: Kollektive Reaktionen auf die Okkupation*, 131-143. Metropol Verlag: Berlin, 1996.

Manoschek, Walter. *Serbien ist Judenfrei: Militärische Besatzungspolitik und Judenvernichtung in Serbien 1941/42*. Munich: Oldenbourg Verlag GmbH, 1993.

Marcot, François. *Dictionnaire historique de la Résistance*. Paris: Éditions Robert Laffont, 2006.

Matsas, Michael. *The Illusion of Safety: The Story of the Greek Jews During the Second World War*. New York: Pella Publishing Company, 1997.

Mayer, Hermann Frank. *Blutiges Edelweiβ: die 1. Gebirgsdivision im Zweiten Weltkrieg*. Berlin: Christoph Links Verlag GmbH, 2008.

Mazower, Mark. *Inside Hitler's Greece: The Experience of Occupation 1941-1944*. New Haven: Yale University Press, 1993.

Mazower, Mark. *Salonica, City of Ghosts: Christians, Muslims and Jews 1430-1950*. New York: Vintage Press—a division of Random House, 2007.

McKinstry, Leo. *Operation Sealion*. London: John Murray Publishers, 2014.

McLean, French l. *The Camp Men: The SS Officers Who Ran the Nazi Concentration Camp System*. Atglen: Schiffer Military History, 1999.

Megargee, Geoffrey P. *War of Annihilation: Combat and Genocide on the Eastern Front, 1941*. New York: Rowman & Littlefield Publishers Inc., 2006.

Mehner, Kurt. *Die Waffen-SS und Polizei 1939-1945*. Norderstedt: Militair-Verlag Klaus D. Patzwall, 1995.

Mendelsohn, John, ed. *Covert Warfare: Intelligence, Counterintelligence, and Military Deception during the World War II Era*, 18 volumes, Vol. 13—*The Final Solution of the Abwehr*. New York: Garland Publishing, Inc., 1988.

Messenger, David A. & Katrin Paehler, eds. *A Nazi Past: Recasting German Identity in Postwar Europe*. Lexington: University Press of Kentucky, 2015.

Messerschmidt, Manfred. *Die Wehrmachtjustiz 1933-1945*. Paderborn: Ferdinand Schöningh Verlag, 2005.

Messerschmidt, Manfred, et al. *The Waldheim Report*. University of Copenhagen: Museum Tusculanum Press, 1993.

Mitcham, Samuel W. *German Order of Battle, Volume One: 1st-290th Infantry Divisions in WWII*. Mechanicsburg: Stackpole Books, 2007.

Mitcham, Samuel W. *Hitler's Legions: The German Army Order of Battle, World War II*. New York: Dorset Press, 1985.

Müller, Rolf-Dieter, and Hans Erik Volkmann. *Die Wehrmacht: Mythos und Realität*. Oldenbourg: Wissenschaftsverlag, 1999.

Muñoz, Antonio. *Army Group South: Rear Area Security and the Holocaust, 1941-1943*. New York: Academic Publishing Group, 2009.

Muñoz, Antonio. *Göring's Grenadiers: The Luftwaffe Field Divisions, 1942-1945*. New York: Europa Books Inc., 2002.

Muñoz, Antonio. *Hitler's Eastern Legions, Volume 1—The Baltic Schutzmannschaft, 1941-1945*. New York: Europa Books, Inc., 2001.

Muñoz, Antonio. *Hitler's Green Army: The German Order Police and their European Auxiliaries, Volume 2*. New York: Europa Books, 2006.

Murphy, David E. *What Stalin Knew: the Enigma of Barbarossa*. New Haven: Yale University Press, 2005.

Neitzel, Sönke ed., *Tapping Hitler's Generals: Transcripts of Secret Conversations, 1942-1945*. St. Paul: MBI Publishing, 2008.

Neulen, Hans Werner. *An deutscher Seite: Internationale Freiwillige von Wehrmacht und Waffen SS*. München: Universitas Verlag, 1985.

Nogueres, Henri. *Munich: "Peace for our Time."* London: George Weidenfeld and Nicholson, Ltd., 1965.

Norden, Albert. *Gestapo und SS Führer: Kommandierten die Westdeutsche Polizei*. Berlin: Ausschus Für Deutsche Einheit, 1961.

Ogden, Alan. *Sons of Odysseus, SOE Heroes in Greece*. London: Bene Factum Publishing Ltd, 2012.

Önsoy, Murat. *The World War Two Allied Economic Warfare: The Case of Turkish Chrome Sales*. Saarbrücken: VDM Verlag, 2009.

Overmans, Rüdiger. *Deutsche militärische Verluste im Zweiten Weltkrieg*. München: R. Oldenbourg Verlag, 1999.

Paris, Edmund. *Genocide in Satellite Croatia, 1941-1945*. Chicago: The American Institute for Balkan Affairs, 1961.

Payne, Stanley G. *Civil War in Europe, 1905-1949*. New York: Cambridge University Press, 2011.

Petrakis, Marina. *The Metaxas Myth: Dictatorship and Propaganda in Greece*. London: I. B. Tauris Publishing, 2005.

Pfund, Albert-Marie. *Wenn Ich Nicht Wiederkomme*. Halle: Projekte-Verlag Cornelius, 2010.

Piotrowski, Tadeusz. *Poland's Holocaust: Ethnic Strife, Collaboration with Occupying Forces and Genocide in the Second Republic, 1918-1947*. Jefferson: McFarland, 1998.

Pohl, Dieter. *Die Herrschaft der Wehrmacht. Deutsche Militärbesatzung und einheimische Bevölkerung in der Sowjetunion*. München: R. Oldenbourg Verlag, 2008.

Porch, Douglas. *The French Secret Services: A History of French Intelligence from the Dreyfus Affair to the Gulf War*. New York: Farrar, Straus and Giroux, 1995.

Reitlinger, Gerald. *The Final Solution: The Attempt to Exterminate the Jews of Europe 1939-1945*. South Brunswick: Thomas Yoseloff, 1968.

Reitlinger, Gerald. *The House Built on Sand: The Conflicts of German Policy in Russia*. New York: The Viking Press, 1960.

Riefenstahl, Leni. *Leni Riefenstahl: A Memoir*. New York: Picador, 1987.

Rigopoulos, Rigas. *Secret War: Greece—Middle East, 1940-1945. The Events Surrounding the Story of Service 5-16-5*. Paducah: Turner Publishing Company, 2003.

Romanko, Dr. Oleg, and Antonio Muñoz. *Hitler's White Russians: Collaboration, Extermination and Anti-Partisan Warfare in Byelorussia, 1941-1944*. New York: Europa Books, 2003.

Rummel, Rudolph J. *Death by Government*. New Brunswick: Transaction Publishers, 1994.

Rutherford, Jeff. *Combat and Genocide on the Eastern Front: The German Infantry's War, 1941-1944*. Cambridge: Cambridge University Press, 2014.

Sabrin, B. F., Editor. *Alliance for Murder. The Nazi-Ukrainian Nationalist Partnership in Genocide*. New York: Sarpedon, 1991.

Safrian, Hans. *Eichmann's Men*. New York: Cambridge University Press, 2010.

Scheffler, Wolfgang and Norbert Kampe. *Die Einsatzgruppen in der besetzten Sowjetunion 1941/42*. Berlin: Drukhaus Hentrich, 1997.

Scheindlin, Raymond P. *A Short History of the Jewish People*. New York: Oxford University Press, 1998.

Schmitz, Peter, and Klaus-Jürgen Thies. *Die Truppenkennzeichen der Verbände und Einheiten der deutschen Wehrmacht und Waffen-SS und ihre Einsätze im Zweiten Weltkrieg 1939-1945*, Vol. 1. Osnabrück: Biblio Verlag GmbH, 1987.

Schoeps, Julus H., ed., *Die Dokumentation zur Goldhagen-Kontroverse um die Rolle der Deutschen im Holocaust*. Hamburg: Hoffmann und Campe, 1996.

Schulte, Theo J. *The German Army and Nazi Policies in Occupied Russia*. Oxford: Berg Publishers, 1989.

Schulz, Andreas, and Dieter Zinke. *Die Generale der Waffen-SS und der Polizei, Band 4*. Bissendorf: Biblio Verlag GmbH, 2009.

Seckendorf, Martin. "Ein Einmaliger Raubzug—Die Wehrmacht in Griechenland 1941 Bis 1944," in *Europa unterm Hakenkreuz, Band 8, Die Okkupationspolitik des deutschen Faschismus in Jugoslawien, Griechenland, Albanien, Italien und Ungarn 1941-1945*, 96-124. Heidelberg: Decker/Müller Verlag GmbH, 2000.

Serban, Mihai. "Special Intelligence Service in the Black Sea Region (1940-1948)," in *Challenges and Opportunities for a Multilateral Cooperation*. Bagheria: Giovanni Mineo Editore, 2012.

Shepperd, Ben. *War in the Wild East: The German Army and Partisans*. Cambridge: Harvard University Press, 2004.

Shirer, William L. *The Rise and fall of the Third Reich: A History of Nazi Germany*. New York: Simon & Schuster, 1960.

Slepyan, Kenneth. *Stalin's Guerrillas: Soviet Partisans in World War II*. Lawrence: University Press of Kansas, 2006.

Stahel, David. *Operation Barbarossa and Germany's Defeat in the East*. New York: Cambridge University Press, 2011.

Streit, Christian. "Wehrmacht, Einsatzgruppen, Soviet POWs and Anti-Bolshevism in the Emergence of the Final Solution," 103–118 in *The Final Solution. Origins and Implementation*, David Cesarani, ed., London: Rutledge, 1994.

Taylor, Telford. *The March of Conquest: The German Victories in Western Europe, 1940*. New York: Simon & Schuster, 1958.

Tech, Nechama. *The Bielski Partisans*. Oxford: Oxford University Press, 1993.

Tessin, Georg. *Verbände und Truppen der deutschen Wehrmacht und Waffen-SS 1939-1945*, 24 Volumes. Osnabrück: Biblio Verlag GmbH, 1973–2002.

Tessin, Georg, and Walter Kannapin, *Waffen-SS und Ordnungspolizei im Kriegseinsatz 1939-1945: Ein Überblick anhand der Feldpostübersicht*. Biblio Verlag GmbH, 2002.

Tomasevich, Jozo. *War and Revolution in Yugoslavia, 1941-1945*. Stanford University Press: Stanford, 2001.

Tooley, T. Hunt. *National Identity and Weimar Germany: Upper Silesia and the eastern border*. Lincoln: University of Nebraska Press, 1997.

Tys-Krokmaliuk, Yuriy. *UPA Warfare in the Ukraine*. New York: Vantage Press, 1972.

Wagner, Patrick. *Hitlers Kriminalisten: Die deutsche Kriminalpolizei und der Nationalsozialismus*. München: Verlag C H Beck, 2002.

Wawro, Jeffrey. *The Austro-Prussian War: Austria's War with Prussia and Italy in 1866*. New York: Cambridge University Press, 1996.

Weinberg, Gerald, et al. *Secret Intelligence and the Holocaust: Collected Essays from the Colloquium at the City University of New York*. Jerusalem: Yad Vashem, 2006.

Westermann, Edward B. *Hitler's Police Battalions: Enforcing Racial War in the East*. Lawrence: University Press of Kansas, 2005.

Wette, Wolfram. *Die Wehrmacht: Feindbilder, Vernichtungskrieg, Legenden*. Frankfurt am Main: S. Fischer Verlag, 2002.

Wette, Wolfram. *The Wehrmacht: History, Myth, Reality*. Cambridge: Harvard University Press, 2006.

Whymant, Robert. *Stalin's Spy: Richard Sorge and the Tokyo Espionage Ring*. London: I. B. Tauris, 2007.

Wildt, Michael. *Generation des Unbedingten: Das Fuhrungskorps des Reichssicherheits-hauptamtes*. Hamburg: Hamburger Edition HIS Verlagsges. mbH, 2003.

Wildt, Michael. *Nachrichtendienst, politische Elite und Mordeinheit. Der Sicherheitsdienst des Reichsführers SS*. Hamburg: Hamburger Edition, 2003.

Wildt, Michael. *An Uncompromising Generation: The Nazi Leadership of the Reich Security Main Office*. Madison: The University of Wisconsin Press, 2003.

Williamson, David G. *The Age of the Dictators*. New York: Routledge Publishing, 2007.

Williamson, Gordon. *German Military Police Units 1939–45*. London: Reed International Books, Ltd., 1997.

Williamson, Gordon. *German Security and Police Soldier 1939–45*. London: Osprey Publishing, 2002.

Winks, Robin W., and R. J. Q. Adams. *Europe, 1890–1945: Crisis and Conflict*. Oxford: Oxford University Press, 2003.

Winter, Robert. *Die Geheime Feldpolizei*. Melchior Historischer Verlag: Wolfenbüttel, 2013.

Winter, Robert. *Täter in Geheimen: Wilhelm Krichbaum zwischen NS-Feldpolizei und Organisation Gehlen*. Leipzig: Militzke Verlag, 2010.

Woodhouse, C.M. *Modern Greece: A Short History*. London: Faber & Faber Publishing, 2000.

Yerger, Mark. *Allgemeine-SS*. Atglen: Schiffer Publishing, 1997.

Zabecki, David T. Editor. *Germany at War: Four Hundred Years of Military History*, Volume I. Santa Barbara: ABC-CLIO, LLC, 2014.

Zöller, Martin, and Kazimirz Leszczyński. *Das Urteil im Geiselmordprozess, gefällt vom Militärgerichtshof V der Vereinigten Staaten von America*. Berlin: VEB Verlag der Wissenschaften, 1965.

Internet Sources

http://www.jewishvirtuallibrary.org/jsource/Holocaust/hitler050441.html, accessed on February 4, 2015.

http://lefthumanism.blogspot.com/2011/08/roth-karl-heinz-die-zerstorung-der.html, accessed on January 27, 2015.

http://lefthumanism.blogspot.com/2011/08/roth-karl-heinz-die-zerstorung-der.html, accessed on January 27, 2015.

http://www1.jur.uva.nl/junsv/ddr/ddrdienststfr.htm, accessed 16 October 2010.

http://www1.jur.uva.nl/junsv/brd/Dienstdeufr.htm, Justiz und NS-Verbrechen, accessed 16 October 2010.

https://www.jewishvirtuallibrary.org/jsource/Holocaust/sephardimsalonica.html, accessed January 11, 2015.

http://www.geocities.com/orion47.geo/WEHRMACHT/HEER/General/GIENANTH_CURT.html, accessed on October 17, 2010.

http://www.ushmm.org/information/exhibitions/online-features/special-focus/holocaust-in-greece/corfu, accessed on January 19, 2015

http://db.yadvashem.org/deportation/transportDetails.html?language=en&itemId=5093698, accessed on January 19, 2015.

http://katyn.ru/index.php?go=Pages&file=print&id=831, accessed on July 1, 2012.

http://www1.jur.uva.nl/junsv/NED/NL-Dienststfr.htm, accessed on March 1, 2015.

http://www1.jur.uva.nl/junsv/ddr/ddrdienststfr.htm, accessed 16 October 2010.

http://www.forum-der-wehrmacht.de/index.php/Thread/8929/ accessed on March 25, 2015.

http://ablhistoryforum.be/viewtopic.php?f=51&t=128, accessed on June 20th 2012.

www.fontanafilm.ch/DOKFILME/argyris/pdf/DI-10062005.pdf, accessed on January 26, 2015.

http://www.alfons-hochhauser.de/bei-der-wehrmacht.html, accessed on March 25, 2015.

http://news.bbc.co.uk/2/hi/europe/3023144.stm, "Greeks Lose Nazi Massacre Claim," accessed January 26, 2015.

http://www.haidari.gr/Default.aspx?tabid=649&language=en-US, accessed on January 12, 2015.

www.znaci.net, accessed on January 25, 2015.

http://mittenwald.blogsport.eu/2010/03/30/auf-zur-befreiungsfeier-nach-mittenwald/, accessed on January 27, 2015.

https://en.wikipedia.org/wiki/Heinrich_Deubel, accessed on July 7, 2015.

https://de.wikipedia.org/wiki/Heinrich_Deubel, accessed on July 7, 2015.

Index

Numbers in *bold italics* indicate pages with illustrations

Abwehrtrupp 150 179
Abwehrtrupp 364 145
Abwehrtrupp von Tarbuk 179
Adrian, *Feldpolizeikommissar* 133
Albert, Ludwig 50–51, 55–57, 82
Albrecht, *Feldpolizeikommissar* *113*
Alexander I, [Greek] King 27, 37
Alexander I, [Yugoslav] King 37
Aly, Gotz 3
Anayeva, Maria 177
Antonescu, Ion 122
Arlt, Kurt 132–133, 167–168, 186
Armee Ligurien 19
Armeeoberkommando Norwegen 151
Army Group "A" 136, 143
Army Group "B" 144
Army Group "E" 46, 53–55, 88, 91, 106–107, 110, 121
Army Group "Courland" [*also spelled:* "Kurland] 63, 162
Army Group "Southern Ukraine" 187

Baar, *Feldpolizeisekretär* 51
Bakos, Georgios 196
Balotescu, Gheorghe 122
Barbie, Klaus 193–196
Bartov, Omer 3
Baucke, *Feldpolizeikommissar* *41*, *113*
Bauer, *Polizeidirektor* 11–14, 17n
Befehlshaber der deutschen Truppen in Kroatien 116
Befehlshaber der Ordnungspolizei Griechenland 101
Befehlshaber der Ordnungspolizei Serbien 119, 208
Befehlshaber der Sicherheitsdienst Belgien und Nordfrankreich 206
Befehlshaber der Sicherheitsdienst Elsass 207
Befehlshaber der Sicherheitsdienst Frankreich 206
Befehlshaber der Sicherheitsdienst Niederlande 206

Befehlshaber der Sicherheitsdienst Norwegen 207
Befehlshaber der Sicherheitsdienst Westmark 207
Befehlshaber der Sicherheitspolizei und des Sicherheitsdienst Griechenland 101
Befehlshaber der Sicherheitspolizei und SD "Paris" 63
Befehlshaber der Sicherheitspolizei und SD Serbien 120
Befehlshaber Rückwartig Heeresgebiet Süd 103 166–167, 169, 185
Befehlshaber Saloniki-Aegaeis 100
Begus, Dr. Otto 50–52, 55–58, 62, 65, 82, 84, 134
Behan, Hans 50–51, 55, 102–103
Behrends, Dr. Hermann 205
Bergner, *Oberleutnant der Schutzpolizei* 208
Beria, Lavrentiy 173
Best, Werner 20
Beuys, *Feldpolizeikommissar* 168
Bewahrungstruppe 999 74
Blomberg, Hans Wilhelm 207
Blume, Dr. Walter 70, 72, 101
Bohlsen, *Feldpolizeikommissar Dr.* 129
Böhme, Franz 119
Bolrova, Anna 175
Bonaparte, Napoleon 154
Bonnes, Otto 205
Boris III, [Bulgarian] King 123
Borissov, Dimitriy 175–176
Bothke, Antmann 208
British 1st Armored Division 38
Brosan, Paul 140
Brosius, *Feldpolizeikommissar* 135, 138
Brown, Paul B. 2–3, 155n, 197–198
Brunner, Alois 99
Bürger, *Hilfsfeldpolizeibeamte* 174
Burger, Anton 111–112
Busse, *Feldpolizeisekretär* 50, 62, 65
Büttner, *Feldpolizeiinspektor* *113*

Canaris, Dr. Constantine 206–207
Chamberlain, Neville 33

Charles, Jean-Leon 3, 197
Chmel, Franz 183
Churchill, Winston 33–34, 38, 89, 136, 190
Ciano, Count Galeazzo 36, 38
Clemens, Hans 198–199
Constantine, Crown Prince 25
Constantine, Peter 84–85, 196; *see also* Schubert, Friedrich
Constantine I, [Greek] King 26–28; *see also* Constantine, Crown Prince

Dallwitz, Johann von 12
Damaskinos, Archbishop [born: Dimitrios Papandreou] 100
Dasnoy, Philippe 3, 197
de Gaulle, Charles 126
Denibir, *Feldpolizeikommissar* 131, 152
Deschmer, Josef 172n
Deubel, Heinrich 50–51, 55–56, 58–59, 73, 86
Dieckmann, Christoph 3
Dinulescu, Radu 122
Distel, *Feldpolizeiinspektor* 131
Dohmen, *Polizei Oberinspekteur* 208
Dollfuss, Engelbert 62
Dollmann, Friedrich 150
Dollmann, *SS Hauptsturmführer und Hauptmann der Schutzpolizei* 205
Dönitz, Karl 20
Dorhage, Hans 101
Dornhecker, *Hilfsfeldpolizeibeamte* 173–174
Dossmann, *Hilfsfeldpolizeibeamte* 174, 177
Dräger, *Feldpolizeidirektor* 128
Drechsler, Willy (Wilhelm) 143
Dreier, *Feldpolizeisekretär* 152
Dreier, *Revier Leutnant der Polizei* 208
Droste, *Hilfsfeldpolizeibeamte* 174–176, 178
Dukat, *Feldwebel* 174
Dunckern, Anton 207

Dunker, *Feldpolizeikommissar* 135
Dykers, Albert 146

Ebert, *Sonderführer* 173
Eder, Leo 50, 59–60, 65, 78–79
Eger, *Feldpolizeikommissar* 152
Ehlers, *SS-Obersturmbannführer* 207
Eichmann, Adolf 111, 122
Eichmann, Ingo 207
18th Army 157
LXXXVIII Armeekorps (88th Army Corps) 116
87th Infantry Regiment 193
Einsatzgruppe A 169
Einsatzgruppe B 169
Einsatzgruppe C 169
Einsatzgruppe D 122, 169, 182
Einsatzkommando 5/II 171
Einsatzkommando 8 116, 181
Eisenblätter, *Feldwebel* 174
[ELAS] Fifth Partisan Division 86
[ELAS] Third Partisan Division 80
11th Air Force Infantry Division 103
11th Army 122, 166, 182
XI Battalion (of the 999th Penal Formation) 47
Engel, Rudi 128, 174
Erdmann, *Revier Oberleutnant der Polizei* 208
Ermark, *Soldat* 174
Erzberger, Matthias 194
Eschweiler, Karl 50–51, 55, 60, 167–168
Esser, *Feldpolizeikommissar* 138
Eube, *Feldpolizeikommissar* 135

Fehlis, Heinrich 207
Feldgendarmerie Abteilung 501(501st Motorized Field Police Battalion) 87–88, 112
Feldgendarmerie Abteilung 683 (683rd Motorized Field Police Battalion) 122, 182
Feldgendarmerie Bataillon 652 [mot.] (652nd Motorized Military Police Battalion) 171
Feldgendarmerie Ersatz Kompanie 1 119–120
Feldgendarmerietrupp (mot.) 616 119
Feldjägerkorps Dresden 194
Feldkommandantur 599 119
Felfe, Heinz, 198, 198n
Fenske, *Feldpolizeiinspektor* 113
Ferdinand II, [King] of Aragon 32
Festungsbrigade 1017 (1017th Fortress Brigade) 107, 111
15th Army 135, 148
Fifth Macedonian Security Battalion [collaborationist militia] 103
57. Panzerkorps (57th Armored Corps) 180

57th Regional Defense Regiment (of the 213th Security Division) 186
Filtchenko, Michail 177
Filtchenko, Vasili 177
Filtchenko, Yegor 177
I. Bataillon / 375. Infanterie Regiment der 454. Sicherungsdivision 186
I. Gruppe / L.G.1 52, 89
First IMRO Battalion [collaborationist militia] 103
1st Parachute Army 183
Fischer, Hans 207
Fischer, Dr. Herbert 17
Fischer, Karl Josef 112
Fishwick, Private 90
555. Sicherungs Bataillon (555th Security Battalion) 177
Flesch, Gerhadt 207
Förster, Jürgen 3
Forstner, 2nd Lieutenant Günther 12
Fortress Division "Crete" 104
454th Security Division 167–168
444th Security Division 167–168
403rd Security Division 167–168, 184
14th Army 19
14th Infantry Division 122
4th Army 143, 178
4. SS Polizei Panzergrenadier Division (Fourth SS Police Armored Infantry Division) 53, 81
4. Tiroler Kaiserjäger Regiment 57
Frank, Hans 20
Frank, *SS Obersturmführer* 205
Franz, *Hauptmann der Schutzpolizei*-208
Franz, Hermann 101
Frederick II, [Prussian] King 8
Frederick III, [German] *Kaiser* 10
Frick, Wilhelm 20
Friedensbacher, Ferdinand 51–52, 60–61, 67, 82–84, 203
Friedrich, *Hauptmann der Wasserschutzpolizei* 209
Fritsch, Werner von 160
Früngel, *Soldat* 173
Fuchs, Dr. Wilhelm 119–120

Gawehns, *Feldpolizeikommissar* 113
Gebhart, *Soldat* 174
Geese, *SS Obersturmführer* 205
Gefangenen-Sammelstelle 20 (Prisoner Collection Camp No.20) 116, 181
Gehlen, Reinhard 3, 57, 197, 198n, 199
Generalkommando der Grenztruppen Oberrhein 144
Generalkommando der Grenztruppen Saarpfalz 145
Gerhardt, *Revier Leutnant der Polizei* 208
Gerhart, *Oberleutnant der Schutzpolizei* 209
Gerlach, Christian 3

George, David Lloyd 27
George I, [Greek] King 24, 26
George II, [Greek] King 28–31, 38
Georges, Pierre 146
Gerhahn, *Feldpolizeikommissar* 168
Gernert, *Feldpolizeikommissar* 113
Gersonde, *Feldpolizeisekretär* 152
Geßner, Klaus 2–3, 197
GFP-1 135, 158, 214
GFP-2 127, 132, 143, 214
GFP-3 115, 135, 137, 144, 214
GFP-7 127, 133, 144–145, 148–149, 214
GFP-8 135, 137, 145, 214
GFP-9 114–116, 119–121, 123, 214
GFP-11 127, 129, 131, 146, 214
GFP-14 127, 132–133, 146, 214
GFP-20 114, 116–118, 123, 127
GFP-30 127, 134, 147–148, 214
GFP-131 135–136, 148, 214
GFP-171 114, 115, 116, 122–123, 136, 214
GFP-312 136, 214
GFP-501 60, 138, 157–158, 163, 214
GFP-510 46–47, 50–51, 55, 60, 63, 69, 92, 98, 102–103, 105–110, 112, 191, 202
GFP-520 133, 158, 163, 171–172, 214
GFP-530 135, 150, 159, 161, 214
GFP-540 18, 135–136, 214
GFP-550 127, 130–131, 148–150, 161, 214
GFP-560 166, 214
GFP-570 18, 158, 172–179
GFP-580 135–136, 158, 179–180, 214
GFP-581 214
GFP-590 133, 135, 214
GFP-603 127, 130–131, 160, 214
GFP-610 131, 136, 146, 214
GFP-611 50, 52–53, 55–57, 59, 61, 63, 65, 75, 82, 84, 87–89, 99, 104, 106–107, 112, 121, 134, 214
GFP-612 134, 158, 214
GFP-621 46, 50, 53–56, 59, 61, 63, 78–79, 81, 90, 92, 98–99, 103–108, 110–111, 191, 215
GFP-625(L) 131, 149–150, 215
GFP-626 122, 131, 158, 166, 180–181, 215
GFP-627 127, 134, 215
GFP-629 136, 215
GFP-632 127, 133, 215
GFP-633 127, 132, 215
GFP-637(L) 19, 116, 138, 215
GFP-639 114, 115, 116–117, 134–136, 158, 181, 215
GFP-640 50, 55–56, 63, 69, 80–81, 114–115, 122
GFP-644 132, 135–136, 215
GFP-647 122, 134, 158, 166, 182, 215
GFP-648 135, 138, 215
GFP-649 127, 131, 215
GFP-701 127, 132, 215
GFP-702 159
GFP-703 158–159, 182
GFP-704 158–159

GFP-705 159
GFP-706 158–159, 168
GFP-707 158–159, 164–165, 182–183
GFP-708 158–159, 166–167
GFP-709 158–159, 164–165
GFP-710 158–159
GFP-711 127, 159, 166, 168
GFP-712 127, 150–151, 215
GFP-713 158–159, 162–163
GFP-714 158–159, 162
GFP-715 158–159, 162, 183–184
GFP-716 135, 158–159, 215
GFP-717 158–159, 184–185
GFP-718 127, 158–159
GFP-719 158–159, 166, 168
GFP-720 122, 158–159, 166, 168, 182
GFP-721 158–159, 167–168, 185
GFP-722 127, 158–159, 162, 188
GFP-723 158–159, 164, 185
GFP-724 127, 158–159, 184
GFP-725 133, 158–159, 161, 167–168, 186–187
GFP-726 159, 166
GFP-727 159, 162
GFP-728 159, 162
GFP-729 158–159, 164
GFP-730 127, 158–159, 167–169
GFP-731 127, 132, 215
GFP-732 127, 133, 215
GFP-733 127, 131, 215
GFP-734 127, 131, 215
GFP-735 136, 151, 215
GFP-736 127, 134, 215
GFP-737 215
GFP-738 138, 215
GFP-739 127, 138, 158, 215
GFP-740 127, 138, 215
GFP-741 19
GFP-742(L) 19
GFP-743(L) 19, 131, 152
GFP-744(L) 19, 51, 63, 163
GFP-745 19
GFP-751 19
GFP Kommissariat 110 65–67, 82–84, 86
GFP Kommissariat 111 65–67, 75, 82
Gienanth, Curt Ludwig Freiherr von 146
Göde, *Feldpolizeikommissar* **113**
Goebbels, Joseph 20
Gonatas, Stylianos 29
Göring, Hermann 19, 96, 139
Gorny, Karl 180
Gounaris, Demetrios 27
Graziani, Rodolfo 35
Greek 5th Infantry Division 39
Greiner, Philip 5, 127–128, 133, 139, 148–149
Grenzschutz-Abschnitt-Kommando 14 146
Grenzschutz Abschnitt Kommando 9 115
Grenzschutz-Abschnitt-Kommando 20 116
Grenzschutz Abschnitt Kommando 2 143
Grieger, Martin **41**, **113**

Grosche, *Unteroffizier* 174
Gruppe Geheimfeldpolizei Condor Legion 18
Gruppe Geheimfeldpolizei z.b.V. 17, 19
Guillaume, Maurice 150; see also Webb, Sidney
Günther, Heinz Gerhard 173
Guryev, Alexander 177
Guryev, Kristina 177

Haas, Hans 69
Hacha, Emil 18
Hafranek, *SS-Standartenführer* 106
Hahnke, Colonel von 14
Haimann, *Feldpolizeikommissar* 168
Hammer, Otto 176
Hannig, Bernhard 130, 150
Hanse, *Oberregierungsrat* Dr. 208
Hansen, *Feldpolizeisekretär* 176–177
Harassti, *Stabsarzt* 208
Hargard, *Feldpolizeikommissar* 131
Harster, Wilhelm 206
Härtel, Paul 51, 61, 78, 135
Hartenstein, *Feldpolizeidirektor* 16
Hartmann, Christian 3
Hartmann, *Feldpolizeikommissar* 51
Hartmann, *Feldpolizeisekretär* 75
Hartung, *Gefreiter* 174
Hasselbacher, *SS-Oberstrumbannführer* 206
Häuserer, Max 134, 146–147, 160, 179
Heer, Hannes 3
Heeresfeldpolizeichef der Wehrmacht 194, 211
Heeresfeldpolizeichef im Oberkommando der Wehrmacht 194
Heeresgruppe "F" 52, 55, 116, 121
Heeresgruppe Mitte (Army Group Center) 157, 183–184
Heeresgruppe Nord (Army Group North) 157, 162
Heeresgruppe Süd (Army Group South) 157, 166–167
Heine, Friedrich 208
Heinrichs, *Feldpolizeikommissar* Dr. 168
Hemmer, Christian 129
Hennemann, *Soldat* 174
Hentschel, *Revier Leutnant der Polizei* 208
Herbert, Ulrich 3
Hergt, *Feldpolizeidirektor* 131, 149
Hermann, Dr. Adalbert 134, 181–182
Herold, Dr. Hermann 129
Heydrich, Reinhard 120
Higgeneyer, *Feldpolizeikommissar* Dr. 150
Hilberg, Raoul 3
Himmler, Heinrich 20, 58n, 59, 73, 100–101, 137n, 149, 158, 189, 192n, 204

Hinterseer, Lieutenant-Colonel 178
Hinterseer, *Oberstleutnant* 172
Hitler, Adolf 2, 6–8, 18–19, 31, 33–40, 42, 44–45, 58, 77, 82, 89, 91, 96, 108–109, 119, 123, 136n, 144, 150, 154, 156, 164, 166–167, 188–190, 193, 201, 203–204
Hitzeroth, Alwin 152
Hochgrabe, *Feldpolizeikommissar* 128
Hochhauser, Alfons Franz Emanuel 68–69
Hoettl, Wilhelm 198n
Höheres Kommando XXXVI 146
Höherer SS und Polizeiführer beim Militärbefehlshaber in Griechenland 100–101
Höherer SS und Polizeiführer Griechenland 100–102
Höherer SS und Polizeiführer Serbien 119, 205
Holst, *Major der Schutzpolizei* 208
Hoppe, *Feldpolizeisekretär* 131
Hoth, Franz 207
Hrabal, Oswald 183
Hull, Dr. Isabel 5
Hultsch, *Oberregierungsrat* Dr. 18
Hunecke, *Feldpolizeisekretär* 152
Hürter, Johannes 3

Infanterie Ersatz Bataillon 600 [supplied GFP personnel] 129, 151
Isabella I, [Queen] of Castile & Leon 32
Isensee, *Feldpolizeisekretär* 174–176
Isselhorst, Erich 207

Jakobs, *Feldpolizeikommissar* 168
Jäger, Emil 107
Janda, *Revier Leutnant der Polizei* 208
Jellositz, *Feldpolizeikommissar* 131
Jennessen, Heinrich 207
Jentzsch, *Feldpolizeikommissar* 135
Jessen, Hans 129, 134
Jetzinger, *Feldpolizeikommissar* 131
Jochum, *Feldpolizeikommissar* 172, 174, 179
Jungmann, *Stabsfeldwebel* 152
Jureit, Ulrike 3

Kaintzik, Joachim 130, 160, 168, 196
Kaiser, Anton 205
Kallenborn, Arthur 131
Kaltenbrunner, Ernst 20
Karhan, *Feldpolizeikommissar* 169
Karpov, Nikolai 175
Kasper, Fridrich 183
Keitel, Wilhelm 40
Keithahn, *Feldpolizeikommissar* 131, 152
Kemal [Ataturk], Mustafa 27n, 29

Killinger, Manfred von 194
Klatt, *Feldpolizeiinspektor* **113**
Kleemann, Ulrich 104
Kleinbaum, *Major der Schutzpolizei* 208
Kleinpaul, Frithjof 140
Kletzke, Kurt 129
Knaus, *Feldpolizeisekretär* 131
Knochen, Helmut 206
Kober, *Major der Schutzpolizei* 208
Koch, Georg 51, 79, 81, 131
Kögl, Franz 183
Kommandant Ost-Aegaeis 46
Kommandeur der Ordnungspolizei Athen 101
Kommandeur der Sicherheitspolizei und SD Belgrad 119
Kommandierenden General und Befehlshaber Südgriechenland 102
Kommandierender General in Serbien 119
Kommissariat Brussels [GFP-743(L)] 152
Kommissariat Lille [GFP-743(L)] 152
Kondaurova, Schura 177
Konstantinidis, Petros 84, 196; see also Constantine, Peter; Schubert, Friedrich
Korff, Modest Graf von 206
Koryzis, Alexandros 31, 38
Kostrowski, Arnold 185
Kraft, *SS Hauptsturmführer* 205
Kraus, Hans 180
Krech, Franz 82
Kreipe, Heinrich von 88n
Krichbaum, Wilhelm 1, 3, 5, 17, 43, 60–62, 72, 129, 150, 191–194, 197–199, 211
Krokidas, Dr. Sotirios 29
Kühn, *Feldpolizeikommissar* 131
Kukawka, Benno 116, 134, 181
Kulakov, Ivan 176
Kunze, *Feldpolizeikommissar* 169
Kupriyanov, Yegor 175
Kurzhals, *Hilfsfeldpolizeibeamte* 174–175
Kutze, *Polizeikommissar* 10

Lamy, *Feldpolizeikommissar* 168, 176
Langsfeld, *Hauptmann der Schutzpolizei* 208
Laubert, *Hilfsfeldpolizeibeamte* 176
Lautenbach, Fritz 81
Lecca, Junius 122
Lehmann, *Major der Schutzpolizei* 208
Leitender Feldpolizeidirektor beim Befehlshaber Heeresgebiet Nord 162
Leitender Feldpolizeidirektor beim Chef des Militärverwaltungsbezirks A 128, 132
Leitender Feldpolizeidirektor beim Chef des Militärverwaltungsbezirks B 128, 146
Leitender Feldpolizeidirektor beim Chef des Militärverwaltungsbezirks C 129, 133
Leitender Feldpolizeidirektor beim Militärbefehlshaber Nord-Frankreich 128–129
Leitender Feldpolizeidirektor beim Oberbefehlshaber Südost 63
Leitender Feldpolizeidirektor beim Paris 129
Leitender Geheime Feldpolizei West 127–128
Leiter der Geheimen Feldpolizei Ost 160
Lenin, Vladimir Illich 28
Lesuire, Karl von 80
Leteit, *Major der Schutzpolizei* 208
Levy, Harry 140
Liebus, *Sonderführer* 175
Ling, Hermann 207
Löhr, Alexander 100
Loos, Roman 50, 60, 62–65, 70, 75, 101
Lorenz, *Hauptmann der Schutzpolizei* 208
Lose, Paul 182
Luckmann, *Polizei Rat* 208
Lüdcke, Dr. Karl 206
Luecke, *Feldpolizeikommissar* **113**
Luftflotte Kommando 3 131
Luftwaffen-Bau-Regiment 6/XIII 177

Mäcker, Corporal 178
Magelle, *Revier Leutnant der Polizei* 208
Makarov, Ivan 179
Malasch, *Gefreiter* 50, 62, 64–65, 67–68, 74–75
Mallmann, Klaus-Michael 3
Manimoff, *Stabsarzt Dr.* 209
Manoschek, Walter 3
Manshausen, Karl 50–51, 54, 108–110, 202
Manstein, Erich von 182
Marine Einsatzkommando 20 54
Märthesheimer, *Hilfsfeldpolizeibeamte* 176
Mau, *Soldat* 174
May, Andreas 208
Mazower, Mark 3, 7, 53, 74
Mehmet II, [Ottoman] Sultan 23
Mehmet V, [Ottoman] Sultan 27
Meissner, Karl-Heinz 117, 168, 181, 185
Melotte, Charles 150
Menzel, *Hilfsfeldpolizeibeamte* 177
Merkel, Angela 91
Metaxas, Ioannis 25–31, 36, 39–40, 201
Meyer, Dr. Ernst-Georg 205, 208
Meyszner, August 119, 205
Michaelis, *Feldpolizeisekretär* 175, 179
Michl, *SS Unterstumführer Dr.-* 205
Michler, *Stabsarzt Dr.* 209
Militärbefehlshaber Belgien-Nordfrankreich 53, 127, 144

Militärbefehlshaber Frankreich 136, 143, 146–147, 151, 181
Militärbefehlshaber Griechenland 67, 80, 102, 200
Militärbefehlshaber Nord-Frankreich 137
Miller, Maria Mark 59
Mohr, *Feldwebel* 174
Mommsen, Dr. Theodore 129, 131
Moritz, Kurt 141
Mosig, Walter 17
Mosley, Sir Oswald 34
Moss, William 87
Müller, Bruno 206
Müller, *Feldpolizeikommissar* 168, 173
Müller, Friedrich Wilhelm 75, 84, 88–89
Müller, Heinrich 194
Müller, *Hilfsfeldpolizeibeamte* - 173–174
Müller, *Oberst* (Colonel) 182
Müller, *SS Obersturmführer* 205
Murrer, *Feldpolizeisekretär* 51, 65, 67
Mussolini, Benito 2, 5–6, 29–31, 34–38, 40, 99, 201
Mytinkova, Uyana 176

Nagel, Gottlieb 101
Naumann, Erich 206
Naumann, Klaus 3
Nedic, Milan 119, 123
Nedwed, Walter 183
Neubacher, Hans 81
Nicholas II, [Russian] Czar 26
Niggemeyer, Dr. Bernhard 130, 150, 161
Nikolai, *Oberst* 14
999th Penal Division 74, 104
967th Fortress Brigade 104
938th Fortress Brigade 104
939th Fortress Brigade 104, 111
9th Army 135, 183
Nizienko, *Hilfsdolmetscher* 174
Nockemann, Hans 206
Ntinoudis, Evangelos 87

Oberbefehlshaber Südost 52
Oberkommando der Wehrmacht 121, 211
Oberkommando des Heeres 121, 183, 210
Oberkommando West 131
O'Connor, Sir Richard 35
Offermann, *Polizei Oberinspekteur* 208
Ohlendorf, Otto 182
189th Reserve Division 145
186th Infantry Regiment 193
105th Hungarian Light Infantry Division 167–168
104th Light Division 103
117. Jäger Division (117th Light Infantry Division) 80–81, 90
164th Light Division 105
121st Infantry Division 157
Orlov, Alexander 178
Ortskommandantur I/882 156

Index

Orth, Karin 3
Ost-Kompanie 612 (612th Eastern Company) 178–179
Ostrowski, *Feldpolizeikommissar* von 130

Paland, Herbert Hugo 173–174, 178
Panzergruppe 1 (1st Armored Group) 180–181
Panzergruppe 3 (3rd Armored Group) 182
Papadakis, P. 86
Papoulas, Anastasios 28
Pätzke, *Feldpolizeikommissar* **113**
Paul, [Yugoslav Regent] Prince 37–38
Paulat, *Feldpolizeidirektor* Dr. 132
Pavelich, Dr. Ante 46, 123
Pederzani, Alois 140
Petain, Henri Philippe 125, 145
Peter II, [Yugoslav] King 37–38
Peterson, German Plenipotentiary for Croatia 115
Petrakov, Yacob 178
Petrescu, Lieutenant-Colonel 122
Petrovici, Grigore 122
Phocas, Cosmetatos 29
Pious XII, Pope 45
Pirrounakis, Georgios 196
Plastiras, Nikolaos 29
Plath, *Sonderführer* 177
Poche, Oswald 207
Pohl, Dieter 3
Polish Independent (Carpathian) Infantry Brigade 39
Polizeiregiment "Mitte" (Police Regiment "Center") 116, 181
Ponger, Kurt 198
Poulos, George 86–87, 196
Poulos Polizei Verband 87
Pranz, Wilhelm 51, 103
Procherov, Nikolai 176
Prokscha, *Unteroffizier* 175
Protopapadakis, Petros 28
Prussian 99th Infantry Regiment 12
Pudewell, *Feldpolizeikommissar* 169
Puls, *Oberleutnant der Schutzpolizei* 208
Pyta, Wolfram 3

Quiring, *Sonderführer* Dr. 179

Radionova, Alexandra 176
Radomski, Paul 112
Rallis, Ioannis 100, 103, 124, 196
Ranck, Werner 182
Rangk, *Soldat* 174
Rassow, Ernst 128, 160, 179, 196
Rath, *SS Hauptsturmführer* 205
Rathernau, Walter 194
Rechenauer, Franz 183
Reichskommissariat Ostland 162
Reighe, *Feldpolizeikommissar* 132
Reinhold, Walter 50, 65, 78
Riesen, Hans 182

Reisl, *Feldpolizeikommissar* 168
Reserve Grenadier Bataillon 350 145
Retzeck, *Feldpolizeikommissar* 128, 132
Ribbentrop, Joachim von 19
Richter, Gustav 122
Riedel, Hans Gerhard Günther 172, 179
Rieß, Volker 3
Rohde, *Feldpolizeikommissar* 51, 55
Röhler, Fritz 151
Romanos IV [Diogenes], Byzantine Emperor 23
Rommel, Erwin 36
Roosevelt, Franklin Delano 33
Röser, 1st Lieutenant 79
Rostalski, *Feldpolizeisekretär* 174
Rückreim, *Feldpolizeikommissar* **113**

Salaw, *Feldpolizeikommissar* 138
Sandkühler, Thomas 3
Sarközy, *SS Untersturmführer* von 205
Sattler, Bruno 120
Savkina, Maria 175
Schäfer, Dr. Emanuel 120
Scheel, Gustav Adolf 207
Schefe, Dr. Robert 171
Schenk, *Feldpolizeisekretär* 51, 65, 67
Schier, *Hauptmann der Schutzpolizei* 209
Schimana, Walter Otto 101
Schletitzki, *Feldpolizeikommissar* 135, 145
Schmatzberger, Josef 183
Schmidt, Cuno 134, 150, 160
Schmidt, *Feldpolizeidirektor* 168
Schmidt, *SS Obersturmführer* 205
Schmidt-Zabierow, Paul 115–116
Schneuer, Albert 129
Schöffler, *Feldpolizeikommissar* 168
Scholz, *Hauptmann der Schutzpolizei* 208
Schöngarth, Karl Eberhard 206
Schubert, Friedrich (Fritz) 51–52, 60–61, 67, 82–84, 196, 203; *see also* Constantine, Peter; Konstantinidis, Petros
Schulze, Bernhard 50–51, 55, 133
Schümer, Karl 81
Schwarz, *Hauptmann der Schutzpolizei* 205
Schweitzer, *Feldpolizeikommissar* 168–169
2nd Army 185
Second Battalion / Grenadier Regiment 989 of the 277th Infantry Division 65
2nd New Zealand Infantry Division 38–39
2. Panzerarmee (2nd Tank Army) 55, 116
2. Zug der Armee Tierklinik 592 (Second Platoon of the 592nd Army Veterinary Hospital) 177

Seconde Brigades Speciale (Second Special Service Brigade) 142
Sekretariat 4 (GFP-510) 108, 110, 112
Sekretariat 6 (GFP-621) 108, 110, 111n, 112
Sensenbrenner, *Feldpolizeiinspektor* 131
Sensenhorst, Felix Tarbuk von 179
[Serbisches] Hilfspolizei Regiment 1 208
[Serbisches] Hilfspolizei Regiment 2 208
Serviciul Special de Informatii 122
17th Army 136, 167, 186
7th Army 135, 149
7th Australian Infantry Division 38
VII Bataillon (of the 999th Penal Formation) 105
Seyss-Inquart, Arthur 20
Shipper, *Feldpolizeisekretär* 152
Sidor, Karol 18
Simeon II, [Bulgarian] King 123
Sithof, Richard 167–168, 196
637th Regional Defense Battalion 16th Army 172
6th Army 143, 166, 168
6th Australian Infantry Division 38
LXVIII Armeekorps (68th Army Corps) 53
65.Grenadier Regiment der 22. Luftlande-Division 84
64. Polizei Bataillon (64th Police Battalion) 119–120
Sonder Kompanie der Geheime Feldpolizei Gruppe 9 115, 120
Sonderkommando Rosenberg 96
Sonka Josef 129–130
Sowa, Friedrich **113**, 128
Speidel, Hans 146
Speidel, Wilhelm 80, 102
Spindelböck, *Regierungsrat* Dr. 208
SS Polizei Gebirgsjäger Regiment 18 62, 78, 101, 103
SS Polizeiregiment 5 120
SS-Sonderkommando 4a 182
SS-Sonderkommando 11a 182
SS Standarte 89 62
SS und Polizeiführer Lettland 119–120
SS und Polizeiführer Serbien 205
Stage, Kurt 207
Stahlecker, Walter 207
Stalin, Joseph 34, 39, 73, 175
Standortkommandantur Belgrad 119
Steinbacher, Sybille 3
Steinhauer, Gustav 10
Stentzel, *Soldat* 174
Stephainski, Hans 160–161, 168
Sterodimas, Dr. Spyros 55
Stockmann, *Feldpolizeikommissar* 176, 178–179
Stoßberg, Karl Heinz 207
Strauch, Edward 207
Strausz, Richard 183

Index

Stroop, Jürgen 100–101
Stubenbeck, *Leutnant der Schutzpolizei* 112
Stumpf, *Major der Schutzpolizei* 209
Sturm Division Rhodes ("Assault Division Rhodes") 105
Stüwe, Wilhelm 205
Sucherdt, *Revier Oberleutnant der Schutzpolizei* 205
Suhr, Friedrich 206
Süsse, Bernhard 51, 62
Szálasi, Count Ferenc 118

10th Army 35
Terboven, Joseph Antonius 20
Thaelmann Bataillon 18
Third and Fourth Companies of 703rd Guard Battalion
3rd Company, Grenadier Regiment "Rhodes" 48
3. Panzerarmee (3rd Tank Army) 184–185
13th Company of 318th Infantry Regiment 186
33rd Mountain Infantry Division "Acqui" 202
Thoss, *Feldpolizeikommissar* 135
359th Infantry Regiment (181st Infantry Division) 178
349th Infantry Regiment (181st Infantry Division) 178
314. Polizei Bataillon (314th Police Battalion) 182
375th Infantry Regiment (of the 454th Security Division) 186
Tiso, Josef Gaspašpar 18
Torgler, *Hilfsdolmetscher* 174–176
Torinus, *Sonderführer* 174
Törkler, Gottfried 50–51, 56, 63, 66, 80
Triantafyllakos, Nokolaos 28
Trikoupis, Charilaos 23
Tsolakoglou, Georgios 196
Tulbure, Emil 122
Turner, Dr. Harald 120, 123
12th Army 51–54, 96n, 121, 134, 138, 143–144, 178, 215
12th Army Corps 178
XII Battalion (of the 999th Penal Formation) 47–48

12th Company of the Third Battalion/*Gebirgsjäger Regiment* 98 of 1st Mountain Division 78–79
20th Mountain Army 151
25 Armeekorps (25th Army Corps) 144
24th Infantry Division 186
XXII. Gebirgs Armeekorps 103, 107
22. Luftlande-Division (22nd Air Landing Division) 82, 104
286th Security Division 182
201st Security Division 183–184
207th Security Division 135, 188
268th Infantry Division 175
265th Infantry Division 144
267th Infantry Division 177
263rd Infantry Division 175–176
213th Security Division 167–168, 186
230th Infantry Division 178
221st Security Division 182
223rd "Royal" Reserve Infantry Regiment 193

Uch, Alois 50–51, 54–56, 63, 92, 98
Ullisperger, *SS Hauptsturmführer und Hauptmann der Schutzpolizei von* 205

Vahdettin VI, [Ottoman] Sultan Mehmet 27
Venizelos, Eleftherios 23–30, 82
Verber, Otto 198
Verwaltungsbezirk "C" der Militärbefehlshaber in Frankreich 144
Vogel, Erich 127–128
Vögler, Heinrich 129
"Volga" Battalion of the "Graukopf Brigade" (Russian volunteers) 178
Voß, *Feldpolizeisekretär* 173n

Wagner, Dr. Ernst 133, 172
Wagner, *Hilfsfeldpolizeibeamter* 177
Waldheim, Kurt 14, 54
Waltz, Jean-Jacques 12–13
Walz, Friedrich 168
Webb, Sidney 150; *see also* Guillaume, Maurice

Wedel, Count Charles von 12
Wehrkreis I 53, 116, 148
Wehrkreis II 143
Wehrkreis IV 150–151, 182, 184–185
Wehrkreis V 116, 144, 148, 181
Wehrkreis VI 115, 143, 145, 180
Wehrkreis VII 171, 181
Wehrkreis VIII 144, 146
Wehrkreis XI 52, 172
Wehrkreis XVII 146
Wehrkreis XVIII 116
Wehrkreis XX 54
Wehrkreis XXI 152
Wehrmacht Befehlshaber Niederlande 116
Weimann, Ernst 207
Weitscharcher, Johann 183
Wengenroth, *Hilfsfeldpolizeibeamte* 174
Werft, *Oberleutnant der Schutzpolizei* 208
Wertel, *Feldpolizeikommissar* 179
Westhauser, Hermann 51
Wiese, *Feldpolizeikommissar* **41**, **113**
Wilhelm, Peter 183
Wilhelm I, [German] *Kaiser* 10
Wilhelm II, [German] *Kaiser* 5, 10, 12, 15n, 25–26, 136
Wilkens, Friedrich 207
Winter, Robert 2–3, 6, 197
Witte, 1st Lieutenant Hans 13
Wonisch, Wilhelm 183

Yakovlev, Michail 178

Zaimig, *SS-Hauptsturmführer* Dr. 129
Zamboni, Guelfo 98
Zellmar, *Stabsarzt* 208
Zimmer, Peter 129
Zimmermann, Hebert 207
Zimmermann, Michael 3
Zog, [Albanian] King 36
Zoufaly, *Hauptmann der Schutzpolizei* 208
Zugnig, *Oberfeldpolizeidirektor* 161

www.ingramcontent.com/pod-product-compliance
Ingram Content Group UK Ltd.
Pitfield, Milton Keynes, MK11 3LW, UK
UKHW050702160426
5217IPUK00038B/1949